Global Capitalism, Culture, and Ethics

This book seeks to deepen the reader's understanding of the complex ethical and social disputes that corporations and managers face in an increasingly globalized world. It reviews the history and nature of global capitalism along with the role of the multinational within the global economy. Special attention is paid to emerging and frontier markets where there is economic potential but also major challenges due to institutional voids.

Globalization is a constantly evolving field. In addition to exploring basic economic concepts and ethical frameworks, this second edition takes into account many new developments across different industries, ranging from "Big Tech" to "Big Pharma." It reviews some of the controversies that have affected those industries including bribery, censorship, the politics of computer networking, sweatshops, divestment, and the intensifying crisis of climate change. The book now includes short case studies to help spur creative reflection. Also, the revised content is highlighted in two new chapters – "Corporate bribery" and "Emerging and frontier markets."

The book is ideal for use as a textbook on globalization, and specifically for courses that want to introduce a social responsibility or ethical component at both undergraduate and postgraduate levels.

Richard A. Spinello is Professor of Management Practice at Boston College, USA, where he teaches courses on business ethics, corporate strategy, and globalization. He has written 14 books on ethics and management topics, and has published in journals such as *Business Ethics Quarterly* and *Ethics and Information Technology*.

"Weaving together themes from economics, history, philosophy, and law, this book successfully presents the topic of globalization from multiple perspectives. Summing up: highly recommended. Upper-division undergraduates and above."

L.J. Cumbo, *Emory and Henry College, in* CHOICE, *October 2014*

Global Capitalism, Culture, and Ethics

Second Edition

Richard A. Spinello

Routledge
Taylor & Francis Group
LONDON AND NEW YORK

Cover image: JamesBrey/Getty Images

Second edition published 2022
by Routledge
4 Park Square, Milton Park, Abingdon, Oxon, OX14 4RN

and by Routledge
605 Third Avenue, New York, NY 10158

Routledge is an imprint of the Taylor & Francis Group, an informa business

First edition published by Routledge 2014

British Library Cataloguing-in-Publication Data
A catalogue record for this book is available from the British Library

Library of Congress Cataloging-in-Publication Data
Names: Spinello, Richard A., author.
Title: Global capitalism, culture and ethics / Richard A. Spinello.
Description: Second edition. | Milton Park, Abingdon, Oxon ; New York,
NY : Routledge, 2022. | Includes bibliographical references and index.
Identifiers: LCCN 2021046566 (print) | LCCN 2021046567 (ebook) |
ISBN 9780367527969 (paperback) | ISBN 9780367527952
(hardback) | ISBN 9781003058427 (ebook)
Subjects: LCSH: Economic policy—Moral and ethical aspects. |
Business ethics. | International business enterprises—Moral
and ethical aspects. | Social responsibility of business.
Classification: LCC HD87 .S7295 2022 (print) |
LCC HD87 (ebook) | DDC 174/.4—dc23
LC record available at https://lccn.loc.gov/2021046566
LC ebook record available at https://lccn.loc.gov/2021046567

ISBN: 978-0-367-52795-2 (hbk)
ISBN: 978-0-367-52796-9 (pbk)
ISBN: 978-1-003-05842-7 (ebk)

DOI: 10.4324/9781003058427

Typeset in Adobe Garamond
by codeMantra

In memory of Carl J. Frappaolo, 1956–2013

Contents

Preface

The primary aim of this second edition remains the same: to deepen the reader's knowledge about the complex moral dimensions of globalization and to expand his or her horizons. While the book focuses on the international economic system and emerging economies, the main theme is the role of multinationals in global economic development. There has been surprising neglect of the ethical realities and conundrums of doing business abroad. Yet there is a valid concern that while globalization promotes economic growth and prosperity, it continues to threaten economic security and basic human rights.

The core idea of this book is that the multinational corporation, which still drives the process of globalization, is an international moral agent that must be guided not just by the laws of host countries, but by the moral imperative to respect and protect universal human rights. Several chapters underscore the deficiencies of a pluralistic approach to ethics. We propose instead "moderate universalism," a moderate set of transcultural norms that are predicated on the equal and intrinsic worth of persons as the foundation of human rights and justice. At the same time, multinationals must be sensitive to the legitimate demands of local culture where they do business.

A secondary objective of this book is to provide a modest defense of global capitalism and free markets. Countries committed to free trade and market liberalization tend to grow faster, and economic growth is one factor that inevitably leads to a decline in the poverty level. A rise in the quantity of economic activity is not a panacea for global poverty, but the impressive growth in emerging economies like China, India, and Brazil has certainly helped to diminish the level of social deprivation in these countries. On the other hand, it is difficult to find a country that has prospered without a commitment to free and open markets.

This book has a definite point of view about ethics, but it is not dogmatic. At the center of the debates about globalization are some striking philosophical controversies that will be objectively and impartially presented: cultural relativism, the scope of moral complicity, the relationship between law and morality, the logic of natural human rights, the proper limits of intellectual property rights, the validity of online censorship, and a suitable vision of ecology. We will seek to bring philosophy's ample resources to bear on these theoretical problems, while always recognizing the practical implications of these issues.

This analysis of globalization will not be confined to a treatment of the moral obligations of multinational corporations, but also reviews the history of globalization, the virtues and deficiencies of capitalism, the interrelationship between states and markets, and the beneficial and detrimental effects of globalization on social welfare. It should be obvious that because of its inter-disciplinary nature, this is not a conventional book. Themes from economics, history, ethics, political philosophy, and law are woven together so that the reader can appreciate the phenomenon of globalization from multiple perspectives.

Globalization is one of the most significant trends in human history, as the world moves from a state of fragmentation to one of deep-seated interdependencies. It is essential, therefore, to appreciate the historical evolution of globalization to grasp the dynamics of this movement and perhaps discern its future. This historical overview presented in the opening chapter unveils the benefits and costs of global capitalism along with the role of multinationals during certain inflection points. Also reviewed are the economic theories of Adam Smith and David Ricardo, which demonstrate that trade within and across borders is critical to economic growth. And that growth is critical to the reduction of poverty. The capitalist system is ideally structured to promote such growth, but capitalism comes in several forms. We analyze the different archetypes of capitalism, such as China's state-guided capitalism, and consider whether the capitalist system can flourish without the West's traditional commitment to civil liberties.

The moral logic of capitalism, predicated on free choice and voluntary exchange, is challenged when market failures lead to impaired choice, environmental degradation, or "slavish" working conditions. Regulations are necessary to fix such failures but they sometimes go unenforced or foster a "compliance mentality." Laws must be supplemented, therefore, by proactive ethical self-regulation that emphasizes individual and corporate responsibility. However, in striving to be morally responsible even conscientious multinationals must confront the challenge of cultural diversity and the tensions between local cultural identity and universal human identity. We claim that the latter is the ground for a set of fundamental, universal human rights that can direct moral choices no matter where multinationals compete. These rights are justified as the conditions of human flourishing and human well-being. In this context, we also consider the challenge of ethical pluralism and the sources of law's moral authority. Finally, what, if anything, do corporations owe to the public good beyond complying with the law and acting within the bounds of moral probity? Is it sufficient to avoid depriving people of their rights and protecting rights from being deprived? Or should a corporation use its resources to correct human rights abuses and rectify social inequities?

With these foundational questions addressed, the book proceeds to apply this rights-based moral framework to specific situations. Two new chapters introduce the challenges of doing business in emerging and frontier markets, such as navigating through minefields of political risk and institutional voids, along with the problem of bribery and corruption. The book then proceeds to the themes of political activism and disinvestment. We demonstrate the dangers of excessive political activism, especially when aimed at regime change. Despite their power and financial resources, however, multinationals have not been successful in manipulating political events in developing countries. The discussion sets the stage for the treatment of divestment, or economic disengagement on moral grounds. Are there countries where multinationals must pursue a strategy of disinvestment because human rights abuses are so pervasive or sovereigns are so corrupt?

The next chapter looks critically at Big Pharma and the importance of industrial patents for innovation. Generous standards of patentability are particularly welcome in the pharmaceutical industry where research investment is so high. Patents, however, are limited monopolies that lead to high prices and lower output. Lower output means that life-preserving drugs will be inaccessible to some of the people who need them. Do pharmaceutical companies have some responsibility to deal with the distributional inequities that arise from these high drug prices, especially in poor countries like India? This chapter also focuses on the World Trade Organization's TRIPS policy that is a condition of membership in that organization. By normalizing intellectual property regimes through this international agreement, the West has exported a set of binding intellectual property rules that may or may not benefit developing nations.

We then review the Orwellian censorship and surveillance regimes found in authoritarian countries like China where the government wants to sustain a monopoly over information. Multinational companies, including Cisco, were instrumental in building China's "Great Firewall," but was its technical assistance morally proper? As Internet custodians like Google and LinkedIn expanded their operations into this market, they had to enforce various censorship laws and other online restrictions. Should social media and search platforms abide by these local laws and help the host country censor the Web? Or should they attempt to follow a higher ethical standard that acknowledges the universal right to free speech?

Chapter 10 scrutinizes environmental issues and corporate responsibilities. It reviews the different species of environmental degradation with a special focus on global warming. It also highlights several environmental debacles in developing countries such as Texaco's pillaging of the Ecuadorean Amazon and the environmental degradation that has occurred in Nigeria's Niger Delta at the hands of companies like Royal/Dutch Shell. To some extent, these problems arose because oil companies have sometimes taken advantage of dysfunctional governments with weak environmental regulations. Oil companies have special obligation not only to decarbonize within a reasonable time frame but to be more socially responsible when extracting gas and oil from foreign lands.

The final chapter does not deal with ethical problems arising from foreign direct investment, but focuses on companies that source their goods from contractors abroad. One of the biggest ongoing scandals in the history of globalization is the chronically poor working conditions in most low-wage countries. There are inferior working conditions in Bangladesh and also in China. But what is the scope of a corporation's responsibility to the workers of its suppliers in these low-wage countries, and how far up the supply chain does that responsibility extend? Issues reviewed in this context include the criteria for determining a decent work environment, the definition of a fair wage, and the intractable problem of child labor.

All of these topics are quite controversial and we try to present both sides of these issues whenever possible. There is copious material here for thinking about and debating the social valences of moral situations and the intricate ethical aspects of globalization. Many of those aspects revolve around the issue of cultural identity. In general terms, the biggest test for the multinational is resolving the tension between respect for cultural diversity and local sovereignty and the protection of universal human rights. How multinationals deal with this tension is decisive for a world that is growing more ambivalent and circumspect about globalization's tenuous future.

Acknowledgments

I wish to thank the Carroll School of Management at Boston College for its ongoing support for my scholarship. My special gratitude extends to the Chairperson of the Management and Organization Department, Judy Gordon, and to Dean Andy Boynton for sustaining an intellectual environment that is conducive for this sort of research. I am grateful to the CSOM students I have taught in globalization courses over the years for the perceptive questions and comments that have helped me to refine several of the arguments in this book. Very special thanks to Ezabel Lynch for assisting me in acquiring the abundant research material necessary to complete this book. My deep gratitude goes to the editors and staff at Routledge, especially to Catherine Scarratt, and to our copy editor, Gareth Vaughan. I am especially grateful to Rebecca Marsh for her confidence in this project, her good cheer, and her guidance in keeping things on the right track. Finally, I reserve my deepest thanks to my wife, Susan, for her patience and gracious support during the long days spent re-writing this book.

The book is dedicated to the memory of Carl "Frapp" Frappaolo, a close friend and colleague for many years. In some respects, this book is about virtuous entrepreneurship, and Carl was the epitome of the virtuous entrepreneur. Carl belonged to the breed of "midnight programmers," working long hours to write computer programs that became the foundation of an exciting new company called the Delphi Group. He was a true pioneer in the field of information technology, but always found a way to bring a sense of humanity, humor, and exuberance to the arid world of databases and knowledge management that occupied so much of his time. Those of us who were privileged to be his friends think of him often and miss him deeply.

Richard A. Spinello
Dedham, Massachusetts
August 2021

Chapter 1

The logic and history of global capitalism

The period immediately after World War II was one of unremitting gloom for many people in war-ravaged Europe. The grim statistics only dimly reflected the human reality of the war's devastation. It was an especially trying time for the citizens of Germany, who wondered how German culture could be revived and how their once powerful economy could ever be restored. Like all institutions, German businesses were in a shocking state of disarray after incessant waves of Allied bombing. Manufacturing plants in the Ruhr valley and in industrial cities like Hamburg and Mannheim were prime targets of the United Kingdom's bombing offensive. Aside from the daunting challenges of re-building factories and supply chains, some companies had to cope with allegations of collusion with Hitler's brutal regime. As Hitler consolidated power, it became increasingly difficult and perilous for businesses to avoid full cooperation with the Nazi government. All foreign and domestic businesses had to comply with the policy of *Gleichschaltung* or total coordination with the state.[1]

The post-war era was particularly challenging for Krupp, the legendary German munitions manufacturer, which was accused of using slave labor during the war, including POWs and civilians from occupied countries like France. These abuses along with the many other war crimes of the Nazi regime demanded justice and fair retribution. After the war the Nuremberg trials were convened to punish Hitler's collaborators and to help exorcise the ghost of the Third Reich. Alfred Krupp and the company's directors were indicted "as the focus, the symbol, and the beneficiary of the most sinister forces engaged in menacing the peace of Europe." Krupp's lawyers protested that the company had no choice – it had to fill Nazi orders for weapons or face dire consequences, and the labor shortage forced the company to rely on foreign laborers. But the Nuremberg judges were not persuaded by this reasoning. Krupp and the directors were convicted for slave labor and for "the plunder of occupied Europe."[2]

DOI: 10.4324/9781003058427-1

The Krupp enterprise traces its roots to a small steel mill built in the city of Essen in 1810.[3] The German company quickly moved into a diverse range of products that took advantage of the industrial age and its insatiable demand for steel to construct buildings, ships, and railroads. Krupp soon became a major manufacturer of steel rollers, ship shafts, and railway tires. Many of Krupp's cast-steel products were vital inputs for the transportation innovations that drove economic development and globalization from the mid- to the late 19th century.[4] But Krupp also specialized in building the tools of war, including rifle barrels and artillery pieces used by the Prussian military. After it perfected these technologies, Krupp became the pre-eminent arms manufacturer in all of Europe.

The entrepreneurial Krupp family also expanded overseas more zealously than most of its competitors. The history of globalization mirrors to some extent what transpired at Krupp from the 1850s until after World War I. Krupp recognized that it needed a presence in prosperous countries like the UK to preserve its competitive advantage in steel and related industries. Fortunately, Krupp's superior technology gave it a big advantage in that market. As word of its quality products spread, the company exported its cast-steel products and weaponry throughout West Europe and Russia. Krupp also invested abroad, purchasing Spanish mines for raw material and a Dutch shipping company as part of its expanding distribution network.

Krupp's global ambitions and economic vitality were disrupted in the early 20th century, however, when a wary German government imposed restrictions on the sale of weaponry to its potential foes. Those restrictions were reinforced during World War I, which unleashed the forces of de-globalization throughout the whole global economy. During the war many of the company's foreign markets were lost thanks to the Allied blockade. After the war, Krupp was forced to renounce arms manufacturing, at least temporarily. The company found itself on the brink of bankruptcy in the mid-1920s, thanks to inflation, overcapacity, and severe labor problems. But the Krupp enterprise was revived, and by 1930 it was back in the arms business. However, daunting challenges remained. The worldwide depression of the 1930s contributed to Krupp's stagnant export business. With the exception of Russia, export orders still languished from most of its major customers. By 1933, Krupp returned to profitability, though not as a result of demand for military products.

As World War II approached, the company began to rebound more strongly as it made weapons for the Nazi war machine. Its *Germaniwert* shipyard filled orders for submarines and destroyers, while its main plants made howitzers and other artillery pieces. Krupp's profits surged in the late 1930s, though they fell off somewhat during the early war years. After Hitler's ignominious defeat there was another reversal of fortune and prolonged turmoil. The victorious British disassembled major Krupp factories and sequestered its coal mines, while the Russians sequestered its *Grusonwerk* factory in Magdeburg.

In later decades, however, Krupp recovered yet again thanks to a new "ethos of globalization" that became the focal point of its corporate strategy. The resilient Krupp enterprise acquired major operations in Italy and Mexico and refined its skills in manufacturing specialty steels.[5] Eventually Krupp merged with Thyssen to become ThyssenKrupp, a trust company, partially owned by a foundation. It remains a major worldwide player in steel mass production and in capital goods such as elevators and industrial equipment.

The Krupp story dramatically mirrors the twisty path of global capitalism, which has been massively thrown off course at times by international conflicts and the forces of economic nationalism. Like Krupp, globalization's fate seems closely tied to politics, as it treads a course marked by sharp discontinuities and an uncertain future. The Krupp saga confirms David Hume's insight that trade and international commerce is "an affair of state."[6] Even in ostensibly free markets, the state is always involved to some degree in the economic welfare of its citizens. Krupp was subject to political intervention because of the nature of its business, but in 19th century Europe, nation states intervened in markets to help forge a global expansion of capital.

Bearing in mind this relationship between commerce and the state, we turn to an examination of economic globalization's past so we can better understand the present moment and perhaps discern its future trajectory. During this discussion we also concisely treat the economic advantages of trade and foreign investment that were perceived so clearly by discerning and resourceful enterprises like Krupp.

The cycles of global market integration

This condensed historical analysis provides a broad context for the remainder of the book and allows us to appreciate the paramount role of the multinational corporation in the globalization process.[7] Some naively think that globalization is a purely contemporary phenomenon that has only recently sprung forth with the help of modern communication and transportation technologies. But this is definitely not the case. Globalization, broadly defined as the "process of increasing integration in world civilization," has a long and tangled history.[8] Since our focus is on economic aspects of globalization, perhaps a more useful definition is the following: "the integration of economic activities across borders, through markets."[9] Globalization represents the triumph of global capitalism over geographical constraints.

Economic integration occurs primarily through both foreign trade and foreign direct investment (FDI). FDI is an especially important dimension of globalization. Multinationals and corporations engage in FDI through acquiring an existing firm in a foreign country or by making a greenfield investment that typically entails construction of a new operation such as a manufacturing plant or a distribution center.

Trade has been aptly described as an "engine of growth." Even in the Middle Ages philosophers recognized the value of free trade and interdependencies between countries. According to Thomas Aquinas, for example, "Trade must not be entirely absent from a city, since one cannot easily find any place so full of life's necessities so as not to need some commodities from other regions."[10] Aquinas, however, also warned about the dangerous side effects of relying excessively on trade. Hence he was skeptical about the net benefits of economic globalization for some countries.

Economists like David Ricardo and Adam Smith have developed viable theories of trade demonstrating that countries enhance their prosperity when they trade across borders. The starting point of Smith's economic theory is two principles: voluntary exchange and the specialization of labor. The division or specialization of labor applies not only to a business but also to an entire country. Smith was convinced that specialization at what a country does best followed up by trade is the key to sustainable economic growth:

> What is prudence in the conduct of every family can scarce be folly in that of a great kingdom. If a foreign country can supply us with a commodity cheaper than we ourselves can make it, better buy it off them with some part of the produce of our own industry, employed in a way in which we have some advantage.[11]

Echoing Smith, Ricardo cleverly demonstrated that countries will benefit from trade if they specialize in what they are *relatively* most efficient in producing and trade for their other needs.[12] Countries should concentrate on products or services where they are comparatively more productive and exchange some of those goods for their other needs. When a country is open to trade for other goods where it does not have such a comparative advantage, its domestic factors of production get the highest returns. In addition, there are static advantages such as economies of scale in production and procurement that can be exploited when trade expands markets. Finally there are dynamic advantages since trade encourages competition and productivity growth. An isolated community, on the other hand, must be self-sufficient and do everything for itself. It must grow its own agricultural products even if the land and climate are unsuited to farming.[13]

Box 1.1 Concepts explained: comparative advantage[14]
Ricardo's theory of comparative advantage

The theory of comparative advantage presented by David Ricardo in 1817 is critical for understanding the positive benefits of trade between countries. Ricardo sought to demonstrate how world trade could increase global consumption and improve living standards. Here is an example of how his simple model works:

Two countries, A and B, each employ 1,000 workers, who make two products: compact cars and syrup. A is more productive – to make a car it needs the labor of 5 workers – whereas B needs 10 workers, and to make a year's worth of maple syrup it needs the labor of 2 workers (vs. 4 for country B). For both countries half the workers are employed in each industry.

	West	East
Cars	10 workers	100 workers
Syrup	2 workers	4 workers

The two countries decide to specialize. A has a more substantial advantage in car-making (10/1 vs. 2/1) and so it devotes most of its resources to that industry, employing 700 workers to make cars and 300 to make syrup; B switches entirely to producing maple syrup.

Both countries are able to consume more of both products if they trade with each other. They negotiate and settle on these terms of trade: 10 cars for 120 vats of syrup.

This table illustrates how both countries are better off than they would be if they did not trade:

	Output w. no trade		Output after specialization		Consumption after trade	
	Cars	Syrup	Cars	Syrup	Cars	Syrup
A	50	250	70	150	60	270
B	4	125	0	250	10	130

Why are both countries better off through free trade? Even though Country A has an "absolute advantage" in producing both cars and syrup, each country has a different comparative advantage. A's greater advantage is in producing cars, while B, although at a disadvantage in both industries, is a relatively more efficient producer of maple syrup. **If each country specializes in producing those goods in which it has a comparative advantage, both countries will benefit from trade.** Thus, countries should specialize in what they are most efficient at doing and trade accordingly.

Thanks to liberal economic policies and the power of Ricardian comparative advantage, the world economy was tightly integrated during the last half of the 19th century, and it seemed to be advancing towards even greater economic integration and global cooperation. Progress was cut short, however, in 1914 and in the turbulent interwar years.

The history of globalization is anti-teleological, because of damaging political and economic choices along with many unintended consequences. It is not marked by some sort of relentless upward spiral. It is instructive to contrast this state of affairs with the views of a philosopher like Hegel who conceived history as a manifestation of the Rational Idea or Reason through time. History is a teleological force, always moving forward toward the final end of absolute freedom. "Freedom," writes Hegel," is the ultimate purpose toward which all world history has continually aimed."[15] Thus, the history of the world, despite whatever appears on the surface, reflects a deeper reality and presents us with a rational process through which the individual subject comes to achieve freedom in the ethical life of the state. History dynamically progresses only in one direction as the person discovers her identity in relation to nature and history.

On the contrary, the history of globalization is distinctly non-linear, a sometimes arbitrary and irrational process. There is no immanent dynamic, no sense that polities, following the arc of history toward its final end, necessarily aspire to construct a fully integrated global economy supported by the proper social systems and multilateral regulations. The history of globalization is much more chaotic, with ebbs and flows, advances and sometimes stunning reversals. Those reversals can occur through economic downturns along with political and ideological conflicts. Accordingly, there is no guarantee that an era of openness and liberal trade policies will not come to an abrupt end, to be followed by a period of disintegration and isolationism. Such an unwelcome turn of events might come to pass if people rebel against the persistence of world poverty or if slower domestic growth in major economies leads to irrational trade wars and fractionalization instead of greater cooperation.

Following the lead of most business historians we can divide this messy history of global capitalism into five discrete periods. The first period extends from the mid-19th century or so until 1914, the outbreak of World War I. The second phase, which extends to the end of World War II in 1945, marks a difficult period of de-globalization. In the third period, from 1950 to 1979, global capitalism was re-built, yet there were still strong forces holding back its progress. For almost three decades, from 1979 to 2008, the world enjoyed a new era of global market integration, with considerable economic growth not only in the West but also in emerging markets. But the final and current period represents an uncertain time in the global economy thanks to the lingering effects of the 2008 recession, a rise in protectionism, and, above all, the 2020 global pandemic.[16]

Globalization before World War I

Although many people think that the current era has exhibited unsurpassed economic integration and growth, the years between 1870 and 1914 represent "the most impressive episode of international economic integration which the world has seen to date ... [thanks to] the largest decline ever in intercontinental barriers to trade and factor mobility."[17] The undisputed center of the world economy during this phase of globalization was Europe. During these years there was relative peace and social order in Europe. After the defeat of Napoleon in 1815, there were no major wars that engulfed European nations. Peace and political concord created the conditions for a high level of economic integration, which occurred through trade, foreign direct investment, short-term capital flows, and the movement of workers across national boundaries. [18]

As economies expanded in European countries such as the United Kingdom, France, and Germany, there was a significant increase in international trade. That expansion of trade was enabled by the adoption of liberal economic policies in most European countries that replaced the reigning philosophy of mercantilism. These countries shunned high tariffs or restrictive quotas and welcomed the advantages of trading with their neighbors. In the UK, protectionism was exemplified by the Corn Laws that banned imports when domestic grain prices dropped below a certain threshold. In 1846 Britain repealed these laws as it transitioned to a more open economy with a stronger free trade agenda. The UK opened its agricultural markets to the world economy and other countries followed in their footsteps. Thanks to liberalization, international trade grew about 16% per year between 1830 and 1870, but decreased somewhat after that period.[19]

One of the chief elements in the evolution of a globalized economy was the abolition of political barriers to trade. However, as Bhagwati points out, the integration of the first global economy "was driven more by technological developments in transportation and communications than by policy changes."[20] The construction of intercontinental railroads and the increasing use of steamships made it easier to move large quantities of goods efficiently and inexpensively. Improvements in communications were also a critical factor in the integration of world markets. Thanks to the telegraph, electronic communications between Europe and the United States were made possible for the first time when a trans-Atlantic cable connection was completed in 1866. The telephone, invented in 1876, was another key technology that connected together disparate parts of the world. The level of global connectivity pales by today's standards, but these primitive technologies were fundamental for the evolution of international commerce. The lower countries can drive transportation and communication costs, the greater the level of economic integration they can achieve.

Globalization was also driven to some degree by imperial ambitions on the part of the United Kingdom and other European countries. European imperialism augmented global linkages as empires accelerated their growth. International rivalries fueled that economic expansion. States were committed to global commerce and to imperial missions in order to finance their military machines. The United Kingdom and France were the principal rivals. They emerged as powerful economic centers, with peripheral colonies like India and African countries supplying raw material and becoming captive offshore markets for the finished goods of their multinational firms.[21] But there was a big difference between these two world powers. Britain was always an empire of free trade whereas France maintained "a tightly centralized mercantilist regime."[22]

After 1880, however, protectionism surfaced throughout Europe, partly inspired by a surge in nationalistic sentiment. The United States also adopted protectionist policies such as the McKinley Act of 1890 which placed tariffs on many manufacturing goods and occasioned a steep rise in prices. This legislation was followed by the Wilson tariff (1894) which went into effect during the worst industrial depression in the United States since the 1870s. Nonetheless, the overall momentum of globalization was not derailed by these policies.

During this same pre-1914 period there was a dramatic increase in capital flows between countries. A high degree of capital market integration typified this first global economy. There were several reasons for this. Adoption of the gold standard minimized foreign exchange risk, since exchange rates were fixed and expressed in terms of gold; a country's domestic money supply was also tied to its gold stock. Hence that standard forced governments to adopt conservative fiscal and monetary policies. The absence of military conflict and political strife also created a climate highly favorable for lending and investment. Political stability and fiscal prudence made it easier for banks and other institutions to lend money to companies in other countries. For the United Kingdom, for example, there are reliable estimates that 32% of its net national wealth was held overseas.[23] Some economists contend that the integration of global capital markets actually reached its pinnacle in 1913 and has not yet been surpassed even in the 21st century.[24]

Foreign direct investment also increased substantially during the pre-war years. There was a high level of multinational manufacturing but also foreign investment in agricultural and raw materials. Buoyed by success in its domestic market, companies like Bayer and Siemens in Germany or Lever Brothers in the UK built manufacturing plants around the world. Bayer became one of the chief foreign manufacturers in the United States. Siemens, which pioneered electricity and telegraph technology, quickly extended its reach into Britain and Russia. Lever Brothers had 33 foreign factories ranging from countries like Canada and the United States to South Africa and Australia. By 1914, Nestlé, the famous Swiss corporation, produced its condensed milk and baby formula in Norway, Spain, Canada, and the United States. The growth in FDI was facilitated by the rapid adoption of international property law, but Europe's colonialism also helped to reduce the risks of foreign investment in developing countries. The UK controlled a sprawling empire with over 400 million inhabitants into which British corporations felt secure in extending their operations.[25] The United Kingdom accounted for 50% of the world's stock of FDI.

By 1913, annual world trade had grown to over $18 billion and integrated world markets existed for many goods.[26] Foreign direct investment reached $14.5 billion, with Europe having a disproportionate share. This investment along with a steady annual volume of exports had accelerated Europe's economic growth. European GDP, which was 47% of world GDP by 1914, grew at a compound annual growth rate of 1.32% between 1870 through 1913. Per capita GDP, however, was much higher in Western Europe than in the countries of Asia and Africa.[27] But as European peace and prosperity gave way to political discord and turmoil and then eventually to war, the forces pushing for open markets were abruptly set in reverse.

The first era of globalization yielded many benefits, including decades of steady economic growth accompanied by a long period of peace enforced by Britain (*Pax Britannica*). The liberal polices articulated by Ricardo and Smith apparently proved to be the right formula as the world thrived on high volumes of trade. Globalization was also driven by technologies that facilitated foreign trade. This era also solidified the "great divergence" between Europe and other economies, especially those in Asia. That divergence had commenced with the Industrial Revolution but became more intense as European economic growth was stimulated by captive overseas markets along with the resources and raw materials of its colonies.[28]

But global economic growth concentrated in Europe had its costs: untamed imperialism, greater global inequities, an intensifying arms race, and the scourge of nationalism. These negative trends sowed the seeds for globalization's rapid demise, as the world stood on the brink of the cataclysm of the "Great War."[29]

De-globalization 1.0

Many believed that the interdependencies created by globalization would insulate Europe from self-destructive conflict and the terrible economic consequences of war. Dependency on international trade and foreign investment made European countries more vulnerable for sustained interruptions in their supply of food and other materials.[30] The business community certainly did not want war but there seemed no way that European countries, locked into tight political alliances, could avert this impending calamity.

The immediate precipitant of the Great War was the assassination of Archduke Ferdinand in June 1914. He was heir to the throne of the Austrian-Hungarian Empire ruled by the Habsburg dynasty. Serbia was a vassal state of that Empire, and blame was rightly cast on this country for harboring the terrorist group that carried out the assassination. The Habsburg ruler, Franz Joseph, declared war on Serbia. When Russia entered the war to support the Serbs, international treaties forced Germany and Italy to also enter the conflict on Russia's behalf. Treaties also compelled France and the UK to align with Austria.

But war seemed inevitable thanks to arms races and a surge of nationalism particularly in central and Eastern Europe. Initially, hopes were high that the war would swiftly come to an end with minimal casualties, but that was not to be. This international conflict dragged on for four long years. By 1916, defense spending in the belligerent countries increased dramatically to over half of GDP, as governments reorganized their economies for "total war." Predictably, these actions led to massive reductions in trade and a sharp curtailment in foreign investment. As a result, the first global economy was fatally disrupted.[31]

During the height of this chaotic world war there was another severe political shock that also contributed to economic turmoil and disintegration. The Russian Revolution, sewn in the intellectual soil of Marxism, commenced in 1917 when Nicholas II, the Czar of Russia, abdicated his throne. The revolution eventually triggered a large-scale sequestration or expropriation of foreign property.[32] The new Russian government nationalized the banking system and confiscated all private enterprises. United States companies like Singer, Kodak, and Otis Elevator lost all of their substantial assets. With these dramatic actions, Leninist Russia became relatively isolated from the global economy. There was some trade with other countries but no foreign direct investment, which was banned until the collapse of the Soviet Union in 1989.[33]

World War I predictably led to a wave of expropriations. After the entry of the United States into the war in April, 1917 on the side of the allies, the German government began to move against U.S. businesses in Germany. By 1918, Germany had sequestered 159 American businesses and properties. In retaliation, the United States executed its Trading with the Enemy Act, cutting off economic relations with Germany.[34] When the war ended, Germany's foreign investments were at high risk for expropriation. Siemens lost both its foreign factories and its patents. And Merck's U.S. operations were expropriated by the American government.

The hostilities ended on November 11, 1918, as an eerie silence fell upon Europe's bloody battlefields. But the political consequences of the war and the Russian Revolution were severe. After the war, the Habsburg army, with many soldiers of South Slav extraction, disintegrated and so did the Habsburg empire which could no longer sustain a sense of imperial identity among East European countries like Poland. The dissolution of the Russian and Habsburg empires meant a collapse of the old world order. This opened the way for nationalist sentiments and passionate ideologies hostile to democratic capitalism.[35]

During the postwar years there was a strong push for protectionism especially in Europe and America. In America, the dreadful Smoot-Hawley legislation was passed in 1930, putting major restraints on American trade. Tariffs were also substantially higher throughout Europe. In 1932, the British government announced a tariff of at least 10% on most imports, bringing to an end almost a century-long tradition of "free trade." As a result of these new tariff walls, the total volume of exports declined steadily, with European exports well below the level of 1913.[36]

Nonetheless, some American enterprises aggressively sought to expand their operations during the 1920s. New international companies emerged such as Aramco International partnership, B.F. Goodrich, and Crown Cork International. General Electric and International Telephone and Telegraph (ITT) also expanded mightily into foreign countries. Attitudes to U.S. investment, however, were mixed and often ambivalent. There was antagonism toward some companies such as the giant oil operation, Jersey Standard. Spain had nationalized its petroleum industry in the 1920s and the threat of further nationalizations seemed possible. The United Kingdom was worried that its worldwide economic power was now being eclipsed by this heavy U.S. foreign investment. In 1922, for the first time, the value of U.S. investment in Canada overtook the value of UK investment there.[37]

Just as the world economy was recovering in the post-war period, the stock market crashed in the United States in 1929. This event, precipitated by a speculative fever that gripped the whole U.S. economy, ushered in a deep economic depression that adversely affected the entire world economy. That crash led to contradiction and panic and ultimately a "contagion of fear," with over four million Americans unemployed by the spring of 1930.[38] America's economic woes contributed to the depression in Britain and weighed down the whole world economy.

In Europe, Germany's devastating depression between 1929 and 1933 left more than a third of the German workforce out of work. Destitute families were everywhere, and the country struggled to get its hyperinflation under control. The depression provoked the rise of the Nazi party as a potent political force and Hitler's victory in 1933. There is little doubt that Hitler's dramatic ascent would have been "unthinkable with the catastrophic effects of the Depression."[39]

At the same time, developing countries began to resist any foreign control over their natural resources. Hence, companies in the extractive industries such as petroleum found themselves in perilous conditions. Standard Oil discovered oil in Bolivia in the 1920s, but a military junta seized all of their properties in 1933. In Mexico, oil production was on the rise during this same period. But in a devastating blow to the oil industry, the country nationalized all foreign oil companies in 1938, citing Article 27 of the Mexican Constitution. The pretext for this sequestration was a dispute over wages and the provision of generous social benefits. The properties of Royal Dutch Shell along with Standard Oil of New Jersey and Sinclair & Standard Oil of California were all nationalized by the Mexican government. The United States ambassador to Mexico described the country's action as a "bolt from the blue," but to the chagrin of U.S. oil companies the American government refused to take action.[40]

The world also had to contend with a fascist economic order with Hitler in Germany, Franco in Spain, and Mussolini in Italy. Relations between business interests and these states were tense and economies suffered due to government controls and the diversion of resources to the military. The Japanese government also assumed many of fascism's worst features. The rise of fascism led to the final shock of World War II, which commenced in Europe in September 1939 when Hitler's troops crossed over the Polish border, and in the United States after Japan's bombing of Pearl Harbor on December 7, 1941. Hitler's belligerence had already led to an exodus of foreign capital from Europe. The heavy resources demanded by the war effort put every world economy under enormous new pressures and severely constrained economic growth. The war impacted international trade policies immediately as trade between warring military blocs ceased completely.[41] This conflict created major complications for U.S. companies operating in occupied countries like France and Belgium. Many ceased operations there while others curtailed them significantly. Combatants also shifted resources to war materials production, placing a further stress on consumption. In beleaguered Britain, U.S. subsidiaries and affiliated companies converted their factories to make munitions for the war effort. Global capitalism was once again in grave peril at this uncertain moment in world history.[42]

Rebuilding global capitalism

Two world wars, sweeping communist revolutions in Russia and China, a wave of protectionism and expropriation, and even a prolonged worldwide depression – all of these forces dealt a harmful blow to global capitalism until the late 1940s. The economic and corporate malaise that ensued after the Great War created a crisis of confidence in capitalism. Many intellectuals concluded that the capitalist system was dysfunctional, and they turned to Soviet-style collectivism as the answer to the world's economic travails.

But global capitalism did not collapse, as some had predicted. Thanks to swift re-building efforts after the war that yielded robust economic growth, globalization began a gradual process of renewal. In the United States President Roosevelt's economic policies eventually brought the U.S. economic depression to an end. Liberalization displaces protectionist policies in some countries, and foreign trade slowly expands.

Many developing countries, however, vigorously resisted this new trend toward greater economic integration and persisted in their closed economies. Countries in Africa and in other parts of the world, which had recently been granted their independence, had tenuous national identities and were anxious to assert their economic and political independence from their former colonial powers.[43] India, for example imposed many restrictions on foreign investment after it won independence from the United Kingdom in 1947. Often this wariness of foreign investment was accompanied by explicit or latent sympathy with socialist ideologies. During Indira Ghandi's leadership from 1966 to 1984, India nationalized mines, banks, and insurance and imposed limits on urban incomes and property. Laws like the Foreign Exchange Restriction Order (FERO) diluted foreign investment in Indian companies. The result of India's government controls and relative isolationism, however, was stagnant economic growth, as per capita income rose a meager 0.3% annually between 1965 and 1975.[44] Things began to change dramatically for India only when it pursued a growth-centered strategy based on a more open and outward-oriented economy.

Similarly, in the Middle East and neighboring regions there was a potent bias against liberal economic policies. Countries like Turkey did not welcome FDI and did not open their markets to trade and imports. The situation was much different in the United States, however, where major corporations like IBM, General Electric, Pepsi, and Ford were making substantial investments in foreign countries. By the early 1970s Pepsi produced its soft drinks in 512 plants located in 114 countries. In that same time frame, 62 of the Fortune 100 American firms had production facilities in at least six nations. And U.S. FDI rose from $11 billion in 1950 to $100 billion in 1972. At this point America, followed by Europe and Japan, was driving the globalization of production.[45]

United States investment in developing countries such as Latin America remained modest, however, thanks to the challenging political climate and economic conditions in those countries. Poverty and crime, currency fluctuations, and political instability created big risks even for adventurous American firms. Some countries severely restricted investment because they feared it might impeded indigenous economic development, leaving its economy exploited and too dependent on multinationals. But there were limited entrepreneurial opportunities in certain Latin American countries like Brazil and Argentina. Both countries implemented laws virtually requiring local production for certain manufacturing goods (such as automobiles), and that proved successful in inducing U.S. firms to commit to building large factories.[46]

These investment conditions in Latin and Central America sometimes created exigent circumstances for investors. As a result, the expansion of American investment overseas had a dark side. This period of corporate history stands out because of the unwarranted political activism of several corporations concerned about the spread of communism in a risky economic environment. Companies, confronted by hostile anti-capitalist policies, sometimes took unorthodox steps to protect their investments. United Fruit Corporation (later Chiquita Banana) was the largest private company operating in Guatemala and accounted for 75% of its banana exports. In the 1950s the banana enterprise found itself embroiled in controversy when a new socialist regime came to power in Guatemala. President Jacobo Árbenz was determined to do something about unequal land distribution and he sought to appropriate some of United Fruit's unused plantations. Consequently, to protect its interests, United Fruit openly supported the overthrow of the Árbenz regime, lobbying the United States State Department and anyone in Washington who would listen that a military coup was necessary. In Chile in the 1970s ITT played a similar role in the overthrow of the socialist Allende government. According to critics, the ITT and UFC cases demonstrated how major corporations had amassed such excessive power that they could actually shape U.S. foreign policy toward those countries where it operated.[47] Thanks to this unfortunate legacy, it is easy to understand why multinationals have been stigmatized in the past as agents of imperialism.

Of course, most multinationals focused their attention on growing their businesses and not on politics or regime change. With domestic markets saturated, they looked for ways to sustain growth by expanding abroad. Like the United States, Japan was particularly aggressive as many of its companies expanded through inexpensive capital available through its insulated financial markets. Japan's targeting of certain strategic industries led to the rise of companies like Hitachi and Fujitsu who challenged IBM on the world stage. Japan, the United States, and Europe were now the leaders in foreign investment.

By the late 1970s tensions were rising in Communist countries. While globalization galvanized growth in many regions those countries were left out. As a result, their epochal revolutions were on the brink of dispersion. The transformation of the Chinese economy was slowly getting underway thanks to the visionary leadership of Deng Xiaoping. The "household responsibility system," which spontaneously emerged in rural China in the 1970s, allowed farmers to sell their goods at free market prices. This policy resulted in a major increase in food production. There were special economic zones in cities like Shenzen where free market principles were introduced. This gradual withdrawal of the government from the economy set the stage for economic reforms that have sustained China's extraordinary economic growth in recent decades.[48] Market forces had already transformed the economies of Hong Kong, Singapore, and Japan, and China was slowly preparing to follow in their footsteps.

At the same time, when the Polish Pope, John Paul II, visited his homeland in the spring of 1979, he contested the moral legitimacy of the Soviet empire. With his bold pronouncements, the Pope helped to set in motion a chain of events that would lead to the collapse of the powerful Soviet Union. In a series of thirty-nine sermons attended by millions of Poles, he rebuked Marxist theories, including the absolute power of the state. As journalist Christian Caryl points out, "Never before had a Communist party in the Soviet bloc endured such a direct public challenge to its ideological and informational hegemony."[49] As a result of the Pope's visit, and many other factors, communism in East Europe began to unravel rapidly, no longer able to suppress the people's longing for truth and freedom.

Thanks in part to visionaries like Deng Xiaoping and Pope John Paul II, the stage was now set for a major transformation in the world's geo-political structure which would reverberate throughout the global economy.

Global capitalism's second wave

Economic historians mark the beginning of the full rebirth of global capitalism around the year 1980. Western Europe, Japan, and North America initially came to dominate this revived borderless global economy, but that dynamic would change in the 21st century as emerging economies like China began to play a more active and substantial role. Globalization in this new century no longer implies that corporations in developed countries invest in emerging economies.

Technology was a principal driver of this prolonged era of globalization. New technical infrastructures that facilitate information flows have reshaped the world economy. Networked computer systems have created a global platform for collaboration and online commerce that transcends national boundaries. The Web has made possible an unprecedented level of information egalitarianism that also opened the way for the further commercialization of cyberspace. However, in one of globalization's many contradictions, this potentially freedom-enhancing technology became a tool for suppression of human rights in authoritarian regimes. From an economic point of view, the revolutionary impact of these technical infrastructure was the reduction of the transaction costs that interfered with the seamless delivery or exchange of goods and services.[50]

The dramatic collapse of Soviet collectivism created vast new opportunities for trade and investment. No longer was there an Iron Curtain dividing East and West Germany and East European markets like Poland were open to the world. In Europe the events of 1989, another pivotal year in world history, culminated in the fall of the Berlin Wall. This set in motion the forces that would allow for a united Germany's full integration into the European and global economies. Similarly, China's economic transformation through its endorsement of free market principles has also been a major factor in globalization's expansion. Casting off the economic principles of Marxist socialism, China began implementing free market policies in the 1980s and joined the World Trade Organization (WTO) in 2001. China's low wages and tax structure became a major impetus behind the sudden rise of offshoring, as companies move their factories abroad to dramatically lower their own cost structure.

There was also an abrupt decline in protectionism and a rise in free trade. To some extent, falling tariffs reflected the growth in regional trade groups such as the European Union, NAFTA (U.S., Canada, Mexico), or Latin America's Mercosur. NAFTA led to explosive growth of U.S. investment in Mexico during the 1990s. However there were still pockets of protectionism as countries sought to protect infant industries or use tariffs and quotas to advance policy agendas. But many developing countries no longer opposed or restricted international firms. Instead, there was a renewed eagerness to attract foreign direct investment, which was seen as a partial solution to poverty and other social ills. Foreign companies are often induced to invest abroad by inexpensive labor and cheap natural resources. From the 1990s there has been a worldwide trend to re-locate labor-intensive industries abroad in countries (like China) where there is an abundance of cheap labor. FDI enables companies to locate different stages of the value chain in different, strategic locations: "marketing where consumers are close at hand, research and development where workers are smart, assembly where they are cheap."[51]

During this period, Europe embarked on a bold adventure to transcend national political entities and achieve greater economic integration through the European Union (EU). One objective of the EU was to harmonize tariffs and to create a single currency for all its members (the euro). But the major goal was to create a single market that facilitated the free movement of labor, capital services, and goods between member countries. The EU, which now has a 27-member bloc, has centralized regulations on matters such as chemical processing, environmental pollution, and privacy. Many firms doing business in Europe obey these standards in other markets to avoid the higher costs of compliance with multiple regulatory standards. Critics say that EU countries lack a common purpose and shared values and question its survival. Nonetheless, despite the EU's fraught history, many see this experiment as the first step toward a unified global political economy.[52]

What differentiates this second wave of globalization from the first wave that ended in 1914 is the high level of foreign direct investment originating from emerging markets. The British tea firm, Tetley, was purchased by India's Tata Group in 2000. Budweiser, America's most popular beer company, was purchased in 2008 by a Belgian-Brazilian conglomerate. In 2010 Volvo was purchased by Chinese car maker Zhejang Geely, and in 2016 Haier purchased the appliance division of General Electric. Thus, unlike the first wave of globalization, the second one is considerably more inclusive; it is bi-directional with FDI flowing to and from emerging economies.

This broader participation deepens interdependencies but should also go a long way in alleviating poverty in those countries that participate in this revived global economy. In India, millions of people have escaped the shackles of poverty as they precariously moved up into the country's burgeoning middle class. Consider the continent of Africa where real income per person has increased by 30% because of improving economic conditions. International firms are attracted by Africa's vast natural resources such as oil and copper. Foreign direct investment has fallen in recent years but was $46 billion in 2019. Poverty and unemployment are still widespread but the continent's economy will continue its upward trajectory so long as it embraces democratic reforms and remains committed to building new infrastructure.[53]

This intensification of globalization beginning around 1979 was accompanied by some notable political and ethical disputes that caught less vigilant companies off guard. There was an endless string of corruption scandals implicating reputable organizations like Siemens, Monsanto, and Avon in acute bribery controversies. In addition, there is a long list of other moral calamities: Union Carbide's chemical spill in Bhopal, the reluctance of many multinationals to depart apartheid South Africa, the callousness of out-sourcers like Nike, the complicity of Yahoo and Google in human rights violations in China, Philip Morris International's manipulation of lax overseas regulations to sell cigarettes without adequate warning labels,[54] Nestlé's dubious tactics in promoting infant formula in developing countries, the environmental irresponsibility of oil companies like Texaco in Ecuador and Royal Dutch Shell in Nigeria. A devastating series of deadly fires followed by a factory collapse in Bangladesh that killed over 1,100 people have underscored the unsafe working conditions for workers making products for Western retailers like Walmart and Benetton. All of these moral crises represent the high social costs associated with globalization and foreign investment. Corporate misdeeds and apparent indifference to the bleak working conditions of their low cost suppliers have stoked fears that global corporations have come to represent an ominous new form of imperial domination. Adolph Berle's remark that multinational corporations "can be thought of only in somewhat the same way we have heretofore thought of nations" would certainly strike a responsive chord with globalization's opponents.[55]

At the same time, there has been increased attention given in the media and academia to corporate social responsibility. International activist groups known as national government organizations or NGOs have also proliferated. These self-governing, non-profit, private organizations represent a "global third sector … pursuing public purposes outside the formal apparatus of the state."[56] NGOs like China Labor Watch focused on globalization issues keep a close eye on corporate performance especially in vulnerable emerging economies. Spar refers to this as the "spotlight effect," which causes strategic decisions to be constricted not by governments but by these determined private organizations with their own social agenda.[57] Social networking technologies have also enabled the rapid mobilization of large groups for political influence. These phenomena were distinctly absent during the first era of global capitalism where a company's overseas operations and misdeeds were far less transparent and concealed from the eyes of its home country. As a result, multinationals have a more difficult time shielding their foreign operations from global scrutiny.

As this second era of globalization progressed forward, there seemed little that could stop its momentum. By 2010 FDI exceeded $1 trillion with the United States, Germany, and France as the top three investing countries.[58] Globalization was also broader in scope, encompassing far more countries than it did in the 19th century. And the balance of power was shifting from Europe and Japan to countries like China, which has become an economic powerhouse and the leading center of manufacturing. But some of the contradictions and tensions that threatened the first era of globalization in 1913 could be found in the second decade of this new century: rising inequities, nationalism, and economic frustration on the part of those who were the "losers" in this global economy.[59]

De-globalization 2.0

The damaging 2008 recession marks the inception of a new phase in global capitalism's history: the return of de-globalization. Globalization has not collapsed but the 2020 pandemic has accelerated forces that were already in motion. While companies still engage in large amounts of cross-border trading, there is a shift to local production that is likely to grow stronger thanks to robotics and automation. Also the China–United States relationship has been impaired and so trade occurs under a cloud of mutual mistrust and suspicion.[60]

The recession was the most serious crisis for the global economy since the Great Depression of 1929. The U.S stock market plummeted and the country's steep economic decline, caused primarily by the subprime mortgage calamity, quickly spread to Europe and Asia. FDI was severely reduced as corporations retrenched. Although apprehension about protectionism turned out to be exaggerated, global trade flows decreased for first time since World War II.[61] There were setbacks for emerging markets which could no longer count on export-driven growth to sustain their fragile economies. Thanks to the excesses of some banks and financial institutions, whose negligent actions precipitated the crisis, there was new distrust in capitalism and its long-term ability to promote social welfare. There was renewed focus on the income disparities and inequities apparently caused by globalization. In addition, the forces of national populism galvanized into a new challenge for Western liberalism.[62]

Brexit, the United Kingdom's decision to sever its ties with the European Union, was another omen signaling globalization's troubled future. Britain was the EU's second largest economy, so its departure puts the bloc's future in some doubt. UK citizens lamented the loss of the country's sovereignty at the hands of EU regulators in Brussels. The EU imposed too many regulations and restrictions that did not yield tangible benefits for the British economy. But now the UK has more latitude to create unilateral trade deals, restrict immigration, and try to revive its manufacturing industries without the shackles of EU regulations. The consequences of Brexit remain to be seen, but for those who saw the EU as the stepping stone to greater international cooperation, this event is a notable setback.

Another blow to globalization has been the trade war between the United States and China that began during the Trump administration (2016–2020). President Trump took direct aim at China's autocratic system of capitalism and unfair trading policies that kept U.S. products, especially agricultural goods, out of China. The president's goal was also to increase U.S. factory production by making Chinese goods more expensive. The 2020 trade deal between the two countries established new U.S. tariffs on imports from China for the foreseeable future. In 2021 tariffs covered half of Chinese exports to the United States, or about $250 billion in goods. China's retaliatory tariffs cover 58.3% of U.S. exports to China.[63]

But by far the biggest blow to globalization's prospects is undoubtedly the coronavirus pandemic that has imposed a new economic reality. The pandemic temporarily shut down the world economy in March 2020. Months later, just as the economy was set to recover, countries had to contend with a costly second wave of the virus. In the face of this global health crisis some countries began to worry about sourcing too much of their medical equipment and pharmaceuticals from China. China, for example, supplied 42% of the world's personal protective equipment, while 75% of Italy's imported blood thinners come from China. The pandemic exposed low inventories and choke points due to reliance on foreign suppliers. In the United States, it is likely that there will be new procurement rules compelling health care providers to purchase American-made products. In general, economists predict that there will be a strong impetus to domesticate more supply chains for the sake of greater economic independence and resilience. As the coronavirus swept through India the prime minister, Narendra Modi, announced that a new era of economic self-reliance had begun.[64]

Capital flows have also diminished thanks to the decline in long-term investment. Foreign direct investment in 2020 fell by 42% to about $860 billion, down from $1.5 trillion in 2019. FDI in developed economies took the biggest hit, falling by 69%. China was the largest recipient of FDI in 2020 with $163 billion in capital inflows. Nonetheless, governments like the United States are more hesitant about investing in China, and countries representing about 60% of the world's GDP have imposed new restrictions on foreign investment.[65]

Much of the retrenchment hurting foreign trade was due to a slump in demand, but travel bans, and quarantines, kept people from traveling. During the height of the pandemic, the number of passengers at Heathrow Airport fell by 97%. Fewer passenger means fewer planes and less room for air freight. Travel restrictions and stricter border controls impeded trade and the free flow of goods across borders.[66] Recovery for the travel and transportation industries will be a long process. All of these conditions, combined with other forces such as resurgent nationalism, will most likely foster a temporary bias toward self-reliance and a period of isolationist policies.

To what extent the world shifts away from free trade and open markets remains to be seen. But the revival of autarky and nationalism is unlikely to optimize social welfare. Interdependencies have their costs, but the lost efficiencies that come with a push toward economic self-sufficiency could be disastrous for the global economy.[67]

Conclusions

The new reality of de-globalization reaffirms globalization's historical contingency. The historical path of global capitalism is not a straight, ascending line but a jagged one with upward spurts and sharp reversals. Moreover, there is no "invisible hand" to foster global economic integration. It requires prudent and deliberate polices that steer countries away from isolationist tendencies and toward global engagement.

What are the other lessons of this non-teleological history of global capitalism besides its contingency? Some are fairly obvious. An abundance of evidence affirms the correlation between rapid expansion of trade, coupled with foreign direct investment, and steady economic growth. This correlation between GDP and economic integration was evident in the first era of globalization that ended in 1913 and is more evident today. Both trade and FDI contribute to economic growth and create better paying jobs. The economic histories of China and India strongly confirm this thesis. Once these countries repudiated a socialist economic model and allowed their citizens to create wealth with the indispensable help of foreign investment and technology transfers, poverty sharply declined. Also, in countries like South Korea and Taiwan, evidence shows how strong economic growth propelled by global trade has "pulled up" the poor into productive employment and out of the depths of poverty.[68] On the other hand, there are no examples of countries that have increased income and standards of living through isolationism. Cuba and North Korea come closest to this ideal of almost total self-sufficiency, but what country would want to emulate their abysmal economic performance? As economists Lindert and Williamson have observed, "There are no anti-global victories to report for the postwar era."[69] The economic growth fostered by trade and FDI may not be a sufficient condition for alleviating poverty but it is almost certainly a necessary condition.

There are some deeper lessons of history that revolve around the paradoxical connection between the state and commerce. The political philosopher, Istvan Hont, asked whether it was appropriate to conceive the economy in a way that is independent of politics – or must the economy be defined in political terms? "Is political economy simply an oxymoron that yokes together two incongruous components without resolving the tension between them?"[70] This "incongruity" between the state and the market economy has been assumed as a tenet of Western capitalism, where the modern state has only an "elective affinity" with free markets and where corporations are strictly apolitical economic entities. But the reality is quite different. The state is deeply involved in economic affairs in some Western economies and most especially in countries like China where there has been a convergence of communism and capitalism. At the same time, as multinationals move into frontier economies where there are many institutional voids, they encounter weak or failed states and must perform tasks that are usually the responsibility of the state such as the provision of security and health care.[71]

Finally, is China's economic model of state-guided capitalism a realistic scenario for the future? China is rapidly transforming the global economic system that elevates the interests of the state and the majority over the interests of its countries' minorities. China seems to have found a way to resolve the tension between the state and commerce, even though it has renounced the liberal order of the West, which it sees as an obstacle to its ascent to global power.[72] But can global capitalism really thrive without a commitment to political liberties that have been at the center of democratic capitalism?

As multinationals navigate this difficult terrain, they encounter enormous political and social challenges, especially the new struggle between East and West. These are accompanied by distinctly moral challenges posed by cultural diversity. Global managers must find a way to respect local culture and different political systems, while always being sensitive to transcultural values that transcend culture and politics. These corporations must balance respect for the sovereignty of their host country with fidelity to ethical ideals and to international standards of decency that no government or international moral agent has a right to cast aside. How multinationals handle the moral tensions inherent in this relationship with foreign governments is intrinsically important but also vital for the future credibility of global capitalism.

Notes

1 William Shirer, *The Rise and Fall of the Third Reich: A History of Nazi Germany* (New York: Simon & Schuster, 1960), 196–202.

2 Quoted in Harold James, *Krupp: A History of the Legendary German Firm* (Princeton, NJ: Princeton University Press, 2012), 2.

3 See, for example, William Manchester, *The Arms of Krupp: 1587–1968* (Boston, MA: Little Brown, 1968). The Krupp family was also the subject of an unflattering film by Luchino Visconti called *The Damned* (1969). A biography of Alfred Krupp by Thomas Mann's son provides two conflicting views of the company's leader during the war: "One is that he cooperated in as much as he needed to hesitatingly and under pressure, and occasionally resisting. The other is that he and his company cooperated willingly and with pleasure, much more intensively than they needed to." See Tilman Lahme, *Golo Mann: Biographie* (Frankfurt: Fischer, 2009), 390. See also James, *Krupp: A History*, 172–173.

4 James, *Krupp: A History*, 43

5 James, *Krupp: A History*, 275.

6 David Hume, "Of Civil Liberty," in *Political Essays* ed. Knud Haakonssen (Cambridge, UK: Cambridge University Press, 1994), 52.

7 A *multinational* is a firm that controls operations or income generating assets in more than one country. This book also considers *international* corporations that are global in scope because they source, sell, or engage in other activities across national boundaries although the firm or organization remains physically in only one location. The term "transnational" is sometimes used as a synonym for multinational. See R. Vernon and L. Wells, *Manager in the International Economy*, 5th ed. (Englewood Cliffs, NJ: Prentice-Hall, 1986).

8 B. Kogut, "Globalization," in *Concise International Encyclopedia of Business and Management* ed. M. Warner (London: Thomson Business Press, 1997), 99.

9 Martin Wolf, *Why Globalization Works* (New Haven, CT: Yale University Press, 2004), 14. Scholars like Peter Berger have analyzed cultural globalization, which is not the axis of discussion in this book. According to Berger, "Globalization is, *au fond*, a continuation … of the perduring challenge of modernization. On the cultural level this has been the great challenge of pluralism: the breakdown of taken-for-granted traditions and the opening up of multiple options for beliefs, values, and lifestyles." See Peter Berger, "Introduction," to *Many Globalizations: Cultural Diversity in the Contemporary World* eds. Peter Berger and Samuel Huntington (Oxford: Oxford University Press, 2002), 16.

10 St. Thomas Aquinas, *De Regno* (Toronto: Pontifical Institute of Medieval Studies, 1949), Bk. 2, Ch. 3 (author's translation).

11 Adam Smith, *An Inquiry into the Nature and Causes of the Wealth of Nations* (Oxford: Oxford University Press, 1976), 457.

12 David Moss, *A Concise Guide to Macro Economics* (Boston, MA: Harvard Business Review Press, 2014, 16–18. See also "Trade Winds," *Economist*, November 8, 1997, 85.

13 Wolf, *Why Globalization Works*, 80–82. See also Bhagwati, *In Defense of Globalization*, 61 and "Donaldson's Difficult Idea," *Economist*, April 22, 2017, 69.

14 Moss, *A Concise Guide to Macro Economics*, 16–20; see also "Trade Winds," *Economist*, 85.

15 G.W.F. Hegel, *Reason in History* (Indianapolis, IN: Bobbs-Merrill, 1978), 25.

16 I follow the framework of Geoffrey Jones, *Entrepreneurship and Global Capitalism* (Boston, MA: Harvard Business School Press, 2019), 2.

17 Kevin O'Rourke, "Europe and the Causes of Globalization, 1790 to 2000," in *Europe and Globalization* ed. H. Kierzkowski (Basingstoke: Palgrave Macmillan, 2002), 65.

18 Geoffrey Jones, *Multinationals and Global Capitalism* (Oxford: Oxford University Press, 2005), 5–15. I am indebted to Jones' insightful treatment of the history of globalization in several key chapters of his book.

19 Ibid.

20 Jagdish Bhagwati, *In Defense of Globalization* (Oxford: Oxford University Press, 2004), 11.

21 Sophus Reinert and Frederica Gabrieli, "Globalization Past, 1850–1914" (Boston, MA: Harvard Business School Press, 2018), 3–5.

22 David Reynolds, *The Long Shadow* (New York: W.W. Norton, 2014), 101.

23 Stephen Broadberry and Kevin O'Rourke, *The Cambridge Economic History of Modern Europe* (Cambridge, UK: Cambridge University Press, 2010), 10.

24 See Maurice Obstfeld and Alan Taylor, "Globalization and Capital Markets," in *Globalization in Historical Perspective* ed. M. Bordo and A.M. Taylor (Chicago, IL: University of Chicago Press, 2002), 66–85.

25 Geoffrey Jones, "Multinationals and the First Global Economy Before 1914" (Boston, MA: Harvard Business School Publications, 2004).

26 Jeffrey Frieden, *Global Capitalism* (New York: W.W. Norton, 2006), 19.

27 Angus Maddison, *The World Economy: A Millennial Perspective* (Paris: Development Center of the Organization for Economic Cooperation and Development, 2001), 3, 264.

28 Per Vries, *State, Economy and the Great Divergence: Great Britain and China, 1680s–1850s* (London: Bloomsbury, 2015). See also Sophus Reinert, "The Great Divergence: Europe and Modern Economic Growth" (Boston, MA: Harvard Business School Publishing, 2018).

29 Reinert and Gabrieli, "Globalization Past."

30 See Norman Angell, *The Great Illusion: A Study of the Relation of the Military Power in Nations to their Economic and Social Advantage* (New York: Garland, 1972). See also Broadberry and O'Rourke, *Cambridge Economic History of Modern Europe*, 137.

31 Reynolds, *The Long Shadow*, xxv.

32 Expropriation is defined as "an act whereby government takes into ownership, by compulsion if necessary, private property for a public use." See M.L. Williams, "The Extent and Significance of the Nationalism of Foreign-owned Assets in Developing Countries," *Oxford Economic Papers* 27 (1975), 261.

33 Geoffrey Jones, "Expropriation in International Business" (Boston, MA: Harvard Business School Publications, 2003), 2.

34 Mira Wilkins, *The Maturing of Multinational Enterprise: American Business Abroad from 1914 to 1970* (Cambridge, MA: Harvard University Press, 1974), 23–26.

35 Reynolds, *The Long Shadow*, 6–15.

36 Angus Maddison, *World Economy in the Twentieth Century* (Paris: OECD, 1989), 98. See also Reynolds, *The Long Shadow*, 149.

37 Wilkins, *Maturing of Multinational Enterprise*, 152–155.

38 Arthur Schlesinger, *The Age of Roosevelt: The Crisis of the Old Order* (New York: Sentry, 1957), 166.

39 Jürgen von Kruedener, *Economic Crisis and Political Collapse: The Weimar Republic, 1924–1933* (New York: Oxford University Press, 1990), xiii.

40 Wilkins, *Maturing of Multinational Enterprise*, 228–229.

41 Frieden, *Global Capitalism*, 212–215.

42 Shale Horowitz, "Restarting Globalization after World War II," *Comparative Political Studies* 37 (2) (2004), 127–151.

43 See Daniel Litvin, *Empires of Profit* (New York: Texere, 2003), 147–148.

44 Jagdish Bhagwati and Arvind Panagariya, *Why Growth Matters* (New York: Perseus Books, 2013), 8.

45 Robert Heilbroner, *The Making of Economic Society*, 5th ed. (Englewood Cliffs, NJ: Prentice-Hall, 1975), 223–225.

46 Wilkins, *Maturing of Multinational Enterprise*, 350–355.

47 Richard Barnet and Ronald Muller, *Global Reach: The Power of Multinational Corporations* (New York: Simon & Schuster, 1974), 81–86.

48 Ronald Coase and Ning Wang, *How China Became Capitalist* (New York: Palgrave Macmillan, 2013), 122.

49 Christian Caryl, *Strange Rebels* (New York: Basic Books, 2013), 237.

50 Julie Cohen, *Configuring the Networked Self* (New Haven, CT: Yale University Press, 2012), 12–13.

51 "Globalization with a Third-World Face," *Economist*, April 9, 2005, 66.

52 "Searching for Meaning," *Economist*, May 16, 2020, 15–17.

53 "Emerging Africa: A Hopeful Continent," *Economist*, March 2, 2013, 4–9. See also World Investment Report 2020, Tralac, January 2020; www.tralac,org/world-investment-report-2020.

54 For more details see "When Health and Trade Policies Don't Jibe," *National Journal*, April 18, 1988.

55 Quoted in Heilbroner, *The Making of Economic Society*, 226.

56 Lester Salamon, "The Rise of the Nonprofit Sector," *Foreign Affairs* 73 (1994), 109.

57 Deborah Spar, "The Spotlight Effect and the Bottom Line," *Foreign Affairs* 77 (1998), 7–12.

58 OECD Factbook, 2012. Available at: http://www.oced-ilibrary.org/sites/factbook-2012-en.

59 Reinert and Gabrieli, "Globalization Past."

60 "Special Report on the World Economy: The Peril and the Promise," *Economist*, October 10, 2020.

61 Binyamin Applebaum, "A Little Noticed Fact about Trade: It's No Longer Growing," *New York Times*, October 30, 2016, B7.

62 Jones, "Entrepreneurship and Global Capitalism," 13.

63 Josh Zumbrum, "U.S. Tariffs Drive Drop in U.S. Imports," *Wall Street Journal*, May 12, 2021, A1, A8.

64 "Torn Apart," *Economist*, May 16, 2020, 57–59. See also "Goodbye Globalization," *Economist*, May 16, 2020, 7.

65 "Goodbye Globalization," 7. See also "China Was Largest Recipient of FDI in 2020," *Reuters*, January 24, 2021, 11.

66 Ibid.

67 "Message in a Bottleneck," *Economist*, April 3, 2021, 9.

68 Bhagwati and Panagariya, *Why Growth Matters*, 24–25. For data on Taiwan, see Arvind Panagariya, "Trade Openness and Growth Miracles: A Fresh Look at Taiwan," in *Ashgate Research Companion to International Trade Policy* ed. Ken Heyden and Stephen Woolcock (London: Ashgate Publishing Limited, 2011).

69 Peter Lindert and John Williamson, "Does Globalization Make the World More Unequal," Paper delivered at Conference on Globalization in Historical Perspective, National Bureau of Economic Research, Santa Barbara, CA, May 3, 2001.

70 Istvan Hont, *Jealousy of Trade* (Cambridge, MA: Harvard University Press, 2005), 3–4.

71 Sophus Reinert, "Globalization," (Boston, MA: Harvard Business School Publishing, 2018), 4. I have benefited greatly from Reinert's reflections on globalization in this chapter.

72 "China Sees its Moment," *Economist*, April 3, 2021, 36.

Chapter 2

Global capitalism and free markets

Students at the University of Chile were bustling about as they prepared for another day of political demonstrations in downtown Santiago. This volatile protest movement had been originally organized by Javier Lopez Layana, a prominent activist and student at the university. Much of the organization took place over social media. The protests began in early October 2019 and continued unabated for many days. What triggered the event was a 30-pesos (4-cent) subway fare increase, but the population's ongoing struggle with low wages and high prices set the stage. "The abuses haven't stopped," declared one protester, "so we're going into the streets."[1]

President Sebastián Piñera watched with mounting dread as social chaos and political turmoil convulsed his country. As the violence escalated, he dispatched the military to restore some semblance of law and order. Piñera sought to placate the incensed protesters with the promise of better health care coverage and higher pensions. He also asked his cabinet to resign and promised a greater effort to eradicate political corruption.[2]

The underlying causes of Chile's unrest are complex and trace back to its transition to a democratic government at the end of Pinochet's military dictatorship. While military rule had ended, the free market policies of the Pinochet era were largely kept in place. But there was growing discontent with political corruption and the apparent failure of the free market system to improve economic welfare for the majority of the population. The country's median salary is $540 per month, and protesters claim with some justification that the country needs economic structural reforms. To some extent, the protests reflected a rising rejection of capitalism itself. But will this impulse to change steer Chile in the wrong direction?[3]

While the arguments of Chile's critics have some merit, there is another side to the story that is neglected by those who applaud this "woke" Chilean moment. Citizens below the poverty rate in Chile have fallen to about 9%, from 68% in 1990.

DOI: 10.4324/9781003058427-2

Income inequality is still a problem, but it too has been coming down. Almost 65% of Chile's population is classified as middle class, a big increase from the mid-1980s. Observers argue that Chile has grown more prosperous than most of its neighbors by sticking with free market principles such as private property, competition, and the rule of law. Yet anti-capitalist forces have gained momentum and want to see the pendulum swing back from the neo-liberal policies initiated by Pinochet in favor of socialist economic policies. They have successfully convinced Chileans to vote for a new constitution that in all likelihood will increase the monopoly power of the state and redistribute wealth. Of course, Chile is not alone. This same drama is being played out in many countries, even in the United States, where some 2020 protests for racial justice promoted class warfare and called for radical economic change.[4]

This chapter will concentrate on the benefits of traditional capitalism as well as its flaws and contradictions. It begins by addressing a fundamental question: what sets capitalism and free market enterprise itself apart from a purely socialist economic system? Since liberal capitalism is so closely linked with globalization, we cannot understand the forces and benefits of globalization without an adequate understanding of capitalism. A secondary aim of this book is to offer a modest justification of global capitalism, despite its well-documented deficiencies. But any efforts to justify globalization or defend it from its most strident critics cannot succeed apart from some treatment of free market capitalism. In addition, it certainly seems that our primary task would be incomplete if we develop an account of a multinational's social responsibility, while ignoring the capitalist context within which its corporate policies and actions occur. Corporate social responsibility should be seen in the light of the moral logic of capitalism, which is sorely tested when there are deviations from the ideal of fair market conditions and efficiencies.

Liberal capitalism is predicated on extensive private property rights along with open and free markets. Labor and capital are unfettered so they can seek out the best returns or opportunities, and that freedom is supported by a matrix of political liberties. Capitalism has a solid record of sustaining economic growth while serving as a catalyst for an expanding global economy. However, even governments that respect and promote free markets need to intervene sometimes when there are market failures, including information deficiencies and negative externalities such as environmental degradation. A key issue, however, revolves around the scope of government involvement in the market. Should government interventions be confined to the correction of market failures or should government adopt a more expansive role by directing certain industries and by correcting inequitable distributions of wealth and capital?

Perhaps one of the greatest trials for Western multinationals is the centralizing impulse of countries like China and Russia. State-guided capitalism has emerged in these countries as an alternative to traditional Western capitalism. State-owned or controlled enterprises flourish in these economies while the door is closed to some civil liberties and any political competition. Can capitalism prosper without the same commitment to human rights and moral principles found in liberal democracies?

And how can multinationals navigate a landscape where economic opportunities are intermingled with human rights abuses? We address these provocative questions in this chapter, but we begin with some reflections on capitalism's primary attributes.

Free markets and private property rights

Defenders of liberal, free market capitalism have cogently argued that economic liberty is a necessary condition not only for high economic performance but also for a person's full personal freedom. Economic liberty includes freedom to choose one's own occupation, freedom to produce and consume goods and services, and freedom to make investments. Countries support this matrix of economic freedoms with institutions like liberal well-defined property rights so that economic agents can acquire, use, and commercialize that property. People clearly value the right to make these economic choices without state interference.[5]

Moreover, as Gaus points out, "there has never been a political order characterized by deep respect for personal freedom that was not based on a market order with widespread private ownership of the means of production."[6] Economic liberty, therefore, is heavily dependent on strong private property rights, the lynchpin of liberal capitalism. While the right to property is not absolute, it is a fundamental right that deserves vigorous protection by the state. Communism, on the other hand, categorically rejects extensive property rights. As Karl Marx emphatically declared, "Communism is the positive abolition of private property."[7]

Thus, the ideal of capitalism is characterized by "maximally extensive feasible property rights." How are these expansive property rights most accurately defined? A property right or right of ownership is actually a collection of rights that are usually separated out in mature legal systems. That collection of rights includes the right to possess (through exclusive physical control or the right to exclude others from use), the right to use, the right to manage, the right to income, the right to alienate (to sell or otherwise dispose of the property), and the right to security (that is, immunity from expropriation). In summary, property rights are best understood as full proprietary rights over tangible or intangible things. Like most rights, property rights can be reasonably restricted and limited by the State for the sake of the common good.[8]

Capitalist systems recognize a broad scope of rights for each individual property owner. But the capitalist system also expands the scope of things that can be privately owned. In contrast to communist systems, capital goods or the goods of production can be owned by private companies or individuals. Natural resources can also be owned by private entities. In an unregulated, laissez-faire market economy, there would be no restrictions on the sort of things people could own. However, a mature and responsible government will prohibit ownership of some things such as people, and hence it will declare slavery to be illegal. But in general the capitalist ideal seeks to maximize the rights of ownership along with the spectrum of objects that can be owned.[9]

Several philosophers have offered thoughtful justifications of these liberal property rights at the heart of capitalism. John Locke's famous theory of property is presented in *The Second Treatise of Government*, which enthusiastically defends the proposition of "natural rights." Locke brought property rights directly to the center of political philosophy, as he demonstrated that these rights were not dependent on the arbitrary claims of a monarch or any civil government. A property right was the corollary of the right to self-preservation: "if everyone has the natural right to preserve himself, he necessarily has the right to everything that is necessary for his self-preservation."[10] A property right is based on self-ownership, that is, ownership of one's body and the labor it produces. Once the labor is "annexed" to common resources, the laborer justly appropriates the end result. Therefore, Locke insisted that property was not a convention of the state, but a God-given, natural right that precedes civil society. It is reasonable to assume, writes Locke, that God "who bid Mankind increase and multiply should ... give them all a Right to make use of the food and Rayment, and other Conveniences of life, the Materials whereof he had so plentifully provided for them."[11]

For Locke, the state exists to protect that natural right along with other natural rights such as life and liberty. As he explains, "The great and chief end, therefore, of Men's uniting into Commonwealths, and putting themselves under Government, is the Preservation of their Property."[12] Locke, who convincingly discarded the divine right of kings as the principle of sovereignty, argued for a limited government that respects the needs and rights of citizens to pursue their own objectives. Since the individual in the state of nature agrees to be governed as a means of protecting his or her rights, "the power of the society or legislature constituted by them can never be supposed to extend farther" than what is necessary for the preservation of those rights.[13]

We can infer from Locke's political analysis that the right to property, which is recognized but not bestowed by the state, is essential for our human flourishing, because it is so closely linked to a person's capacity to apply his or her intellect and will to material and intellectual objects, to set plans and goals, and to be good stewards of possessions. In general, property contributes to our capacity for self-determination, to put our distinctive personal mark on the sphere of nature. Property rights ensure security of possession and thereby support entrepreneurial freedom and independence, the right to start and operate a business as one sees fit without state interference or the risk of confiscation. Collective ownership, on the other hand, is unworkable and usually turns into ownership by an elite, privileged political class. While collective ownership breeds dependence on the state, private property rights give people autonomy and independence that is a necessary stimulus for creativity.[14]

Thus, property rights disperse power and give people an opportunity to properly exercise their autonomy and invest things with a personal meaning. Hegel emphasizes this logical connection between property rights and freedom throughout his political philosophy. One of the most important institutions that constitute the ethical life (*Sittlichkeit*) of a people is property. Hegel explains that a person must be able to control and shape objects in his or her environment over time; otherwise the world will remain an alien place. The human subject requires "the right of putting his will into any and every being and making it his property."[15] The person cannot be free without this ability to overcome the opposition between self and world by projecting his or her personality into external objects. Property rights, which safeguard secure possession and stability of ownership, are necessary to protect this freedom and to inspire the extension of someone's will and personality into the external world. Hegel agreed with his predecessor, Immanuel Kant, that freedom of choice requires freedom of action and freedom of action requires the right to possess.[16]

Hegel would disagree with Locke's views on the minimal role of the state, but Locke's paradigm has prevailed within the liberal tradition. Despite Locke's minimalism, there is a firm acknowledgment of the necessity of the legal order. Laws give people space to pursue their objectives, preserve strong but limited property rights, and help settle disputes over rights. As Hayek explained, "law, liberty, and property are an inseparable trinity."[17]

In addition to broad property rights that enable economic liberty, capitalism also depends on free and open markets. The presumption is that free or voluntary exchange of the goods in the marketplace by property holders yields the most efficient economic outcome. Individuals and companies "reassign" their property rights when goods are exchanged. These markets will also set wages and prices. The forces of supply and demand determine the market clearing price of a product along with the efficient quantity to be produced. The entrepreneur must face the discipline of the market and satisfy the consumer's needs at the appropriate price if he or she is to remain in business and make a reasonable profit. In this "commercial society," there is a formal equality as jobs are open to all based on talent and ability.

As Adam Smith has explained, division of labor and voluntary exchange are the keys to a prosperous economy. Even though the workers and other market participants in that economy are motivated by self-interest, under certain conditions the free market allocates resources efficiently, producing the right outcome that maximizes social welfare by allowing society to get the most out of its scarce resources. Society is guided to this optimal result by an "invisible hand" that directs uncoordinated individuals to supply the right amount of goods that are demanded by consumers at the appropriate price. According to Smith,

> The natural effort of every individual to better his own condition, when suffered to exert himself with freedom and security, is so powerful a principle that it is alone … capable of carrying on the society to wealth and prosperity. … Every individual endeavors as much as he can to direct … industry so that its produce may be of the greatest value, … neither intend[ing] to promote the public interest, nor know[ing] how much he is promoting it. He intends only his own gain, and he is, in this, as in many other cases, led by an *invisible hand* to promote an end that

was no part of his intention. By pursuing his own interest he frequently promotes that of society more effectually than when he really intends to promote it.[18]

Competition fueled by self-interest brings about the most effective coordination of individual efforts. Socialist governments often feel ill at ease over the chaotic and disorderly free market and its apparent lack of coordination. As a consequence, they seek to nudge it in one direction or another, though sometimes this intervention is counterproductive. But Smith, who agreed with Locke in the need for governmental restraint, believed that economic liberty supported by property rights along with free markets created their own social order that was not imposed by the state but resulted *spontaneously* from the cooperation and competition of ordinary people.[19]

The alternative to free markets and broad property ownership is constrained property rights and central planning where the omniscient and omnipotent state owns and controls virtually all means of production and sets all wages and prices. Collectivism or communism, defined as the "abolition of private property," eliminates the market and subjects the entire economy to the management of "associated producers" controlled by the state.[20] These producers represent "socialized man" who is finally free and no longer at the mercy of "the blind forces of Nature."[21] The planners in these economies attempt to organize all of society as if it were one large factory. In communist handbooks we find comments like the following: "We must know in advance how much labor to assign to the various branches of industry; what products are required and how much of it is necessary to produce; how and where machines must be provided. These and similar details must be thought out beforehand, with approximate accuracy at least; and the work must be guided in accordance with these calculations."[22]

As Friedrich Hayek has been at pains to insist, however, the central planner suffers from a "fatal conceit," a sort of "synoptic delusion," believing that he or she could somehow know and evaluate all the relevant information necessary to operate and control an efficient economy. Policy makers can never possess such perfect knowledge about the behavior of people and must always deal with the unintended consequences of their policies. Moreover, Hayek explains that economic planning has broad and possibly inhumane consequences: "Economic control is not merely control of a sector of human life which can be separated from the rest; it is the control of the means for all our ends."[23]

The failure of both the Soviet Union and China's command economy under Mao sounded the death knell for collectivism. But new modalities of socialism have taken its place. Modern proponents of democratic socialism recognize the difficulty of purging the economy of private corporations. Nonetheless, this ideology proposes "state ownership of certain industries," where elected officials would decide what to make and what prices to charge. But a socialist economy with some private corporations under greater state control is most likely a transitional phase on the way to communism and the abolition of capitalism and free, open markets.[24]

For Hayek, of course what is far superior to central or even industry-wide planning is a decentralized system of production that relies primarily on private capital and unencumbered labor. Capitalism creates economic opportunity since it encourages competition, innovation, and efficiency through market rewards. It rewards the entrepreneur for creating value and for efficiently serving the wants and needs of others. Socialist systems, however, not only provide few incentives for innovation that benefit individuals but also foster dependence on the state and on the schemes of its planners. As a result, those systems have not been able to drive economic growth in the same way as democratic capitalism.

Within the thought of Locke, Smith, and Hayek, one finds the rudimentary ideas of classic liberalism, which is committed to a "thick" conception of economic liberty, supported by strong and expansive property rights, and to formal equality or equality of opportunity within the marketplace.[25] Economic liberty implies liberty of labor ("the liberty to employ one's body and time in productive activity one has chosen or accepted") and liberty of transacting (the freedom to manage one's own economic affairs).[26] The classical liberal tradition also accepts the efficacy of free markets and a limited role for the state in economic affairs. The state is a referee in the marketplace but not a direct player.

Inequality and the socialist challenge

Critics of classical liberal capitalism claim that extensive property rights and free markets are incompatible with the ideal of social justice. The unrestricted ownership of productive or capital goods along with modestly regulated markets produces asymmetries of wealth and power to the great disadvantage of vast numbers of people. According to philosophers who advocate this perspective, sometimes referred to as "high liberalism," social justice demands that excessive wealth must be redistributed if real justice is to be achieved.

Along these lines, an objective but pungent critique of capitalism is found in the work of Thomas Piketty, who concludes that the dynamics of private capital accumulation are leading to a dangerous concentration of wealth in very few powerful hands. To some extent, this plutocracy comes about because the countervailing forces of competition, economic growth, and technological progress have been unable to reduce that inequality.[27] Consequently, what was once a moderately egalitarian society is becoming more aristocratic with a small coterie of plutocrats exercising disproportionate political influence. This trend is a threat to democracy and to the social values on which it is based.

Piketty's study, *Capitalism in the Twenty-First Century*, is premised on a central contradiction of capitalism that can be concisely captured in the following formula: $r > g = I$ where r is the rate of return on capital, g is the rate of economic growth, and I is widening inequality. His principal argument is that "when the rate of return on capital exceeds the rate of growth or output and income, as it did in the nineteenth century, and seems quite likely to do again in the twenty-first, capitalism generates arbitrary and unsustainable inequalities."[28] Piketty uses "wealth" and "capital" as synonymous terms, even though capital is a factor of production and wealth can include assets such as art works that have no productive value.[29]

Piketty's grand theory assumes that those whose income derives exclusively from their labor will be given wage increases that are tied to the economy's productivity increase, which is usually a little less than the overall economic growth rate. On the other hand, the wealthy, those whose income comes primarily from returns on their accumulated wealth, earn "r" percent on their money. These prosperous individuals are less disposed to consume more than a small percentage of that income. Piketty's analysis concludes that when the rate of return (r) on capital is higher than the economic growth rate (g), the income and accumulated wealth of the affluent will grow much faster than the income from derived work. As a result, the gap will widen between the very rich and the workers in the lower and middle classes of society. Thus, thanks to a resurgence of inherited wealth and low economic growth we are now headed towards an era of peerless wealth concentration.[30] Of course, flagrant inequality is nothing new in the history of global capitalism, which has seen a succession of inequitable regimes.

For many, the excessive inequities described by Piketty are inconsistent with a just society. John Rawls, among others, has persuasively argued that a well-ordered and just society will provide equal liberties for its citizens and will permit social and economic inequalities only to the extent that they benefit the least advantaged. Preferable to an equal and uniform distribution of wealth and income, however, is the toleration of certain inequalities if they improve the condition of those who have the least. But Rawls believed that a necessary condition of justice as fairness was that "property and wealth must be kept widely distributed."[31] Piketty would concur, and he proposes the imposition of much higher taxes on the rich, perhaps running as high as 90% on society's biggest fortunes.

According to this paradigm, the redistribution of concentrated wealth is necessary even if it means the attenuation of economic liberty. The tradition of high liberalism or social democracy, reflected in the work of Rawls and Piketty, affirms a thin conception of economic liberty, a more "substantive conception of equality" that requires goods to be distributed in ways that benefit the least advantaged. It also proposes a much broader role for the state in regulating the market.[32]

Another acute criticism of classical liberal capitalism is that free markets are not conducive to the development of good moral character because they breed individualism and consumerism. Corporations are quite adept at generating demand for their products by expanding consumer "needs" and desires through advertising and marketing. Capitalism educates people to conceive of themselves as consumers. The capitalist creed proposes that the acquisition of material goods is the key to a fulfilling life. According to Alasdair MacIntyre, capitalism is an immoral system because it induces people to regard greed as a virtue rather than a vice. As an Aristotelian, MacIntyre believes that our final end can be pursued only by human beings cooperating and acting together in a community where there is solidarity toward others. Yet, in his estimation, capitalism militates against such efforts.[33] People who pursue wealth even to excess are rewarded and esteemed by their peers for following their acquisitive impulses. Consequently, atomized individualism along with the avaricious pursuit of wealth becomes normative. Capitalism, therefore, unlike economic systems that promote equality and solidarity, is tainted by greed and the drive to accumulate.[34]

Free markets and thick property rights also tend to breed corporate malfeasance. Public corporations are the "property" of the shareholders who pressure corporate managers for high returns on their risky investment. Corporate managers are easily prone to opportunistic behavior in their rent-seeking activities. The relentless drive for profit maximization accounts for steady progression of corporate scandals in the global economy. While some corporations have consistently acted conscientiously, others have willingly produced unsafe products, engaged in fraudulent marketing campaigns, looked the other way when their suppliers mistreated workers, and encroached upon privacy rights with impunity. For a number of years too many corporations were also derelict in their duty to avoid degrading the natural environment. There are few countervailing forces to curtail their acquisitive impulses. Self-moderation is not a virtue of the capitalist system.

A more thorough treatment of free market capitalism's deficiencies is well beyond the scope of this book. But let it suffice to say that there is certainly some merit to these familiar objections. As we saw in the previous chapter, some companies go too far in their pursuit of property and profits. They exploit workers and harm consumers along with other stakeholders. But most of the worst excesses are found in uncompetitive and dysfunctional markets. Moreover, for Adam Smith, the virtues of justice and prudence were intrinsic to a well-functioning commercial society. Harmful individualism and opportunism that undermine "free" markets ensue when these virtues are discarded.[35]

Authentic capitalism gives primacy to the entrepreneur as it rewards hard work and creative innovation. Entrepreneurial opportunity has the potential to build character rather than destabilize it. Authentic capitalism is predicated on free market clarity so consumers can judge the value and quality of products offered for sale. Authentic capitalism also demands financial validity without wild gambles on the anomalies of the global economy. Opaque markets full of abstract financial derivatives and other forms of speculation are a deviation from capitalism as it was originally conceived by Adam Smith and others. The challenge is to reform free market capitalism so that it fosters unrestricted entrepreneurship and prudent competition, rather than pursue a socialist agenda that abolishes or radically curtails market mechanisms.[36]

In addition, the myopic moral vision of individualized and unrestricted property rights to be exercised without concern for others is not faithful to the intellectual roots of liberalism, which is disposed toward some measure of distributive equity. Contrary to Piketty's claims, capitalism is not based on a neo-proprietarian ideology that absolutizes private property rights.[37] John Locke, for example, contended that property rights must be limited by what he called a "charity proviso," which recognizes that the poor sometimes have a claim on the assets of valid property holders. Thus, a commitment to property rights and economic liberty does not preclude a concern for social justice issues. Implicit in Locke's analysis is the need for corporations and other property holders to accept charity as an ethical duty, an intrinsic constraint on their property rights. For example, when patents interfere with the distribution of life-preserving medicine, pharmaceutical companies must be prepared to concede their property rights for the sake of the common good.

Abuses of economic power and marketplace transactions should not undermine our appreciation of the free market's role in the economy. Productive resources, including labor and capital, are guided to their optimal use by market prices and by profits and losses. But the market economy needs to be complemented by the distribution of essential goods such as life-saving medicine, which should be managed by appropriate government agencies. Ideologies that transform the market into an absolute discard humanitarian dimensions of production and distribution. They also reject virtually all political and social intervention in markets. These ideologies, however, are untenable because they deform the economy's harmony and justice. The free market is essential for the global economy, though it must be supplemented by just government policies.[38]

Responsible theories of capitalism affirm the need for government intervention in the marketplace to provide a safety net and to fix market failures. Markets sometimes fail to allocate resources efficiently and those failures often require prudent government action. Even realistic market fundamentalists do not deny the need for such targeted intervention in markets that cannot fix themselves. The warrant for government engagement in situations of market failure should be twofold: the failure must be serious and harmful and there is a high probability that government policies will be welfare enhancing such that benefits will exceed the cost of those policies. Market failures are real and sometimes appreciably reduce social welfare. If government can effectively correct those failures, it can create value just as corporations do.[39]

Box 2.1 Concepts explained: market failures[40]

Markets sometimes fail to function properly. Market failure does not suggest a complete collapse or some sort of radical malfunction, but simply implies that the market is producing less than optimal results. A market failure is a deviation from the ideal of economic efficiency. That ideal supposes many buyers and sellers (no monopolies), no entry barriers, no differentiated goods or services, clearly assigned property rights, perfect information, and no switching costs. Since markets function properly and efficiently only under these conditions of perfect competition, which are hard to satisfy in the real world, market failures are commonplace and typically require some type of government intervention. The first form of market failure is inadequate competition that most often occurs in concentrated industries dominated by fewer and bigger companies. In the absence of competition, monopolies and oligopolies under-produce and charge higher prices in order to reap monopoly rents. The centralization of high-tech commerce into the hands of Facebook, Amazon, and Google are the most contemporary examples of industry consolidation. Negative externalities constitute side effects of production that impose costs involuntarily on others who are powerless to affect the decisions about that production. Markets often ignore externalities such as pollution, which leads to the underpricing and overproduction of goods. If a chemical company's manufacturing processes heavily pollute the local environment, that manufacturer imposes a cost on others (for example, damage to their health) that is not reflected in the price of the chemicals nor in the amount of those chemicals to be supplied. If the manufacturer had to cover these externalized costs, the price of its products would go up and the amount consumed would be reduced. However, this chemical manufacturer has no incentive to internalize these costs and therefore is not likely to do so unless coerced by regulatory constraints. Information deficiencies are another source of market failure. Efficient markets rely on available information so when there are information asymmetries, one party (the seller) is in a position to exploit the other party (the buyer). In these situations the seller is better informed than the potential buyers about the quality of goods he is attempting to sell. Buyers will then be forced to expend resources to confirm the quality of these goods, and sellers will also be tempted to invest resources to convince a skeptical public about the quality of their merchandise. Since these activities do not create value, they amount to an inefficient allocation of resources from the market's perspective. Finally, some goods such as "public goods" cannot be adequately supplied by independent markets. These public goods exhibit two chief qualities. First, their consumption is non-rivalrous. This means that unlike private goods (such as a cake), one person's consumption of a public good (a cake recipe) does not reduce what is available for others. These goods are also non-excludable, which means that it is difficult to exclude or keep out those who haven't paid. Markets reward producers for the private goods they produce but not for the public goods they preserve. Since public goods, including information-based goods, are vulnerable to free riders, they tend to be under-produced in unregulated markets that lack some sort of protection, such as patents and copyrights.

Finally, it is far from obvious that a more socialistic economic system or excessive regulation that grants government undue powers will suddenly eliminate corruption, greed, and bias from marketplace interactions. Most forms of democratic socialism, committed to distributive equity, favor constraints on private economic freedom in order to open the door for government's expanded role in the marketplace. The constraints on economic freedom, the right of citizens to freely produce and consume goods and services of their choice, is a core principle of socialism. Some "democratic socialists" still yearn for a system where democratically elected workers or officials decide what products to make and what prices to charge.[41] Yet there is a strong correlation between economic freedom and economic performance. Countries that cut back on this liberty are more likely to experience serious economic decline. They can also slide toward a more radical totalitarianism as we have witnessed in places like Cuba and Venezuela.[42] Even countries like China have perceived that pure socialism is a recipe for economic stagnation, so the Communist Party reformed itself to include basic economic liberties along with entrepreneurship.

Those protesting in Chile and the United States against the evils of capitalism seek structural changes to the global economic system. The implacable foes of capitalism want to realize Marx's utopian vision of an egalitarian and classless society. Once social classes are eradicated, conflict will subside. If everyone is to be equal, then everyone will need to receive the same wage. But if everyone receives the same wage why would anyone be motivated to choose a dangerous occupation or a dirty job like cleaning the sewers? Everyone will want pleasant and easy jobs. Will people be motivated to spend years studying to enter the medical profession if they will end up receiving the same wage as a lifeguard? Wages set by the market, on the other hand, direct the right people, those with the proper interests, talent, and resources, into the right jobs. The incentive problem is not easily resolved by communism or even by democratic socialism, which might simply tax income above a base level to achieve its egalitarian objectives.[43] Egalitarianism may be achieved by these means, but at what cost?

The archetypes of capitalism

Now that we comprehend the tradition of liberal capitalism and what sets it apart from the economic systems associated with collectivism, we can review the different modalities of capitalism. In *Good Capitalism, Bad Capitalism*, Baumol and his co-authors argue that globalization enhances economic performance and reduces poverty. As we noted in the previous chapter, it is quite difficult to find examples of countries where poverty has waned without free markets that drive sustainable economic growth. That growth depends to a large degree on innovation and technological progress, but what economic conditions are conducive for stimulating innovation? The short answer is capitalism, but what type of capitalism?[44]

There are four fundamental archetypes of capitalism: state-guided capitalism; oligarchic capitalism; big firm capitalism; and entrepreneurial capitalism. While these models are quite distinct, they share in common capitalist principles such as the recognition of private property rights, including the right to own capital goods and the means of production. Also, in all these versions of capitalism, a preponderance of productive assets is usually controlled by the private sector. However, in Baumol's view, not all of these capitalist systems are "good," since there is only one sure path that can avoid economic stagnation and decline.[45]

In state-guided capitalism, government complements and directs market mechanisms rather than replace them. The public sector takes the lead in deciding which industries deserve an influx of capital investment because of their potential for growth or strategic significance for the economy. Policy makers in these governments often strive to support "national champions," companies with the most promise and potential. Sometimes the state exercises direct control by owning a majority of shares in the targeted companies. It can also support such enterprises by means of tax breaks, subsidies, government contracts, and other mechanisms. Examples of state-guided capitalism include countries in South East Asia and Latin America, and, of course, China. In China, four state-owned banks dominate the financial system, and the government has an ownership stake in many other companies. The allocation of capital is strongly influenced by those state-owned banks. China boasts 109 corporations listed on the Fortune Global 500 list, but only 15% of those are privately owned.[46]

Milanovic describes this economic system as "political capitalism," where the strong state harnesses the forces of the weaker market. The main objective of these bureaucratic systems is to realize higher economic growth by means of tight control over the private sector and its open markets. Milanovic and other economists suggest that China's economic model is a potential alternative to the traditionalist capital economy.[47]

According to Baumol, companies in most state capitalist systems typically thrive not through innovation and true entrepreneurship, but by importing foreign technology and combining it with their own low-cost labor. The primary defect with this system is that governments do not have a good track record in picking winners and losers. When countries approach the "technological frontier," where there are no market leaders to follow and imitate, they tend to falter and to make major investment mistakes. Finally, once a state has committed its resources and reputation to a particular project, it can be difficult to "pull the plug."[48]

The second archetype is oligarchic capitalism where government policies are oriented toward the promotion of the vested interests of a small segment of the population, such as the family and cohorts of the ruling autocratic dictator. The goals of economic growth and the welfare of workers and consumers are secondary to the goal of wealth aggrandizement for the privileged few. What oligarchic economies have in common is extreme inequality in the distribution of wealth, which is usually found only in the hands of the political elite. These economies are plagued by cronyism, pervasive corruption, and intolerance of internal dissent. Moreover, within these economies there tends to be considerable "informal activity," such as construction without permits and informal systems of property rights.

Some African countries, such as Angola and Equatorial Guinea, which suffer from the "resource curse" of superabundant oil, clearly resemble oligarchic capitalism. These regimes use oil or some other resource to enrich themselves rather than benefit their impoverished citizens. At the same time, the sale of these natural resources raises the value of the currency and makes the country's other goods too expensive on world markets. Hence the notion that abundant natural resources can be a curse rather than a blessing for a national economy. The Obiang regime in Equatorial Guinea, for example, permits foreign oil companies to exploit the country's oil reserves with little benefit to anyone beyond Obiang and his family and cronies. This is a nominal democracy with a capitalist system, but mismanagement of that system assures poor economic performance.[49]

Big firm capitalism, on the other hand, thrives in stable and predictable markets where there is an established basis for competition and little risk of imminent disruption.[50] This sort of oligopolistic capitalism is found predominantly in Western Europe, the United States, and Japan. Big firm capitalism typifies industries like auto manufacturing or semiconductors that can absorb fixed costs by taking advantage of scale economies. Scale matters a great deal in the express mail industry where the biggest players, FedEx and UPS, have driven subscale competitors out of the market. Some of Europe's biggest firms include Nokia, BP, Novartis, and Nestlé. Large firms prosper by keeping costs low and usually by concentrating only on incremental innovations rather than disruptive ones. There is a certain enduring logic to bigness and the low-cost structure that supports price cuts that increase volume. But large firms have many other advantages. They have the resources to buy and experiment with new technologies and to borrow at cheaper rates. They also tend to spend more on R&D.[51]

Finally, entrepreneurial capitalism is a system in which many small firms consistently innovate and take the initial steps necessary to commercialize their innovations. Radical rather than incremental innovations occur within this capitalist framework where the risks and expense of innovating can lead to high economic rents. These innovations would not exist without entrepreneurs who perceive an opportunity to sell a bold new product or service that often changes an entire industry. Thanks to brilliant innovators like Steve Jobs, Apple, Inc. falls in this category, and so too does Tesla, the car company founded by Elon Musk. Musk has pursued a dream of making electric cars with glamor and style. Tesla now produces about 300,000 cars a year. Just as Steve Jobs reinvented the phone, so Musk has reinvented the car industry. Not only has he effectively changed the car's energy source, but he has also developed computer-assisted or "self-driving" vehicles.[52] When entrepreneurs like Musk succeed they grow into big firms, as measured by market capitalization.[53]

While China could be described as a mix of big firm and state-guided capitalism, the United States represents "a unique blend of entrepreneurial and big firm capitalism."[54] Entrepreneurs prosper in this dynamic environment where change and innovation quite often disrupt entrenched industries and established technologies. Economies cannot survive without an entrepreneurial spirit. Radical innovations such as 5G technology fuel new waves of economic growth. Experts believe that 5G could become the foundation for a vast, interrelated system in which everything from cars to kitchen appliances seamlessly streams information.[55] But big firms like Qualcomm are still necessary to efficiently produce and market the innovations conceived by these entrepreneurs. The U.S. system epitomizes liberal capitalism with its commitment to maximum economic freedom and minimal state involvement.

This unique blend of entrepreneurial and big firm capitalism is a prime example of "good capitalism" because it promotes both innovation and efficiency. According to Baumol, "bad capitalism" is state-guided or oligarchic capitalism. Oligarchic capitalism has no redeeming features and has spelled disaster for many countries in Africa. Oligarchic capitalism marginalizes the goal of economic growth and it is not committed to globalization. But what about state capitalism, which is different from traditional liberal capitalism? Are Baumol and his co-authors correct in their assessment that this is also a bad form of capitalism, since the invisible hand is being replaced by the visible hand of the public sector?

Elements of state-guided capitalism have surfaced in the past, especially in the rise of Japan in the 1950s and 1960s and in Singapore in the 1980s. Singapore's version of state capitalism was crafted by Lee Kuan Yee who planned an information technology infrastructure and an economic environment that proved to be attractive to foreign investors. But thanks to China state-guided capitalism now plays a much larger role in the global economy. Roughly half of China's economy is in the hands of government. The Chinese state is the primary shareholder in the country's 150 biggest corporations. The Chinese government subsidizes its state-owned enterprises (SOEs) that constitute 40% of the country's GDP. It directs money to favored industries and works closely with Chinese companies that have invested abroad.[56]

Like Singapore, the Chinese system attempts to integrate national planning and free market forces. But, unlike Singapore, China has at its disposal more capital and more sophisticated capitalist tools which the country does not hesitate to deploy. The Chinese government usually keeps state-owned firms in the hands of professionally trained managers rather than turning them over to cronies and state bureaucrats.[57]

State capitalism has been successful in building infrastructure and in producing aggressive corporations like Lenovo or Huawei that compete effectively in global markets. Huawei, founded in 1987, is the world's largest manufacturer of telecommunications equipment with revenues of $136 billion in 2020. Some of China's SOEs are also among the world's leading companies. They include Sinopec, Bank of China, China Telcom, and China Mobile. China Mobile is the world's largest cellular phone company.[58]

In the past, state-owned (or controlled) companies have been less innovative than private companies. According to one economist, governments may be "good at providing the seedcorn for innovation ... but they are bad at turning that seedcorn into bread."[59] Notable failures include Malaysia's ill-advised investment in biotechnology (BioValley) and Russia's high-tech park known as Skolkovo. Several high-profile and large-scale projects in China, such as a \$91 billion industrial project in Caofeidian, have also failed because they were redundant and simply created overcapacity in steel, concrete and other industries.[60] Also, China's SOEs and other corporations in which the government has a stake are sometimes more inclined to respond to political imperatives than dynamic market forces.[61]

For some economists, therefore, this hybrid form of capitalism is defective because it centralizes far too much power in the hands of the authoritative state and engenders cronyism. Politicians can dictate strategies to big companies and even impose restrictions on entire industries. Russia's Gazprom, for example, which is owned in part by the Russian government, has been a political instrument for Putin and his cronies. The expansive role of the state in the market also creates an unlevel playing field where well-managed private firms are at a disadvantage to competitors that have the benefit of subsidized capital.

Nonetheless, China's state capitalist system can boast many economic successes, especially in high tech, with firms like Lenovo, Huawei, and ByteDance (owner of TikTok). Appliance maker Haier and Geely Automotive are also world-class competitors. Huawei has overtaken U.S competitors like Cisco and is a leading force in the deployment of 5G technology. Huawei joins other Chinese companies that have become more adept at innovation. The Chinese e-commerce firms are bigger, more creative, and more competitive than their counterparts in other countries, including the United States. China's three major players include Alibaba, JD.Com, and Pinduoduo. These firms fuse together e-commerce and social media to become "on-line shopping emporia" for China's 850 million digital customers. For example, social media apps like WeChat, owned by Tencent, direct traffic to JD.Com and Pinduoduo in which they own a stake. As a result, the line between social media and shopping websites is being slowly erased. Overspecialized Western firms (like Facebook), on the other hand, are unlikely to emulate China's success because they prefer to focus on their core business.[62]

The return of pure socialism, command and control economies, is highly unlikely. But state-guided capitalism, despite its deficiencies, seems to have a bright future. As the *Economist* points out, the "defining battle" of the 21st century will not be between capitalism and socialism but between these different versions of capitalism.[63]

Conclusions

We have presented the traditional arguments that liberal capitalism, which has historically been linked with globalization, is superior to pure socialist collectivism or communism that relies on a command system of central planning rather than free and open markets. Capitalism respects extensive property rights and modestly regulated markets, while communism seeks to replace market mechanisms and severely limit property rights. As philosopher Charles Taylor observes, however, economic history in the previous century has demonstrated that "market mechanisms in some form are indispensable to an industrial society, certainly for its economic efficiency and probably also for its freedom."[64]

According to critics, the problem with liberal capitalism is that it tolerates an arbitrary distribution of essential goods along with substantial disparities in wealth. Also, the conception of the corporation as the property of shareholder-owners fosters a viewpoint that corporate managers must promote the financial interests of the owners. The pressure to do so is often the catalyst for corporate misdeeds and opportunism. But there is a disposition within classical liberalism to preserve economic liberty and property rights without neglecting distributional equity and the requirements of natural justice. In the spirit of Locke's charity proviso, multinationals should assert property rights, but in a way that takes account of the relevant needs of others and does not allow familiar points of moral orientation to dissolve.

Unlike command and control collectivism, capitalism preserves economic liberty, but not all forms of capitalism are created equal. We must differentiate between different forms of capitalism. The United State is a unique blend of entrepreneurial and big firm capitalism. Both are necessary to ensure that there is radical innovation and that those innovations can be produced efficiently. The synthesis of big firm and entrepreneurial capitalism is "good capitalism," because it is focused on innovation, the key to sustainable economic growth.

While state-guided capitalism, which explicitly directs resources to favored industries or national champions, has its defects, it continues to advance in China, Russia, and other countries. State-owned firms have typically been less innovative than their counterparts in the West, but in China many corporations like Huawei and Geely are global competitors and some have pioneered new technologies and business models. This economic success suggests that the China model, which integrates national planning with free market forces, will be a formidable challenge for Western forms of democratic capitalism. Of course, every form of capitalism will struggle to resolve the proper boundary between the state and the market. In general, a presumption in favor of free markets whenever possible seems sensible in order to avoid starting down the well-trodden road to serfdom.

Notes

1 Amanda Taub, "'Chile Woke Up:' A Legacy of Economic Inequality Incites Mass Protests," *New York Times*, November 4, 2019, A8.
2 Ibid.
3 Ibid.
4 Mary Anastasi O'Grady, "Chilean Capitalism on Trial," *Wall Street Journal*, October 28, 2020, A15. See also Mary Anastasi O'Grady, "Chile's Suicide Mission," *Wall Street Journal*, October 19, 2020, A15.

5 Jorge Jraissati, "A Tale of Two Countries: How Norway Embraces Markets while Venezuela Does Not," *Public Discourse*, September 9, 2020.

6 Gerald Gaus, "Coercion, Ownership, and the Redistributive State: Justificatory Liberalism's Classical Tilt," *Social Philosophy & Policy* 27 (2010), 252.

7 Karl Marx, *Economic and Philosophical Manuscripts of 1844* in Marx/Engels Collected Works trans. T. Bottomore vol. 4 (London: Lawrence and Wisehart, Ltd., 1959), 293.

8 Lawrence Becker, *Property Rights: Philosophic Foundations* (London: Routledge & Kegan Paul, 1977), 18–22. For a full specification of ownership rights, see A.M. Honore, "Ownership," in *Oxford Essays in Jurisprudence* ed. A.G. Guest (Oxford: Clarendon Press, 1961), 107–147.

9 Gerald Gaus, "The Idea and Ideal of Capitalism," in *The Oxford Handbook of Business Ethics* ed. George Brenkert and Tom Beauchamp (Oxford: Oxford University Press, 2010), 73–99.

10 Leo Strauss, *Natural Right and History* (Chicago, IL: University of Chicago Press, 1950), 233. Strauss goes on to explain that food and other basic goods are necessary for our "comfortable self-preservation," but this natural right to appropriate such things as our property "must be limited if it is not to be incompatible with the peace and preservation of mankind," 236.

11 John Locke, *Two Treatises of Government* ed. Peter Laslett (Cambridge, UK: Cambridge University Press, 1988), §41 (original work published 1698).

12 Ibid., 124.

13 Ibid., 98.

14 Rev. Robert Sirico, *Defending the Free Market* (Washington, D.C.: Regnery, 2012), 28–36.

15 Georg W.F. Hegel, *Philosophy of Right* trans. T. Knox. (London: Oxford University Press, 1952), §39.

16 Robert Merges, *Justifying Intellectual Property* (Cambridge, MA: Harvard University Press, 2011), 72. See Merges' thoughtful account of Kant's views on property, 68–101.

17 Friedrich Hayek, *Law, Legislation and Liberty: Rules and Order* (Chicago, IL: University of Chicago Press, 1973), 107. Quoted in John Tomasi, *Free Market Fairness* (Princeton, NJ: Princeton University Press, 2012), 19.

18 Adam Smith, *An Inquiry into the Nature and Causes of the Wealth of Nations* (New York: Penguin, 1973), 162.

19 Tomasi, *Free Market Fairness*, 6. See also David Skeel, "God and Mammon," *Wall Street Journal*, October 24, 2020, C9.

20 Marx, *Economic and Philosophical Manuscripts*, 132.

21 Karl Marx, *Capital* (New York: International Publishers, 1967), vol. III, 820.

22 Quoted in Michael Ellman, *Socialist Planning* (Cambridge, UK: Cambridge University Press, 1979), 9.

23 Friedrich A. Hayek, *The Road to Serfdom* ed. Bruce Caldwell (Chicago, IL: University of Chicago Press, 2007), 127.

24 Stephen Miller, "The Fantasy of 'Democratic Socialism,'" *Wall Street Journal*, October 27, 2018, A11.

25 Tomasi, *Free Market Fairness*, 22–26.

26 James Nickel, "Economic Liberties," in *The Idea of Political Liberalism: Essays on Rawls* ed. Victoria Davison and Clark Wolf (Lanham, MD: Rowman and Littlefield, 2000), 155–167.

27 Thomas Piketty, *Capitalism in the Twenty-First Century* (Cambridge, MA: Harvard University Press, 2014), 1–2.

28 Ibid., 26.

29 Robert M. Solow, "Thomas Piketty is Right," in *After Piketty* ed. Heather Boushey (Cambridge, MA: Harvard University Press, 2017), 50.

30 Ibid., 54–56.

31 John Rawls, *A Theory of Justice* (Cambridge, MA: Harvard University Press, 1971), 225.

32 Tomasi, *Free Market Fairness*, 51.

33 David Schaengold, "Defending Alasdair MacIntyre's Economics," *Public Discourse*, March 14, 2011.

34 Paul Oslington, "Why are Philosophers and Theologians So Hostile to Economics," *Public Discourse*, July 28, 2020, 5.

35 Samuel Gregg, "Putting Adam Smith Back Together," *Public Discourse*, March 6, 2019.

36 Judy Shelton, "A Capitalist Manifesto," *Wall Street Journal*, October 13, 2008, A19.

37 "A Modern Marx," *Economist*, March 7, 2020, 75.

38 Carlos Massini-Correas, "The Rule of Law and the Foundation of Democracy," in *Fundamental Rights and Conflicts of Rights* eds. P. Azzaro and Mary Ann Glendon (Steubenville, OH: Franciscan University Press, 2020), 148–179.

39 Forest Reinhardt, "Conceptual Overview: 'Business and the Environment'" (Boston, MA: Harvard Business School Publishing, 1999), 8.

40 Gregory Dees, "Responding to Market Failures" (Cambridge, MA: Harvard Business School Publications, 1996), 2–4. See also Robert Spence, "Job Market Signaling," *Quarterly Journal of Economics* 87 (1973), 355–374.

41 Stephen Miller, "The Fantasy of Democratic Socialism," *Wall Street Journal*, October 27, 2018, A11.

42 Jraissati, "A Tale of Two Countries," 4–5.

43 Trent Horn and Catherine Pakaluk, *Can a Catholic Be a Socialist* (El Cajon, CA: Catholic Answers Press, 2020), 28–29.

44 William Baumol, Robert Litan, and Carl Schramm, *Good Capitalism, Bad Capitalism, and the Economics of Growth and Prosperity* (New Haven, CT: Yale University Press, 2007), 21–25. For empirical evidence supporting a positive correlation between economic growth and poverty reduction, see David Dollar and Art Kraay, "Growth is Good for the Poor," *Journal of Economic Growth* 1 (2002), 195–225.

45 Baumol et al., *Good Capitalism, Bad Capitalism*, 60–61.

46 Amir Guluzube, "Role of China's State Owned Enterprises Explained," World Economic Forum, May 7, 2019.

47 Branko Milanovic, *Capitalism, Alone* (Cambridge, MA: Harvard University Press, 2019). See also Joseph Sternberg, "Inclined Toward Inequality," *Wall Street Journal*, January 21, 2020, A15.

48 Baumol et al., *Good Capitalism, Bad Capitalism*), 62–70.

49 Ibid., 71–79.

50 Martin Reeves, Knut Haanaes, and Janmejaya Sinha, *Your Strategy Needs a Strategy* (Boston, MA: Harvard Business Review Press, 2015), 28–32.

51 "The New Geopolitics of Business," *Economist*, June 5, 2021, 20–22. See also Baumol et al., *Good Capitalism, Bad Capitalism*, 80–84.

52 Gregg Easterbrook, "A Revolutionary Old Product," *Wall Street Journal*, August 28, 2019, A13. See also Edward Niedermeyer, *Ludicrous: The Unvarnished Story of Tesla Motors* (San Diego, CA: BenBella, 2019).

53 Baumol et al., 85–88.

54 Ibid., 90.

55 "The Qualcommunist Manifesto," *Economist*, February 15, 2020, 59.

56 Michael Pillsbury, *The Hundred-Year Marathon* (New York: St. Martin's, 2016), 169–176.

57 "The Visible Hand: State Capitalism," *Economist*, Special Report January 21, 2012, 3–7.

58 Pillsbury, *Hundred-Year Marathon*, 171–172.

59 "The Visible Hand: State Capitalism," 14.

60 Dinny McMahon and Bob Davis, "Troubled Megaproject Spotlights China Woes," *Wall Street Journal*, July 25, 2013, A7.

61 Pillsbury, *Hundred-Year Marathon*, 171.

62 "The Future of E-Commerce: The Great Mall of China," *Economist*, January 2, 2021, 47–50.

63 "The Visible Hand: State Capitalism," 18.

64 Charles Taylor, *Ethics of Authenticity* (Cambridge, MA: Harvard University Press, 1992), 10.

Chapter 3

Cultural diversity and cultural relativism

In a classic article written for the *New York Times Book Review* called "The Opening of the American Mind," the distinguished American historian, Arthur Schlesinger, made a compelling case for overthrowing transcultural and universal moral standards. In this essay, which typifies the arguments advanced by thoughtful proponents of relativism, Schlesinger eloquently exposed the perils of moral absolutism. He argued quite forcefully that it can breed intolerance, imperiousness, and an arrogant disregard for other cultures and religions. This uncompromising inflexibility has been the source of endless strife and social discord, particularly when the moral absolutes have their roots in religious beliefs. He praised the American mind, shaped by thinkers like Ralph Waldo Emerson and William James, which is by nature pluralistic and relativistic, and so has little use for the pretensions of absolutism. While moral absolutism is abstract, rigid, and ahistorical, relativism is "concrete, pluralistic, inductive, historical, skeptical, and intimately bound up with deference to experience."[1]

This debate about universalism and pluralism is not new and extends back to the days of ancient Greece. In ancient Athens the Sophists taught rhetoric and boasted that the study of this art was a great good because it provided the orator with an opportunity to exert power and influence over others. What mattered was the orator's rhetorical skills and not the moral quality of the value judgments he articulated. Rhetoric for the clever Sophists was all about persuasion, never about what was right or wrong, because judgments of this sort were matters of subjective opinion, not matters of truth. While the Sophists relativized morality, Plato and Aristotle were moral realists who saw the precariousness intrinsic to this line of reasoning. They argued vigorously against ethical conventionalism and nihilism, and insisted on the need for general virtues and specific moral absolutes that were necessary for the good life.[2] While ethics for Aristotle has a certain indeterminacy, the first principles of practical reason that forbid taking innocent life, adultery, and theft leave no room for ambiguity. Many modern philosophers, however, like John Rawls, follow the lead of Mr. Schlesinger. They prefer a "wide reflective equilibrium" when it comes to moral issues and explicitly reject moral absolutes and appeals to any *a priori* or first principles that reflect a fixed moral order.[3]

The philosophical thesis of meta-ethical skepticism alluded to in Schlesinger's essay may seem abstract, but actually has great relevance for the policies of multinational corporations as they extend their operations into foreign countries with different cultures. The key axis of concern revolves around respect and appreciation for cultural diversity. How can multinationals transfer their technologies, strategies, and managerial techniques to these different environments without diluting that country's cultural integrity? But by far the most vexing question is whether multinationals should adapt to the local culture or seek to reform that culture when its moral and social norms appear to be deficient. Does a European manager export high safety standards to a frontier economy if the workers in his plant and even the host country's government resist those standards? There seems to be something wrong with "imposing" one's home country standards around the world, but are there some occasions where the host country's norms should not be followed because they undermine the common good? Hovering over this practical consideration that has surfaced for many multinationals is the theoretical issue of cultural moral relativism. Are there absolute and universal values that apply in every cultural context, or are moral values historically and culturally conditioned? Is cultural moral relativism simply a pretext for corporate self-interest or is it a legitimate response to cultural diversity?

It seems essential to clarify these demanding questions, even if we cannot completely resolve them. If relativism is really a plausible theory, if there are no objective and cross-cultural values, moral discourse between cultures becomes pointless and futile, an interminable exchange of subjective opinions. More importantly, if morality itself differs by culture and country, it is impossible to defend the validity of global ethical standards for multinationals operating across borders. When moral dilemmas arise, their response can only be to follow the well-known maxim "when in Rome do as the Romans do." But this approach is unsettling and cannot be easily defended when the "Romans" are engaged in acts that abuse basic human rights. Should retailers sourcing apparel and other goods from India accept forced child labor as part of this country's cultural reality? Hence we must explore more deeply the premises and rationale for relativism, which, if accepted, would imply that even the most foundational ethical ideals cannot be applied in cross-cultural contexts. But we begin this clarification by looking first at the issue of cultural diversity and how this factors into corporate decisions about morality.

Cultural diversity and its challenges

Investing abroad is always a risky affair. Aside from the specter of economic risks, there are political and ethical risks that virtually always accompany foreign direct investment. In crossing borders, firms encounter alien practices, policies, and cultures, along with a different set of moral norms and laws. One author tersely expresses this experience as "the liability of foreignness."[4] The extent of this liability correlates to the distance between the multinational's home country and the host country where it chooses to make an investment. According to Ghemawat, there are four dimensions of this "distance": political, geographic, economic, and cultural. Each type of distance can affect businesses in different but dramatic ways.[5]

Political distance is created by an unfamiliar political and public policy environment along with the absence of a shared monetary and political association. The power dynamics of one-party, communist rule in China is markedly different from Western democracy, and this difference adds complexity for American firms doing business in China. Political distance is also fostered by policies that create barriers to foreign investment, such as tariffs and trade quotas. Geographic distance is increased by physical remoteness and major climate differences along with weak transportation and communications infrastructure. American and European companies, for example, have not had an easy time of expanding into the desolate and frigid region of Siberia. The International Paper Co., headquartered in Memphis, Tennessee, entered into a joint venture in the Siberian city of Bratsk in order to harvest logs cheaply. Labor costs are low and there are rail connections to China. However, the company must deal with hazardous weather conditions such as extreme temperatures that plummet to 65° below zero Fahrenheit.[6] Economic differences include disparities in consumer income and also in the quality of a country's infrastructure and human capital. Cultural distance includes dissimilarities in linguistic heritage, religious or philosophical beliefs, ethical standards, and social norms.[7] There is certainly a major cultural difference between the Sinosphere and the Anglosphere. Cultural affinity, on the other hand, "supercharges communication," and fosters trust.[8]

While we focus to some extent on political and public policy issues, our main axis of discussion in the latter chapters of this book is on how the multinational corporation can accommodate this cultural distance by handling differences in ethical and social norms with both moral sensitivity and strategic effectiveness. It's imperative, however, that multinationals do not overcome cultural distance at the expense of human rights and the common good.

Culture is defined as what rational people add to nature by their chosen ways of living, thinking, and acting. Cultures are not homogenous. They differ, sometimes radically, but that diversity is a great benefit to the global community. People have diverse gifts, resources, and talents that can enrich their authentic human flourishing. When considering the complex interaction between a local culture and a foreign business, two prominent issued need to be addressed. The first involves the impact of multinational operations and technology on that local culture. How will that technology or marketing campaign effect changes or subvert valid cultural norms that have evolved over generations? The second involves the extent to which a multinational enterprise should adopt the ways and norms of that culture. In effect, as we have suggested, corporations must typically make a difficult choice: *either adapt to new cultural and moral standards or challenge the status quo even if it threatens a host country's sovereignty.*

Countries are sometimes prone to regard multinationals suspiciously, as a threat to local cultural values. These corporations are large and powerful entities that are disposed to export foreign values, strange technologies, and foreign management techniques. When Toys "R" Us wanted to start selling its toys in Japan it was described in ominous terms as the "Black Ship of Kawasaki." The toy store's entry into Japan was seen as a vehicle for the imposition of American cultural values through the sale of American toys and artifacts. "Toys are culture," proclaimed one of Japan's disgruntled toy sellers.[9] Toys "R" Us' use of the discount retailing format was also seen as a threat to the survival of an important cultural tradition: the small "mom and pop" toy store that provided service and convenience to its customers. At a minimum, the giant toy company has obligations to be sensitive to the cultural issues connected with the toys and other products it sells in its Japanese stores.

The people in many developing countries have often regarded these large vertically integrated behemoths as an alien external force that will inordinately unsettle or corrupt the local culture. Regrettably, this apprehension became a stark reality in parts of Nigeria for the indigenous tribes who had to contend with the petroleum industry invading their lands. There is little doubt, for example, that Royal Dutch Shell drastically disrupted the native culture of the Ogoni people in the Niger Delta with its drilling operations, which polluted the land and lit the sky through gas flaring. It became far more difficult to farm the land and fish the waterways in accordance with tribal customs under these severe conditions. Saudi Arabia offers another example of the threat rapid industrialization poses to local culture. The Trans-Arabian Pipeline constructed by Aramco, a coalition of American oil companies, interfered with many Bedouin traveling routes, while its oil wells disrupted centuries-old migration patterns. Also, the sudden wealth of this developing country occupied by indigenous cultural groups clearly frayed the country's delicate social fabric.[10] Unfortunately, multinational corporations have usually been obtuse about the social and cultural changes caused by their investments.

Thus, the potential impact of a multinational operation on a local culture and on the ways of indigenous people is a pertinent normative issue, and it must be a key factor in ethical decision making. Ideally, this can be managed by the host country's government, which can control and restrict a multinational corporation's movements so that cultural concerns are duly respected. Government can also make sure that the investment helps out these indigenous people economically. The African country of Botswana is a good example of this sort of management. This country tightly controls multinationals such as DeBeers in order to minimize the negative impact on its local culture. Botswana also invests diamond revenues in health care, education, and infrastructure so that all people benefit, not just the ruling elite.

A second challenge for the multinational along these lines arises from the conflict between local cultural values and universal human rights, which are not always respected outside of developed liberal democracies. Multinationals can find themselves in the middle of a collision between local standards and international human rights, such as property, free speech, and life and health that are recognized by the United Nations and other international bodies. Expectations are often high as multinationals struggle to reconcile this tension.

Consider the experience of technology firms operating abroad where they encounter vastly different free speech standards. These companies often find it difficult to preserve their commitment to open communication and free expression in these contexts where they are instructed by local law to censor different content. When companies refuse to censor objectionable content from their sites they can easily risk a confrontation with the host country's government. In India, both Google and Facebook have been taken to court for not blocking content that is forbidden by an austere Indian censorship law (at least by Western standards). That law prohibits blasphemy, ethnic disparagement, and any threats made to the public order. Google, which owns YouTube, ran afoul of Indian law because it failed to remove a video showing someone relating a Hindu story that had been edited to incorporate obscene language. Google has regarded YouTube as a platform for a broad range of free expression and is not inclined to censor it for blasphemous speech. The company is supported by civil libertarians who object that India's Information Technology Act (2008) represents an unjust stifling of free speech. But others argue that India has a right to set its own speech standards and that Internet companies must follow the laws and customs of the land.[11]

Who's right in this debate? Is there a universal right to free expression that Google should seek to respect no matter where it does business, or should it adapt and comply with the letter of the Indian law which reflects a non-Western cultural tradition? And is there a common principle that companies caught up in such dilemmas can follow? The question is complicated by the legacy of colonialism and the pressure on Western firms in this post-imperial world to respect each country's self-determination.

Given this complex moral universe, it is safe to assume that multinationals should avoid two extremes. In Enderle's terms, they should avoid being cast as the "Empire Type," which exports home country values to any cultural context usually without any adjustment and concern for negative consequences.[12] It would be a mistake, for example, to expect that people in an Islamic culture should adopt liberal, Western sexual mores or alter their convictions about interactions between men and women. The imposition of one country's values on another country echoes the European imperialism that shaped the first era of globalization. This problem can arise even when human rights are at stake. Western governments and corporate institutions are often perceived as appealing to human rights merely as a means of advancing their own vested interests. Rights are construed as a neo-colonial effort to universalize a particular set of "Western" moral ideals aimed at taming the social and economic progress of emerging economies.[13] However, multinational corporations cannot violate objective norms of morality merely to avoid the perception of imperialism.

Similarly, multinationals should eschew the "Foreign Country Type," which adjusts its policies and strategic choices to whatever is socially acceptable or conventional within a given culture. For this type of company there is nothing to limit the "moral free space" allowed by the host country culture.[14] In countries where rights are ignored or subordinated, a corporation's field of action sizably expands and becomes far more indeterminate. For example, according to this paradigm, oil companies would have more latitude in countries that ignore the health risks of weak environmental standards. However, while companies must respect cultural diversity and local norms to a degree, they cannot succumb to opportunism and be a party to the deprivation of basic human rights. Sometimes multinationals will be doing business in countries where corruption and bribery are not anomalous but a routine way of doing business. They cannot abandon their moral principles and bribe their way to commercial success. The questions for multinationals like Google is whether or not they can stake out an acceptable middle ground between these polarities of the local and the universal.

Of course, there are not only potential conflicts between multinationals and their host countries, but also between countries and even between a country and the global community. According to Ignatieff, environmentalism, based on a moral vision to preserve our common home, is an example of "moral globalization" in action. At the same time, this unified movement reveals the limits of globalization. Some states admit the urgency of this need to save the planet, but claim that their local needs and norms take precedence.[15] Since 2019, many world leaders have expressed outrage over the Amazon forest fires. Thousands of fires that sometimes get out of control have been deliberately set by ranchers and farmers to clear the land and make it more arable and productive. The rapid deforestation has caused global alarm, since the Amazon rainforest serves as a "carbon sink" that absorbs carbon dioxide and keeps global temperatures from rising. But Brazil's leaders, including President Bolsonaro, claim that the denuded forests are essential for the livelihood of small farmers and ranchers who export large amounts of beef and soy to the rest of the world. They also accuse other global leaders of neo-colonialism for telling Brazilians how they should steward their land. The Amazon fire controversy represents a vivid tension between the universal and the local. It also suggests problems for international commerce. Should companies refuse to do business with exporters of goods from deforested ranches in order to protest this environmental degradation? Or does Brazil have the right to control its land as it sees fit?[16]

How we address the sensitive matter of adjustment to a country's different cultural and ethical standards turns on the philosophical issue of relativism. Perhaps there is some benefit to the Foreign Country Type. Its pluralistic philosophy at least seems to overcome the trap of ethnocentrism, which insists on subtly coercing other people to conform to our beliefs and values. In addition, companies sometimes face internal and external pressures to behave abroad as if they were confirmed cultural relativists, operating according to prevailing local standards by respecting all of the values, beliefs, and practices of other cultures. But can actions and policies contingent on cultural standards be morally justified if normative relativism is not philosophically tenable? With these questions in mind, we turn to a theoretical treatment of normative relativism and ethical pluralism.

Moral relativism

Moral relativism has several different permutations, so sometimes it is difficult to know what a person means when he or she uses this term. In its most extreme form, relativism denies that there are any universal basic moral demands and supposes that morality can differ at the level of each individual person. Different people are subject to different moral demands, depending upon many factors including the customs, practices, belief systems, and values that they accept.[17]

Thus, the theory of individual ethical relativism presumes that the good is not necessarily the same for all persons. Each of us has different beliefs and sentiments about the moral good, although often those beliefs overlap. However, the relativist opines, who are we to question another person's experience or perception about what is good? The individual person is "free" to determine for herself what is good or evil. "Man is the measure of all things," said the ancient philosopher Protagoras, so the good is whatever a person declares it to be. In similar terms, the Romantic writer Johann Herder claimed that each individual is his "own measure" for how to live and how to behave.[18] Accordingly, each moral agent is the standard bearer and the source of his or her own particular moral code. In summary, the thesis of relativism as it is generally understood could be formulated this way: if someone believes that it is right (or wrong) to do A, then it is right (or wrong) for him to do A.[19]

Relativists of this stripe argue, therefore, that morality is purely a matter of personal preference. Morality is reduced to individual, subjective opinion, and what is right for one person may be wrong for someone else. Relativists typically claim empirical support for this viewpoint by citing the plentiful evidence of moral diversity in society – if people cannot agree even on critical moral issues like abortion, euthanasia, and human cloning, how could there possibly be any single moral truth? The frequency of ethical disagreement and conflict about basic moral issues seem to undermine the possibility of objective moral truth to which *all* can give their assent. In a universe where man is the measure of all things, the best one can hope for is to make agreements with others to arrive at some social conventions to which the majority can assent, at least provisionally.

Much of the recent momentum for ethical relativism emanates from postmodern philosophy. Postmodernism is notoriously difficult to define, but Lyotard characterizes this movement as an "incredulity toward metanarratives."[20] Postmodernists like Lyotard and Derrida rebuke the grand narrative, that is, any attempt to find a totalizing or systematic explanation of reality. There is no room in their philosophy for some universal set of norms or standards of belief and practice that goes beyond anyone's individual, idiosyncratic narrative. Even more moderate versions of postmodernism are committed to these principles. They are suspicious of the motives behind universal theories and skeptical that an overarching moral theory articulating the requirements of justice for all humanity could ever be validated. As Zygmunt Bauman writes, "the foolproof – universal and unshakably founded – ethical code will never be found … and ethics that is universal and 'objectively founded' is a practical impossibility."[21]

The postmodern tradition, therefore, has given ethical relativism new voice and vogue and lent support to an ideology of radical pluralism. There is actually a two-pronged attack on traditional morality that is inspired by this philosophy. First, there is an attack on the metaphysical assumptions of moral philosophy such as the existence of common humanity as the ground of universal human rights. Postmodern philosophy rejects a fixed or common human nature that serves as the foundation of a universal morality or "law of nature." Nor are there essential truths about human flourishing and rationality to provide a theoretical support for a universal moral law. Richard Rorty, for example, contends that there is no theoretical grounding for human rights because there is no theoretical foundation for any system of beliefs or values.[22] Second, this philosophy fosters an abiding skepticism about the possibility of an objective moral system that expresses the basic requirements of justice for all humanity. That skepticism has implanted itself in modern culture where it is expressed as a non-judgmental stance on the whole spectrum of moral issues. Hence a foundationalist and universal ethic, a system that tries to explain right and wrong in terms of the natural law or some other unifying principle such as natural rights, is considered suspect and invalid.

The bottom line is that people have a plurality of different preferences and desires, and those preferences constitute the only reasonable basis of morality. According to the relativist, the simple truth is that our moral beliefs do not provide evidence of any independent realm of values and moral obligations.[23] Those who favor relativism claim that objectivism has a tragic flaw because it is too dogmatic and has failed to give enough attention to the "politics of difference" and the potential for defining one's own moral and social identity.[24] Multiculturalism, therefore, which inspires a more pluralistic approach to morality, is preferable to the moral certitudes of a shallow objectivism which asserts that there is a single set of moral truths for all men and women.

Thus, the relativist claims that any form of moral absolutism or universalism is false and unproveable. Indeed, all the empirical evidence points to the contrary. There is no ideal moral code or moral law that applies to everyone. There are no moral demands that everyone has a sufficient reason to follow, regardless of their customs and cultural experiences.[25] As a result, there is no normative foundation for society's laws, because law is only a social fact of power and practice.[26] We are left with the reduction of morality to our immediate desires, personal preferences, and subjective opinions. As Mackie concludes, there is nothing that is in truth either good or bad; rather, "'good' and 'evil' are words which express only the relation of things to the speaker's desires."[27]

Social or cultural relativism

The most popular form of relativism, however, is somewhat less extreme. It is known as cultural ethical relativism or as social relativism. The normative cultural relativist argues that morality cannot be reduced to an individual's subjective opinion. There are some durable social values that go beyond individual preference, but they are relative to a given culture or social context. Different cultures have different moral norms or standards, and a person's moral obligation is to conform to the norms of his or her culture. What's right, therefore, is always measured in terms of social custom and cultural tradition.

There are two levels or versions of cultural relativism. The first level is descriptive cultural relativism, which states that moral values and practices differ in a significant way from one culture or social group to another. These differences generate deep-seated moral disputes that cannot be rationally resolved.[28] Descriptive relativism is not a philosophical thesis but an anthropological one, because it is based on making scientific generalizations about a certain culture. Some anthropologists, like Ruth Benedict, are convinced of this thesis: "Morality differs in every society, and is a convenient term for socially approved habits."[29] Similarly Herskovits asserts that cultural relativism is the logical consequence of recognizing the "enculturative conditioning in shaping thought and behavior."[30] How significant and deep are these differences? This is an empirical question about which there has been much debate and disagreement. The strong version of descriptive relativism argues that these differences are fundamental. Weaker versions claim that while there are clearly moral differences on the surface, there is some underlying agreement on core moral beliefs (such as the sanctity of life). What all versions of descriptive cultural relativism have in common is their neutrality regarding the moral principles or norms under consideration. It makes no judgments about the suitability or validity of those norms.[31]

Support for the thesis of descriptive relativism is complicated by the heterogeneity that often exists within particular cultures. Regional variations in social customs make it difficult sometimes to determine whether or not there is true cultural consensus for a moral practice. It is not so easy to construct a reliable description of the moral practice of an entire culture, a description that would warrant a valid judgment juxtaposing one culture's moral beliefs with those of other cultures.[32]

Normative cultural relativism goes beyond descriptive cultural relativism. It contends that whatever moral standards happen to prevail in a given culture have their own validity. Moral judgments are relativized not to the individual but to each culture's prevalent ethical standards. If Filipinos believe that euthanasia is always morally wrong, then euthanasia is morally wrong within the Filipino culture. But if Canadians are convinced that euthanasia is morally acceptable, then it is morally right within Canada. Thus, the same kind of act may be right within one society and wrong in another. Culture, rather than the individual person, is now the measure of all things. As Herskovits explains, moral evaluations "are relative to the cultural background out of which they arise."[33] Beyond cultural consensus, there is no independent or objective criterion to determine what is morally right or wrong. Everything depends on the social context. Although normative cultural relativism does not follow logically from descriptive relativism, it does rely on the latter as intellectual support for its arguments.

In summary, the doctrine of normative cultural ethical relativism asserts that the moral rightness or wrongness of actions varies from one society to another, and that there are no absolute universal moral standards binding on all people at all times; this doctrine also affirms that whether or not it is right for an individual to act in a certain way is contingent on the society to which he or she belongs.[34] There is no transcultural, objective standard of morality, no transcendent set of principles that can be invoked to judge one society's moral norms as superior or preferable to another's. All cultures, all ways of life, are equal in moral stature, and any attempt to judge or rank them is a form of discrimination and a veiled attack on human equality.[35]

Ethicists who embrace this philosophy tend to regard moral norms on the same level as custom and social convention. Like customs, moral norms are "prescriptive" – they are cultural action guides that prescribe certain behavior and tell us what to do. The authority of a moral norm is equivalent to the authority of local customs. It logically follows, therefore, that ethical norms and judgments can have only local validity. They are distinct from the propositions of mathematics and natural science, which have universal validity.[36] Just as the customs of Japan are not followed in the United States, the same could be said for the ethical norms of Japan, which are based on Japanese tradition and values and therefore have validity and normative force only within Japan. The repudiation of moral objectivism implies that moral disputes between cultures are fundamentally irreducible and irresolvable.

Another implication of normative cultural relativism is the need for tolerance. The virtue of tolerance sensitizes us to cultural and *moral* differences that deserve our recognition and respect. Just as the visitor to a foreign country must adapt her behavior to take into account that country's customs, so too that visitor must adapt to their ethical norms. It is arrogance to imperiously judge the normative codes of conduct of other cultures and demand that this code be changed to conform to our way of doing things. This is the fatal error of ethnocentrism. Paradoxically, for some relativists, tolerance becomes an objective and transcultural moral standard.

The principle of cultural moral diversity cannot be easily defended. But we should never discount the need for an attitude of openness or tolerance when dealing with other cultures, no matter how diverse they may be. Multinationals can also learn a great deal from other cultures. The real challenge is discerning how to respect cultural diversity without tolerating or supporting injustice.

Evaluating cultural relativism

The doctrine of normative cultural relativism that denies transcultural moral standards continues to be influential, thanks in part to its linkage with multiculturalism and the deconstruction of objectivism. But is this a tenable theory and is it logically justified? The theory is certainly attractive and seems to be a remedy for the dogmatism of ethnocentrism. Respect for ethical pluralism and diversity, some argue, is the key to social order, cooperation, and world harmony. Insensitivity to cultural diversity and local customs can sometimes be embedded in the mentality of the multinational enterprise, so perhaps endorsing this thesis of relativism can promote greater global harmony and a different face for global capitalism.

However, while normative cultural relativism has not lost its salience or superficial attractiveness, it is difficult to see how it can withstand critical scrutiny. The objections against this form of relativism are powerful, and supporters have been able to mount only a thin defense. The principal argument against this thesis is that the relativist has to tolerate any behavior as morally acceptable, so long as it conforms to a cultural consensus and constitutes part of a society's normative code of conduct. But are supporters of this theory really prepared to accept its brutally harsh ramifications? Some cultures, for example, may well believe that a campaign of genocide against some disabled segment of the population or some ethnic minority is morally warranted based on the premise that these individuals are sub-human. Unfortunately, this is not just a remote possibility. The progression of history has been correctly referred to by Hegel as a "slaughter bench," where people are continually sacrificed for some elusive "greater good."[37] Genocide has been justified in Nazi Germany and elsewhere. As one author explains, German culture (though certainly not all Germans) saw itself as "liberated from such 'outmoded' concepts as pity and Christianity," and it viewed humanity "sorted into a table of races, with Aryans and Nordics at the top and Jews and Slavs consigned to the status of vermin."[38] The German elite believed that they were caught up in a life and death struggle for racial superiority and so embarked on its campaign to purge the world of the Jewish race.

In Africa several brutal regimes have been guilty of ethnic cleansing and ethnic massacres. Sudan's deposed president, Omar al-Bashir, has been credibly accused of extensive ethnic cleansing that targeted rival African groups such as Masalit, Fur, and Zaghawa. Mr. al-Bashir faces a trial at the hands of the International Criminal Court which contends that he inflicted on each of these groups "conditions of life calculated to bring about the group's physical destruction."[39]

How could anyone accept such perverse moral reasoning that gave rise to the "new morality" of Nazi Germany or the practice of ethnic cleansing and genocide found in countries like the Sudan? Yet the relativist, whose own culture would assuredly reject such ideas, cannot reasonably object. Otherwise he would be imposing his own culture's moral code on Germany, which is incompatible with normative cultural relativism. Instead he must tolerate this difference in moral opinion, no matter how repulsive he finds it. The central problem is that there is no universal and transcendent moral truth to which he can appeal in order to demonstrate why another culture's moral beliefs and practices are woefully misguided. Moral authority is reduced to cultural solidarity. The consistent relativist cannot raise his or her voice in disagreement or protest, since cultural agreement alone determines right and wrong. If a majority within a particular culture has determined that genocide and ethnic cleansing are warranted as part of the Darwinian struggle for survival, these practices become morally valid within that culture.

Thus, the cultural relativist who is true to his or her beliefs has to acknowledge all sorts of extreme behavior as morally permissible, including torture, slavery, rape, and so forth. The need to tolerate this behavior in the name of cultural consensus underscores the implausibility and irrationality of normative cultural relativism. Accepting normative cultural relativism means rejecting the authority of universal human rights that are valid for every human person regardless of their cultural background.[40]

Perhaps the most fatal conceptual problem for social relativism is the determination of a proper standard or "unit of measure." Is morality relative to an entire culture, a society, a nation, or a country? And within a country is morality further relativized to an ethnic group with its unique cultural standards, a religious sect, or even a tribe? How precisely do we determine cultural consensus that is the sole arbiter of morality? In some African countries, for example, the plurality of tribes and their different belief systems make it exceedingly difficult to determine some uniform standard for a particular country or nation. The Karamajong tribe in Uganda clings to its ancient cultural tradition that claims the world's cattle are its property. They seize cattle wherever they find it and place them in the center of their homesteads with their huts on the periphery. Other tribes regard them as rustlers.[41] Hence these conflicting tribal beliefs complicate the identification of proper moral standards for a country like Uganda. Second, what is the proper level of agreement for determining a "consensus?" If 51% of the people in a certain country agree that euthanasia is morally acceptable, is that slim majority enough to declare that there is a consensus on this issue? And how exactly can we reliably determine this number? As Oderberg points out, normative social relativism is arbitrary in two ways; the determination of a valid standard and the degree of measurement to be used within that standard.[42]

A related problem with relativism is its incompatibility with the notion of moral progress. How can we argue that a particular culture has achieved either moral progress or regression if we have no common yardstick by which to make such a judgment? It would be impossible to judge our own historic culture as a good one and to measure its social and moral progress, if there are no objective and transcultural standards of comparison. The best we can do is to criticize a society for not living up to the normative ideals it has chosen, but the ideals themselves cannot be criticized.[43]

Finally, cultural relativism is inattentive to the compelling philosophical arguments supporting our common humanity. The inescapable truth is that despite cultural and ethnic diversity we are all essentially similar as rational human beings. Skeptics and postmodernists may scoff at this line of reasoning. But if there is no human species and every human being is unique in kind we are vulnerable to the human rights abuses that often emerge from a separatist and racist mentality that sees superficial differences such as skin color as the mark of superiority. On the other hand, if we accept the highly credible assumption of a universally shared humanity that expresses itself in many cultural forms, we can quickly deduce that there must be *some* substantive, universal goods that we all seek out, such as friendship and knowledge. According to the philosopher, Philippa Foot,

> Granted that it is wrong to assume identity of aim between people of different cultures; nevertheless there is a great deal that all men have in common. All need affection, the cooperation of others, a place in the community, and help in trouble. It isn't true to suppose that human beings can flourish without these things – being isolated, despised or embattled, or without courage or hope. We are not therefore simply expressing values that we happen to have if we think of some moral systems as good moral systems and others as bad. Communities as well as individuals can live wisely or unwisely, and this is largely the result of their values and the codes of behavior that they teach. Looking at these societies, and critically also at our own, we surely have some idea of how thing work out and they work out as they do.[44]

Some philosophers would go deeper than Foot by arguing for a rational nature as the metaphysical basis to our common humanity and profound equality. Aristotle conceived an immutable human nature as the ground of a "universal law" or "natural justice" binding on all human persons.[45] We cannot address this debate here, but surely our lived experience bears out Professor Foot's balanced conclusions about our shared humanity along with a common normative code of conduct that supports the needs and aspirations of all human persons. In addition, the notion of a common human nature is not confined to the Western philosophical tradition. The Confucian tradition gives prominence to the notion of *ren* or humanity, and some Chinese scholars regard the Mencian concept of common humanity as a critical link between classical Confucian philosophy and modern human rights discourse.[46]

This conception of a common humanity and universal goods defies the popular postmodern vision that has argued so vehemently for moral conventionalism and nihilism. Space constraints make it impossible to explore these issues further. However, we should not be intimidated by postmodernity's renunciation of objective truth and objective morality. The denial of metanarratives seems to refute itself since that very denial and its rationale is also a metanarrative, articulating a truth presumably universal in its significance. When these philosophers claim that there is no truth, either they are claiming to inform us of a truth, what really *is* the case, or their assertion is also culturally, historically, and linguistically conditioned such that this statement too is relativized, just another opinion that need not really concern us.[47] As Bernard Williams has observed, the postmodern skeptic "holds up before the reader's lens a sign saying that something is true or plausible or worth considering, and then tries to vacate the spot before the shutter clicks." [48]

Even in the face of these convincing arguments, extreme cultural relativism still has its vocal defenders. However, many philosophers are unwilling to follow this line of reasoning to its logical conclusion of pure moral nihilism. Far more plausible and defensible is the more nuanced doctrine of modified cultural relativism. This thesis maintains that there are at least some cross-cultural norms, some common elements of morality, though there is a large gray area where cultures disagree over what is right and wrong. There are certain universal moral rules or rights that apply to all nations and peoples. The key question is not whether there are objective cross-culture norms that constrain the behavior of all international agents (including multinational corporations), but what is the content and scope of those obligations.[49]

Donaldson and Dunfee prefer to speak about these cross-cultural objective standards as "hypernorms," which represent the global norms by which all others are to be judged. Hypernorms constitute a "thin universal morality," but they also respect intercultural diversity by setting broad parameters for a "moral free space."[50] They argue for procedural hypernorms such as the "right of voice," structural hypernorms such as the right to property (which may be defined differently by different societies), and substantive hypernorms such as respect for human dignity and promise keeping. While these various hypernorms might reflect what human beings tend to have in common, they are not grounded in human nature. Rather, they depend on "widespread consensus": conformity with global industry standards, conformity with the standards of regional government organizations, and a general consistency with the precepts of major religions and philosophies. This approach is pluralistic in its acceptance of a broad range of ethical viewpoints that may be chosen by a culture, yet it rejects the relativistic notion that any cultural norm is routinely permissible.[51]

This pluralistic moral philosophy supports a minimal set of universally binding moral principles as an antidote to moral relativism, and it recognizes the need for an appropriate balance between "ethical universality" and the "cultural particularity," which is ignored by normative cultural relativism. At the same time, it repudiates extreme universalism (or moral absolutism), which argues for a single set of universal moral principles or laws that capture and define *all* normative issues of global significance. Hypernorms give some recognition to our shared humanity, but preserve a zone of moral free space that respects the unique identity of particular peoples or cultures.[52] Cultures are free to determine their own moral standards so long as these hypernorms are not violated.

Despite the clear advantages of this nuanced theory, it still raises some pressing questions. Is it adequate to ground these universal moral norms in an overlapping consensus when such consensus is always subject to change? Or can we find a stronger basis for a moral objectivism that can serve as a reliable defense against moral nihilism and the hegemony of cultural consensus? In the next chapter we argue for a *moderate universalism*, a set of universal natural rights that express *many* normative issues of global significance, grounded not in overlapping consensus but in fundamental human goods. This perspective narrows moral free space more than the theory proposed by Dunfee and Donaldson, but it still leaves adequate room for cultural diversity and the implementation of those rights within a given culture.

Conclusions

Managers and executives of multinational corporations must often confront the reality of moral and cultural diversity when they do business abroad. This is part of the liability of foreignness that makes crossing borders so tenuous even for well-prepared corporations. The extent of this liability correlates to the distance between the home economy of a multinational and the host economy. There are four dimensions of this "distance": political, geographic, economic, and cultural. Our primary concern has been cultural distance, which is sometimes difficult to bridge.

Multinationals must assess the effects of their transactions on the integrity of local cultures and factor this assessment into their strategic decisions. Corporate strategies should always reflect a suitable appreciation for cultural diversity. A more daunting challenge for multinationals is how to deal with the normative diversity that can exist between two different social environments. Multinationals often find themselves in awkward situations where the moral norms in the host country conflict with their own moral standards and the standards of their home country. U.S. social media companies like LinkedIn, for example, must contend with a Chinese government that wants to control free expression on their respective platforms. Should they adapt to the host country's norms or abide by "universal" standards, even if it means exporting those standards to another cultural context?

Those who promote the universality of moral norms like human rights recognize that there must be room for the different cultural expression of those rights. But while this flexible, pluralist approach to universal norms is warranted, unbounded pluralism that effectively negates certain rights is not acceptable.[53]

In order to appreciate the theoretical underpinnings of these practical questions, we explored in some depth the issue of moral relativism, especially the more popular form of cultural relativism. Our main axis of discussion has been normative cultural relativism, which insists that moral rightness or wrongness differs from one society or culture to another and that prevailing moral standards are equally valid. There are no universal moral standards, only a cultural consensus on what is right or wrong. We demonstrated the philosophical problems with this approach since it implies that any behavior, no matter how indecent or extreme, is morally permissible so long as it meets with cultural approval. Far more intellectually coherent is the thesis of modified cultural relativism which acknowledges a minimal set of moral standards that have normative force across different cultures. Those standards can be expressed in terms of hypernorms that constitute some limits on cultural consensus as the basis for moral judgment. A better alternative is moderate universalism that proposes a thick set of natural rights. The foundation of those rights is not some arbitrary global consensus but the basic human goods constitutive of human flourishing.

Moral systems predicated on a minimal normative code of hypernorms or even on a strong set of universal natural rights are not attempting to override all cultural differences or promote dogmatic ethnocentric standards that will homogenize diverse cultures. Rather, they seek to recognize and respect both cultural particularity and universal humanity. The challenge for the fair-minded multinational corporation and its managers is to combine respect for people in their cultural diversity with a steadfast refusal to tolerate any injustice. Cultural diversity does not deserve respect when it appears to manifest itself as ethnic cleansing, forced labor, or torture.[54] To be sure, this is a difficult terrain even for the most savvy and nimble multinational enterprise.

Notes

1 Arthur Schlesinger, "The Opening of the American Mind," *New York Times Book Review*, July 23, 1989, 1, 26–27.
2 Despite the claims of some contemporary Aristotelian scholars, Aristotle, who described virtue as the capacity to choose the intermediate or the mean between the vices of defect or excess, was particularly clear that certain actions are always wrong. According to Aristotle: "But not every action nor every passion admits of a mean; for some have names that already imply badness, e.g., spite, shamelessness, envy, and in the case of actions, adultery, theft, murder … It is not possible, then, ever to be right with regard to them; one must always be wrong." *Nicomachean Ethics* trans. William Ross, John Ackrill, and W. Urmson (Oxford: Oxford University Press, 1934), 2.6.
3 Kevin Flannery, *Acts Amid Precepts* (Washington, D.C.: Catholic University of America Press, 2001), 16–23.
4 S. Zaheer, "Overcoming the Liability of Foreignness," *Academy of Management Journal* 38 (1995), 341–363. See also Geoffrey Jones, *Multinationals and Global Capitalism* (Oxford: Oxford University Press, 2005), 4–6.
5 Pankaj Ghemawat, "Distance Still Matters: The Hard Reality of Global Expansion," *Harvard Business Review*, Sept–Oct (2001), 138–152.
6 James Hagerty and Paul Sonne, "Paper Titan's Big Bet Hits a Frosty Siberia," *Wall Street Journal*, July 17, 2013, A1, A12.
7 Ghemawat, "Distance Still Matters," 140–146.
8 "The Power of Tribes," *Economist*, January 28, 2012, 68.
9 David Turner, "Toys 'R' Us Goes to Japan," *Wall Street Journal*, February 7, 1990, B1.
10 Daniel Litvin, *Empires of Profit* (New York: Texere, 2003), 192–195.
11 Amol Sharma, "Google, Facebook Fight India Censors," *Wall Street Journal*, March 18, 2012, B1–2.
12 George Enderle, "What is International? A Topology of International Spheres and its Relevance for Business Ethics," Paper presented at the annual meeting of the International Association of Business and Society, Austria, July 1995. See also Thomas Donaldson and Thomas Dunfee, *Ties that Bind: A Social Contract Approach to Business Ethics* (Boston, MA: Harvard Business School Press, 1999), 217–220.
13 Mary Ann Glendon, "The Universal Declaration of Human Rights at 70," in *Fundamental Rights and Conflicts among Rights* eds. Pierluca Azzaro and Mary Ann Glendon (Steubenville, OH: Franciscan University Press, 2020), 227–243.

14 Enderle, "What is International?" 217–220.

15 Michael Ignatieff, *The Ordinary Virtues: Moral Order in a Divided World* (Cambridge, MA: Harvard University Press, 2017), 18–19.

16 Manuela Andreoni and Ernesto Londono, "Despite World's Outrage, Farmers in Amazon Remain Defiant," *New York Times*, August 27, 2019, A4.

17 Gilbert Harman, "Is There a Single True Morality," in *Moral Relativism: A Reader* ed. Paul Moser and Thomas Carson (New York: Oxford University Press, 2001), 165–184.

18 Johann Herder, *Herders Sämtliche Werke* ed. Bernard Suphan 15 volumes (Berlin: Weidmann, 1913), vol. 13, 291.

19 Richard Brandt, "Ethical Relativism," in *Moral Relativism*, 26.

20 Jean-Francois Lyotard, *The Post-Modern Condition: A Report on Knowledge* (Minneapolis, MN: University of Minnesota Press, 1984), xix.

21 Zygmunt Bauman, *Life in Fragments: Essays in Postmodern Morality* (Cambridge, MA: Blackwell, 1995), 8.

22 Michael Freeman, *Human Rights* (Cambridge, UK: Polity Press, 2011), 62.

23 Harman, "Is there a Single True Morality," 170.

24 Charles Taylor, *Multiculturalism and the Politics of Recognition: An Essay by Charles Taylor* (Princeton, NJ: Princeton University Press, 1992), 42.

25 Harman, "Is there a Single True Morality," 172.

26 According to Coleman and Leiter, "what count as law in any particular society is fundamentally a matter of social fact or convention." See Jules Coleman and Brian Leiter, "Legal Positivism," in *A Companion to Philosophy of Law and Legal Theory* ed. Dennis Patterson (Oxford: Oxford University Press, 1996), 241. See also John Finnis, "Natural Law Theories," *Stanford Encyclopedia of Philosophy*. Available at http://plato.standord.edu/entries/natural-law-theories.

27 J.L. Mackie, *Hume's Moral Theory* (London: Routledge & Kegan Paul, 1980), 150.

28 Michelle Moody-Adams, *Fieldwork in Familiar Places* (Cambridge, MA: Harvard University Press, 1997), 15.

29 Ruth Benedict, *Patterns of Culture* (Boston, MA: Houghton Mifflin, 1934), 223.

30 Melville Herskovits, *Cultural Relativism: Perspectives in Cultural Pluralism* (New York: Random House, 1972), 32. See also Moody-Adams, *Fieldwork in Familiar Places*, 99.

31 Kenneth Goodpaster, "Note on Relativism in Ethics," in *Polices and Persons* Supplement eds. Kenneth Goodpaster, John Matthews, and Laura Nash (New York: McGraw-Hill, 1991), 358–366. See also Richard Brandt, "Ethical Relativism," in *Moral Relativism*, 25–31.

32 Moody-Adams, *Fieldwork in Familiar Places*, 103.

33 Melville Herskovits, *Man and His Works* (New York: Knopf, 1948), 63.

34 John Ladd, *Ethical Relativism* (New York: Wadsworth, 1973), 1.

35 Pierre Manent, *Natural Law and Human Rights* (Notre Dame, IN: Notre Dame University Press, 2020), 4.

36 Goodpaster, "Note on Relativism in Ethics," 360–361.

37 Georg W.F. Hegel, *Die Vernunft in der Geschichte* ed. J. Hoffmeister (Hamburg: Niemeyer, 1955), 80.

38 Roger Moorhouse, "The League of Races," Review of *The SS: A New History*, *Financial Times*, July 24, 2011, F3.

39 "A Day of Reckoning Nears," *Economist*, February 15, 2020, 44.

40 Manent *Natural Law and Human Rights*, 5.

41 Jane Perlez, "A Fierce Uganda Tribe, Rustlers of the Old School," *New York Times*, September 18, 1995, A6.

42 David Oderberg, *Moral Theory* (Oxford: Blackwell Publishing, 2000), 22–23.

43 Rachels, "The Challenge of Cultural Relativism," 58.

44 Phillipa Foot. "Moral Relativism," in *Moral Relativism*, 195–196. See also Steven Rockefeller's "Comment," in *Multiculturalism and the Politics of Recognition*, 87–98.

45 Aristotle, *Rhetoric* in *The Basic Works of Aristotle* ed. Richard McKeon (New York: Random House, 1941), 1373b5. See also David Oderberg, "Natural Law and Rights Theory," in *The Routledge Companion to Social and Political Philosophy* eds. Gerald Gaus and Fred D'Agostino (New York: Routledge, 2013), 375–386.

46 See Grace Kao, *Grounding Human Rights in a Pluralist World* (Washington, D.C.: Georgetown University Press, 2011), 24–25. See also Irene Bloom, "Fundamental Intuitions and Consensus Statements: Mencian Confucianism and Human Rights," in *Confucianism and Human Rights* ed. Wm. Theodore De Bary and Tu Weiming (New York: Columbia University Press, 1998), 94–116.

47 See W. Norris Clarke, *Explorations in Metaphysics* (Notre Dame, IN: University of Notre Dame Press, 1994), 154–155.

48 Bernard Williams, *Truth and Truthfulness: An Essay in Genealogy* (Princeton, NJ: Princeton University Press, 2002), 19.

49 Thomas Donaldson, *The Ethics of International Business* (New York: Oxford University Press, 1989), 17–18. See Donaldson's insightful discussion of normative cultural relativism, which influenced my own views on this subject.

50 Donaldson and Dunfee, *Ties that Bind*, 43.

51 Ibid., 49–82.

52 Ibid., 79.

53 Glendon, "The Universal Declaration of Human Rights at 70," 235.

54 See John Finnis, "Virtue and the Constitution of the United States," *Fordham Law Review* 69 (2001), 1596. I am indebted to Finnis' analysis of civic virtue for helping me formulate some of the issues in this chapter.

Chapter 4

Law, morality, and natural rights

Multinational investment is one of the primary drivers of globalization. These investments have created many positive effects, including higher employment, and accelerated transfers of technology and managerial skills. These jobs have helped to lift many people out of poverty. In many cases these foreign operations create an export industry and links to the global economy.

However, some multinationals have acted without restraint or moral prudence in foreign markets. The result has been a series of ethical morasses that have damaged corporate reputations and cast a shadow over global capitalism itself. These scandals range from bribery and corruption to unsafe sweatshops and environmental degradation. To the casual observer, the multinational corporation seems to be an entity with unchecked and limitless power, an amoral "empire of profit," which seeks to extend its tentacles into foreign countries to exploit workers and find incremental markets for its goods. It is not uncommon to see multinationals castigated as "increasingly rapacious" and predatory.[1]

Multinational corporations can reform and alter their tarnished image with a deeper commitment to corporate social responsibility (CSR). While CSR may be a matter of enlightened self-interest, it is still instructive to think about it in terms of constraints on the wealth-creating activities of the multinational enterprise. In this chapter we review those constraints that take the form of legal and moral obligations. Some might argue that the law is a sufficient guide to responsible behavior, a worthy surrogate for corporate integrity. But there are institutional voids in emerging markets that often take the form of weak legal frameworks. Hence the need for ethical self-regulation and a corporate commitment to justice and the common good. In the previous chapter we demonstrated the logic and credibility of moral objectivism. It is possible to speak intelligibly of hypernorms or universal natural rights that are not

DOI: 10.4324/9781003058427-4

culturally conditioned. We now consider more specifically the moral expectations of multinationals that operate so extensively outside their home country's borders.

Above all, multinational corporations, like all moral agents, have an obligation to do no harm to anyone. One of the most fruitful avenues for specifying the obligation to do no harm is the delineation of basic human rights and the correlative duties associated with those rights. We advocate a modest list of rights that is neither too thick nor too thin, but moderate and adequate to ensure the most basic requirements of international justice. Rights, which are grounded in intrinsic human goods, are principles that inform our actions so they respect a person's welfare and dignity.[2]

Finally, it is important to briefly consider the scope of a corporation's social responsibility beyond common decency and respect for basic human rights. Should a multinational enterprise also have a social agenda that goes beyond the norm of justice to solidarity and corporate charity? Should a multinational attempt, for example, to help those who have been deprived of their rights? We address these questions in the final portion of this chapter.

Corporate responsibilities

Corporate responsibilities flow from the corporation's purpose. That purpose should not be conceived as profit maximization or as the optimization of stakeholder equity. The profit-making corporation is a voluntary, private association organized for a common end. This organization brings together different groups and individuals who cooperate in various activities to create value and to receive specific economic benefits. Thus, corporate purpose, the principle underlying the responsibilities of corporate managers, is the common good of that business as a community of persons.[3] And the common good is best defined as *efficient economic cooperation* in the value-creation process, along with *fairness to all participants*, who contribute to the financing, production, marketing, and distribution of the firm's products or services. All of these cooperating constituencies, including investors, managers, employees, suppliers, and customers, deserve a fair reward commensurate to their contribution and the risks they take. Investors, for example, who take risks by providing capital, deserve a reasonable rate of return on their investment. With this definition of corporate purpose, the emphasis is shifted away from false notions of shareholder primacy and the notion that everyone with a "stake" in the corporation, however transient or superficial, has a right to shape corporate policy and to share in the rewards of successful corporate performance. Only those who participate in the business have these legitimate claims, although it is sometimes difficult to identify participating stakeholder groups, given the ecology of the modern firm.[4]

It follows from the corporation's purpose and its moral agency that every corporation has *three fundamental duties*: to pursue their economic mission through the efficient allocation of resources that creates value and enhances shareholder wealth; to follow society's rules and laws; and to recognize and respect human rights and other moral principles that ensure justice and social harmony. This triad of duties will direct a corporation to responsibly achieve its purpose by realizing the common or shared good of the stakeholder groups that cooperate in this corporate enterprise.[5]

We can refer to this model as *fair market capitalism*, because it emphasizes not only the need for ongoing cooperation to efficiently create value but also the requirement of justice in all participants' interrelationships. Justice includes a fair and equitable sharing in the burdens and benefits that come from this cooperation.[6] In addition, the corporation has the same general moral obligations as any other moral agent. Hence, it must avoid harmful environmental degradation, rectify its past injustices through affirmative action policies, avoid bribery payments in emerging economies, and so on. The corporation must act with justice and prudence in all its marketplace interactions.

The first of these three duties is to allocate resources in a way that efficiently creates value in the marketplace. According to modern economic theory, value is added by creating the biggest differential possible between willingness to pay for a product and the supplier opportunity cost. Willingness to pay is the most that consumers will pay for a product and usually corresponds to the price. Almost any activity in the value chain can influence a customer's willingness to pay. A luxury car manufacturer, for example, focuses on high-quality components and intangibles to boost willingness to pay for its product. Efficient companies strive to keep the cost of supplier inputs as low as possible, and hence they do not pay those suppliers any unnecessary premiums. Supplier opportunity cost is defined as the least suppliers will accept for their goods. The bigger the difference between willingness to pay and supplier opportunity cost, the bigger the added value. Efficient corporations will also be disciplined in reducing the costs of adding such value (labor cost, overhead, etc.). As a result, they will be able to capture a large amount of the value they have created and generate sizable corporate profits.[7]

The authority of law

These value-added activities must be carried out within the rules of the game, general laws, and specific regulations that govern a particular industry. Like all persons, corporations are agents that must follow society's laws. Thomas Aquinas' definition of law as "a rule and measure of action" captures its essence. As a rule, the law tells us what to do or how to behave and as a measure it provides a standard by which our actions can be judged.[8] Law promotes and preserves the common good of the community, and when laws are properly formulated and justly implemented, they possess intelligence and authority. Laws are both directive and coercive. Recalcitrant parties need the incentive of coercion to abide by the law when an appeal to the reasonableness of preserving the common good fails to persuade.[9]

For Aristotle (and Aquinas), morality and law are closely connected, since positive laws are valid only if they are just. The purpose of law, explains Aristotle, is to make citizens good and virtuous. Thus, the act of formulating law should be guided by objective moral principles rather than by social conventions or arbitrary standards. Laws can change. But some laws reflecting essential aspects of our human nature, such as the laws that protect innocent human life, cannot be radically revised or abolished.[10]

The legal order is paramount. In the *Politics* Aristotle insisted that we must follow "the rule of law and not of men," and his admonition suggests the dangers of a retreat from the primacy of the legal order.[11] The legal system remains our common pathway for achieving the common good, which is defined as a set of conditions that allow members of the political community to realize their reasonable objectives and values. Its promotion and enforcement is essential for the welfare of every member of that community.[12] Without the law and the effective authority of the state, it would be impossible to prevent rights from being deprived and to promote the common good among those determined to act against it.

Basic legal requirements of corporations would include honoring contracts, avoiding fraud, and refraining from the payment of bribes. In foreign countries multinational corporations are governed by the national laws of the host country. Thus, if a multinational operates a manufacturing plant in India through a subsidiary, that operation must follow Indian law. Executives welcome law's transparency, but multinationals with operations in many different countries must be prepared to deal with a bewildering array of legal and regulatory frameworks.

In developing countries, laws can be weak and inadequate, or the rule of law is arbitrary and unfair. A deficient legal system opens the door for opportunistic behavior. But companies cannot exploit their workers and pillage the environment just because the host country laws are weak or the legal infrastructure has poor enforcement mechanisms. Rather, multinationals must resist such behavior and abide by internal ethical standards that go beyond the external guidance provided by law.

In some cases, home governments will introduce laws or regulations to control the behavior of their firms operating abroad. As a result of multiple corporate scandals, the Foreign Corrupt Practices Act (FCPA) was passed into law in 1977. This regulation outlaws payments to foreign officials to retain or obtain business or to achieve an "improper advantage." Multinationals are also subject to international laws and regulations. However, since there is an inability among national governments to reach consensus on most issues, there is a lack of codified international law that governs interactions between host governments and multinationals. One of the few examples of multilateral regulation is Trade Related Aspects of Intellectual Property Rights (TRIPS). TRIPS, which harmonizes patent laws as well as other intellectual property standards, is controversial and will be reviewed more thoroughly in Chapter 8.

The lack of international law and global standards has prompted victims of multinational transgressions to rely on the arcane Alien Torts Claims Act of 1789. This law states that "The district courts shall have original jurisdiction of any civil action by an alien for a tort (civil wrong) only, committed in violation of the law of nations or a treaty of the United States."[13] Previous interpretations of the law allowed non-citizens to sue in U.S. courts for violations of international law that were committed overseas. In 1980, a Paraguayan immigrant successfully used the ATCA to sue a former Paraguayan police officer for torturing and killing her brother in Paraguay. The ATCA was also used to sue Unocal for human rights violations committed during its construction of a pipeline in Burma. However, a more recent Supreme Court ruling in a case involving Royal Dutch Shell and Nigeria decided that the statute only covers violations of international law in the United States. But the Court left open the possibility that some acts abroad could so severely "touch and concern the territory of the United States," to thereby "displace the presumption" against the statute's use.[14]

Ethical standards

Corporations must also abide by moral norms that are not codified in laws or regulations or even in voluntary codes of conduct. Even in countries with mature institutions, law is reactionary and sometimes fails to protect basic human rights. In emerging economies with institutional voids, legal rules may be unclear and unstable and not backed by appropriate sanctions. But a morally responsible corporation is attuned to the demands of justice regardless of what the law allows. Multinationals should avoid the trap of "legalism," which implies an inclination to "get around" laws if possible and which regards those laws as mere social conventions.[15] As moral agents, corporations can and should be held accountable for exploiting legal loopholes (assuming the law in question is just) and for moral transgressions that inflict harm on others. Arguably, a multinational that is able to create value while staying within the boundaries of law and morality will be better able to sustain its competitive position in the world, by avoiding scandal and reputational damage.

But what precisely are the moral principles by which moral agents such as corporations should be governed? This is a controversial issue over which philosophers and ethicists have had profound disagreements. It is impossible to consider all of the normative theories of ethics and justice that have been proposed. Instead, we will review only the most prominent theoretical avenues for addressing moral dilemmas in the corporate environment.

Utilitarian reasoning

One immensely popular approach for resolving ethical dilemmas centers on the argument that justice can be expressed by the theory of utilitarianism, which is sometimes called consequentialism. According to this theory, first presented in the works of Jeremy Bentham and John Stuart Mill, the right or just course of action is to promote the general good or maximize happiness. The general good can be described in terms of "utility," and this principle of utility is the foundation of morality and the ultimate criterion of right and wrong. The term "utility" simply refers to the net benefits (or good) created by an action. According to Frankena, utilitarianism is the view that "the sole ultimate standard of right, wrong and obligation is the *principle of utility* or *beneficence*, which says quite strictly that the moral end to be sought in all that we do is *the greatest possible balance of good over evil* (or the least possible balance of evil over good)."[16] Thus an action or policy is right if it will produce the greatest net benefits or the lowest net costs (assuming that all of the alternatives impose some net cost) for all the parties affected by that action.

Seifert refers to classical utilitarianism as the "ethics of success." The decisive principle of this theory is that the moral worth of an action is contingent on whether or not its outcome is the best one possible. Antecedent to the moral agent's choice is an attempt to measure the immediate effects to be realized by that action along with more remote ones.[17] The agent must engage in a moral calculus, a cost benefit analysis, that will determine which option or choice produces the greatest net benefits for all affected groups or individuals. For example, let's assume that a manager who runs a plant that makes telecommunications equipment is considering outsourcing jobs to cut costs and wants to focus on the moral dimension of that decision. There are two options: outsource jobs to Malaysia and cut production costs by 60%, or keep the jobs in the U.S. The first option will mean higher profits, more money to invest in R&D, and a more secure future, but it will lead to social costs such as layoffs, hardships for workers and their families, and economic chaos for the local community. The second option will avoid those hardships but the company's high operating cost structure will make it more difficult to compete with Japanese and European companies that have already outsourced many of their jobs. The conscientious manager must weigh all of these diffuse costs and benefits and choose the alternative that maximizes net benefits.

Critics of consequentialism argue that the theory's primary deficiency is an insensitivity to basic human rights and justice. There are no intrinsically unjust or immoral acts since any act can be justified if it maximizes the good. When human rights conflict with utility they can be compromised or put aside. Basic liberties such as freedom of speech can be suppressed for the sake of the general good. Even an act of torture or rape can be justified if utilitarian calculation demonstrates that it will promote the greater good. There is nothing in utilitarianism that would prevent these abuses from happening as long as a cogent and objective case is made that the benefits flowing from these moral choices would exceed the costs. In addition, consequentialism is impractical since it is quite difficult for decision makers to predict remote consequences and to suppress their own biases and partialities as they work through this "objective" moral calculus. As Paine observes, "for all its aura of objectivity and precision, cost-benefit analysis is highly vulnerable to distortions and biases that cloud the moral issues."[18]

Moral duties

A reasonable alternative to consequentialism is moral reasoning that is informed by respect for moral duties. Prudent, moral action is motivated not by the optimization of consequences but by discerning and obeying one's duties to others and to oneself. Sandel describes three categories of duties: (i) particular voluntary obligations; (ii) particular obligations of solidarity; and (iii) universal natural duties.[19]

The first category, voluntary obligations, derives from our consent and includes promises, commitments, and contractual agreements. If a software engineer signs a non-disclosure agreement that prohibits disclosure of her work to competitors, then she has an obligation to abide by this voluntary agreement. Similarly, if a person receives a loan and voluntarily promises to repay that loan within six months, he or she is obliged to live up to this self-imposed obligation. The second category, obligations of solidarity, constitutes those duties that arise because of one's membership in particular communities, such as the family, the corporation, the local town where one resides, and the country where one is a citizen. Family members, for example, have definite duties of care and loyalty to each other, particularly in times of urgent need. The political community or state also assumes certain responsibilities to care for the welfare of its citizens. The government of such a political community must be just in all its affairs, but owes a particular obligation of solidarity towards its own people, which leads to a deeper level of care and concern. At the same time, citizens owe their countries gratitude and are bound by ties of loyalty and love of *patria*.[20]

Finally, there are natural duties that are owed to others by virtue of their humanity or rational personhood. These duties can be derived from Immanuel Kant's moral philosophy, which argues that the moral law is determined by pure reason alone. Kant 's reasoning begins with the principle that actions only have moral worth when they are done for the sake of duty. Only the motive of duty bestows worth on an action because only then does a moral agent do the right thing in the right spirit. Results, effects, or consequences have no role to play. And all rational beings have one moral duty: to follow the moral law, which, like all rational laws, must be universal, since universality represents the common character of rationality and law. Authentic moral action must proceed out of respect for this law and not be tainted by lesser motivations such as compassion or self-advantage. And this universal moral law takes the form of a categorical imperative: "I should never act except in such a way that I can also will that my maxim should become a universal law." The imperative is "categorical" because it is unconditional and does not allow for any exceptions.[21]

This maxim in Kant's formula is an implied general principle or rule underlying a particular action. If, for example, I usually break my promises, then I act according to the private maxim that promise breaking is morally acceptable when it is in my best interests to do so. But can this maxim be transformed into a universal moral law that holds for me as well as others? That universal law would stipulate that everyone can break a promise when it's in their best interest. Such a law, however, is fraught with contradiction, since the maxim permitting a false promise becomes self-defeating if it is universalized. According to Kant, with such a universal law allowing everyone to make a false promise, "I immediately see … that with such a law there would be no promises at all, inasmuch as it would be futile to make a pretense of my intention of my future actions to those who would not believe this pretense."[22] Unless I can will that my maxim becomes a universal law, it must be rejected. In view of the contradiction involved in universalizing promise breaking, we have a duty to keep all of our promises.

Also, from the categorical imperative we can derive other "universal natural duties," such as the duty to keep contracts, to tell the truth, and to refrain from theft of another's property. For example, no one would enter into a contract if he or she believed that the other party had no intention of honoring that contract. Kant would maintain that each of these duties is also categorical, admitting of no exceptions, since the maxim underlying such an exception cannot be universalized. Thus, Kant's universalizablity principle expressed in the categorical imperative can be used to test the validity of specific corporate and individual actions. If they cannot be logically and practically universalized, those actions violate the moral law. The bottom line for Kant is that we must not disregard or disobey a universal duty, even if by doing so we could bring about a "better" state of affairs.

Kant presents a "compass" or guide for human reason that allows us "to distinguish what is good, what is bad, and what is consistent or inconsistent with duty."[23] His ethics emphasizes fairness to others and impartiality. Perhaps the most serious defect in Kant's austere moral philosophy is the conclusion that the absolute norms derived from the categorical imperative allow for no exceptions. Even if lying will prevent injury to someone else, I am still forbidden from doing so, since the maxim, "it's permissible for me to tell a lie," cannot be universalized. According to Kant, "Truthfulness in statements that cannot be avoided is the formal duty of man to everyone, however great the disadvantage that may arise for him or for any other."[24] The austerity and abstractness of Kant's grand theory undermines its usefulness as a practical avenue for addressing intricate moral issues.

Rights: thick or thin?

A third approach to ethics focuses on basic human rights. According to this perspective, moral reasoning should be governed by respect for individual rights and a philosophy of fairness. A rights-based analysis of moral problems should consider whether a particular action or policy violates an individual's natural or legal rights such as the right to privacy, the right to own property, or the right to subsistence level wages. And where two rights conflict, ethical reasoning must determine which right is more urgent and deserves priority.

In some cases, when rights are not at stake, it is necessary to think about right action in terms of the duties outlined by Sandel and the moral compass provided by Kant. However, it is unrealistic to expect managers to routinely engage Kant's abstract theory to determine their specific duties. In international affairs, moral issues typically pertain to human rights and their correlative duties. And so we give special attention to this framework because of its relevance for globalization issues.

Commitment to human rights has evolved thanks to a broad moral consensus of the globalized world. Rights are distinctive because they take priority over other social and economic considerations and because of their mandatory character.[25] Rights language is at the center of many national and international constitutions. Prominently enshrined in the United States Constitution is a Bill of Rights that guarantees every citizen certain entitlements such as free speech and religious liberty. The Universal Declaration on Human Rights (UDHR), ratified by the General Assembly of the United Nations in 1948, attempted to shift attention to the universality of human rights rather than local cultural norms. The UN Declaration has been widely endorsed and it was the model for European Convention for the Protection of Rights and Fundamental Freedoms (1952). Article 1 of the UDHR declares that all human beings are equal in dignity and rights. The UDHR goes on to stipulate a plethora of basic human rights such as the right to freedom of movement, the right to be free from slavery and torture, the right to work, the right to own property, and the right to just remuneration.

However, the international human rights movement appears to be in some peril. In emerging economies, the promotion of rights has rekindled old resentments associated with colonialism. Western countries and their multinationals are perceived as promoting rights only to advance their own self-interests. Rights advocates are accused of ethno-centrism by quashing local cultural values. According to this reasoning, the Declaration was a cleverly disguised attempt to universalize Western ideals and norms.[26] When the UDHR was being developed in 1947 the American Anthropological Association warned those working on the project of the danger of producing "a statement of *rights* conceived only in terms of the values prevalent in Western Europe and America."[27]

In addition, there is growing skepticism about human rights in some Western democracies, which is partly due to the mixed results of supranational institutions in safeguarding those rights. The spread of moral cultural relativism in Western institutions works against the affirmation of universal moral principles. These principles imply ranking cultures in terms of their commitment to basic rights, and this prospect is anathema to most progressive thinkers. And as the pressure to respect cultural diversity increases, there are renewed questions about how to identify and defend universal rights in a pluralistic world.[28]

Concerns also persist about the philosophical grounding of universal human rights. Neither the United States Constitution nor the United Nations Declaration provides any foundation or normative justification for the rights that they declare. These rights are merely asserted as necessary and self-evident. Thus, while the UN Declaration remains influential, its efficacy is limited by the fact that while the rights it proposes are plausible, they are not philosophically justified. Without that justification, rights appear to be arbitrary and provisional.[29]

Nonetheless, is it still possible to defend the UDHR's extensive or "thick" set of rights, or can we only defend a minimal or "thin" list of rights in the face of cultural pluralism? Before we evaluate these various options, it is necessary to briefly review the definition of a natural right that may or may not be implemented in the law. Rights are powerful normative considerations that typically prevail against competing interests. Rights are assumed to be universal because a person has those rights by virtue of his or her personhood. And rights imply duties that are independent of their recognition by governments or by other people.[30]

Hohfeld distinguishes between a "claim right," or right in the "strict sense," and a liberty right. According to Hohfeld, A has a claim right that B should do Ø if and only if B has a duty to A to do Ø.[31] The key point is that when claim rights are at stake, the action in question is an action on the part of others and not on the person who has the right. A claim right is either a right to be given something, to be "assisted in some way," or a right not to be interfered with or dealt with in a certain way.[32] Otherwise, in Hofheld's terms, we would be talking about a liberty or a "privilege" instead of a claim right.

Thus, rights are *justified claims* that a person or group of persons can make upon other individuals or upon society. These claims entail *correlative duties* on the part of other individuals. If one possesses a right, one is in a position to determine, by one's choices, what others should or should not do. In Hohfeld's framework, for example, privacy would be considered a claim right such that one individual (the right holder) has a claim on another (the duty bearer) to assist in the process of restricting access to the right holder's personal information or not to interfere with the right holder's efforts to restrict such access.

These natural or moral rights, which reflect the constitutive elements of the well-being and fulfillment of human persons and their communities, are antecedent to just laws. These are rights people possess by virtue of their humanity, and everyone is bound to respect those rights as a matter of justice.[33] A natural right, therefore, has its own moral authority, which must be asserted even if that right is not reflected in the legal structure of a particular political community. But how is it possible to specify those rights for peoples across the globe within different historic cultures and holding conflicting moral beliefs? And how can we avoid the dangers of a purely Westo-centric approach to rights that obscure those differences?

In the *Law of Peoples*, Rawls articulates an account of justice between and among "peoples," and attempts to sketch out a theory of universal rights that is devoid of a Western bias. The "law of peoples" constitutes political principles of international law that govern interactions among different societies. Rawls uses the term "people" to refer to what is commonly called a nation or political community. He assumes that a shared culture is central to being a certain people who are united among themselves by certain common traits and "sympathies" that they do not share with others. Rawls differentiates between a just, well-ordered liberal society (such as Western democracies) and a decent society. And he distinguishes both from a rogue or "outlaw" society that violates the norms of decency.[34]

But what makes a society "decent" rather than an outlaw state that deserves to be shunned by other nations? Rawls argues that there are two broad conditions necessary for decency. First, this society does not have aggressive ambitions and it recognizes that it must achieve its objectives through diplomacy and other peaceful means. Second, a decent society secures for all of its citizens basic human rights. A social system that systematically violates rights cannot postulate a just or "decent" scheme of political and social cooperation. A decent society may not be quite as just and morally reasonable as a well-ordered liberal one, but it deserves the toleration and cooperation of other peoples or nations.[35]

Rawls sketches out basic rights that are the condition for having a decent society. Since these universal rights cannot be peculiarly liberal or unique to Western cultures, Rawls recognizes only a "special class of urgent rights" as moral rights in the proper sense.[36] These rights include the right to life, integrity of person, and security along with the right to the means of subsistence; rights to liberty of the person (understood as freedom from slavery, serfdom, and forced occupation); the right to own personal property; the right to a "sufficient measure" of liberty of conscience to protect to some degree freedom of religion, thought, and association; and the right to "formal equality," and equal protection under the law (understood as the right to due process, a fair trial, etc.). For Rawls, decent societies need not affirm the equality of its citizens or provide political rights such as the right to vote.[37]

In contrast to Rawls, it is philosophically cogent to propose a broader set of rights and correlative duties binding on all moral agent, including multinational corporations. To be sure, the UDHR list is too extensive because it includes some questionable economic rights such as rights to social security insurance or the right to "periodic holidays with pay" (art. 24). On the other hand, Nickel and Donaldson present criteria for determining universal rights that allow us to go beyond Rawls while also avoiding the excesses of the UDHR. They argue that a natural right that requires legal implementation must satisfy three conditions to have full legitimacy:

1. The right must protect something of great importance (Nickel).
2. The right must be subject to substantial and recurrent threats (Nickel).
3. The obligations or burdens imposed by the right must satisfy the fairness-affordability test (Donaldson).

The first condition implies that rights refer to goods of critical importance. Rights protect a person's most fundamental interests or a "secure claim to life." Second, Nickel believed that rights must involve human goods subject to threats or the list of rights would be too expansive. If there were no ethnic or racial discrimination within a particular society, it would not be necessary to call attention to a right against discrimination. But Nickel insists upon a low "threat threshold." Even if a society experiences very little discrimination, it will be necessary to recognize and support a moral and legal right against such discrimination.[38]

Donaldson interprets the third condition in terms of a fairness affordability test. This means that international agents, including multinationals, must be able under ordinary circumstances to assume the burdens and duties that they inherit in honoring positive rights that require the provision of certain goods and services. If the implementation of a specific right imposes a serious burden on people, that implementation might violate norms of justice that determine the distribution of burdens. Declaring a universal right to a college education would impose too big a burden on poor countries whose governments would have to implement that right. [39]

Satisfying all three conditions qualifies a presumptive rights claim as a fundamental human right, which must be codified in a legal framework and respected by individuals, organizations, and nation states.

Nickel's first condition for recognizing a right is also suggested in the legal philosophies of H.L Hart and John Finnis. According to Hart, "the core of the notion of rights is neither individual choice nor individual benefit, but basic or fundamental individual needs."[40] In Finnis' terms, rights involve basic aspects of human flourishing. They protect basic human goods such as life and health or knowledge without which human flourishing is impossible. Hart and Finnis, therefore, concur with the logic of rights implicit in Nickel's analysis. Rights proceed from our understanding of basic human goods and protect those goods that are "something of great importance" for human well-being. Rights provide a way of speaking about what is just "from the viewpoint of the other to whom something is owed or due, and who would be wronged if denied that something."[41] In contrast to Rawls, there is no basis to exclude a traditional liberal right if that right protects a good fundamental for human well-being. Our own proposed list of rights is more expansive than Rawls because it gives priority to Nickel's first condition and has a more subtle view of how rights are threatened.

Given these conditions and mindful of the fact that our focus is on rights that all international agents must honor, we propose a list of fourteen fundamental rights. Some of these rights are suggested by Donaldson and Nickel, though we sometimes formulate them differently, and virtually all of them are included in the United Nation's UDHR. This list is not necessarily exhaustive, but the rights enumerated here express quite well the most basic demands of justice:

- ■ Right to freedom or political liberty
- ■ Right to be free from slavery or servitude
- ■ Right to ownership of property
- ■ Right to freedom from torture
- ■ Right to equality before the law and to a fair trial (due process)
- ■ Right not to be subject to arbitrary arrest or detention
- ■ Right to nondiscriminatory treatment
- ■ Right to life, health, bodily integrity, and security of person
- ■ Right to freedom of speech and association
- ■ Right to political participation

- ■ Right to minimal education
- ■ Right to subsistence ("a standard of living adequate for health and well-being," art. 25, UDHR)
- ■ Right to privacy
- ■ Right to freedom of thought, conscience, and religion

These rights must all be precisely specified and limited by other rights and by certain aspects of the common good such as public order. Rights are inviolable but they are not limitless. Therefore, they may be *infringed* under certain conditions but not *violated*. Someone infringes on another's right when she interferes with the exercise of that person's right. A right is violated if that infringement is wrong and unjust. Not every infringement constitutes a violation but a violation is always an infringement. Rights must sometimes be violated when there are conflicts or a collision of rights. It may be necessary, for example, to trespass on someone's property without their consent to get access to water that will save one's life. Rights can be infringed in these well-defined and exceptional circumstances where the more urgent right prevails because it is more essential for the preservation of one's dignity and well-being. The right to life and health trumps property rights, and so unless there are other extraordinary factors at work, that property right may be respectfully and carefully violated for the sake of these higher goods.[42]

Very few of these rights are absolute and exceptionless. Since human life is an irreducible human good, a critical aspect of one's real well-being, it is always unreasonable to choose directly against that good. Hence the absolute right of an innocent person not to have his or her life taken directly either as a means or as an end. Similarly, the right not to be tortured should allow for no exceptions since intentional damage to bodily integrity or health is intrinsically wrong. Finally the right not to be deliberately sentenced to prison or condemned on false charges qualifies as absolute.[43]

Duties are correlative to rights, and, according to Shue, there are three categories of duties that apply for every basic right. All of these duties must be carried out if the right in question is to be fully respected, but not necessarily carried out by the same individuals or institutions. It is impossible for any right to be "fully guaranteed unless all three types of duties are fulfilled."[44]

These correlative duties include: 1) Duties to avoid depriving; 2) Duties to protect from deprivation; and 3) Duties to aid the deprived. For example, with respect to the right of physical security, there is a duty not to directly abolish a person's security (by assaulting or raping that person), a duty to protect people against deprivation of security by other people, and a duty to provide security for those unable to provide their own. While all of these duties might apply to certain institutions, such as the state, we can safely assume that a multinational corporation's duty should only fall within the first two categories. Corporations are not required to assist those deprived of rights and correct rights abuses, since they are unsuited for this task, which may sometimes require them to educate the young and care for the sick. Thus, a multinational corporation should *avoid depriving* people of these rights and avoid cooperation in such deprivation by another party. This means that a multinational corporation cannot cooperate with a government that denies freedom of speech to some of its citizens. In many cases, where corporate activities are concerned, multinationals must also help *protect* rights from being deprived. A corporation that uses an overseas contractor employing very young children is not directly depriving those children of an education. But given its proximate relationship with the contractor, that corporation has a duty to protect the right to a minimal education from being deprived.[45]

The advantage of moderate universalism is that it strikes a reasonable balance between the maximalist scheme proposed by the United Nations in its Declaration (which includes twenty-nine rights) and the minimalism recommended by Rawls. This compromise goes beyond more pluralistic approaches that allow for a broader range of ethical viewpoints and that predicate transcultural hypernorms on overlapping consensus. On the contrary, according to this theory, rights are grounded in the irreducible aspects of human well-being so there is less free space for cultures to determine valid local norms. However, moderate universalism and its modest set of rights respect cultural diversity. Local custom can assume moral authority so long as these rights are not violated, and cultural factors can play some reasonable role in the implementation and specification of these rights.

A normative foundation for natural rights

The list of rights we have proposed offers a clear and concrete delineation of a multinational's basic obligations as a moral agent. These universal rights proceed from an understanding of basic human goods ("something important" in Nickel's words), and we must now demonstrate the relationship between the good and these human rights. More foundational than rights are certain intrinsic goods, valued for their own sake, which identify the basic reasons for our actions. A theory of rights is incomplete unless it attends to those goods that are necessary for our human flourishing.[46]

The word "good" refers to what people want and desire. Aquinas explains that the first principle of practical reason, which directs us to act in certain ways, is "good is to be done and pursued, and the bad is to be avoided."[47] The "good" means what is intelligibly worthwhile, authentic possibilities for our flourishing as human persons. We can specify the good by identifying irreducible aspects of human well-being and fulfillment, which include knowledge, friendship, health and life. These specific goods guide and direct our actions by providing reasons to consider certain choices as intelligible and "choice worthy." These "basic human goods" are basic not because we need them to survive but because we cannot flourish as human beings without them. Hence these goods are intrinsically valuable, and we recognize that they are choice worthy not as means to other ends but as ends in themselves. These goods are the primary reasons for action and the ultimate source of normativity. [48]

If a good is not intrinsic to human fulfillment, it cannot qualify as a basic human good. External or material goods are important, but they are not basic for fulfillment. Even freedom cannot be classified as a basic human good, since freedom, though quite important, is not a good that offers people fulfillment. What are these irreducible human goods? The list begins with several substantive goods: bodily life (including aspects of life's fullness: health, bodily integrity, and safety); knowledge and aesthetic appreciation; skillful performance or excellence in work and play. In addition there are relational goods such as friendship or harmony between persons and groups of persons; marriage; religion or harmony with God; and harmony between human persons and the wider sub-personal reality or physical environment the person inhabits. And finally there is the good of self-integration or inner harmony between one's judgments and behavior (authenticity) and between one's judgments and inner feelings (integrity).[49]

These goods, which we all seek in one form or another, represent basic aspects of human flourishing that reveal the permanent features of human reality. If human nature, which is prior in reality to these goods that fulfill it, were radically different, so would the basic human goods. There are countless ways of participating in or sharing basic human goods. Knowledge will always be a basic human good, but the scope and quality of humanity's knowledge along with methods for appropriating and disseminating that knowledge have clearly evolved throughout the course of history.[50]

Morality can begin to claim objectivity because the good, that is, this discrete set of basic human goods, is not subjective, subject to cultural differences or arbitrary preference. Each good such as knowledge, life, or friendship, is an *objective perfection* because it fulfills any human person and makes that person better off.

By reflecting upon these fundamental goods that are constitutive of our well-being, we can derive principles of justice or basic human rights. These rights come to be when there are principles of practical reason that direct us to act or refrain from acting in certain ways out of respect for the well-being and dignity of persons whose reasonable interests are affected by our actions. These rights cannot be compromised or "trumped" for purely utilitarian reasons. The goods of life and health are essential for our welfare, so justice demands that we desist from harming people or taking an innocent life. This duty or principle of justice can be expressed as a right: the right of an innocent person not to be directly killed or injured.[51]

Each of the other rights proposed on the list of fundamental international rights can be defended more forcefully by reference to these intrinsic human goods or to instrumental goods like freedom that enable the pursuit of those various forms of fulfillment. All of these goods constitute the moral foundation for the precepts of justice. We can rely on intermediate moral principles such as "one should not do harm to any other human being," or the Golden Rule, to assist in this process of deriving principles of justice or rights from these goods.[52] For example, since knowledge is indisputably a basic human good, essential for human flourishing, one should not choose in a way that is contrary to that good by depriving another person or group of persons of a basic or minimal education so that they can extricate themselves from a state of ignorance. Depriving someone of a basic education either through a deliberate choice or through moral inertia impedes the good of knowledge and cannot be consistent with the "do not harm" principle. Given the critical importance of knowledge for human well-being, there is a duty to educate all human persons, which can be expressed as the right to a minimal education. This right, of course, needs to be properly qualified and specified. The duty to educate belongs to the family and the state, but in relevant circumstances, corporations might have a duty to protect this right to a minimal education from being deprived.

A Social agenda?

One final word about a corporation's moral and social responsibility. Many ethicists and activists have maintained that corporations have obligations that exceed respect for international rights and rational moral principles such as the Golden Rule. They envision the multinational corporations as a social entity committed to a broad social agenda that includes fixing social problems. According to this view, corporations are not just bound to avoid depriving people of their rights but they must also correct human rights abuses even if this means working for the aim of distributive justice.[53] Corporations must pledge some of their plentiful resources for public purposes such as culture and the arts, education, or community health.

Although there is sometimes an overlap between these ethical and social obligations, it is useful to keep them distinct. Ethical obligations, as we have presented them, prohibit the deprivation of human rights and the protection of those rights from being deprived. But social obligations in the thick sense are more philanthropic and proactive in nature, and hence they can be classified as corporate charity. They go beyond the demands of decency and respect for human rights, and involve large commitments of time and resources to altruistic activities or the correction of social injustice. Coca-Cola, for example, does not just conserve water in its own operations, but is also committed to promoting water conservation and collaborates with environmental groups to conserve seven major freshwater river basins.[54]

However, not everyone concurs that corporations should have such a broad social agenda. Milton Friedman and those who endorse the doctrine of shareholder primacy resist the idea that a corporation, which is privately owned by its shareholders, is obliged to resolve public problems no matter how severe. According to Friedman, "there is one and only one social responsibility of business – to use its resources and engage in activities designed to increase its profits so long as it stays within the rules of the game, which is to say, engages in free and open competition, without deception or fraud."[55] Managers who sacrifice profits for the public good or select social causes are imposing an unfair tax on the shareholders. The only responsibility for private corporations is to increase long-term profits within the framework of the law and within certain bounds of ethical probity that preclude fraud and deception.

Friedman also believed that the markets themselves would solve many of the "social" problems that resulted from market failures such as negative externalities. When this doesn't happen, legal regulations may be necessary to fix the problem so that resources are directed to their optimal social use. Hence corporations can count on markets and the law as a guide to their proper social behavior. For Friedman, correcting market failures is the government's domain.

The problem, of course, is that markets and government regulators often react too slowly to fix these failures and, in emerging economies, sometimes they don't react at all. In some countries the rule of law is not upheld. Nonetheless, although there may be a regulatory vacuum, corporations have an ethical obligation to do something about market failures caused by their actions and policies, especially when those failures lead to the abridgement of rights. A corporation has a duty to inform its customers about the risks of using its products, regardless of what the market or the law allows, because basic human goods like health are at stake. Similarly, companies are obliged to fix and compensate for negative externalities even if they are not legally required to do so because of a country's low environmental standards. And that obligation might mean support for community development as compensation for the more disparate and indirect environmental harms to which a community is exposed. It's not completely clear what Friedman means by "rules of the game," but it seems that he does not go far enough in respecting the ethical dimension of a corporation's overall social responsibility.

The prime thrust of Friedman's critique is that corporate social responsibility in the strong sense (or corporate charity) is invalid. His theory advocates restraint on a corporation's philanthropic impulses and its willingness to commit corporate resources to solve social ills in a way that implicates public involvement in corporate management. His reasoning is that these corporate executives are spending the shareholders' money and foregoing profits in violation of their fiduciary obligation to make money for those shareholder-owners.

There are many valid objections to Friedman's theory, such as his misplaced faith in the resiliency of markets. Nonetheless, there is some merit to his argument, especially if corporate philanthropy comes at the expense of reasonable returns for the firm's shareholders. Also, free market logic will be profoundly challenged if private corporations are conceived as public entities in which multiple stakeholders have a "pseudo-ownership" interest.[56]

Thus, while a social agenda might be commendable for some companies, there are a few caveats worth mentioning. First, social responsibility or corporate philanthropy programs should not distract corporations from their ethical obligations to respect human rights. Multinationals can't take credit for opening medical clinics in Bangladesh, but then allow their suppliers to pay below subsistence level wages in unsafe facilities. Second, in most situations, corporations are not competent to privatize public policy as they attempt to remedy distributive injustice by weighing competing social and economic goals. They also lack the democratic credentials to engage in this sort of work, which is the function of government, the real custodian of public interest.[57] Third, the pursuit of a profitable business that creates value for its customers does a service to society and advances the public good in its own right. By adding value through the creation of goods and services people are willing to pay for, corporations enhance social welfare, and this primary obligation should not become a "sideshow" to more noble, philanthropic activities.[58] As Adam Smith pointed out centuries ago, these companies or cooperative enterprises benefit society by acting in their own economic self-interest.

Conclusions

Corporate purpose should be conceived in terms of the organization's common good: *efficient economic cooperation* in the value-creation process, along with *fairness to all participants*, who contribute to the financing, production, marketing, and distribution of the firm's products or services. It logically follows from the corporation's purpose and moral agency that it has three fundamental obligations: to create value or wealth, to follow the relevant law, and to observe ethical standards of fairness and justice. The corporation's goal of maximizing the value of the owners' assets is constrained by law and by moral norms, which above all ensure fairness for direct stakeholders involved in the value-creation process.

The rule of law is necessary for justice and for a well-ordered society. But law is sometimes reactive, riddled with loopholes, and even unjust. Thus, in the marketplace, companies should also be guided by appropriate ethical standards. For multinationals, the framework of universal human rights is the most fruitful avenue for ethical analysis since it does not suffer from the indeterminacy of utilitarianism or the abstractness of Kantianism. A company that sincerely respects rights will do no harm, follow the Golden Rule, and live up to the primitive moral standard of "common decency."

The framework of natural rights provides a useful way of expressing the requirements of morality. The United Nations has given the world an extensive set of universal rights while social philosophers like Rawls argue that only a thin set of universal rights is warranted. In contrast to the polarities of thick and thin rights, we made the case for a moderate universalism, a modest set of fourteen rights that must be honored by all international moral agents. Rights, which protect "something very important," can be derived from principles of justice that direct us to act or refrain from acting in ways that respect the well-being of others. The constitutive aspects of our well-being are the basic irreducible human goods essential for human flourishing. The principles of justice or rights guide our choosing toward those goods and away from their deprivation.[59] Therefore these basic human goods are the foundation of rights and the ultimate source of normativity.

The fourteen basic rights that constitute moderate universalism have three general correlative duties, all of which must be carried out if a right is to be properly respected. Multinational corporations have a duty not to deprive people of their rights and in some cases to protect rights from being deprived. But they do not have a duty to correct human rights abuses and resolve distributional inequities, since they lack the democratic qualifications and the competencies to deal with the demands of social justice.

Corporations may conceive their ethical or social obligations more broadly than the mandate to respect and protect the rights of others. They might opt for social responsibility in the strong sense, which involves a substantial commitment to corporate charity and to promoting social causes. But they should bear in mind the complexity of privatizing public policy that requires the weighing of competing social and economic goals. Moreover, they should not let this social agenda distract them from more fundamental moral obligations.

Notes

1 Alan Wolfe, "The Snake: Globalization, America and the Wretched Earth," *The New Republic*, October 1, 2001, 31.
2 John Finnis, *Philosophy of Law* (Oxford: Oxford University Press, 2011), 115.
3 Germain Grisez, *Difficult Moral Questions* (Quincy, IL: Franciscan University Press, 1991), 454–456.
4 Ibid., 455–459. See also Robert George, "Natural Law," *American Journal of Jurisprudence* 52 (2007), 55–70.
5 Lynn Sharp Paine, "Guide to Leadership and Corporate Accountability" (Boston, MA: Harvard Business School Publications, 2007). See also Goodpaster, "Business Ethics and Stakeholder Analysis," 70 and Grisez, *Difficult Moral Questions*, 455.
6 Grisez, *Difficult Moral Questions*, 496.
7 Pankaj Ghemawat, *Strategy and the Business Landscape* (Reading, MA: Addison-Wesley, 1999), 58–60.
8 Thomas Aquinas, *Summa Theologiae*, translated by the Fathers of the English Dominican Province (New York: Benziger Bros., 1947–1948), I–II, q. 90, a. 1. See also J. Budziszewski, *Commentary on Thomas Aquinas's Treatise on Law* (New York: Cambridge University Press, 2014), 36–37.
9 John Finnis, *Natural Law and Natural Rights* (Oxford: Oxford University Press, 1980).
10 Kevin Flannery, *Acts Amid Precepts* (Washington, D.C.: Catholic University of America Press, 2001), 187–190.
11 Aristotle, *Politics*, in *The Works of Aristotle* ed. R. McKeon (New York: Random House, 1941), III, 10.
12 Finnis, *Natural Law and Natural Rights*, 155.
13 Alien Tort Claims Act 28 U.S.C. §1350.
14 Jess Bravin, "Justices Limit Law's Reach for Acts Overseas," *Wall Street Journal*, April 18, 2013, A5. The case is *Kiobel v. Royal Dutch Petroleum Co.* 133 U.S. 1659 (2013). See also *Doe v. Unocal Corp.* 963 F. Supp 880 [C.D. Cal 1997]. In the *Kiobel* case, the Court affirmed that "there is no indication that [ATCA] was passed to make the United States a uniquely hospitable forum for the enforcement of international norms," 1685.
15 Flannery, *Acts Amid Precepts*, 188.
16 William Frankena, *Ethics* (Englewood Cliffs, NJ: Prentice-Hall, 1963).
17 Josef Seifert, *The Moral Action* (Irving, TX: International Academy of Philosophy Press, 2017), 34–35.

18 Lynn Sharp Paine, *Value Shift* (New York: McGraw-Hill, 2003), 222.

19 Sandel, *Justice*, 225.

20 Ibid., 225–230. See also Thomas Aquinas who refers to this gratitude and love of *patria* as a form of *pietas* or piety, *Summa Theologiae*, II–II, q. 101, a.1, ad.2.

21 Immanuel Kant, *Grounding for the Metaphysics of Morals* trans. Lewis Beck (Cambridge, MA: Hackett Publishing, 1993).

22 Ibid., 19.

23 Ibid., 20.

24 Immanuel Kant, *On the Supposed Right to Lie for Philanthropic Concerns* (Cambridge, MA: Hackett Publishing, 1993), 64.

25 James Nickel, *Making Sense of Human Rights: Philosophical Reflections on the Universal Declaration of Human Rights* (Berkeley, CA: University of California Press, 1987), 18.

26 Mary Ann Glendon, "The Universal Declaration of Human Rights at 70," in *Fundamental Rights and Conflicts of Human Rights* ed. Mary Ann Glendon (Steubenville, OH: Franciscan University Press, 2020), 228–229.

27 "Statement on Human Rights," *American Anthropologist* 49 (1947), 539–543. See also Nickel, *Making Sense of Human Rights*, 68.

28 Glendon, "The Universal Declaration of Human Rights at 70."

29 Michael Freeman, *Human Rights* (Cambridge, UK: Polity, 2011), 41–42. Philosopher Jacques Maritain who helped craft the UDHR called attention to this glaring deficiency but hoped that agreement would be reached "not only on the enumeration of human rights, but also on the key values governing their exercise." Jacques Maritain, "Introduction," in *Human Rights: Comments and Interpretations* ed. UNESCO (Westport, CN: Greenwood Press, 1949), 17.

30 Nickel, *Making Sense of Human Rights*, 3.

31 W.N. Hohfeld, *Fundamental Legal Conceptions* (New Haven, CT: Yale University Press, 1919), 140–144.

32 Finnis, *Natural Law and Natural Rights*, 200. I am indebted to Finnis' treatment of rights throughout this brief discussion.

33 Robert George, "Natural Law, God, and Human Dignity," in *Natural Law Jurisprudence* eds. George Duke and Robert George (Cambridge, UK: Cambridge University Press, 2017), 59–60.

34 John Rawls, *The Law of Peoples* (Cambridge, MA: Harvard University Press, 1999), 62–65. See also Samuel Freeman, *Rawls* (Oxford: Routledge, 2007), 429–430.

35 Rawls, *The Law of Peoples*, 64–65.

36 Ibid.,79.

37 Ibid., 65. See also Freeman, *Rawls*, 429–431.

38 Nickel, *Making Sense of Human Rights*, 111–112.

39 Thomas Donaldson, *The Ethics of International Business* (New York: Oxford University Press, 1989), 72–77.

40 H.L. Hart, "Bentham on Legal Rights," in *Oxford Essays in Jurisprudence: Second Series* ed. A. Simpson (Oxford: Oxford University Press, 1971), 171–185.

41 Patrick Lee, "Interrogational Torture," *American Journal of Jurisprudence* 51 (2006), 131. See also Finnis, *Natural Law and Natural Rights*, 205.

42 David Oderberg, *Moral Theory* (Oxford: Blackwell Publishing, 2000), 76–85.

43 Finnis, *Natural Law and Natural Rights*, 225.

44 Henry Shue, *Basic Rights: Subsistence, Affluence, and U.S. Foreign Policy*, 2nd ed. (Princeton, NJ: Princeton University Press, 1996), 53.

45 Ibid., 52–53. See also Thomas Donaldson, "The Perils of Multinationals' Largess," *Business Ethics Quarterly* 4 (3) (1994), 367–371.
46 John Finnis, "Natural Law: The Classical Tradition," in *The Oxford Handbook of Jurisprudence* eds. Jules Coleman and Scott Shapiro (Oxford: Oxford University Press, 2002), 24–25.
47 St. Thomas Aquinas, *Summa Theologiae*, I–II, q. 94, a. 2.
48 Germain Grisez, "A Contemporary Natural Law Ethic," in *Normative Ethics and Objective Reason* ed. G. McLean. Available at http://216.255.45.103/book/Series01/1–11/chapter_xi.htm. See also Robert George, "Natural Law," *American Journal of Jurisprudence* 52 (2007).
49 John Finnis, "Liberalism and Natural Law Theory," *Mercer Law Review* 45 (1994), 691–692. See also George, "Natural Law, God, and Human Dignity."
50 Germain Grisez, "Natural Law and Human Fulfillment," *American Journal of Jurisprudence* 46 (2001), 3–21. See also Finnis, "Natural Law: The Classical Tradition."
51 Robert George, "Natural Law, God, and Human Dignity," in *Natural Law Jurisprudence* eds. George Duke and Robert George (Cambridge, UK: Cambridge University Press, 2017), 57–75.
52 St. Thomas Aquinas, *Summa Theologiae*, I–II, q. 100, a. 3c.
53 See, for example, Kevin Jackson, "Distributive Justice and the Corporate Duty to Aid," *Journal of Business Ethics* 12 (1993), 547–551.
54 "Just Good Business," A Special Report on Corporate Social Responsibility, *Economist*, January 19, 2008, 6, 20.
55 Milton Friedman, *Capitalism and Freedom* (Chicago, IL: University of Chicago Press, 1962), 133. See also Friedman's celebrated article, "The Social Responsibility of Business Is to Increase Its Profits," *New York Times Magazine*, September 13, 1970, 32–33, 122–126.
56 Henry Manne, "Milton Friedman Was Right," *Wall Street Journal*, August 23, 2010, A24.
57 "The Good Company," *Economist*, January 22, 2005, 22. See also "Curse of the Ethical Executive," *Economist*, November 17, 2001, 70.
58 "Just Good Business," 8.
59 Robert George, "The Genesis or Meaning of Natural Law," in *Fundamental Rights and Conflicts among Rights*, 119.

Chapter 5

Emerging and frontier markets

The Republic of Zimbabwe, a landlocked country located in southern Africa, is rich in natural resources and well endowed with arable farmland. There is no reason why its people should suffer from hunger and economic destitution. Yet Zimbabwe has been a beleaguered nation for many years. It forms part of an African landscape spoiled by thwarted hopes and shattered reveries of post-colonial independent states where people hoped to flourish and enjoy the basic rights of democracy.

For a long time, this country, once called Rhodesia, was one of Africa's most prosperous nations. There was consistent economic growth, despite its colonial heritage. But everything changed when Robert Mugabe became Prime Minister in 1980. This autocratic leader, who misgoverned and impoverished Zimbabwe, served in that role until his forced resignation in 2017. When the army finally seized power, they prevented his young wife, Grace Mugabe, from taking over the presidency and continuing his corrupt legacy. He died two years later in Singapore where he was seeking treatment for various ailments.

Mugabe seemed to have the right credentials to lead Zimbabwe as it transitioned away from the state of Rhodesia governed by a white minority. Rhodesia was the unofficial successor state to the British colony of Southern Rhodesia, which had been self-governing or independent since 1923. Named after the imperialist diamond and gold explorer, Cecil Rhodes, this territory was originally chartered to his British South Africa Company. After criticizing the Rhodesian government in 1964 Mugabe was imprisoned for more than a decade and held without a trial or any due process. In 1973, while still in prison, he was selected as the president of the Zimbabwe African National Union (ZANU), of which he was a founding member. After his release from prison, Mugabe went to Mozambique where he organized a military campaign against the white-ruled government of Rhodesia. The Rhodesian regime, led by Ian Smith, was defeated in 1980 after a seven-year civil war. During that same

DOI: 10.4324/9781003058427-5

year, Mugabe's impassioned, anti-imperialist speeches along with his lofty promises helped to assure his victory as Prime Minister. He advocated peaceful co-existence and reconciliation with the remaining white residents of his country. Supported by foreign aid, global goodwill, along with plentiful harvests, Zimbabwe continued to thrive for a while.[1]

However, under Mugabe's chaotic leadership, the state security forces guided by the Central Intelligence Organization (CIO) soon began to terrorize his unfortunate critics and opponents. Many fell victim to the CIO's violent campaigns and human rights violations. The Prime Minister was hypersensitive to criticism and quick to demand a violent response to those who sought to exercise their political liberties. Mugabe's intolerance led to the unleashing of those security forces on the Ndebele tribe, which he considered to be disloyal. Thousands of these civilians were raped, tortured, and murdered. This atrocity became known as the Matabeleland massacre. It set a precedent for the Mugabe regime, which never hesitated to use military power to stifle even the slightest opposition or dissent. Mugabe soon compelled the opposition party, ZAPU, into accepting a one-party state, when it became known as ZANU-PF.[2]

While Mugabe's speeches evoked hope and prosperity, his political and economic policies were a complete disaster. He destroyed the country's civil service and hollowed out its legal system. His own political party was reduced to little more than a personality cult. His land reform program that took land from productive farmers and gave it to inexperienced citizens was naive and disordered. It devastated agricultural production, even in the most fertile areas of the country. He neglected Zimbabwe's weak infrastructure and made inadequate investments in human capital. There was little capital investment in agriculture and manufacturing. Mugabe essentially took a country that was once the most prosperous in Africa and reduced it to ruin. As a result of his policies and neglect, Zimbabwe has been in economic decline since the 1990s, experiencing several economic catastrophes, famines, and bouts of hyperinflation. Thanks to hyperinflation and other macroeconomic woes, most local industries collapsed and unemployment soared. This economic malaise was followed by a diaspora as a quarter of the population left this destitute country.[3]

Like some other African leaders in this post-colonial era, Mugabe enriched himself and his leading allies with proceeds from his country's mineral wealth, especially the Marange diamonds. Leaders of the Zimbabwean army, the police force, and the CIO have been linked to mining companies with rights to mine those precious stones. As one United States diplomat observed, "In a country with corrupt schemes, the diamond business in Zimbabwe is one of the dirtiest."[4]

Mugabe frequently relied on socialist rhetoric to explain away the country's problems. His blazing polemics always attributed Zimbabwe's economic woes to the machinations of conspiring Western capitalist countries rather than to his own incompetence. The message resonated with Zimbabwe citizens who had experienced inequities and predation at the hands of colonial powers. Prominent African political leaders were reluctant to criticize Mugabe, because of his political connections and his strong socialist pedigree.

With Mugabe's departure, there was renewed hope that his malignant influence would be dissipated. This emerging economy had an opportunity to revitalize itself and transform its political structure. Like many other African countries, Zimbabwe has a plentiful share of the continent's minerals, including gold, nickel, platinum, and diamonds. Perhaps now these resources will benefit the majority of the country's citizens and not just the elite class, hand-picked by Mugabe. With proper management, the country's agricultural production can also be restored.

But Mugabe's successor, Mr. Mnangagwa, who once served as the former president's intelligence chief, has not yet embarked on a path of radical reform. The tragic history of Zimbabwe underscores the importance of democracy, where citizens have a voice in who governs them. It also crystallizes the plight of many African countries, which suffer from despotic rulers and unenlightened policies, despite their great economic potential. The tale of Zimbabwe is only one strand in the narrative of Africa's tragic history with all its perils and promise.[5]

This chapter is dedicated to the topic of emerging and frontier economies like Zimbabwe. It has a special focus on Africa where so many of these fragile markets exist. By 2013, emerging economies accounted for more than half of the world's GDP (based on purchasing power). The rapid growth in these countries has been described as "the biggest economic transformation in modern history."[6] Emerging economies represent significant opportunities for private enterprise. But with those opportunities comes formidable challenges that are one of the primary themes of this chapter. After we provide a definition of an emerging economy we review the theme of institutional voids which often plagues these economies and deters their progress. Also considered is the resource curse, the politics of industrialization, the need for contextual intelligence, the role of national populism, and the question of marketization in more primitive environments. Along the way, we highlight the unique trials that emerging and frontier economies face, especially in light of the competitive and anarchic tendencies of geopolitics. We conclude with a discussion on how countries like China and Russia vie for political and economic influence over low-income, emerging economies through strategies such as China's Belt and Road program.

What are emerging and frontier economies?

Emerging markets stand in contrast to developed ones, which can rely on multiple external institutions to minimize market failures or high transaction costs. An emerging market is one that shares some of the features of a developed market, but does not fully meet its standards. The category includes markets that may become developed markets in the future or were so in the past.[7] When an emerging market economy makes progress, it usually becomes more integrated with the global economy. Its trade volume increases and it has a greater ability to attract additional foreign investment. As these economies mature, there is also a steady evolution of modern financial and regulatory institutions. Thus an emerging market economy is in the process of transition from a low-income, underdeveloped, and typically pre-industrial economy towards a modern, industrial one with a higher gross domestic product (GDP) and stronger economic fundamentals.[8]

Antoine van Agtmael coined the term "emerging markets" in order to convey a sense of "progress, uplift, and dynamism." Some equity funds specialize in equities from companies in emerging economies. The MSCI EM is the most popular equity benchmark and now includes twenty-four countries. Among those countries are the high-income BRICs, Brazil, Russia, India, and China, which are the four biggest emerging economies. Other high-income emerging economies include Taiwan and Qatar. Most emerging economies are classified as upper middle or lower middle income. The most notable emerging market economies in those categories include Mexico, Pakistan, Philippines, South Africa, Chile, and Malaysia.[10]

Frontier markets, on the other hand, are less advanced and prosperous than emerging markets. These markets are more mature than the least developed countries (LDCs), but they are still less established than emerging markets. They are too

---

Box 5.1 Concepts explained: Gross Domestic Product[9]

What is GDP (gross domestic product)?

A country's wealth is measured by its output, that is, the goods and services that it produces. Wealth is not measured by money printed by governments. The measurement of a country's output is gross domestic product. How is GDP calculated?

GDP is defined as the market value of the goods and services that are produced within a country over the course of a given year. This measurement includes household consumption (C), business investment (I), government spending on goods and services (G), exports (Ex), and imports (Im).

National Output or GDP = C + I + G + Ex − Im.

Consumption includes all household spending, but investment includes only expenditures for productive assets such as machinery and equipment. Since imports represent the purchase of foreign-made products, they must be subtracted from GDP.

GDP is measured in terms of current market prices. Nominal GDP may change either because there has been an increase in prices or an increase in quantity of goods produced and consumed; if there are big price increases (inflation) and yet no increases in the quantity consumed/invested from one year to the next, GDP will increase but national output will not. Real GDP, on the other hand, takes inflation into account and uses a constant set of prices. Real GDP increases only when there is an increase in quantity.

small and they have very poor macroeconomic fundamentals, such as exceedingly low GDP, illiquidity, and high debt. Frontier markets, also known as "pre-emerging markets," are only now beginning to invite more attention from investors and multinationals looking for new growth opportunities.[11] Frontier markets have the potential to stabilize and mature over the course of decades. However, it is also possible for established, emerging markets to regress to frontier market status. Cyprus, Ukraine, Croatia, Estonia, Kuwait, Nigeria, Botswana, Kenya, Ghana, and Argentina are all current examples of frontier markets.[12]

State failures are common in frontier economies and least developed countries, especially on the continent of Africa. Dysfunctional state governments impede economic growth through corruption and regressive policies. Somalia, for example, with an exceedingly low nominal GDP of $4.9 billion (2020), has been in complete disarray since its protracted civil war.[13] Essential state institutions, conceived by political philosophers like Hegel and Max Weber, are absent, and the resultant political turmoil keeps the country in a state of destitution. For Weber, the state's most critical functions include "the enactment of law (legislative function), the protection of personal safety and public order, the protection of vested rights, [and] the cultivation of hygienic, educational, social-welfare, and other cultural interests."[14] Without that institutional support, economic development is highly unlikely.

Emerging economies performed well until the 2020 pandemic recession with steady GDP growth and currencies strengthening against the U.S. dollar. But many of these economies are in a precarious position. One source of instability is the commodity cycle. It is always difficult to properly manage a commodity-based economy. The sharp drop in oil prices in 2014 and again in 2020 led to severe economic problems in Russia and other countries that depend on exports of crude oil. Many of these countries have little else to support their economies, so when petro dollars vanish, there is typically a big deficit in the current account. Budgets are stressed and investors take flight. Other commodity markets fell off substantially as the pandemic took hold in 2020. The result was rising fiscal pressures and market skepticism in countries like Brazil and Argentina.[15]

Another problem looming on the horizon for both emerging and frontier markets is the rise of automation and robotics. The only "natural resource" in some countries is labor. Countries like Pakistan and Mexico offer the benefit of cheap labor that attracts labor-intensive manufacturing. But robotic technology may erode that advantage and lead to "premature deindustrialization." Factory automation has decimated jobs in some industries, and, as this technology matures, it could cause economic duress for countries that have just begun to industrialize. Robotic technology, for example, threatens the garment industry in countries like Bangladesh. Although robots are common in many industries, they are rare in clothes making because these machines have a hard time with soft material. However, as advances are being made in robotic dexterity, robots rather than low-paid workers may one day fill the factories of Western manufacturers to the detriment of countries like Bangladesh and Malaysia.[16]

The final threat is the resurgence of protectionism, which has the potential to limit access to some of the world's biggest markets in the U.S. and Europe. For example, President Trump's threat to impose tariffs on a number of products exported from Mexico induced Ford to locate the manufacturing plant for its Focus cars in Flat Rock, Michigan instead of in San Luis Potosi, Mexico. Tariffs on washing machines, designed to protect U.S. companies like Whirlpool, have led to lower imports from countries like Thailand and Vietnam. China has also paid a price from this new wave of protectionism. In 2018, the Trump Administration began taxing $200 billion in imports from China. Thanks to these tariffs, Americans have purchased fewer Chinese goods due to rising prices.[17]

Challenges for multinationals

One of the major problems with some emerging markets and most frontier markets is the presence of "institutional voids." In developed markets, buyers and sellers can easily transact business thanks to intermediary institutions that provide necessary information, quality assurances, and contract enforcement necessary to complete the transaction. Emerging or developing markets often fall short of these requirements and markets do not function efficiently. Buyers and sellers may have a hard time attaining reliable information about each other, and, when contract disputes arise, there are limited means of reaching a settlement due to an overburdened or deficient legal infrastructure. Supply chains can be weak and inadequate. For example, there may be no intermediaries or distributors which can help farmers get their produce to markets such as restaurants and hotels.[18]

Along with the absence of reliable information and ineffective judicial systems, these voids also include unstable or non-existent capital markets and usually an uncertain and arbitrary regulatory environment. Institutional voids are sources of market failure and they restrict foreign direct investment. Another common void is poor or absent physical infrastructure, including roads, bridges, telecommunications networks, power plants, and running water supplies. Without proper physical infrastructure it is difficult for workers, suppliers, distribution networks, and consumers to function effectively.[19]

As an example of institutional voids and their negative impact, it is instructive to consider the African country of Nigeria. Nigeria has vast oil and wealth reserves and it is also one of the world's more prospective mining frontiers with a plentiful supply of many valuable commodities. But defective infrastructure hampers its efforts to accelerate industrialization. For example, the entire country of Nigeria produces only as much electricity as a single mid-size European city. The problem is primarily gas shortages and old, decaying transmission lines. As an *Economist* survey of the Nigerian economy concludes, "given cheap and reliable energy, other parts of the economy, from manufacturing to film-making and e-commerce, could take off."[20] Nigeria also suffers from other infrastructure problems. The major parts in the capital city of Lagos are overcrowded and highly inefficient. There is no longer a railway and most of the major roads are in disrepair. In the north, where there is ample arable farmland, agribusiness factories have halted production because they cannot move their goods to the south. The World Bank estimates that Nigeria must begin to invest $50 billion a year on infrastructure to remedy these woeful conditions.[21]

Institutional voids go beyond deficient infrastructure. In extreme cases, the rule of law is jeopardized thanks to the unjust schemes of despotic and highly partisan rulers. In these legal systems, laws are unenforced, incoherent, inconsistently applied, and not sufficiently stable to guide the population.[22] This more chaotic situation is typical in primitive frontier markets, like Somalia or the Republic of the Congo, which remain on the fringes of the global economy. In Congo, for example, criminal networks, unchecked by law, are the link between its cobalt, copper, and gold mines and world suppliers. Somalia, on the other hand, is the classic example of a failed state where the rule of law is subservient to tribal authorities.[23]

Finally, it is not uncommon for some states with a weak institutional structure to abdicate sovereignty to private corporations, which must fill the void and assume certain state functions. In these environments, "corporations rather than states are *de facto* sovereign."[24] In Liberia, for example, corporations sign concession agreements. They are given an area in which they can extract resources such as iron ore but in that concession area they are required to take full responsibility for security, along with the health care and education of their workers and their families. Firestone has a large concessionary area in Liberia where it harvests rubber trees. During the Ebola crisis, Firestone was forced to develop prevention, treatment, and education plans for its employees, essentially taking over the public health function of the state. There are similar situations in other African countries. Nestlé's food factory in Agbara, Nigeria must generate its own power, clean up its own water and provide health care for its many employees.[25]

Companies need to develop coherent strategies for handling these voids, including the lack of infrastructure, that often constrain business development in emerging and frontier markets. "Contextual intelligence" is a necessary condition for market success in these environments. Multinational corporations cannot operate the same way they do in developed markets – they must adapt to the peculiar conditions of each emerging market they serve and in some cases reconceive their business model. As Khanna points out, contextual intelligence may even require moving beyond the institutional context of a country into areas such as aesthetic preference, attitudes toward power, and assumptions about free markets.[26] Sometimes these voids can create opportunities because the firms or entrepreneurs that can fill them efficiently often erect barriers to entry through which they achieve first mover advantages in promising markets.

The resource curse

Many resource-based emerging markets suffer from the so-called "resource curse." The concept can be traced back to the work of Harvard economists, Jeffrey Sachs and Andrew Warner, who presented research showing that resource-rich economies grow more slowly than countries that are not so well endowed. They demonstrated how economies with a high ratio of natural resource exports to GDP in 1971 (the base year) tended to have low growth rates during the subsequent period 1971–1989. The paper also explored the possible causes underlying this negative relationship by studying the cross-country effects of resource endowments on trade policy and other aspects of economic growth.[27]

The discovery of oil or other valuable resources in impoverished countries has the potential to reverse their dismal economic fortunes. Yet while countries like Angola and Equatorial Guinea abound in oil, they remain immersed in poverty because the people have been denied the tangible benefits of the revenues accruing from the country's oil. These countries also struggle to remain internationally competitive. But why the negative consequences of natural resource wealth?

One problem is that the capital invested in the extraction of resources like oil or precious metals draws investment funds away from other sectors of the economy such as agriculture and manufacturing. The mineral wealth creates good paying jobs and exports, so there are low incentives for more broad-based economic development. As a result, the economy becomes less diversified and overly dependent on a single industry. Once the oil or other natural resource runs out, there will be dire consequences, unless other manufacturing sectors can pick up the slack.

Oil extraction, the most common source of the resource curse, is capital intensive and the large influx of foreign capital also tends to inflate the country's exchange rate. The overvalued exchange rate usually makes other industries less competitive. This currency appreciation therefore leads to a country's dependency on a resource such as oil or gold, which becomes the core of its economy. This phenomenon is known as the "Dutch Disease." With no other manufacturing or high growth industries to offset resource dependency, countries become victims of the commodity cycle as prices climb, bottom out, and then rebound in an M- or V-shaped cycle. Economic volatility, therefore, is a major aspect of the resource curse. [28]

In these environments, the country is essentially transformed into a rentier state that is very heavily dependent on revenues from its natural resources instead of income or corporate taxes. The firms operating in these export-oriented environments strike a bargain with the resource-rich country. They will extract a resource and in return pay royalties and taxes to the state, which shares in the rents or above-average profits of these companies. Governments in these high-rent states have little incentive to tax domestic corporations or their citizens since there is adequate revenue flowing in from its ensemble of rentiers. In addition, the public sector often becomes the primary employer with autocratic rulers often indulging in nepotism and patronage to preserve their power.[29]

Finally, the extraction of oil or other valuable commodities almost always provokes a lethal fight for the rents generated by these resource-based industries. The influx of big royalty payments inspires greater corruption and damages unstable political institutions. As Burgis observes, "the resource industry is hard-wired for corruption."[30] Resource rents very often lead to the concentration of wealth and power in the hands of autocratic leaders and their cronies. In Angola, the Democratic Republic of the Congo, Equatorial Guinea, and Zimbabwe people live in extreme poverty despite their country's vast mineral wealth. While the resource curse is not confined to Africa, it seems to be the most insidious on this continent, which is paradoxically the world's poorest and its richest.[31]

Equatorial Guinea, for example, is the third-largest oil producer in sub-Saharan Africa and its GDP has grown from a paltry $130 million in 1991 to over $11 billion in 2020. Its per capita income is about $37,000. Yet this prosperity has not reached the citizens of Equatorial Guinea or improved their overall welfare. The vast majority of the population still live in abject poverty. It ranks 138th out of 188 countries on the Human Development Index. The government invests only 2–3% of its budget on health and education. There are few jobs outside of the oil industry and most people subsist on farming the land.[32] The oil money has enriched the country's leader, President Obiang, along with his family and cronies, but it has not flowed to the people. Similar tales can be told about other autocratic leaders such as dos Santos in Angola, Kaddafi in Libya, and Mobuto in the Democratic Republic of the Congo.

What these leaders conveniently ignore is that a country's natural resources belong to its people, not to those who happen to govern that country. Leaders who make deals and sell off a country's resources must be accountable to the owners of those resources, its citizens. If a government like Angola decides to strike an agreement with foreign companies to extract oil or some other resource, the government must be held accountable for the agreement and the use of royalties and taxes that are generated by those companies. This accountability can be dealt with through the customary mechanisms of democracy. If a majority of citizens disagree with government policies, those policies will be altered to reflect the will of the people. Leif Wenar refers to this principle as "popular resource sovereignty." The principle stipulates that "all peoples may, for their own ends, freely dispose of their natural wealth and resources."[33]

It is possible to counteract some of the most damaging consequence of natural resource wealth. To mitigate the effects of the Dutch Disease, some countries have established Sovereign Wealth Funds (SWF). These funds are defined as "special purpose investment funds or arrangements owned by the general government, [and] created for macroeconomic purposes."[34] Thus, SWFs are investment funds owned by the government, managed independently of other financial and political institutions, and invested in a diverse set of financial assets with a significant proportion of those investments made in international markets.[35] Mineral-rich countries can rely on these funds for a dual purpose: to prevent inflation and the Dutch Disease precipitated by excess spending of revenues derived from resource extraction and to preserve some of these revenues for future generations. SWFs help achieve the objective of inter-generational equity, which is often overlooked by avaricious or short-sighted leaders. The tension for some states, especially frontier economies, is the need for current spending to develop infrastructure and human capital juxtaposed to intergenerational justice and avoidance of the Dutch Disease.[36]

Of course, abundant commodities like oil do not necessarily undermine the economies of countries that extract and export those resources. They can be a "blessing" and even a platform for technological innovation.[37] Consider the country of Guyana, South America's third poorest country. Its fate could be dramatically transformed by the oil and gas that has begun to flow from the Liza-1 offshore oil well, which lies within the oil-rich Stabroek block. By 2030 the Guyana government could reap rents of $10 billion in real terms, which is double the country's current GDP. But there are valid worries that the Guyanese economy, like the economies of its neighbor Venezuela, will be subverted by corruption. Does this new "petro-state" have mature enough institutions and prudent leadership to avoid the resource curse so its oil enriches poor Guyanese citizens and not just the country's elite leadership?[38]

What role should multinational corporations, especially those in extractive industries, play in countries prone to the resource curse? Arguably, there is an obligation to counter some of the forces contributing to the exploitation of a country's natural resources and the corruption of its leaders. Western banks, for example, that accept money from the leaders of countries with ample natural resources like oil are often deliberately blind to its provenance. Companies that mine resources like diamonds or gold pay royalties but they too do not concern themselves with how those royalties are managed by a country's leaders.

This issue has been especially controversial in the oil industry, where companies adopt a strategy of political neutrality. Consider the case of ExxonMobil, which has benefited enormously from the vast oil reserves in the impoverished country of Equatorial Guinea. ExxonMobil controlled the Zafiro oil field off the coast and from which it extracted 160,000 barrels of oil per day. At one point oil from Equatorial Guinea accounted for 10% of the company's total worldwide production. Exxon's royalty payments were deposited at Riggs Bank (and several others) in Washington, D.C. They were transferred into accounts controlled by the country's president, Teodoro Obiang. Most of that money has been used to enrich President Obiang along with his family and friends, and very little has flowed back into the country. According to UN Development Programme officials working in that country, Obiang has failed to utilize the country's oil wealth to develop a desperately needed economic infrastructure or to provide for the education, health care, and general well-being of its citizens.[39]

A U.S. Senate investigation chastised ExxonMobil for contributing to the corruption and predatory behavior of Equatorial Guinea's leadership. But the company has consistently disavowed any responsibility for its actions. According to an Exxon spokesperson, "We are private investors, and it is not our role to tell governments how to spend their money." Thus, the company's position is that it bears no accountability for the negative consequences caused by its oil extraction. As long as a dictator like Obiang keeps them in the oil production business, ExxonMobil refuses to address the effects of the malignant resource curse.[40]

However, a strong case can be put forth that Exxon is complicit in the abuses associated with the Obiang regime. Through its decision to drill for oil in the country and pay royalties to Obiang with no conditions, the company has enabled the harm caused by this corrupt leader. During Exxon's early years in Equatorial Guinea it became cognizant of Obiang's behavior and yet it renewed contracts without any restrictive stipulations regarding transparency or the use of those royalty funds. Equatorial Guinea lacks the technological capability to engage in offshore drilling, so it needs the capital investment and expert assistance of companies like Exxon. The enabler's (ExxonMobil) actions are a necessary condition of the principal actor's (Obiang) producing the harm that takes the form of robbing the country of its oil wealth. In general, oil companies that operate in countries where corruption is rampant cannot turn a blind eye to the perverse consequences caused by oil extraction. They are complicit in Obiang's wrongdoing and corruption because they refuse to take action, such as imposing some conditions on its royalty payments that will lead to a more just outcome.[41]

National populism and other political risks

Within the last decade "populist revolts" have taken place in many countries. National populism is responsible for Brexit, the vote by British people to leave the European Union, and the election of Donald Trump in America. Both the UK vote to leave the EU and the Trump election reflect a re-assertion of the nation state as the primary unit of social and political order. Frustrated British citizens certainly did not want to deconstruct the country's political institutions. But workers felt that interactions between the EU and Parliament along with other factors meant that "people like them" no longer had a voice in their own government. Above all British citizens wanted to reclaim national sovereignty from alien transnational forces like the EU.[42]

Other national populists include Marine Le Pen in France, Matteo Salvini in Italy, Viktor Orbán in Hungary, and Rodrigo Duterte in the Philippines. Populists typically win elections because they incite resentment and promise to prioritize domestic jobs along with local economic needs. This populist policy agenda challenges the fundamentals of globalization. National populists also seek to reclaim national identity over a broader and more amorphous transnational identity and "to reassert the primacy of the nation over distant and unaccountable international organizations." Critics say, however, that nationalists risk framing national identity too narrowly.[43]

Emerging and frontier economies that have suffered in the past from colonialism and the predation of developed countries are especially susceptible to nationalistic rhetoric and ideologies. Many of these countries want to re-assert their national sovereignty in a more forceful way. The rise of populism and nationalism in emerging markets may pose acute political risks for multinational corporations doing business in those markets or multinational corporations that have investment aspirations. National populism can also shape emerging markets for good or ill, but usually it is an exclusivist and regressive force that leads to diminished economic integration.

The forces of nationalism and socialism have destroyed Venezuela's economy, once one of the fastest growing in the world. At the turn of the last century, Venezuela still ranked as Latin America's most prosperous country. But in 1999 President Hugo Chavez convinced his country to give nationalistic socialism a try. Oil revenues supported his massive social spending for a time, but when oil prices plunged and money ran out, Venezuela became mired in totalitarianism. Military force was the only way to sustain the country's bankrupt socialist policies.[44]

Various versions of national populism, which resist political and economic globalization, have also hobbled economic growth for countries such as Argentina, Brazil, and Uruguay. Populist governments usually indulge in a high level of public spending that is financed by borrowing. Prices are often frozen, local industries are protected from imports, and wage hikes do not correlate with productivity gains. In the long run these reckless economic policies are unsustainable and the result is economic instability and political division.[45]

Geopolitical turmoil has taken a big toll on countries such as Uruguay, which has experienced a reversal of economic fortunes. The populist leader there, Hector Edgardo Novick, presidential candidate for the People's Party, has followed the lead of President Trump by emphasizing the urgency of preserving and expanding domestic jobs. "I want to start defending Uruguayans' jobs," he said in one of his campaign speeches.[46] But this nationalist philosophy comes at the expense of downplaying trade and even some forms of foreign investment. Uruguay's past success, however, has been contingent on a more open economy and access to foreign markets.

Unfortunately, Mexico appears to be regressing back to "energy nationalism," and as a result its hopes for vigorous economic progress have dimmed. Mexico is a classic case of an underdeveloped emerging economy that needs fast growth to lift many more of its citizens out of poverty. To its credit, the Mexican government has transformed an economy dependent on oil to one that is based on manufacturing products such as vehicles, car parts, and computers. In 2018, crude oil exports were less than 7% of total exports. Experts agree that Mexico must continue to expand its industrial base, but that requires access to low-price energy sources, both foreign and domestic. However, Mexico's Pemex monopoly is too inefficient to exploit the country's abundant energy resources, and this is why former Mexican President Enrique Nieto opened the energy industry to foreign competitors. But in the name of nationalism new President Andres Manuel López Obrador has put a moratorium on foreign investment. The President wants to protect an inefficient and debt-burdened Pemex from more competitive foreign companies. Nationalists applauded Mexico's revival of autarky, but others warn that this decision will only interfere with the country's social and economic aspirations.[47]

Marketization in the frontier economy

Can capitalism become entrenched in the most primitive frontier economies where markets are acutely underdeveloped? Is *homo economicus* ("economic man") a reality or just a theoretical abstraction? According to this principle, all people are naturally inclined to act in their own rational, economic self-interest. The theory of the *homo economicus*, who instinctively seeks his or her own personal interests and material gains, has its roots in the political philosophy of Adam Smith. Following those instincts is most likely to produce a merchant or laborer who fits well within a capitalist commercial society. But Smith emphasized the need for two limitations on the pursuit of one's economic self-interest: justice and sympathy for one's fellow human beings. He also underscored the importance of division of labor and voluntary exchange, which suggest our need for others if we are to survive and prosper materially.[48]

In some primitive economies or frontier markets, where there is little trace of markets and commerce, there is a need to build the most foundational economic structures. This is the case, for example, in countries like East Timor, which won its independence in 2002 from Indonesia. The country depends on oil as its main source of revenues but seeks to diversify to avoid the resource curse and provide broad economic opportunities for its citizens. Many residents of this island nation live in huts without running water and are very poorly educated. How can they become the entrepreneurs and managers of the future? If the *homo economicus* thesis is true it should be easy to convert these individuals into self-serving capitalists.[49]

Similarly, indigenous peoples in the Amazon jungle remain isolated from capitalist influences, some in regions where there are significant agribusiness markets. Other peripheral areas include the dense jungle highlands of New Guinea in South East Asia, along with the West Papua region in Indonesia, where there are about forty tribes. How can these countries and regions at the peripheries of the global economy become better integrated into that economy? Is it possible to transform these remote regions into what Adam Smith calls a "commercial society"? And should such a transformation even be attempted? Or would such attempts to integrate these people into global capitalism disrespect their indigenous traditions and way of life?[50]

Many economists have critiqued the notion of *homo economicus*, especially later versions that portray the person as isolated and self-centered, only accidentally related to others. According to von Mises, "No man is exclusively motivated by the desire to become as rich as possible, [and] many are not at all influenced by this mean craving."[51] Even Smith recognized the intrinsic value of human sociability and proposed an understanding of the human person that transcended an exclusively economic conception of free choice and action.[52]

Others argue that capitalist principles must be taught and assimilated over time. As Sophus Reinert points out, people in such primitive areas will need to be "socialized" into capitalism and its customs if their economic condition is to improve. Through education, directed development, and other means they must become convinced of the benefits of marketization and the production of goods for others. Through that socialization process they could eventually become active buyers and sellers in order to launch a market society and, arguably, improve their quality of life. They must also learn the value of free exchange. For Smith, the propensity "to truck, barter, and exchange one thing for another" is closely tied with the inclination to pursue our economic self-interest.[53] But without the proper socialization and assimilation of market principles, an authentic commercial society can never emerge.[54]

Thus, capitalist values are not innate, but they are built on certain human propensities. It is unintelligible to speak about *homo economicus,* if that means that the human person is instinctively capitalistic and motivated exclusively by the prospect of material gain. As Charles Taylor has pointed out, the "value put on commercial activity" can be traced back to the 18th century: the rising esteem of commercial life was accompanied by the "recession of the aristocratic honor ethic." The new self-regulating system of production and exchange became the basis for the notion of political economy we have today.[55] However, while the commercial life is not innate, the socialization process can be quite effective since people are generally inclined to act in their own self-interest. As legal philosopher Hart has observed, the person is a creature "moved by the calculations of long-term interest" (i.e., self-interest).[56] A person's own welfare will have ample claim on his or her interest, concern, and effort, even if there are limits imposed by justice and sympathy.[57] And if one becomes convinced that the material gains associated with the merchant's way of life best suits those long-term interests, one is more likely to turn to capitalist structures to enhance one's overall well-being.

Economic and political partners

Low-income, emerging, or frontier economies often look for external assistance as they try to build the necessary infrastructure that will transform their society into a developed economy. They can seek out Western institutions such as the International Monetary Fund (IMF) or the World Bank for loans and other types of financial aid. Debt-ridden Angola, for example, turned to the IMF for a bailout in 2018 in exchange for implementing certain structural political reforms.

But the West's role as a global beacon of hope and reliable resource has been in retreat for some time. As a result, emerging and frontier economies are more reliant on aid and direction from China and Russia. This trend has caused much consternation among Western political leaders, but shows no signs of abatement. In Africa, where some countries face utter destitution with no relief, international powers like China and Russia offer significant opportunities to make infrastructure improvements and to implement economic reforms. As the United States has pulled back from the continent, Russia has expanded its presence, especially in insecure countries rich in mineral wealth. Its goal is to assert itself more prominently in global affairs and reap some financial benefits. In the Central African Republic, where gems and diamonds are trafficked by rebels, Russia is working with the government to regain control of the diamond industry. Russian mercenaries train local soldiers and help negotiate deals between local warlords and the government. Russia's representatives have also worked out deals to mine diamonds where the trade is legal. But some of the country's lawmakers have voiced concerns about human rights violations by Russian mercenaries. "What kind of army are we going to have if they are trained by Russians?" remarked one member of Parliament.[58]

China also has ambitions on the African continent. When Angola was on the brink of bankruptcy, its president, José Eduardo dos Santos, initially appealed to the West for funding to rescue his economy. But Western institutions insisted on certain conditions so the money would not end up in the bank accounts of dos Santos and his inner circle. The President refused these conditions and looked to China instead. In 2004 China signed an agreement with Angola: it would lend the country $2 billion to fund public works and the loan repayments were to be made in Angolan oil.[59] Some economists applauded the move because it offered Angola the opportunity to escape "the grip of the IMF and World Bank," and their free trade globalization agenda. In the years after its deal with Angola, China signed multibillion dollar "resources for infrastructure deals" in the Congo and the Sudan.[60]

China's largesse in Africa is reflected in its Belt and Road Initiative (BRI) strategy, a fusion of China's commercial and military interests introduced in 2013 by President Xi Jinping. This imperial enterprise is designed to link the economies of Asia, Europe, and Africa with highways, railways, and power plants. Many poor countries are in desperate need of infrastructure but lack the ability to make the necessary investments in these expensive projects. The program, which builds linkages around the world, is described as the centerpiece of China's foreign policy. China's government under Xi Jinping provides a mix of infrastructure and financial assistance to distressed economies, including Malaysia, Sri Lanka, Pakistan, Laos, and Uganda. These countries no longer implore the U.S. for substantial aid since U.S. leaders now regard these regions strictly through the narrow prism of national security.[61]

The BRI is formally defined by the World Bank as "a China-led effort to improve connectivity and regional cooperation on a trans-continental scale through large-scale investments." Since the BRI was announced in 2013, China has signed $460 billion in construction contracts that span 140 countries. According to a World Bank report, the Belt and Road Initiative has the potential to substantially improve trade, foreign investment, and living conditions in those emerging economies that participate. But the report adds a caveat: those positive consequence depend on the adoption of deeper policy reforms by participating economies that increase transparency, improve macroeconomic fundamentals (such as lower debt), and mitigate environmental, social, and corruption risks.[62]

In Laos, Chinese investment includes a 260-mile, $5 billion rail line that will extend from Laos into Thailand. The railway will also connect landlocked Laos with the Chinese rail network, which will bring that country more tourism and property investment. China has given priority to its Laos project in its Belt and Road Initiative because it regards Laos as a pathway for rail and road connectivity that encompasses Thailand and other South East Asian countries. These projects constitute a key part of the "Silk Road economic belt," a network of railroads and highway that will eventually link China to Central, South East, and South Asia and then to Europe.[63]

The "flagship" BRI project was supposed to be in Pakistan. The China–Pakistan economic corridor (CPEC) was considered so transformative that it "could wean the populace from fundamentalism." The $60 billion project was designed to build new roadways, power plants, and railways; also included was the modernization of the port of Gwadar. But the project alienated Pakistan's rival, India, which has still not signed on to BRI. In addition, CPEC has been far costlier than expected and the financing portion to be assumed by the Pakistani government is beyond its means. In 2018, the Pakistani rupee slid and the economy collapsed, and this has complicated Pakistan's capacity for contributing to the various projects. In addition, one of the major projects completed by China, a new port in Baluchistan, has been a disappointment, since very few goods have arrived at its docks. China has not abandoned CPEC but it has reduced its commitments.[64]

Many Western institutions, including the World Bank, view BRI rather benignly, and concentrate on its economic benefits. Of course, along with those benefits political bonds are strengthened between China and other nations, and this unnerves some in the West. Diplomats, political leaders, and economists have therefore voiced concerns about BRI. The United States' National Security Strategy claims that BRI is an exercise in "predatory economics."[65] To be sure, China's imperial exploits are an assertion of its political power. The creation of infrastructure abroad primarily to sustain the flow of goods in and out of China "is intrinsic to cementing the nation's path to power and competing with the United States."[66] For Mr. Xi, BRI is an effective means of negating the U.S.'s residual political influence in East Asia and Europe.

But there is possibly something more fundamental at stake. Arguably, China's leaders are using BRI to directly challenge the West's global pre-eminence and the liberal status quo. In its place, China will reshape a new world order that is more amenable to the country's vision of political economy. BRI is consistent with China's more authoritarian and centralized approach to global capitalism, a distinct alternative to traditional free market capitalism that minimizes the public sector's involvement in economic affairs. Countries that are enmeshed in BRI are beholden to China and dependent upon it to support their infrastructure investment. One day China may leverage this obligation for political advantage. Those countries may be more inclined to set their political agenda in the direction of China as a model for their political economies. There is little doubt that China's ability to amass vast sums of capital for public purposes gives this communist country a valuable mechanism for cultivating political power. The Chinese model, where government directs economic growth and downplays political liberties, is apt to be quite appealing in certain regions of Africa and Asia.[67]

Is China the avatar of a new social order where capitalist principles prevail but without traditional political liberties or human rights associated with liberal democracy? If so, there will be dramatic change in global political and economic structures. As a communist nation, China's guiding philosophy is based not on the political theories of Locke or Adam Smith that emphasize economic freedom and individualism, but on those of Marx and Hegel. Hegel, for example, argues for the priority of the state over the individual and the need for the organic integration (*Bezwingung*) of each individual into the majestic unity of the state and its institutions.[68] Liberal democracy once looked almost unassailable, but the rise of China certainly raises new questions about the contingency of liberal ideals.

Paradoxically, Africa's abrupt turn toward China comes at a time when many of the continent's residents are hopeful that their countries will initiate democratic reforms. In a 2019 poll of thirty-four countries, 68% of Africans stated that democracy is the optimal form of government. There is growing frustration over the persistence of authoritarian regimes in most countries. Some predict that the tension between these leaders and their citizens will become more intense. Protests, inspired by demands for political freedom and a long list of economic grievances, have sprung up in countries like Sudan and Malawi. But following in the footsteps of China will mean that Africans citizens, like their Chinese counterparts, will not have the same opportunities for democratic self-expression as citizens in Western countries.[69]

Case study: China's "Belt and Road Initiative" in the Philippines

Rodrigo Duterte was elected President of the Philippines in 2016. He is the sixteenth President of the Philippines and succeeded Benigno Aquino III. His term extends to June 30, 2022. Duterte, the oldest person ever to be elected to this office, is the first President from the Mindanao region, which encompasses the large island of Mindanao plus smaller islands in the southern Philippines. The island is home to many ethnic minorities but has been the sight of civil unrest and terrorism for many years. Duterte had served as the mayor of it largest city, Davao, prior to his election as President.

Duterte seemed like an unusual choice but Filipinos were simply unhappy with the status quo. When the dictator Ferdinand Marcos (1965–1986) was driven from office, there was hope among Filipinos that the restoration of democracy would finally bring about social and economic progress. But that progress was insufficient, and corruption became rampant in the post-Marcos era. Exhausted by the corruption and status quo, Filipinos turned to the aggressive populist candidate Duterte, who immediately launched a country-wide campaign against corruption and illegal drugs. The commitment to fight the illegal drug trade and take on powerful drug dealers was at the center of Duterte's election campaign.[70]

The Philippines is an island country of South East Asia that sits in the western Pacific ocean, 500 miles off the coast of Vietnam. The country is an archipelago that consists of 7,100 islands and inlets. The capital city of Manila is located on the largest island, Luzon. The country's current population stands at 107 million. Under Duterte's regime, economic performance has been adequate. GDP, which was $331 billion in 2019, has increased at a rate of about 6% per year since Duterte's election in 2016. It has decent macroeconomic fundamentals, including manageable debt.

The country's economy depends on a number of manufacturing monopolies that are protected by high tariffs. The Philippines is considered to be one of the more promising growth prospects in the area. But despite the strong economic performance, there is a dark side to the Duterte regime. He has intimidated the media and in 2020 the President annulled the franchise for the media giant ABS-CBN. He claimed that the company was responsible for "highly abusive practices." In addition, Duterte has not delivered on his promise of providing deep-rooted change to his country. The unreformed political system remains largely unresponsive to the people's needs.[71]

Duterte's predecessors, including the popular Mr. Aquino, invested few funds in the country's decrepit infrastructure, but Duterte is committed to remedy this oversight. Shortly after his election, he initiated his "Build! Build! Build!" economic plan, which is supposed to launch this "Golden Age of Infrastructure." The aim is to make repairs where necessary and to construct new roads, bridges, and airports. The beneficial side effects of this massive investment should also include a reduction in poverty, enhanced economic growth, and less congestion in the capital city of Manila.

Like other governments with limited funds and lofty ambitions, Duterte has turned to its neighbor, China, for assistance. China has promised $9 billion in infrastructure investment. At this point only $900 million has been agreed to in formal contracts between the two countries. Two Chinese-funded infrastructure projects have already begun: the construction of two bridges over Pasig River in Manila and the Chico River Pump Irrigation Project in the northern Philippines. China has said that it sees "common aims" between BRI and the infrastructure needs of the Philippines. Filipino leaders such as former President Gloria Arroyo have described BRI as "China's broadest platform for collaboration and cooperation," noting that its new "Silk Road" fits perfectly with the "Build, Build, Build" infrastructure project.[72]

Initially there was public opposition to an alliance with China, a country perceived in the past as a threat to this island nation. But the Philippine public's perception of China has begun to change, with more Filipinos convinced that China (and not the United States) is the world's leading economy, and so cooperation is vital. Linkages to China provided by BRI will give Filipino companies better access to Chinese markets and position Manila directly on the radar screen of Chinese investors and creditors.[73]

Duterte's tentative commitment to this partnership with China and BRI comes at a propitious time because the Philippines economy has paid a steep price for its severe infrastructure problems. Its infrastructure deficiencies have become a major roadblock in promoting industrial and national development. The World Economic Forum's Global Competitiveness Index ranked the infrastructure of the Philippines (roads, railroads, ports, air transport, electricity, and telecommunications) seventh out of nine ASEAN countries. From a security perspective, BRI could be highly advantageous for addressing insurgency incidents and the political instability in the Mindanao region.[74]

Although a proportion of the Filipino population has done an about-face, there is still apprehension in some quarters about China's imperial ambitions. Duterte's commitment to China represents a decisive break with the Aquino government, which had challenged China's claims in the South China Sea. The Philippines and China have conflicting territorial claims over the sea, based on various accounts of history and geography. China's bold claim of sovereignty over much of the sea and its estimated 11 billion barrels of untapped oil has been a source of ongoing tension between the two countries. But Duterte has put those difference aside. He has even said (perhaps jokingly) that in the future the Philippines could end up becoming a "province" of China.[75]

Study questions

1. Discuss the costs and benefits of participating in China's BRI. What are the dangers for the future of the Philippines?
2. If you had been advising Duterte about this decision, what advice would you have given him?

Conclusions

Emerging and frontier economies are anxious to expand their economies and enjoy the fruits of globalization: higher GDP and enhanced social welfare. Foreign trade and prudent politics that foster FDI will make this progress possible. However, the Covid-19 pandemic has dimmed the hopes for some countries, especially those dependent on the export of commodities. In addition, dysfunctional politics in some countries has interfered with higher economic performance.

Multinationals recognize opportunity as well as peril in these immature markets where they must contend with vexing institutional voids and other hazards in order to penetrate these markets. Success depends on cultivating contextual intelligence and on a heavy dose of adaptability.

One of the biggest problems for emerging and frontier economies can be overcoming the resource curse. The Dutch Disease of currency overvaluation is accompanied by insufficient investment in other industries as the political elite fight for rents generated by the sale of resources like diamonds or oil. As we have argued, multinationals, including oil companies, cannot deflect their responsibilities in these countries by insisting on their political neutrality. Instead they must exhibit more solidarity with the people of countries from which oil is extracted because those people rightly own that resource.

Emerging economies, especially those that have been the victim of colonial power abuses in the past, are prone to national populism, which is a threat to economic growth. Populist governments often prioritize domestic jobs and resist economic globalization. They are critical of failed trade policies and foreign investment and often proclaim the virtue of economic self-sufficiency. Some populist leaders indulge in extravagant public spending projects that throw their economies into further chaos. Populist leaders are not advocating a new social order, but some of their arguments about trade and FDI continue to resonate with the citizens of their respective countries.

Fragile economies like the ones considered in this chapter have turned away from the geopolitical West towards China for aid, especially for funds to remedy infrastructure deficiencies. China's imperial aspirations for regional and global dominance are manifest in its Belt and Road Initiative, which follows in the footsteps of past global empires but probably overreaches.[76]

Notes

1 "Fall of the Dictator," *Economist*, November 18, 2017, 12.
2 Ibid.
3 Peter Godwin, "From the Start, a Brutal Regime," *Wall Street Journal*, November 25, 2017, C4.
4 Tom Burgis, *The Looting Machine* (New York: Public Affairs, 2015), 235.
5 Godwin, "From the Start."
6 "Briefing: Emerging Economies," *Economist*, July 27, 2013, 20–22.
7 MSCI Market Classification, June 2014.
8 Jim Chappelow, "Emerging Market Economies," *Investopedia*, March 16, 2020. Available at https://www.investopedia.com/terms/e/emergingmarketeconomy.asp.
9 David Moss, *A Concise Guide to Macro Economics* (Boston, MA: Harvard Business Review Press, 2014), 8–12, 39–42.
10 "Emerging Markets: What's in a Name," *Economist*, October 7, 2017, 6.
11 James Chen, "What are Frontier Markets, *Investopedia*, October 15, 2019. Available at https://www.investopedia.co/term/frontier-market.asp.
12 Segin Obarumng, "Differences between an Emerging Market and a Frontier Market," July 2, 2019, *Nairametrics*. Available at nairametics.com/2019/07/03/differences-between-an-emerging-market-and-a-frontier-market.
13 Somalia GDP, Trading Economics. Available at tradingeconomics.com/Somalia/gdp.
14 Max Weber, *Economy and Society* ed. Guenther Roth and Claus Wittich (Berkeley, CA: University of California Press, 1978), 905.

15 "Material Losses," *Economist*, March 7, 2020, 70.

16 Oren Cass, *The Once and Future Worker* (New York: Encounter Books, 2018), 59–60. See also "Premature Industrialization: Sew What Now?" *Economist*, October 7, 2017, 16–17; and "Emerging Markets: Out of the Traps," *Economist*, October 7, 2017, 4.

17 Jane Perlez, "China, Facing U.S. Hostility, Vows to Come Out Swinging," *New York Times*, September 24, 2018, A1, A10. See also "Anti-trumping Duties," *Economist*, October 7, 2017, 18–19; and "Rinse and Repeat," *Economist*, February 13, 2021, 73.

18 Tarun Khanna and Krishna Palepu, *Winning in Emerging Markets* (Boston, MA: Harvard Business Press, 2010), 13–14.

19 Ibid., 14–17.

20 "Special Report Nigeria: Opportunity Knocks," *Economist*, June 20, 2015, 5.

21 Ibid., 10.

22 John Finnis, *Natural Law and Natural Rights* (Oxford: Oxford University Press, 1980), 270.

23 "Treasure and Turmoil," *Financial Times*, December 16, 2010, 11.

24 Sophus Reinert, "Globalization and Emerging Markets" (Boston, MA: Harvard Business School Publishing, 2018).

25 "Nigeria: Opportunity Knocks," 8.

26 Tarun Khanna, "Contextual Intelligence," *Harvard Business Review* 92 (9), 2014, 58–68.

27 Jeffrey Sachs and Andrew Warner, 1995, "Natural Resource Abundance and Economic Growth," NBER Working Paper 5398, Natural Bureau of Economic Research.

28 "Commodities: A Drag, Not a Curse," *Economist*, October 7, 2017, 14–15.

29 Eric Werker, "4Ms: Four-Market Analysis for Emerging Economies" (Boston, MA: Harvard Business School Publishing, 2014).

30 Burgis, *The Looting Machine*, 5.

31 Ibid.

32 Sarah Saradoun, "Ill-Gotten Gains: Equatorial Guinea Is a Case Study in Self-Dealing," Human Rights Watch, June 20, 2017.

33 Leif Wenar, *Blood Oil: Tyrants, Violence, and the Rules that Run the World* (Oxford: Oxford University Press, 2016), 344.

34 International Working Group of Sovereign Wealth Funds, "Sovereign Wealth Funds: Generally Accepted Principles and Practices" (Washington, D.C.: International Monetary Fund, 2008).

35 Sophus Reinart and Julie Kheyfets, "Sovereign Wealth Funds" (Boston, MA: Harvard Business School Publishing, 2016).

36 Ibid.

37 "Commodities, A Drag, Not a Curse," 16.

38 "Guyana: An Opportunity to Score," *Economist*, February 29, 2020.

39 "Making a Killing: The Curious Bonds of Diplomacy," Center for Public Integrity, May 19, 2014. Available at https://publicintegrity.org/national-security/making-a-killing/the-curious-bonds-of-oil-diplomacy.

40 Rachel Maddow, *Blowout* (New York: Crown, 2019), 110–115.

41 Gregory Mellema, *Complicity and Moral Accountability* (Notre Dame, IN: University of Notre Dame Press, 2016), 45–54.

42 Roger Eatwell and Matthew Goodwin, *National Populism: The Revolt against Liberal Democracy* (New York: Penguin, 2018), xi, 69.

43 Ibid., xxxii. See also Jason Willick, "Against the Liberal Empire," *Wall Street Journal*, October 10, 2018, A15.

44 Daniel Pipes, "Venezuela's Tyranny of Bad Ideas," *Wall Street Journal*, August 27, 2018, A15.

45 "Movements in EM Major," *Economist*, October 7, 2017, 19.

46 "Edgardo Novick: La Gente Quiere un Cambio," *Republica.com.uy*, November 10, 2016. Available at www.republica.com.uy/novick-la-gente-quiere-un-cambio.

47 Mary Anastasia O'Grady, "Mexico's Energy Hara-Kiri," *Wall Street Journal*, December 16, 2019, A17.

48 Samuel Gregg, "Putting Adam Smith Back Together," *Public Discourse*, March 6, 2019, 5.

49 Sophus Reinert and Dawn Lau, "East Timor: Betting on Oil" (Boston, MA: Harvard Business School, 2017). See also the Teaching Note for this case, 2, 8.

50 Ibid.

51 Ludwig von Mises, *Human Action: A Treatise in Economics* (New Haven, CT: Yale University Press, 1949), 82.

52 Gregg, "Putting Adam Smith Back Together," 6.

53 Adam Smith, *Wealth of Nations* (New York: Penguin, 1979), 343.

54 Sophus Reinert, *The Academy of Fisticuffs: Political Economy and Commercial Society in Enlightenment Italy* (Cambridge, MA: Harvard University Press, 2018), 392–396.

55 Charles Taylor, *The Sources of the Self* (Cambridge, MA: Harvard University Press, 1989), 285–286. See also Reinert, *Academy of Fisticuffs*, 396.

56 H.L.A. Hart, *The Concept of Law* (Oxford: Oxford University Press, 1961), 198.

57 Finnis, *Natural Law and Natural Rights*, 107.

58 Dionne Searcey, "The Russian Playbook in Africa: Win Hearts and Reap Diamonds," *New York Times*, September 30, 2019, A1, A9.

59 Burgis, *Looting Machine*, 85–87.

60 "The IMF Comeback in Africa," *Deutsche Welle*, September 14, 2018. Available at https://www.dw.com/en/the-imf-comeback-in-africa/a-45489734. See also Burgis, *Looting Machine*, 136.

61 Keith Bradsher, "China Tiptoes on Belt and Road," *New York Times*, January 23, 2019, B3. See also James Areddy, "China Makes Gains in West's Backyard," *Wall Street Journal*, November 6, 2018, A1, A14.

62 Michelle Ruta, et al., "Belt and Road Economics: Opportunities and Risks of Transport Corridors," The World Bank, June 18, 2019. See also Jonathan Hillman, "China's Imperial Overreach," *Wall Street Journal*, October 3, 2020, C17.

63 Chris Horton, "Chinese Investment Transforms Capital of Laos," *New York Times*, September 25, 2018, B6.

64 William Galston, "Is It Too Late to Counter China's Rise," *Wall Street Journal*, April 3, 2019, A15. See also "The Belt: Tighten Up a Notch," *Economist*, February 8, 2020, 5–6.

65 Charles Clover, "Xi Jiping Signal Departure from Low-Profile Policy," *Financial Times*, October 20, 2017, 4.

66 Jane Perlez, "With Allies Feeling Choked, Xi Loosens His Grip on China's Global Building Push," *New York Times*, April 26, 2019, A1, A8.

67 "China's Belt and Road: Return to Centre," *Economist*, February 8, 2020, 3–5. See also David Runciman, "China's Challenge to Democracy," *Wall Street Journal*, April 28, 2019, C1–2.

68 G.W.F. Hegel, *Natural Law* trans. T.M. Knox (Philadelphia, PA: University of Pennsylvania Press, 1975), 94–98. For Hegel, the individual person is free only inasmuch as he overcomes his singular properties and becomes a living member (or organ) of the Universal, the whole people organized into the State. "For the individual is singularity, and freedom is the annihilation of singularity" (*Natural Law*, 90).
69 "Democracy in Africa: Generation Game," *Economist*, March 7, 2020, 44–46.
70 "Briefing on the Philippines: Still the People's Choice," *Economist*, February 22, 2020, 24–26.
71 World Bank Group, Philippines Data. Available at https://data.worldbank.org/country/PH. See also "Briefing on the Philippines," 25.
72 Li Xia, "Philippines's Arroyo Describes China's BRI as 'Broadest Platform for Collaboration'," *Asia and Pacific News*, July 26, 2019. Available at Xinhua.com/English/2019-07/26/c_138261/09.htm. See also "Briefing on the Philippines," 25.
73 Aaron Jed Rabena, "The Complex Interdependence of China's Belt and Road Initiative in the Philippines," *Asia and the Pacific Policy Studies*, August (2018). Available at https://doi.org/10.1002/app5.251.
74 Ibid.
75 "Briefing on the Philippines," 25.
76 Hillman, "China's Imperial Overreach," C17.

Chapter 6

Corporate bribery and the Foreign Corrupt Practices Act

On a bright but chilly Sunday afternoon in February, Eli Black's chauffer drove him from his Park Avenue Apartment to his office in midtown Manhattan. Black was Chairman of the Board and CEO of United Brands (later known as Chiquita Banana), the largest banana enterprise in the entire world. His office was on the 44th floor of the distinctive Pan Am building on the East side of New York City. As he left his limousine and entered the building, the security guards who greeted him had no idea of the turbulence surrounding his life at this moment. Mr. Black took the elevator to his office and spent a few minutes at his desk. But then he suddenly smashed the large office window with his briefcase and plunged to his death on Park Avenue as horrified pedestrians scurried out of the way.

What would induce a powerful and prestigious CEO like Mr. Black to suddenly take his own life? As a Securities and Exchange Commission official remarked, "Guys don't just drop out of windows for nothing." Shortly after this 1975 incident, United Brands was compelled by the SEC to make public a notorious bribery scandal. The banana industry had always been quite unattractive with high fixed costs, price volatility, and the political complexities of dealing with corrupt countries like Honduras and Guatemala. United Brands had been losing money, and Black was determined to reverse this trend. But, in 1974, a catastrophic hurricane in Honduras wiped out the crops at United's banana plantation, and the company lost $70 million. Also, Honduran officials were set to impose a dollar-per-box tax on all exported fruit, including bananas. Black realized that this tax would have a devastating effect on his company's bottom line and crush his turnaround efforts. Consequently, despite his misgivings, he reluctantly agreed to authorize $1.25 million in secretive payments

DOI: 10.4324/9781003058427-6

to the country's president, General Oswaldo López. In return, López reduced the banana export tax to $0.25 per box. Bribery is shameful business, and Mr. Black was acutely aware that news of the bribery scandal would one day leak out, sullying the reputation of United Brands and undermining his leadership. Burdened by guilt and remorse, Mr. Black, a former rabbi, apparently believed that suicide was the only answer to his awful predicament.[1]

Several weeks after the revelation of the United Brands payoff, Mr. Robert Moore, the CEO of a competitor, Castle & Cooke, told the *Wall Street Journal* that Black's payments to the Honduran general were a "deplorable development" for the whole industry. He was at a "loss to understand" how this could happen. Yet months later, Castle & Cooke, the producer of Dole bananas, confessed that it too had made bribery payments to Latin American officials for favorable treatment.[2]

The actions of both companies may have been morally reprehensible but they were not illegal, at least in the United States. And these two scandals in the banana industry were accompanied by many others. Gulf Oil, Ashland Oil, and Lockheed were all implicated in bribery scandals in the 1970s. Gulf Oil paid $4 million in bribes to the Democratic Party of South Korea to win new contracts. In a highly publicized case, Lockheed executives admitted making payments of $12.5 million to Japanese government officials to win a lucrative contract from Nippon Air for its TriStar plane. When word of these bribes leaked out, Lockheed rationalized these payments as an "acceptable" way of doing business in Japan where bribery was supposedly a common practice. Yet in Japan the payments caused a public scandal, so it is doubtful that this practice was as customary or acceptable as Lockheed had claimed.[3]

In this chapter we review the issue of bribery especially in emerging markets where bribery and corruption has sometimes become normative. A particular focus of the chapter is the Foreign Corrupt Practices Act (FCPA), which was enacted in 1977 to deter multinationals from making payments to foreign officials to win a new contract or retain business. Self-regulation had failed and the authority of law with its coercive force was deemed necessary to secure justice in international business transactions. Despite the FCPA and other laws, bribery in foreign markets has certainly not disappeared. Why is this problem so intractable? We consider this question along with some of the more recent bribery scandals in this chapter. It concludes with a case study on the pharmaceutical firm, Schering-Plough.

Bribery: a definition and moral evaluation

Bribery has a very long and undistinguished pedigree in the history of the world's commercial relationships and legal proceedings. Bribery was rampant in the ancient kingdoms of Egypt and Mesopotamia. In Ancient Rome appeals to justice seemed cynical because bribery and corruption were so pervasive. At least in Rome, some statesmen resisted this trend. In 74 B.C. the Roman Senator, Cicero, voiced his complaints about a corrupt judge who took gifts that transformed him into a "zealous partisan" for someone being prosecuted for attempted murder.[4]

In this era, bribery seems more common in undeveloped and emerging markets, where corruption is not an isolated event but is instead the norm for doing business. It is also more customary in international commerce rather than domestic commerce. The "prototypical bribe" involves a corporation or its agent making a payment to a foreign government official to induce that official to make a decision in that corporation's interest rather than in the public interest.[5]

But why is bribery so wrong, and how can we define bribery more precisely? Also, how can a bribe be differentiated from a gratuity or some type of charity? According to Noonan, what constitutes a bribe changes with the culture and this makes bribery difficult to define. But at its core bribery is an "inducement improperly influencing the performance of a public function meant to be gratuitously exercised." Specifying the common elements of a bribe, "inducement," "improper influence," "public function," may depend to some extent on conventions, local laws, and practices, but bribery in this form constantly recurs in every cultural setting.[6]

Stuart Green provides a more formal and precise definition. According to Green, X is bribed by Y if X accepts or consents to accept something of value from Y in exchange for X's acting or consenting to act to further some interest of Y's by violating some duty of loyalty owed by X as a consequence of X's office, official position, or involvement in some practice. Thus, the briber (Y) offers or gives something of value in exchange for some service provided by the bribee (X). That "something of value" should be broadly understood. Most often it is money, but it could also be a job offer, tickets for a concert or sporting event, a paid vacation trip, or even sexual favors. Bribes are sometimes difficult to differentiate from gifts or gratuities, but a gift is given without any condition of reciprocation. A bribe, on the other hand, always involves reciprocity between the payer and the receiver.[7]

What about cases where the bribe receives payment or something valuable from the briber, but does not permit herself to be influenced by that payment. This turn of events happened in the Monsanto bribery case that unfolded in Indonesia. A $50,000 payment was made to a senior government official. In exchange for the payment that official was to use his influence to stop an environmental study of cotton crops grown from Monsanto's genetically modified cotton seed. The government official took the money but never did anything to halt the environmental study.[8] Although the U.S. Securities and Exchange Commission classified this payment as a bribe, it seems self-evident that we are not talking about bribery in cases like this one. If an official or an alleged bribee accepts money for an act he has no intention to carry out, that person has not engaged in bribery but fraud. On the other hand, if someone accepts payment to perform a certain action that he has every intention of doing but is unable to perform that action, this individual has indeed accepted a bribe.[9]

In some legal statutes, the bribee can only be a public official, but this provision seems too restrictive. From a moral perspective, it is also wrong to bribe employees or managers of private firms. Bribery payments made to a retail buyer or to other private sector agents in exchange for "something of value" are just as immoral as payments made to government officials.[10] In a foreign context, multinational corporations sometimes depend on bribes to obtain or retain government contracts or to reduce taxes or fees. A company might be under great duress to make such payments, especially if it assumes that bribery is the customary practice and that its competitors are following that practice. In these situations, there may be local laws prohibiting bribery. But perhaps the rule of law is weak or the country's bribery laws are unenforced and ignored by government officials. Should multinationals adapt to these different cultural norms when doing business in these countries? Or is a bribery payment, the offer of something of value in exchange for some service, intrinsically wrong and morally unacceptable no matter where a company does business?

To address that question it is instructive to consult the ethical theories reviewed in Chapter 4. Utilitarianism appeals to total consequences or aggregate social welfare as the ultimate moral criterion. From this perspective, it may appear that bribes are justifiable under some conditions. If bribes truly enhance aggregate welfare and bring about the best possible outcome, they would be a morally valid means of doing business. Sometimes managers, especially in certain emerging markets, confront a complex set of conflicting demands and constraints. They reason that based on local practices, host country expectations, and market pressures, the optimal solution is to pay a bribe to win a new contract or retain business, even if that payment violates their personal values (and perhaps even the company's code of conduct). Utilitarian reasoning, however, is too often distorted by rationalization, a justification of bribery based on self-interested calculations. Moral agents, including managers, have a great capacity to contrive rationalizations for deviating from reasonable ethical standards to secure what's in their best self-interest.[11]

The decisive problem with a utilitarianism rationale for bribery is its failure to provide a coherent account of the victims of a bribery scheme. The moral calculus rarely takes into account the adverse effects of bribery on competitors who try to compete fairly and openly. It also rarely takes into account the systemic inefficiencies of bribery, which often lead to the misallocation of resources and other social costs. When companies and individuals engage in voluntary exchange on the basis of price and product quality, the market allocates resources efficiently. However, when bribery enters the picture, the buyer makes a purchase not on the basis of price and quality, but on the basis of how much he will be paid "under the table" for making this purchase. Thus, the whole market mechanism is distorted and economic efficiency is undermined.[12]

Most economists confirm the efficiency argument. They also concur that a pattern of bribery hurts a country's economic growth and development. Corrupt economies get a high score on the corruption index and consequently struggle to attract new foreign investment. Multinationals are wary of those countries where bribery and corruption have become normative. Hence they defer investment despite that country's valuable natural resources, low labor costs, or the opportunity for market expansion.[13]

From a more balanced, non-utilitarian perspective, it is even more difficult to reach the conclusion that bribery is morally permissible given the harm that is caused to multiple stakeholders. There are two grounds for establishing the moral wrongfulness of bribery. First, engaging in bribery to win contracts or close a business deal represents unfair competition. The briber is attempting to beat out the competition not on the basis of a better price or on the merits of the company's product but by paying a bribe. Those who accept the bribe share in this harm of unfairness that also distorts value between the briber and bribee. Bribery disrupts any semblance of market fairness, which depends on open competition. In a fair marketplace all companies compete on equal terms. No company has a preferential advantage and everyone has an equal chance to sell their goods.[14] Such fairness and equality of opportunity is the essence of justice, which precludes arbitrary self-preference in pursuit of the good. Bribery does not advance the common good of the relevant community because it rewards the briber in disregard for the welfare of others.[15]

From a Kantian or duty-based perspective, the practice of bribery could not be universalized, because the briber's maxim promotes an action that would be inconsistent with his purpose if everyone tried to act on it. If everyone accepted and paid bribes, those bribes would offset each other, and the briber's payment would not have the intended effect of gaining a special advantage. In this case, there is a pragmatic contradiction since the briber is acting on a maxim ("it's acceptable to make a bribery payment to win this contract") that, if universalized, defeats the purpose behind the maxim.[16] As Korsgaard points out, Kant's theory prohibits those actions "whose efficacy in achieving their purposes depends upon their being exceptional."[17]

Also, it is important to underscore that bribery often interferes with the duty of loyalty or fidelity that public officials owe to their government. They are paid to promote the best interest of the government institution or agency that employs them. When bribes are accepted by such officials in exchange for some favorable treatment there is a breach of that loyalty. A foreign government worker who takes a bribe from a multinational to approve the purchase of its military equipment for the country's police force is not being loyal to his country and not acting with its economic well-being in mind. At the same time, the person or corporation offering the bribery payment is morally liable for encouraging someone to breach his or her duties.

There are, of course, gray areas involving overseas payments. Ethical quandaries arise when it becomes difficult to differentiate a gift or gratuity from a bribe. When does a corporate donation that ostensibly does not involve reciprocity constitute a bribe or an attempt at influence peddling? Drawing this line between a gift or charitable contribution and an outright bribe will depend to a great extent on the intentions of the giver and the perception of the recipient. Lobbying government officials is also a gray area. There is nothing wrong with trying to influence regulators by speaking the truth about the impact of proposed regulations on a particular industry. Sometimes, however, it is difficult to discern whether or not an amenity offered to a government official is just a disguised influence payment.

The Foreign Corrupt Practices Act

As a result of the many bribery scandals such as Lockheed and United Brands along with the political corruption that surfaced in the wake of the infamous Watergate investigation, the U.S. Congress finally took action. Quite simply, it decided to police the overseas behavior of corporations, even if the home countries where those multinationals operated did not forbid or restrict bribery payments. Many corporate executives argued that the law was controversial and unnecessary. But as one of the law's architects, Senator William Proxmire, pointed out: "Certainly there are subtleties and complexities in the foreign bribery issue, but we should be able to agree … that the time has come to provide a remedy for an act as simple and outrageous as bribery."[18]

The Foreign Corrupt Practices Act was passed into law in 1977 with virtually no opposition. U.S. lawmakers agreed with Senator Proxmire's conclusion that the only way to secure justice and fairness in international business transactions was the authority of a law that applied to domestic companies when doing business in foreign markets. The rules of law bring more definition, clarity, and predictability into these commercial interactions.[19] The law also plays a symbolic role, "putting down a marker indicating that this kind of behavior is unacceptable."[20]

The FCPA consists of two main sections: the anti-bribery provisions and the accounting standards. The accounting provisions of the law require corporations to maintain and keep records that accurately reflect the corporation's financial transactions. They are also obliged to develop a satisfactory system of internal accounting controls. The anti-bribery provision essentially outlaws the payment of bribes by "domestic concerns" to foreign officials for the purpose of obtaining or retaining business. A domestic concern includes any individual or firm along with any officer, director, employee, or agent of that firm acting on its behalf.[21]

According to the FCPA, domestic corporations, along with their employees and agents, doing business outside their home country must avoid bribes of any kind. A bribe is categorized as an "offer, payment, promise to pay, or authorization of the payment of any money, or offer, gift, promise to give, or authorization of the giving of anything of value to any foreign official for purposes of influencing any act or decision of such official in his official capacity … [or] inducing such foreign official to use his influence with a foreign government or instrumentality thereof to affect or influence any act or decision of such government … in order to assist such domestic concern in obtaining or retaining business."[22] In addition these domestic concerns cannot use these various means to attain some kind of "improper advantage." Thus, to violate the FCPA the bribery payment (or offer, promise to pay, etc.) had to be made to a "foreign official" for the express purpose of obtaining or retaining business or to achieve an improper advantage. The term "foreign official" is quite broad, and generally refers to all foreign government employees, including employees of state-owned or controlled corporations.

The FCPA statute uses morally neutral language such as "payments" and "gifts" or "offers" to avoid any confusion over the definition of the word "bribe," which may vary from country to country. The law's jurisdiction is broad. It applies to any U.S.-based corporation, any corporation listed on U.S. stock exchanges, and any foreign firms operating on American territory. Enforcement was to be ensured by accounting requirements: companies were required to keep books reflecting their foreign transactions in "reasonable detail."[23]

A typical strategy for corporate executives ensnared in bribery scandals has been to profess ignorance about the foreign payments. When four GlaxoSmithKline executives were arrested in China for paying bribes to doctors and hospital officials to obtain their business, executives in London claimed that they had no knowledge of this massive bribery scheme in China. That may be so. But if executive ignorance is determined to be "willful blindness," that claim cannot be the basis of a valid defense.[24]

The FCPA is enforced by both the Securities and Exchange Commission (SEC) and the U.S. Department of Justice (DOJ). The DOJ usually prosecutes violations of the anti-bribery statute. Both criminal and civil penalties could be imposed on those found guilty of violating this statute. Individual managers or others caught up in foreign bribery incidents could be fined up to $100,000 and they could also be sentenced to prison for up to five years. Corporations faced the prospect of much bigger fines that could amount to the financial gains that were accrued from the bribery payment.[25]

For several decades the FCPA was not strictly enforced. Between 1977 and 2005 the DOJ prosecuted only thirty-seven FCPA cases.[26] But things began to change shortly after the turn of the century thanks to new anti-corruption treaties, an increase in the number of multinationals, and a new law requiring companies to more carefully verify the accuracy of their financial statements. That law was the Sarbanes-Oxley Act of 2002, which holds public corporations accountable for illegal conduct anywhere that corporation does business.

As a consequence, federal prosecutors have made the FCPA a high priority. Enforcement of this statute "has gone from a carriage trade into what the Justice Department has said at times is its No. 2 priority behind terrorism."[27] For U.S. companies the cost of compliance has skyrocketed as they spend vast sums of money investigating and defending bribery allegations. Corporations in a broad range of industries have added compliance committees to corporate boards and taken other aggressive measures to ensure that money is not being improperly used in their overseas operations.[28]

The FCPA has not been a popular piece of legislation. After the law was passed many U.S. firms protested and argued that as long as the laws of competitor countries fell short of the FCPA, they would be at a disadvantage in bidding for contracts abroad. Many companies have claimed loss of business to rivals who won contracts through graft and kickbacks. Andrew Pincus, general counsel for the Department of Commerce, told Congress in 1998 that U.S. corporations had lost $30 billion in foreign contracts and business because their foreign competitors were still resorting to bribery payments.[29] Some independent scholars feared that stricter enforcement might have unintended consequences such as deterring multinationals from investing in emerging economies where corruption is more rampant and bribes are commonly required as a means of doing business. And if U.S. corporations cut back on investing in those economies corporations from other nations not as committed to fighting bribery and corruption will fill the vacuum.[30]

Some U.S. companies also contended that certain "payments" to "foreign officials" were sometimes necessary for the smooth running of their overseas operations. In many countries civil servants like customs workers are poorly compensated and seek to supplement their meager salaries through small payoffs. U.S. lawmakers were eventually forced to take the latter issue into account. A 1998 amendment to the FCPA exempts "facilitation payments," that is, small payments made to speed up things such as clearing some goods through customs or obtaining permits. Unlike a bribe, these payments merely expedite "routine government actions" and do not lead to an "improper advantage" or the awarding of a new business contract. Some critics claim, however, that there is little distinction in practice between these facilitation payments and bribes, and that the former represent the initial step toward more morally serious payments aimed at getting a special advantage.[31]

International regulations

Other countries were unusually slow and quite reactive in dealing with bribery payments offered by their corporations doing business abroad. They were remiss in crafting their own anti-bribery laws that mirror the FCPA. This tardiness was a source of acrimony for U.S. multinationals. As a result, U.S. policy makers and business executives urged other countries to take action. They insisted that as long as legislation in other countries fell short of the FCPA, U.S. corporations would be at an unfair disadvantage in bidding for international contracts.[32]

But by 1999 other industrialized countries finally followed the lead of the United States and forged an agreement to outlaw commercial bribery. This was accomplished through the Organisation for Economic Co-operation and Development (OECD), an international organization formed in 1961 to help administer the Marshall Plan for the further reconstruction of Europe. The OECD Anti-Bribery Convention was signed by its thirty-seven member-countries, including Australia, the United States, Canada, France, and Germany, and seven others mostly from Latina America. The OECD boasts that this convention is the only international anti-corruption measure that focuses on the "supply side" of bribery transactions – the individual or entity offering, promising, or giving a bribe. The signatory countries were required to reform their respective laws and enact legislation that outlaws commercial bribery payments to foreign public officials. They also pledged to cooperate in international corruption investigations. The OECD has no authority or capability to enforce the stipulations of the convention, but monitors implementation and enforcement by participating countries through its Working Group on Bribery.[33]

Most countries, like France and the UK, ratified the OECD Convention quickly, and adapted their laws to comply with the Convention's requirements. The French Penal Code has criminalized active and passive bribery of foreign officials and international judicial staff since 2007. In 2010, the United Kingdom Parliament enacted comprehensive anti-bribery legislation; The Bribery Act of 2010 is designed to deter corruption and graft abroad. The UK law parallels the FCPA and prohibits bribing of government officials in foreign countries. The crime of bribery is committed under this Act if a person intends to influence a foreign public official in his capacity as such, and if he or she intends to obtain or retain business (or gain some advantage involving that business). The UK law also penalizes the failure to prevent bribes that are made or offered on a company's behalf. However, the scope of the UK Bribery Act is broader than that of the FCPA. While the FCPA applies only to the corruption of foreign officials, the Bribery Act includes bribes offered or given to *any* person. Also, it is an offense under the UK law to request, agree to receive, or to accept a bribe. The FCPA, on the other hand, applies only to persons giving or offering a bribe and not to those accepting one.[34]

In 2018, Transparency International published an independent assessment of how well countries are enforcing the OECD Anti-Bribery Convention. The results are disappointing. The study found that only 25% of the world's exports come from countries where there is active enforcement of companies paying bribes in foreign markets. There are twenty-two countries where there is little or no enforcement, including China, South Korea, India, Spain, Mexico, and Finland. Eleven countries, including France, Canada, the Netherlands, and Austria, have limited enforcement. The report concluded that too many countries have "significant deficiencies that impede enforcement." The main deficiencies are insufficient resources, the low skills of enforcement agents, and weak whistleblower protection. The report further concludes that many countries, those party to the OECD Convention and others, need to make big investments to scale up their enforcement of corporate bribery in foreign markets.[35]

Recent scandals

The Transparency International assessment confirms that despite the ratification of the OECD Anti-Bribery Convention and a proliferation of anti-bribery statues, enforcement remains a critical problem. Corporate corruption scandals abound, and many managers still believe that in some emerging economies a company has to pay bribes in order to conduct business. An OECD study uncovered over 400 bribery cases that were investigated and closed between 1999 and 2014. Most of these bribery cases involved larger companies, especially in four industries: construction, resource extraction, transportation, and IT/communications.[36] And there have certainly been many other high-profile bribery cases since 2014.

It is instructive to review some of these shameful scandals in order to understand the dynamics of overseas bribery payments and the motivations that still drive some companies to violate well-defined legal and moral standards. Studies reveal that the oil and gas industry leads the list for bribery scandals with over eighty confirmed cases between 1977 and 2020. The health care industry (including pharmaceutical companies) is a close second.[37]

The communications industry has also had its share of corporate bribery and corruption. In 2007, for example, Lucent Technologies admitted that it provided funding for 1,000 Chinese officials, who were employed by Chinese telecom firms, so they could travel to Las Vegas and other destinations. In exchange, Lucent hoped to win lucrative telecom contracts. Several years earlier, Lucent was accused of making $15 to $21 million in payments to Saudi Arabia's telecommunications minister to obtain business in that country. Lucent was awarded over $5 billion in contracts, far more than any other telecom company in the world. The government had laid out plans for a telecommunications system "to help bring the kingdom into the next century." Siemens AG, L.M. Ericsson, and other multinationals bid on the multibillion dollar contract but Lucent was the big winner.[38]

In 2007, BAE Systems, one of the world's largest defense companies, was entangled in a high-profile bribery case. It was investigated by the UK and the U.S. Department of Justice. BAE was accused of making questionable payments and violating the FCPA regarding business deals in countries such as Chile, the Czech Republic, Qatar, Romania, South Africa, and Tanzania. BAE admitted to making false statements about FCPA compliance and paid the U.S. government a $400 million fine. It was also fined $50 million by the British government.[39]

In 2010, the DOJ and SEC made public a long-running investigation into the personal computer manufacturer, Hewlett-Packard (HP). HP allegedly paid out $44.5 million in order to secure a contract with the office of the Prosecutor General of the Russian Federation. The lucrative contract was for the delivery and installation of a full-scale information technology network. Since the payments were made to government officials they would constitute a violation of the FCPA. The investigation was extended to similar questionable payments in Mexico and Poland. U.S. investigators uncovered a slush fund for bribes set up by executives at an HP subsidiary in Russia. In Poland, HP employees gave a government employee a free trip to Las Vegas and provided him with "bags of cash," which changed hands in a Warsaw parking lot. In 2014, HP pled guilty to violating the FCPA in three countries and was ordered to pay a fine of $108 million.[40]

Also, in 2010, the German car manufacturer, Daimler-Benz, was accused of bribing foreign officials in twenty-two different countries. The bribery payments amounted to "tens of millions of dollars" in order to win vehicle contracts in several countries, such as North Korea, China, Vietnam, and Nigeria. The U.S. Department of Justice claimed that Daimler secured over $50 million in profits due to this elaborate bribery scheme. The company pled guilty to these bribery charges and paid a fine of $185 million.[41]

In June 2013, Chinese officials accused GlaxoSmithKline, the British Big Pharma multinational, of several crimes, including commercial bribery, tax evasion, and embezzlement. In Shanghai, four senior GSK executives, all Chinese nationals, were detained by Chinese police. They were later charged with making bribery payments of $489 million to Chinese doctors and hospital employees between 2010 and 2013. The purpose of the payments was to increase sales for GSK's prescription drugs. The money was laundered through local travel agencies. The low base salaries of Chinese doctors incentivized them to accept these illegal payments. Moreover, China's public hospitals generate much of their revenues from the sale of drugs. They have a virtual monopoly on drug sales, and this creates fertile ground for bribery payments by Big Pharma companies like GSK.[42]

GSK's payments to doctors and hospital officials violated both the FCPA and the UK Bribery Act along with local Chinese laws. One year later, in 2014, a Chinese court found the UK drug maker guilty and fined the company $500 million. Five executives, including the head of GSK's China business, were convicted of bribery and received suspended prison sentences. GSK also paid a heavy fine to the United States for violating the FCPA. During this same period, U.S. regulators also brought FCPA charges against other Big Pharma firms, including Pfizer, Eli Lilly, and Bristol-Myers Squibb.[43] Why do these reputable companies resort to bribery payments in countries like China? According to one Chinese pharma executive, "Because the others all pay. If we do not pay we lose market."[44]

More recently, it has come to light that the Brazilian construction firm, Oderbrecht, SA has been entangled in multiple bribery scandals, primarily in Latin American countries. The firm has admitted to U.S. prosecutors that it paid $800 million in bribes throughout Latin America and other countries in order to win lucrative infrastructure contracts. From 2001 through 2016, the company paid bribes on 100 projects in countries including Angola, Argentina, Columbia, Ecuador, Mexico, Venezuela, and Peru. Oderbrecht received several billion dollars from contracts in these and other countries.[45]

One of the most infamous cases has apparently happened in Peru. Four former presidents have been placed under investigation. Ollanta Humala and his wife Nadine Herediaare are facing potentially lengthy prison sentences for allegedly receiving payments to fund his presidential campaigns in 2006 and 2011. Alan García, who served as president from 1985 to 1990 and again from 2006 to 2011, committed suicide as police came to arrest him over credible allegations that he accepted bribes from Odebrecht.[46]

Odebrecht has also admitted to paying bribes in Peru to secure big construction contracts. Former President Alejandro Toledo governed the country from 2001 to 2006. Toledo allegedly received $20 million in bribes from Oderbrecht. The money was wired to offshore accounts owned by one of Toledo's close friends.[47] Odebrecht benefited greatly from its political connections in Peru. Under President Toledo leadership, Odebrecht began construction of the Interoceanic Highway running across the country. The highway cost $4.5 billion, which was four times over budget. Those exorbitant overruns were approved by an official in the Toledo administration.[48]

Odebrecht's cost overruns in Peru reflect its approach in many countries including Peru. They sought to win contracts through exceptionally low bids and then by means of bribes and other corrupt practices secure big cost increases through contract amendments. Oderbrecht concentrated especially on public–private partnerships (PPPS), which are typically adopted for large expensive infrastructure projects such as highways or public highways. Researchers have determined that 78% of all transport PPPS in Latin American countries were re-negotiated with an average cost increase of $30 million per contract amendment. There were twenty-two amendments to the Peru contract, which was initially approved for about $1.2 billion. These researchers have concluded that these contract changes are quite often "fertile ground for corruption."[49]

In addition, Oderbrecht allegedly donated $1 million to the President of Columbia's re-election campaign in exchange for contracts for projects including a road that links the country's interior region to the Magdalena highway. Oderbrecht's brazen bribery routine also created a political scandal in Brazil, which led to the impeachment of its former President, Dilma Rousseff. In 2016, Oderbrecht settled with the U.S., Brazil, and Switzerland for up to $4.5 billion. U.S. prosecutors pursued the construction company for violating the FCPA. These fines represent the largest anti-corruption settlement in history.[50]

Another major bribery scandal erupted in Italy in 2018 when Italian prosecutors claimed that a $1.3 billion "license fee" paid by Eni SpA for rights to a prized oil field in Nigeria was mostly a bribe. Eni Spa, one of the oil industry's "supermajors," is an Italian firm that worked on this deal along with Royal Dutch Shell. The prosecutors alleged that Eni and Shell executives approved payments to the Nigerian government knowing that most of the money would be transferred to a company controlled by one of the country's ex-oil ministers. The prosecutors maintained that these executives knew the former oil minister would pay off Nigerian officials and even send some kickbacks to certain Eni executives. Payments were allegedly made to more than 100 recipients, including then Nigerian President Goodluck Johnson. Eni and Shell have admitted to paying the government, but claim that they did not know the money would be used for bribes. According to an Eni spokesperson, "it was at the discretion of the Nigerian government to decide how to use funds received from Eni and Shell."[51] Criminal proceedings in the Italian court system have not yet resolved this case.

Also in 2018 a complex bribery scheme involving Goldman Sachs and the Malaysian government was exposed. The Asian country set up a government fund to stimulate economic growth. It was called 1 Malaysia Development Bhd. or 1MDB. Goldman helped the government sell $6.5 billion in bonds for the fund. Goldman earned $600 million in fees to arrange the bond sales. More than $2.7 billion raised for the fund has been embezzled. Most of its was stolen by an advisor to the fund but $700 million ended up in bank account of the country's Prime Minister who was convicted of "abuse of power" by a Malaysian court for his role in this scandal. During the investigations into this incident it was revealed that the former head of

Goldman's South East Asian business and another senior banker had paid bribes to government officials, including expensive jewelry gifts to Malaysia's first lady, to obtain the government's business. Goldman has blamed the debacle on this pair of rogue employees but critics point out that the exorbitant fees, well above what is typical for arranging bond sales, should have been warning sign that something was amiss. The company has admitted to wrongdoing in the affair and has paid a $2.8 billion fine to the DOJ.[52]

Finally, in 2020, Airbus SE, a global provider of civilian and military aircraft based in France, agreed to pay fines of a record $4 billion to resolve foreign bribery charges that violated anti-bribery laws in the United States, France, and the United Kingdom. Airbus is the second largest aerospace company worldwide and a major competitor of the leading U.S. firm, Boeing. The Airbus bribery scheme relied on third-party business partners to bribe government officials, as well as some airline executives in order to win new contracts. Airbus engaged in this prolonged bribery campaign to fortify its market share in as many foreign countries as possible. According to one U.S. official, "Airbus's fraud and bribery in commercial aircraft transactions strengthened corrupt airlines and bad actors worldwide, at the expense of straightforward enterprises." Additionally, the U.S. contended that the bribery of foreign government officials, specifically those who were involved in the procurement of U.S. military technology, posed a national security threat to both the U.S. and its allies.[53]

According to court documents, the Airbus bribery scheme began in 2008 and continued until at least 2015. Airbus paid bribes to key decision makers, including foreign government officials, to win commercial airline business from both privately owned enterprises and state-owned and state-controlled businesses in countries like China. In order to conceal and to execute its bribery plans, Airbus used a network of agents operating from a cell in Paris. Between 2013 and 2015, for example, Airbus employed one of those agents or "business partners" in China to work as an intermediary. It made payments to that individual that were intended to be used as bribes to Chinese government officials. The payments were made to induce those officials to approve the purchase of Airbus aircraft for several airlines owned or controlled by the state. As a means of covering up the payments and the employment of its business partner in China, Airbus did not pay the business partner directly but instead made payments to a bank account in Hong Kong in the name of a company controlled by another business partner.[54]

Fallout from the $4 billion payouts reverberated around the world, and investigations were initiated in many foreign counties where those bribes allegedly took place, without the knowledge of those countries' leaders.[55]

It seems evident from these ongoing bribery incidents that corporations must do a better job of reforming their cultures from within to prevent employees from engaging in this unlawful and predatory behavior. Sales executives are rewarded for the revenues they generate, but rarely are they rewarded for turning away from corrupt deals. Refusing bribes and kickbacks may result in lost sales in the short run, but companies should concentrate more on creating value and building a competitive business that derives its profits ethically and without the durable taint of bribery and corruption.[56]

Case study: Schering-Plough in Poland

The New Jersey corporation, Schering-Plough, once a subsidiary of Schering AG in Germany, was a sizable pharmaceutical firm that merged with Merck & Co. in 2007. Schering was best known for several blockbuster drugs such as the allergy drugs Claritin and Clarinex along with the anti-cholesterol drug Vytorin. Before the merger with Merck, Schering had about 1.5% share of the U.S. drug market, well below bigger firms such as Merck and Pfizer.

Between February 1999 and March 2002 Schering-Plough Poland, a branch office of Schering's wholly owned Swiss subsidiary, "donated" 315,800 zlotys ($76,000) to a Polish charitable foundation. The money was given to the Chudow Castle Foundation, which was established in 1995. Its aim was to restore castles and other historic sites in the Silesian region of Poland. The founder and president of the foundation was the director of the Silesian Health Fund, which was one of the sixteen regional health agencies in Poland responsible for the financial management of health care. The Silesian Health Fund provided funding for the purchase of pharmaceutical products. It also influenced the purchase of those products by hospitals and other health care providers by negotiating contracts for drug purchases. Thus, the Silesian Health Fund Director had decision making authority that could influence the sale of Schering-Plough products.[57]

The gifts to the Chudow Castle Foundation began shortly after its founder and director was appointed as the Director of the Silesian Health Fund. Schering Plough Poland sold many drugs in Poland at the time, including cancer therapies such as Intron. The payments made to the Chudow Foundation were described by the manager of Schering's Polish office as "support for a health campaign" within the region. They were recorded on the books as charitable donations.[58]

Thanks to these and other gifts, the foundation was able to initiate reconstruction and excavation works. By 2004, the castle tower was re-built with a whole new roof. The monuments obtained during the archeological research and excavation were refurbished. The walls around the courtyard were raised and the gates were renovated.[59]

In its subsequent investigation into these events, the Securities & Exchange Commission (SEC) conceded that these payments were made to a bona fide charity. However, in their estimation, they were made to influence the Director of the Silesian Health Fund to implicitly persuade him to purchase

Schering's products. While there was no direct proof of an explicit *quid pro quo*, Schering-Plough Poland's sales of Intron A and another oncology drug called Temodal increased "disproportionately" compared with sales of those two products in other regions of Poland. According to the SEC, by 2002, "53% of Intron A and 40% of Temodal sold in Poland were in Silesia."[60]

Schering-Plough never admitted to the allegations of bribery, but it worked out a settlement with the SEC. Defenders of Schering-Plough have pointed out that its Polish subsidiary was simply trying to improve the region within which it worked by supporting the foundation. The pharmaceutical company was simply acting as an exemplary corporate citizen. Also, although most bribes are usually cash payments made "off the books," these payments in Silesia were duly recorded in the company's accounting system. Perhaps the Polish office had no intention to increase sales, which were just an unforeseen side effect of its generous donation. Others have argued that these were bribery payments cleverly disguised as charitable donations.

Study questions

1. Are these payments a violation of the FCPA?
2. Do these payments fit the definition of bribery or are they merely a gift?

Conclusions

In this short chapter we have reviewed the issue of bribery and corruption, and provided a concise definition of bribery, which, unlike a gift, always entails reciprocity. A bribe is a mutual agreement between two parties. The briber offers or promises to provide something of value in exchange for some service or action to be provided by the bribee. That "something of value" has been broadly construed by government authorities. Ambiguities arise sometimes because the distinction between a gift and a bribe is not always easily discernible. Whether a payment of some sort qualifies as a bribe depends to some extent on the intention and motivation of the giver along with the perception of the recipient.

While utilitarian reasoning might appear to validate bribery payments under some circumstances that optimize consequences, there are no convincing moral arguments that bribery advances the common good in ways that make it morally justified. Bribery undermines fair and open competition and disrupts free markets. Bribery fuels "unpredictability and the misallocation of resources."[61] Bribery is unjust because the parties do not preclude arbitrary self-preference in their pursuit of the good. Bribery also has many negative effects on an organization's internal dynamics, since it can damage morale and undermine confidence.

The normalization of bribery in foreign markets led to the genesis of the FCPA. U.S. legislators seized the authority to outlaw bribery payments in foreign markets, as self-regulation yielded to the coercive authority of the law. The hope was that tangible incentives to follow the law would be more effective than appeals to the moral urgency of promoting the common good. The FCPA forbids payments (along with offers, promises of payment) to "foreign officials" for the purpose of obtaining or retaining business or for some type of "special advantage." The term "foreign official" is quite broad, and generally refers to all foreign government employees, including employees of state-owned or controlled corporations.

The Unites States is not alone in its fight against international bribery. The OECD Anti-Bribery Convention, which took effect in 1999, also directed its forty-four signatories to revise their laws to outlaw commercial bribery in foreign markets. Many countries such as the United Kingdom have passed comprehensive anti-bribery laws, but enforcement of those laws in some countries remains weak.

However, despite new laws and vocal commitments to end graft, combating corporate bribery in foreign markets continues to be an intense challenge. International bribery remains a serious obstacle for the realization of fair and free global markets. It continues to be a particular menace in emerging economies, as reflected in the GSK, Odebrecht, Eni Spa, Goldman Sachs, and Airbus scandals. In Africa, for example, some countries have no sound bribery laws, and in other countries those laws are unenforced. Recalcitrant multinationals have had no qualms in exploiting this legal vacuum. There is some evidence of short-term gains for a corporation from its illicit bribery payments. But the calculus changes if enforcement intensifies and there is increased likelihood of getting caught. Yet without greater resolve to eradicate bribery from the global economic system, it remains, in the words of the *Economist*, "the worm that never dies."[62]

Notes

1 Dan Koeppel, *Banana: The Fate of the Fruit that Changed the World* (New York: Penguin Group, 2008), 169–175. See also Eugene Soltes, *Why They Do It* (New York: Hachette Book Group, 2016), 34.
2 Soltes, 34–36.
3 Edwin Reischauer, "The Lessons of the Lockheed Scandal," *Newsweek*, May 10, 1976, 20–21. For a more detailed account of this scandal see David Boulton, *The Grease Machine* (New York: Harper & Row, 1978).
4 John T. Noonan, *Bribes* (Berkeley, CA: University of California Press, 1984), 31–33.
5 James Weber and Kathleen Getz, "The Future Status of Bribery in International Commerce," *Business Ethics Quarterly* 14 (4), 2004, 696.
6 Noonan, *Bribes*, xi.
7 Stuart P. Green, *Lying, Cheating, and Stealing* (Oxford: Oxford University Press, 2006), 194–200.
8 For a full discussion of this case see Richard A. Spinello, *Business Ethics: Contemporary Issues and Cases* (Los Angeles, CA: SAGE, 2019), 389–393.

9 Green, *Lying, Cheating, and Stealing*, 201. For a legal case that comes to a different conclusion see *United States v. Myers* 692 F. 2d 823 (2nd Cir 1982).

10 Ibid., 195–196.

11 John Finnis, *Religion and Public Reason* (Oxford: Oxford University Press, 2011), 42–55.

12 Thomas Donaldson and Thomas Dunfee, *Ties that Bind* (Boston, MA: Harvard Business School Press, 1999), 228–229.

13 "Graft Work," *Economist*, December 6, 2014, 73.

14 Richard De George, *Competing with Integrity in International Business* (Oxford: Oxford University Press, 1993), 99–102.

15 John Finnis, *Natural Law and Natural Rights* (Oxford: Oxford University Press, 1980), 161–165.

16 Norman Bowie, *Business Ethics: A Kantian Perspective* (Oxford: Blackwell Publishers, 1999), 26–27.

17 Christine Korsgaard, *Creating the Kingdom of Ends* (New York: Cambridge University Press, 1996), 92.

18 Statement of Senator William Proxmire, Foreign and Corporate Bribes, Hearings before the Committee on Banking, Housing, and Urban Affairs, United States Senate, 94th Congress, April 5–8, 1976 (Washington, D.C.: U.S. Government Printing Office, 1976), 76.

19 Finnis, *Natural Law and Natural Rights*, 260–268.

20 Robert Theobald, "Should the Payment of Bribes Overseas be made Illegal," *Business Ethics: A European Review* 11 (2), 2002, 381.

21 Richard Cassin, *Bribery Abroad* (Singapore: Cassin Law Publishing, 2011), 14–15.

22 The Foreign Corrupt Practices Act, Pub. L. No. 95–213, 91 Stat. 1464 (1977) codified at 15 U.S.C. §78, 78m, 78dd-1, 78ff.

23 Noonan, *Bribes*, 678–679.

24 Cassin, *Bribery Abroad*, 15.

25 Criminal Division, U.S. Department of Justice, "A Resource Guide to the Foreign Corrupt Practices Act, November 2012.

26 David Montero, *Kickback: Exposing the Global Corporate Bribery Network* (New York: Viking, 2018), 33.

27 Joe Palazzolo, "Law's Long Path: Nixon, Carter, Bush," *Wall Street Journal*, October 2, 2012, B1, B4.

28 Joe Palazzolo and Christopher Matthews, "The Cost of Compliance Grows," *Wall Street Journal*, October 2, 2012, B4.

29 Montero, *Kickback*, 34.

30 Dionne Searcey, "In Antibribery Law, Some Fear Inadvertent Chill on Business," *Wall Street Journal*, August 16, 2009, A9.

31 "Bribery and Business: The Short Arm of the Law," *Economist*, March 2, 2002, 63–65.

32 Ibid.

33 "OECD Anti-Bribery Convention," Organization for Economic Cooperation and Development. Available at oecd.org/corruption-integrity/anti-bribery-convention. See also Montero, *Kickback*, 33–34.

34 Geoffrey Gauci and Jessica Fisher, "The UK Bribery Act and the US FCPA: Key Differences," Association of Corporate Counsel, June 2011.

35 Gillian Dell and Andrew McDevitt, "Exporting Corruption: Progress Report 2018 Assessing Enforcement of the OECD Anti-Bribery Convention," Transparency International, October 2018. Available at www.transparencyinternatinal.org.

36 Laura French, "A History of Bribery," *World of Finance*, March 6, 2015. Available at http://www.worldfinance.com/comment/a-history-of-bribery.

37 "A Closer Look at Greasy Palms," *Economist*, August 29, 2020, 51.

38 Christopher Rhoads, "Lucent faces Bribery Allegations in Giant Saudi Telecom Project," *Wall Street Journal*, November 16, 2004, A1, A18. See also French, "A History of Bribery."

39 French, "A History of Bribery."

40 Joseph Palazzolo, "H-P Bribe Probe Widens," *Wall Street Journal*, September 10, 2010, B1. See also Spencer Ante and Don Clark, "H-P Settles Bribery Investigations," *Wall Street Journal*, April 10, 2014, B1–2.

41 French, "A History of Bribery."

42 Montero, *Kickback*, 71.

43 Hester Plumridge and Laurie Burkitt, "GlaxoSmithKline Found Guilty of Bribery in China," *Wall Street Journal*, September 19, 2014, A1.

44 Montero, *Kickback*, 82.

45 Luciana Magalhaes and Ryan Dube, "Builder Faces Bans Across Latin America," *Wall Street Journal*, January 6, 2017, A14.

46 "Odebrecht Case: Politicians Worldwide Suspected in Bribery Scandal," *BBC News*, April 17, 2019.

47 Ryan Dube, Luciana Magalhaes, and Rogerio Jelmayer, "Graft Probes Grow in Latin America," *Wall Street Journal*, March 9, 2017, A20.

48 Nicholas Casey and Andrea Zarate, "Brazilian Graft Scandals Echo Across Continent," *New York Times*, February 15, 2017, A3.

49 Bello, "Rage against the Bribes Department," *Economist*, February 4, 2017.

50 Casey and Zarate, "Brazilian Graft Scandals Echo Across Continent." See also Ryan Dube, "Brazilian Bribery Scandal Shakes Up Latin America," *Wall Street Journal*, December 23, 2016, B3.

51 Sarah Kent and Eric Sylvers, "Billion-Dollar Bribery Scandal Sweeps through Oil Industry," *Wall Street Journal*, February 14, 2018, A1, A11.

52 Matthew Goldstein, "Goldman Sachs to Admit Mistakes in 1MDB Scandal," *New York Times*, October 23, 2020, B1, B3. See also David Michaels, "Goldman to Settle Federal Probe on 1MDB," *Wall Street Journal*, October 21, 2020, A1, A6.

53 "Airbus Agrees to Pay over $3.9 Billion in Global Penalties to Resolve Foreign Bribery Case," Department of Justice, January 31, 2020.

54 Ibid.

55 Tim Hepher and Laurence Frost, "Airbus Bribes Scandal Triggers New Probes Worldwide," *Reuters*, February 3, 2020.

56 Montero, *Kickback*, 247–250.

57 Securities and Exchange Commission (SEC) v. Schering-Plough Corporation, case no. 1:04CV00945, District of Columbia, U.S. District Court, June 2004.

58 Ibid.

59 Chudow Castle, Wikipedia. Available at https://en.wikipedia.org/wiki/Chud%C3%B3w.

60 SEC v. Schering-Plough.

61 Donaldson and Dunfee, *Ties that Bind*, 137.

62 "The Anti-Bribery Business," *Economist*, May 9, 2015, 62–63.

Chapter 7

Political risk, corporate collusion, and divestment

Not far from Thomas Watson's hotel room, crowds of Germans were mesmerized by the intoxicating spectacle of S.S. troops marching briskly in lockstep at a customary Berlin party rally. The IBM CEO was in Berlin in 1935 to celebrate the accomplishments of IBM's successful German subsidiary known as Dehomag. After enjoying a lavish dinner at the ornate Hotel Adoni, Watson consulted with his German staff about how corporate headquarters in New York could further help its prosperous German operations. Watson was especially proud of Dehomag and his cooperative relationship with the German government.

This German subsidiary was almost as old as the IBM corporation itself. IBM began as the Tabulating Machines Company (TMC) in 1896. The company was started by Herman Hollerith who developed a machine that tabulated census data using punch cards. Hollerith's versatile machines were used in the 1890 U.S. census with great results. Hollerith licensed his technology to foreign entrepreneurs, including Willy Heidinger who established *Deutsche Hollerith Machinen Gesellschaft*, which became known as Dehomag. Heidinger paid a royalty to TMC based on the revenues generated from the machines imported from the U.S. TMC was sold to the Computer-Tabulating-Recording Company where the young Tom Watson was employed as the general manager. In 1924 Watson changed the name of CTR to IBM or International Business Machines Corporation.[1] He built up a strong corporate culture and spoke often of the "IBM Family."

Shortly after Watson became CEO of IBM, he set his sights on the acquisition of Dehomag. In April 1933, after Hitler came to power, the Third Reich announced that a new census would take place for all Germans. The regime sought basic demographic data for the forty-one million Germans living in Prussia. To expedite this arduous process, the government turned to Dehomag, which secured the RM 1.35 million contract to conduct the Prussian census. The company customized its

DOI: 10.4324/9781003058427-7

technology to meet the requirements of the census by producing a sixty-column card to accommodate the demographic information sought in the census (each column represented a biographical characteristic). With the help of these cards, the census tracked the following data: county, community, gender, age, religion, mother tongue, current occupation, and so forth.[2]

The company's simple punch-card technology was sold to many other customers besides the Third Reich. Among Dehomag's major clients were the German Post Office and the Ministry of Defence. Private sector customers included Siemens and Daimler-Benz. But the German government's census contracts offered the biggest financial bonanza for Dehomag. Sensing the potential for growth, Watson authorized additional investments in 1935 for printing presses that produced the punch cards.

Under Hitler's autocratic leadership, things became increasingly tenuous for Jews living in Germany. There was a concerted effort to dismiss those of "Jewish extraction" from government jobs.[3] Jewish businesses were routinely boycotted. It also became virtually intolerable for foreign businesses to retain Jewish workers. There was immense pressure to remove Jews from any management positions. With Watson's blessing, IBM followed this trend. In response to criticism over this policy, Watson said in an interview, "I am an internationalist. I cooperate with all forms of government, regardless of whether I can subscribe to all their principles or not."[4]

IBM never divested its holdings in Germany or disassociated itself from Dehomag in the years leading up to World War II. On the contrary, it increased its investment and entered into a strong commercial alliance with the government and several of its agencies. Watson authorized the construction of a new factory in Berlin to produce the Dehomag machines, and in 1935 additional investments were made for specialized printing presses, which allowed Dehomag to print its own punch cards. By 1937, fifty-nine presses, shipped from Europe and the United States, were installed throughout Germany. In May 1938, after Germany's annexation of Austria – known as the *Anschluss* – Watson visited the country again and approved Dehomag's extension into Austria.

Was IBM morally lax in putting its technology at the disposal of the Nazi party for the purpose of the 1933 Prussian census? Perhaps it is expecting too much for IBM to have foreseen that one purpose of that census was the identification and tracking of the Jews who were so despised by the regime. However, IBM's willingness to increase investment in Dehomag operations throughout the 1930s is another matter. During the early years of the Nazi regime, Hitler's evil intentions to exterminate the Jewish race were not yet known. However, as early as 1933 there were portentous manifestations and hints of the malicious intentions of this racist regime. Countless headlines in newspapers like the *New York Times* reported on the growing persecution of the Jews. In April 1933 the paper reported that 10,000 Jews had already fled Germany in the face of persecution, home invasions, and even torture at the hands of the Brown Shirts.[5] On April 1, 1933 Hitler ordered a national boycott of Jewish shops. He declared that "Jews were not Germans," and issued laws that banned them from public service, universities and schools, journalism, farming, theater, and films. In 1934 they were summarily expelled from Germany's stock exchanges, and soon after they could no longer openly practice law or medicine. In September 1935 the Nuremberg Laws were passed, depriving the Jewish people of citizenship and forbidding marriage between Jews and Aryans. By the summer of 1936, historian William Shirer estimates that over one half of the Jewish population was without any means of livelihood.[6]

IBM managers must have perceived the virulence of the anti-Semitism infecting Germany during the Nazification of its culture in the 1930s. That anti-Semitism was invading the workplace and every aspect of German social life. Surely, by 1938, the time frame for the second German census authorized to help implement the Nuremberg Laws, IBM would have recognized the implications of complicity with this regime. Many American and European businesses faced the same dilemma as IBM: suspend business in this totalitarian state despite the expected pecuniary rewards, or conduct business as usual and face the risk of disapprobation at home.

This brief account of IBM's experience in Nazi Germany evokes one of the primary themes of this chapter: are there countries so politically corrupt or morally offensive that the only viable ethical strategy is disinvestment? The issue of disinvestment suggests the intimate connection between politics and economics, and that connection raises another question to be addressed in this chapter: to what extent can multinational corporations shape the local political environment to their advantage? This issue assumes some urgency if the political environment transitions to socialism or extreme nationalism and a company's assets are in peril of being seized. A multinational has every right to protect its property abroad so long as its means are just. But sometimes it overreaches and intrudes too deeply into a host country's internal political affairs. We begin our discussion with several examples of such excessive political activism.

Political risk and corporate activism

Multinationals encounter various economic risks associated with foreign direct investment (FDI), trade, and outsourcing. Sometimes that risk is exceptionally high. Consider the supermajor oil companies, such as Chevron and ExxonMobil, which invest billions in capital expenditures for exploration and production. However, their expensive projects in foreign locales can yield minimal economic benefits. In some cases, their efforts to find oil or natural gas are futile and they end up forfeiting their substantial up-front investment in exploration. Or because of geology (gas and oil buried deep underwater) the resources are hard to access and so they must expend more capital to get less output. If the oil is mixed up with tar sand or similar substances it must be subject to the expensive process of separation. While oil is an especially risky proposition, most companies have to contend with major economic risks when doing business abroad, and they plan accordingly.[7]

But companies are often ill-prepared to manage political and ethical risks associated with FDI and trade. They lack local knowledge about political matters and too often they are deluded by the appearance of political stability. Autocratic governments, for example, often seem quite stable but then rapidly collapse. Political risk simply refers to the possibility that political decisions or events in a particular country will cause foreign investors there to lose money or fail to capture their expected returns. Political risk is rife in emerging economies. It usually arises from immature legal systems, provisional institutions, volatile urban areas, and unstable political regimes.[8]

Doing business in most Middle East countries entails a particularly high level of political risk. There are weak institutions and poor infrastructure, but in addition corporations must navigate a thicket of ethnic and religious tensions. Businesses can easily be caught in the middle of conflicts between Sunni and Shia Muslims. Corruption is also a problem thanks to the tradition of informal business deals and paying commission to middlemen that can incur the risk of violating home country anti-bribery laws.[9] In countries like China and Russia, where state-owned or controlled business is often used as an instrument of political power, there is a different breed of political risk. For example, consummating a fair business deal with Russia's state-controlled natural gas giant, Gazprom, will be easily clouded by political considerations. Through its natural gas monopoly Russia can exercise significant leverage over foreign investors in the energy sector. Other political risks of doing business in Russia include its economic volatility, authoritarian leadership, ongoing corruption, and its opaque legal system. Russia has been described as an "impossible country," a society where basic government institutions do not function properly.[10] In China, government favoritism of state-controlled companies will make it difficult for foreign investors to gain a competitive advantage in most markets. In general, whenever government policy decisions or political events can affect the profitability and security of foreign investments, political risk exists.

Aside from wars and regional conflict, the biggest risk for foreign investors is the loss of assets through expropriation or nationalization. That risk was greatly magnified when socialist rule came to Venezuela, thanks to Hugo Chavez. Many foreign companies, such as General Motors, have departed Venezuela after government authorities seized their plants and other assets. Chavez and the current ruler, Nicolas Maduro, have nationalized more than 1,400 companies and private assets since taking power in 1999.[11] Multinationals are obliged to protect their assets and promote their interests especially when they believe in good faith that those interests align with the common good of the host country. But how far can companies go to defend their investments from severe political risk, including the threat of expropriation?

We consider this vexing issue by focusing on three multinationals that used their corporate power in ways that were ethically problematic and ultimately self-defeating. None of these companies navigated political risk responsibly and all of them played at least an indirect role in regime change. Unfortunately these and other examples illustrate how foreign policy can sometimes be driven by the vested interests of multinationals.

The first case involves the Boston Fruit Company, which traces its origins back to 1885 when a young entrepreneur began importing bananas from Jamaica. In 1908 Boston Fruit merged with another enterprise to form United Fruit Company (UFC). With more capital and resources, the newly formed corporation expanded into Central America to meet the rising demand for bananas in the United States. By the late 1920s, United Fruit was worth well over $100 million. It had 67,000 employees, owned 1.6 million acres of land, and had business interests in thirty-two countries.[12]

UFC had built up extensive operations in Central America and it soon became the largest employer in Guatemala. In most Central and Latin American countries where it operated UFC exercised considerable economic influence. Its CEO was so powerful that he became known as "the uncrowned king of Central America."[13] Nonetheless, periodic labor disputes ruffled feathers at UFC's corporate headquarters in Boston and even at the U.S. State Department, which wanted to keep the region secure for American business. UFC saw itself as a benign and paternalistic employer, but many Guatemalans perceived their country as a captive of this giant foreign corporation.[14]

From the United States' perspective, the political environment in Guatemala began to deteriorate when Jacobo Árbenz Guzmán was elected president. Árbenz has been described as a nationalist seeking to reform an "oligarchic society." He assumed the presidency in March 1951 and immediately set about the task of land reform and income redistribution. In 1950, the annual per capita income of agricultural workers was a meager $87. Moreover, 2.2% of landowners owned 70% of the country's land, but less than a quarter of that land was in use.[15]

Árbenz's goal of transforming his country into a modern socialist state clashed with the economic interests of UFC. By now, United Fruit was the largest property owner in the country with 550,000 acres on both coasts. But 85% of the land was uncultivated. As part of his agrarian reform and land redistribution program, Jacobo Árbenz sought to purchase some of UFC's unused land. In March 1953, 209,842 acres of UFC's uncultivated land was appropriated by the Árbenz government for a payment of $627,572. UFC claimed that the land was worth about $16 million, but the government believed that it had offered a fair price. UFC paid $1.48 an acre for this land and the government's offer amounted to $2.99 an acre.[16]

When negotiations with the Árbenz regime collapsed, UFC initiated a propaganda campaign designed to convince Washington lawmakers of Árbenz's Communist sympathies. UFC hired a shrewd public relations expert, Edward Bernays, to plant stories in the press favorable to UFC and to hype the story of Soviet communism's role in Guatemala's government. Bernays flew journalists into Guatemala for "fact finding junkets." The result was numerous articles that portrayed Guatemala's leadership as a dangerous threat to U.S. security because of its communist affinities.[17]

United Fruit also funded the printing of a book written by John Clements called *Report on Guatemala – 1952* that presumably documented this alleged "Moscow-directed communist conspiracy" taking place in Guatemala. The hastily written book was sent to every member of Congress, their staff, and other influential Washington policy makers.[18] There were communists working in the Guatemalan government and Árbenz clearly tolerated communist influence as a counterweight to the conservative forces in the country. But there is no evidence to suggest that Árbenz was subject to any foreign control or even had any substantive contact with communists in countries like Russia. Nonetheless, the thesis of Soviet influence in Guatemala echoed loudly in Washington thanks to the palpable fears of communism stoked by Joe McCarthy and others. All of UFC's subversive efforts succeeded in creating a climate of deep suspicion about the Árbenz government.[19]

Thanks in part to UFC's public relations campaign and its aggressive lobbying, the Eisenhower Administration approved a plan crafted by the Central Intelligence Agency (CIA) to overthrow Árbenz. A group of rebels, funded and supported by the United States, was organized to "liberate" Guatemala from communist influence. The hand-picked leader of the rebel army was Colonel Carlos Castillo. Árbenz's supporters were no match for Castillo's well-armed militia. Within two weeks, the rebel armies prevailed, and Árbenz was forced into exile. Castillo became the country's new president. The former Guatemalan president was convinced that American corporations were instrumental in his demise:

> The United Fruit Company, in collaboration with the governing circles of the United States, is responsible for what is happening to us … In whose name have they carried out these barbaric acts? What is their banner? We know very well. They have used the pretext of anti-Communism. The truth is very different. The truth is to be found in the financial interests of the fruit company and the other U.S. monopolies which have invested great amounts of money in Latin America and fear that the example of Guatemala would be followed by other Latin countries.[20]

The UFC case represents an egregious ethical transgression because it undermines a basic right of the Guatemalan people. As we observed in Chapter 4, a person or group of persons has the right to political participation, which implies the right to national self-determination. Yet by helping to subvert a democratically elected government, UFC cooperated in depriving people of this right to national self-determination. It is not surprising that this coup led to anti-American demonstrations throughout Latin America. The overthrow of the Árbenz regime remains a focal point in Guatemala's unsettled history and still casts a dark shadow over corporate investment in Central and South America.

Not too long after these events, Union Minière, a prominent Belgian mining company founded in 1906, became enmeshed in a political quagmire in the Congo. Union Minière mined the abundant resources of the Katanga province in the southern part of the Congo. Its mining operations included minerals such as copper, cobalt, and uranium. The mining company employed over 20,000 workers, most of whom lived in a company town called Elizabethville. Like UFC, Union Minière regarded itself as a benevolent and paternalistic employer that provided jobs, security, and benefits for its workers.[21]

In June, 1960, the Congo was granted independence from Belgium. Belgium's former king, Leopold II, had established "one of the most violent and exploitative colonial regimes" in the late 1800s. The charismatic Patrice Lumumba was the first democratically elected Prime Minister of this new post-colonial nation. He was committed to a vision of a unified Congo functioning as a centralized state. In his inauguration speech, the new president vowed to "put an end to the humiliating slavery that force imposed on us … and to show the world what the black man can do when he works in freedom." But Western leaders, including U.S. President Eisenhower, were suspicious of Lumumba because of his communist leanings.[22]

In addition to Western opposition, Lumumba had to cope with severe political divisions within his own country. The leader of the mineral-rich Katanga province, Moise Tshombe, seceded several weeks after Lumumba's inauguration. Tshombe sensed an opportunity and declared this secession in order to advance his own political agenda. He was far more sympathetic to Belgium's corporate interests and to companies like Union Minière. The company worried about the anti-colonialist tone of Lumumba's heated rhetoric. Consequently, Union Minière executives enthusiastically endorsed this secession as a means of protecting themselves from the uncertain political developments in this country. The company paid its substantial taxes and duties (1.2 billion Belgian francs) to the Katanga regime. Union Minière's monetary and political support for Tshombe gave that regime resources and credibility. Union Minière also provided funding for a Katanga delegation in Belgium to enhance the fledgling regime's status, and even made some efforts to fund and support the military forces of Katanga. The company always insisted, however, that it was not meddling in the internal affairs of the Congo.[23]

Thanks in part to the financial support of Union Minière, the Katanga secession gained traction, and Lumumba soon found himself without enough resources to quash this rebellion. He sought the help of the United Nations, but its leader, Dag Hammarskjold, worried about his socialist pedigree, turned him down. Twelve weeks after he became president, Lumumba was deposed in a coup, and in January 1961 he was assassinated. While Union Minière was not directly involved in these events there is some evidence that Western governments, including Belgium and the United States, orchestrated the assassination plot behind the scenes. The secession attempt ended after Lumumba's death, but when Mobutu seized power in 1965 he nationalized Union Minière's properties as part of a strategy to consolidate his power by reducing the risk of another secession in this region, which contained the huge asset of this Belgian company's mining empire.[24]

While Union Minière's interference is perhaps less egregious than UFC's, there is little doubt that the multinational went too far in attempting to protect its vulnerable assets in this volatile African country. Union Minière had little acumen for dealing with political matters. The company was simply "bewildered by the pace of events, and had little experience in other countries to provide perspective."[25] As a consequence, its political maneuvers and neocolonialism backfired, and its "empire" in the Congo was lost.

The third case involves the International Telephone and Telegraph Corporation (ITT) conspiracy to overthrow the Allende regime in Chile. ITT, which began operating in 1920, quickly became a major international provider of telephone switching equipment and telecommunications services during the pre-war years. Like IBM, ITT apparently saw no ethical problems in doing business with the Nazi regime. It supplied communications equipment to the German armies through its subsidiary, Focke-Wulf, and did so even for a short time after the United States entered the war.[26] From 1960 to 1977, under the leadership of Harold Geneen, ITT became a diversified conglomerate, acquiring more than 350 companies. The portfolio of businesses included Sheraton hotels, Avis Rent-a-Car, and Hartford Insurance. Thanks to Geneen's aggressive management, ITT grew into a powerful global corporation with $17 billion in sales.

One of ITT's many foreign-owned properties was Chitelco, the Chilean Telephone Company. ITT had a 70% interest in this company, while the remaining 30% was held by the Chilean Development Corporation. The estimated value of ITT's investment was about $153 million. When Marxist candidate Salvador Allende Gossens was elected president of Chile in October 1970, ITT knew that its property was in danger. Allende had campaigned on a platform calling for the expropriation of American businesses. In September, 1971, Allende, true to his word, took possession of Chilteco. Like UFC, ITT sought to use its political influence to protect itself against Allende.

Prior to Allende's election, ITT had offered over $1 million to the CIA to support opposition candidates such as the conservative leader, Jorge Alessandri. The CIA rejected ITT's offer. But the company still found a way to contribute $350,000 to the Alessandri campaign. ITT also supported a right-wing newspaper known as *El Mercurio* by means of increased advertising. The aim was to prop up revenues for the paper and boost the circulation of its anti-Allende editorials throughout Chile and the rest of Latin America. Those editorials were sometimes planted by the CIA. In 1970, Geneen and others at ITT considered a plan proposed by the CIA to create "economic chaos" in Chile, but rejected that plan as unworkable. After ITT's property was expropriated by the Allende government, ITT pressured the Nixon Administration to take some sort of covert action against this socialist regime. William Merriam, head of ITT's Washington Office, proposed another plan to U.S. officials on behalf of the company to "accelerate economic chaos" in Chile with the hope of destabilizing the regime. That plan, which proposed specific measures such as loan restrictions, delaying purchases, using American copper instead of buying from Chile, was never implemented by the Nixon Administration.[27]

In September, 1973 a coup led by General Augusto Pinochet succeeded in overthrowing the Allende regime. The CIA was informed of the coup but took no part in the overthrow of the government. Similarly, ITT was not involved in this coup in any way, but the company had sought to persuade the U.S. government and the

CIA to manipulate the outcome of the Chilean election, both before and after that election took place.[28]

All of these unfortunate cases exemplify the worst apprehensions and suspicions about the abuse of power by large multinational corporations, which are willing to go to great lengths to retain their assets within a host country. The multinational corporation as a political actor on the global stage suddenly became a frightening prospect for those who were already nervous about the excesses of corporate power.[29] Even more frightening was the likelihood of an umbilical connection between multinationals and the U.S. federal government. The rogue political activities of ITT and UFC, which were aimed at overthrowing democratically elected governments, cannot be morally justified because they erode the sovereignty of these weaker nations and interfere with the will of the people who have freely chosen their own form of governance.

The key lesson is that multinationals should avoid such overt involvement in political affairs, and they should not attempt to influence political events without scrupulous consideration of a country's common good. And the preservation of human rights along with the public order are basic components of that common good. A company like Union Minière is entitled to protect its valid property rights by vigorously petitioning the local government for justice or by seeking the peaceful intervention of its home government. But it cannot use unjust means, such as support for a secession or rebellion, to achieve this end. Like Árbenz, Lumumba was a democratically elected leader, and through its material support for the secession, Union Minière helped to undermine that election along with the right of the Congolese people to national self-determination. The Katanga secession declared by the opportunistic Tshombe was orchestrated for his own political gain. It did not serve the country's common good, understood in the Aristotelian sense as the common advantage which contributes to the "living well" of all the citizens who are joined together in a political community.[30] Therefore, this rebellion should not have been endorsed by Union Minière, even though the Tshombe regime was more responsive to its economic interests.

In response to the intrusive political engagement of Union Minière, UFC, and ITT, multinational corporations moved to the polar opposite position: a principle of strict "non-involvement" in a country's social or political affairs. Companies vowed to respect national political sovereignty and not to meddle in internal politics. Royal Dutch Shell, for example, adopted "non-involvement" as one of its core values, and relied on this principle to defend some of its actions in Nigeria. To some extent, these multinationals took the advice of Milton Friedman, who urges corporations to eschew the realm of politics where they have no competence.

However, a philosophy of unconditional political neutrality is unrealistic. First, no corporation can conduct business in any country in a purely apolitical manner. It must submit to established government regulations and interact with government and local officials. It has a right to lobby policy makers in good faith on behalf of its own legitimate economic interests. Second, a stance of neutrality on moral and social issues has negative ethical implications, especially if it becomes a means of deflecting one's moral obligations. Multinational corporations have two fundamental duties: they should never deprive people of their rights, and in some situations they must be held accountable for safeguarding those rights when threatened by others. The former obligation also means that they must not cooperate in the deprivation of basic rights.

This moral duty to respect and protect rights implies a certain degree of political engagement, such as refusing to obey unjust laws that violate basic rights. The critical question is how to determine the correct balance between too much or too little activism, and how to decide which forms of activism are morally and politically appropriate. Activism oriented toward the protection of rights for the common good is morally acceptable, but, absent the most exigent circumstances, activism that aims to change the state's identity from one form of government to another or to tendentiously take sides in internal political conflict is presumptively unacceptable.

Divestment decisions

Corporations must sometimes consider the need for disinvestment when a host country is involved in human rights violations or other reprehensible activities. Disinvestment is one form of "divestment," which can be broadly defined as economic disengagement on moral grounds. This disengagement is meant to convey disapproval for certain policies within a host country. Divestment can include selling off the shares of companies which do business under these questionable conditions. Divestment, which can also include decisions about avoiding collusion with nefarious regimes, is the broad concept that will be the axis of discussion in this section.[31]

There are two conditions under which divestment should be considered. The first is when a country's leaders are corrupt, repressive, and unjust to their own people. Perhaps these leaders acquire great personal wealth at the expense of their citizens or divert foreign aid into their own pockets. The second is when the whole social system might be corrupt, rife with unjust and repressive laws along with systematic human rights abuses.[32]

The most drastic form of economic disengagement is disinvestment, that is, exiting an operation in a foreign country purely on moral grounds and foreclosing future investment until the situation is resolved. In the early 1980s many European and U.S. companies abandoned South Africa over its racist apartheid policies. Similarly, in the late 1990s companies left Burma (Myanmar) because of the repressive and anti-democratic policies of the ruling military junta.

But economic disengagement is not always so extreme and sometimes it means refusing to collude with a corrupt regime. For example, government bonds are bought and sold every day. But what if the seller is the Venezuelan government, which has been squeezing imports of necessities like food and medicine in order to make debt payments? The issue came into focus when the Goldman Sachs Group's investment division bought bonds held by the country's central bank. Despite the risk, the 24% yield on these bonds makes them very attractive. But should investment banks like Goldman Sachs purchase these bonds when the controversial Venezuelan regime of Nicolas Maduro is electing to pay interest on debt rather than feed the people? The moral calculus in this case is particularly complex. Without banks to purchase the bonds, yields will go even higher, thereby making it harder for the government to borrow. In the case of default, creditors could seize oil shipments and cut off the country's primary source of revenues. On the other hand, isn't it unethical to profit from this country's humanitarian crisis by purchasing these high-yielding bonds?[33]

Another contentious case is Iran. Many countries, including the United States, imposed sanctions on Iran because of alleged human rights abuses and the country's close ties to terrorist organizations. Yet Iran is a promising market of eighty million people. When sanctions were lifted in 2016 in exchange for restrictions on Tehran's nuclear weapons program, Asian and European firms moved in, but U.S firms remained cautious. One exception was Boeing. In 2017, Boeing negotiated a deal with the Iranian government for the sale of sixty of its most popular jets to an Iranian airline. But critics of the deal have pointed out that despite the lifting of official sanctions, Boeing should refrain from selling aircraft to Iran. Iran remains a staunch ally of Syria, which is a notorious abuser of human rights. A U.S. congressman observed that Boeing's deal with Iran was announced the same day Syria was credibly accused of using chemical weapons against some of its citizens. There are also concerns about ongoing human rights abuses within Iran and the role of Iran's powerful Revolutionary Guard Corps, a hardline paramilitary force with members who have wide and sometimes opaque economic interests. The Trump Administration re-imposed sanctions on Iran, but when those are lifted U.S. firms will have to decide whether to invest in this country despite its troubling policies and political alliances.[34]

From a practical viewpoint, companies have three broad options for making disinvestment decisions. The first option is unrestricted engagement in countries, even where there are systemic human rights violations and oppressive policies. This policy option is often supported by cultural relativism, a willingness to follow local norms in its business conduct. Theoretical support also comes from ethical egoism that emphasizes the need for a corporation to follow its economic self-interest without violating the rule of law.[35]

Second, a multinational could opt for a strategy of constructive engagement. This solution is usually justified by utilitarian reasoning that demonstrates how continued investment will optimize consequences for all parties involved and further social development for the country in question. Critics of this solution have underscored the ambiguity of "constructive engagement." Is it enough for companies to dialogue over questionable practices and perhaps coordinate industry support to oppose rights abuses? Or should this "engagement" also include a substantial contribution to social development in order to offset some of the rights-abuses? Despite these legitimate questions, there may be merit in some circumstances to a strategy based on engagement of political and cultural diversity.[36]

The final option is principled non-engagement. In this case a company is probably guided by core values that it refuses to compromise in any foreign situation. Rather than ethical egoism or utilitarianism, the ethical orientation for such a strategy of voluntary withdrawal and deferment of direct investment is an uncompromising commitment to a set of universally binding moral norms that could be expressed as natural rights or as hypernorms. Companies which choose this option refuse to cooperate in any way, even remotely, in human rights violations.[37]

Moderate universalism, which favors a fairly thick set of rights, implies that disinvestment must become a serious option when these rights are consistently and blatantly abused by a host government. Of course, companies must strive to tolerate cultural differences but they must do so in a way that does not accommodate injustice and systemic corruption. Before we specifically delineate the circumstances that should warrant withdrawal, we consider the case of business investment in Myanmar where companies have been forced to make hard choices about divestment.

Doing business in Myanmar

The American oil and gas company, Unocal, was founded in California in 1890. After decades of steady but modest growth the company ran into financial problems in the 1980s, as it attempted to compete with its bigger competitors like Exxon and Texaco. In its effort to replenish oil and gas reserves and cultivate new opportunities, Unocal expanded its global presence. The company had just begun to focus its attention on South East Asia when it faced a major divestment decision. The decision involved the country of Burma, also known as Myanmar, located in Southeast Asia. In the mid-1990s Unocal entered into a joint venture with the state-owned Myanmar Oil and Gas Enterprise (MOGE), closely linked to the country's military leaders. Also included in this venture was the French energy company, Total SE, and PTT, the energy company of Thailand. Unocal's stake in the $1 billion project was 28%. The objective of this joint venture was the extraction of natural gas from the Yadana gas field located off the coast of Burma. The pipeline from the field would supply gas for the domestic market and for export to Thailand. The low risk project has generated over $500 million of revenues per year since it became operational in 2000.[38]

Burma, now known as Myanmar, gained its independence from the United Kingdom in 1948, and occupies a vital geostrategic position, which should have made it a prosperous country. However, Burma could never fully live up to its economic potential. There has been sporadic civil unrest since 1948, and the country's "Burmese Way to Socialism" is one of the root causes of its dysfunctional economy. From 1988, Burma has been run by a military junta known as the State Law and Order Restoration Council (SLORC). The SLORC nullified the democratic elections held in 1990 and placed the leader of the opposition party, Aung San Suu Kyi, under house arrest. The autocratic SLORC ruled with an iron fist, closing down universities and forbidding any public gatherings for the sake of securing public order. The SLORC ended the Burmese Way to Socialism and began to welcome private enterprise and foreign investment. However, the effort to reboot the sluggish economy was not a success.[39]

This poor economic performance accounts for the importance of Yadana, described as "the one project that really matters to the military junta."[40] But the Yadana pipeline project was the source of fierce criticism by human rights advocates for a number of reasons. Aside from the environmental issues, the SLORC had been accused of human rights violations such as the use of forced labor to build roads, a railway, and other supporting infrastructure in the pipeline areas. The SLORC had also been credibly accused of forcefully relocating large segments of the civilian population in the area to make way for the pipeline and production operations that supplemented the offshore drilling operations. The troops that protected the pipeline construction used brutal tactics, including kidnapping and torture, to deal with sabotage or any subversive activities.

These human rights violations were not confined to the Burmese villages that were scattered along the route of the pipeline. Rather, human rights violations were pervasive throughout all of Burma. The Burmese government consistently relied on forced labor to build up its roads and weak infrastructure and it continued to suppress free speech and punish dissenters. There was even military conscription of children. No attention was paid to securing justice through procedural rights such as a fair trial and due process.[41]

As foreign governments watched this display of military aggression, some took decisive action. In 1997, the United States banned future investment in the country, but it did not compel multinationals that had already invested to withdraw. The European Union removed Myanmar's preferential trade status, and in 2000 the United Kingdom's Foreign Office demanded that Premier Oil cease doing business in Burma. Other countries were not keen on imposing penalties, and the demand for further sanctions and economic isolation never achieved multilateral consensus.

In the midst of this evolving controversy companies were forced to decide about whether to disinvest. U.S. foreign investment in Burma was sizable at the time, estimated at just over $6 billion. As the abuses worsened with no end in sight, many companies such as Apple Computer Company, PepsiCo, Levi Strauss, and J. Crew chose to leave. Other companies including Deutsche Telecom, Siemens, ARCO, British Petroleum, and Acer chose to stay.[42] Both Total and Unocal (later acquired by Chevron) also chose to stay and to persevere with the Yadana project. By 2000, construction was complete, and natural gas began flowing through the pipelines into Burma and Thailand. Criticism subsided as NGOs and other rights groups turned their attention to other hot spots around the globe.

Both companies defended their decision to remain by vehemently denying that they sanctioned any human rights abuses. But critics pointed out their tacit approval by virtue of their ongoing participation in the joint venture with the MOGE, which was closely tied to the government. Both Total and Unocal benefited from those human rights abuses since they made money from the pipeline. They were the beneficiaries of the infrastructure, the roads and railway, built for Yadana with forced labor. They benefited from the SLORC's heavy-handed pipeline security, which minimized sabotage and other disruptions. Moreover, Total and Unocal provided state-of-the-art technology and know-how that enabled the Burmese military regime to generate much needed capital and thereby sustain its power. And their continued presence in Burma helped the military government retain some residue of credibility during the crisis precipitated by corporate departures in the late 1990s.[43]

A decade later, things began to change dramatically in Myanmar. The new president, Thein Sein, instituted democratic reforms in 2011, and the country now aspired to "open democracy." Aung San Suu Kyi was released from house arrest and served as president of the National League for Democracy (NLD) party. The country's leaders relaxed their tight grip on the media. Burma was no longer a pariah state in the eyes of the world. The country's dire economic straits that resulted from failed economic policies of the junta appeared to be the basis for this change of direction.[44]

In 2015, Aung San Suu Kyi and the NLD won enough seats in the country's first truly free election in many decades to form a government. Kyi could not be named president due to a constitutional rule that forbade anyone from holding the office of the presidency who had foreign family members (she had been married to a British citizen). But she was the de facto leader of her party, which looked to her for guidance and inspiration The NLD sought to capitalize on reforms and re-build the economy by opening up further to foreign businesses.[45]

But turmoil erupted in Burma again in 2017 when the Burmese military initiated a counterinsurgency campaign against the Rohingya Muslim minority. This violent, disproportionate response was triggered by an attack on three police posts. By 2018, the Burmese military forced 700,000 refugees to flee across the border into Bangladesh. The French humanitarian agency *Médecins Sans Frontières* estimated that at least 6,700 Rohingya men, women, and children were slaughtered in their villages. The ongoing repression of this Muslim minority has been portrayed in the media as an epic humanitarian crisis. Burma's commander-in-chief insisted that refugees would be detained indefinitely in Bangladesh and prevented from renewed "Islamic aggression."[46]

Aung San Suu Kyi defended the military forces that had once persecuted her. She denied credible reports of atrocities by Burma's military, even though outside observers continued to accuse Burma of genocide. Protecting minority rights among Burma's Buddhist majority was an unpopular position in the country and she aligned herself with the majority. When this violence against the Rohingya was exposed, Suu Kyi claimed that she was not a human rights activist but a politician.[47] Part of Suu Kyi's motivation was her desire for a stronger alliance with the country's powerful military leaders, although this détente never happened. According to Human Rights Watch, "she failed a great moral test by covering up the military's atrocities against the Rohingya."[48]

Things in Myanmar took a more dramatic turn for the worse in 2021 when the military, known as the Tatmadaw, once again seized control of the government.

In November 2020, Suu Kyi's party (NLD) won a big victory over the Union Solidarity and Development Party, a proxy for the Tatmadaw. The military alleged that there was election fraud and before Parliament was due to convene it staged a coup. The country's short era of democratic rule rapidly unraveled, as the country returned to full military rule. Party leaders of the NLD, including Suu Kyi, were once again put under house arrest. The military claims that they can reverse Myanmar's dysfunctional economy, but their poor track record does not inspire much hope.[49]

When Myanmar opened to the West in 2011, many thought this would be an exciting new market for European and American firms. Some companies recognized its economic promise – low wages, a growing middle class, and many self-made entrepreneurs detached from the crony capitalism of the old regime. From 2017 through 2020 the garment sector had boomed, with a big investment coming from Asian countries. Western companies, on the other hand, did not make the financial commitment that was anticipated due to a difficult regulatory environment. Nonetheless, clothing brands such as Sweden's Hermes & Mauritz and Italy's Benneton Group source their garments from Myanmar.[50]

Those companies that invested in Myanmar after its transition to a more democratic government now faced a new challenge. Should they continue to do business in Myanmar and preserve those jobs that are helping Myanmar citizens to escape from poverty? Or should they divest and abandon their investment to protest the ongoing repression of the Rohingya minority and the military takeover of the government? Renewed attention has been focused on the energy giants, Chevron and Total SE, which continue to profit from the Yadana pipeline. They are under pressure to stop transferring revenues to their state-owned partner MOGE and to stop paying taxes and royalties to the military government, which amount to over $120 million a year. The pipeline is one of the military's primary revenue streams. The U.S. State Department urged companies like Chevron to look at their investments and "reconsider them as a means of denying the military the financial support it needs to sustain itself against the will of the people."[51]

The condition of business principle

There is no conclusive evidence to affirm that Myanmar changed its ways in 2011 because of the disinvestment of responsible corporations such as PepsiCo, Amoco, and Levi-Strauss. Nonetheless, a plausible case can be made that this was a contributing factor to the country's growing economic chaos, and that chaos led to the dramatic reforms of the Thein Sein regime. Consequentialist reasoning, therefore, might be a promising avenue for the ethical analysis of disinvestment as an effective vehicle to induce social changes. When there is severe injustice, companies should disinvest in order to bring about a greater aggregate social good.

However, a stronger case can be put forth for disinvestment than one based purely on utilitarian grounds. Consequentialism is ultimately indeterminate, since it is so difficult to definitively prove that multilateral disinvestment and trade sanctions will lead to a certain result. But even if one cannot assure a good result there are non-consequentialist reasons why transacting business with a country that is based on a mutual advantage is morally unacceptable under certain conditions. What are those conditions and how do responsible multinational enterprises determine which regimes should be avoided in a world of ethical pluralism and cultural diversity?

As a guideline for the multinationals immersed in these situations, Donaldson proposes a condition of business principle that is predicated on the violation of human rights. The violation of basic rights causes great harm and multinationals should not collude in the deprivation of those rights. Of course, rights violations occur to some extent in every country. The United States, a country with a reasonably strong record of respecting human rights, was accused of violating privacy rights by passing the Patriot Act after the terrorist attack on the World Trade Center on September 11, 2001. Hence it is more realistic to argue that a country must be a *systematic violator of basic human rights* before it is subject to trade sanctions or other forms of economic disengagement. These right include the right to life and health, the right to own property, and the right to be free from slavery and torture. Recall that these fundamental rights, which are rooted in our common humanity, were defended as necessary conditions of human flourishing. Although there is some room for a culturally informed interpretation of how to specify and properly limit some of these rights (like free speech), there comes a point where such limits become unreasonable if they virtually nullify the right in question.

The general moral principle at stake is that one must refrain from harming others but also not help another party (even indirectly) to harm others. It is immoral, therefore, to assist a corrupt government in violating the rights of its citizens. The evil of such cooperation is compounded when the cooperating agent also benefits as a consequence of these activities that violate rights. There may be some circumstances where business transactions do not benefit rights violators but actually cause them some harm. If a Western news organization were able to penetrate into Myanmar and operate an underground newspaper critical of the military regime, the continuation of such an enterprise would be fully justified. Also, an exception must be made for the genuine possibility of a moral catastrophe that might ensue if a company stopped trade or terminated its investment. In virtually all cases of trade sanctions and disinvestment some innocent people will be harmed to some degree. But significant harm to an appreciable group of innocents should validate an exception. For example, if a drug company like Merck were to depart Myanmar and leave people without life-preserving medicines, its departure could lead to great suffering end even death. Under these conditions, the company should obviously remain in the country. This assumes that Merck determines in good faith that no other domestic or foreign companies can fill the void left by its absence.

With these critical exceptions in mind, we offer this modified version of Donaldson's condition of business principle:

> *Ceteris paribus*, business transactions of company X with country Y are morally impermissible when Y is a systematic violator of fundamental human rights, unless those transactions actually discourage the violation of rights, harm country Y in consequence of its rights-violating activity, or the termination of these transactions would cause a moral catastrophe or severe injury to innocent people.[52]

The exemptions from the condition of business principle must be carefully applied. When a business departs a country some harm is done because people are deprived of its products. But only something "catastrophic" such as the deprivation of life-saving medicine justifies collusion with a rights-violating regime. The general principle is that it is unjust to transact business within corrupt regimes that systematically violate the human rights of their innocent citizens. These transactions presuppose a mutual advantage between the multinational and the host country, and multinational corporations should not promote or support such an improper advantage.

The exemplary case for divestment in accordance with this principle is South Africa. In 1948 the National Party in South Africa, dominated by white Afrikaners, instituted a system of "apartheid," a formalized system of racial segregation. Black political movements such as the African National Congress (ANC) were suppressed, and all schools, restaurants, restrooms, dining halls, and public gathering places were segregated. Blacks, who represented 83% of the population, could only own land in their homelands, areas known as the "native reserves," which comprised only 13% of South Africa's land surface. Apartheid laws banned blacks from holding skilled or managerial jobs if those jobs gave them any authority over whites. Despite efforts at constructive engagement by means of the Sullivan Principles, which committed corporations through their actions and public statements to work for reform, the main pillars of apartheid could not be demolished. As a result, the vast majority of corporations doing business in South Africa came to the conclusion that because of these repressive laws and systematic rights abuses they had no choice but to exit.

While the condition of business principle provides a useful compass for companies faced with tough disinvestment decisions, there are sometimes complications and mitigating factors. Consider the case of Chevron in Myanmar. It would be relatively easy and risk-free for retail companies like PepsiCo to pull out of Myanmar. But how easy would it be for Chevron to disengage and walk away from its investment in the Yadana pipeline? There is certainly good grounds for taking this action. The taxes paid by Chevron and its partners support a repressive military junta that systematically suppresses the rights of Myanmar's citizens. Denial of this revenue stream would definitely damage the Myanmar government. But if Chevron did not pay its taxes in protest, it stands in breach of contract, which could put its local employees at risk of criminal charges and imprisonment. Chevron's departure could also mean that the pipeline would be shut down at least temporarily. Yadana, which supplies half the electricity for Myanmar's largest city of Yangon, is a mature field that requires maintenance by experienced Chevron workers to sustain its future production. It is much more difficult for companies supplying essential products to disengage from this country, especially when those products are delivered through a complex infrastructure or supply chain. Prudent companies will need to weigh the hardships imposed on people because of their departure against the obligation to avoid complicity in human rights abuses through their material support of a corrupt regime.[53]

Case study: Disney and the Uighur Muslims

In March 2020, Disney, the famed entertainment conglomerate, premiered a move called *Mulan*. This was the first Disney-branded film to include an all-Asian cast. *Mulan* is a remake of a twenty-two-year-old animated movie, and it cost the studio over $200 million to produce. The live-action movie is based on the "Ballad of Mulan," a folk tale about a woman who disguises herself as a man to go to war in place of her ailing father. After twelve years at war, Mulan returns to her Chinese village along with her comrades who are stunned to learn that she is a woman.[54]

Some of the movie was filmed in Xinjiang, a region in the western part of China that is home to the Uighurs, a Muslim, Turkic-speaking, ethnic minority. There is ample evidence of a government-directed indoctrination campaign against this minority group. About one million people (one in ten Uighurs) have been put into indoctrination camps where they have been compelled to disavow extremism along with belief in God. In this gulag, they are forcefully taught to put their faith in "Xi Jinping Thought" rather than the Koran. They are chosen for this "training" because of habits such as praying too often to Allah or exhibiting too much enthusiasm for their Turkic culture. There is also evidence that hundreds of thousands of children have been temporarily displaced into boarding schools where they learn this "thought" of the Chinese leader, and where they are punished for speaking their own language.[55]

Several countries have rebuked China for this arbitrary round up of the Uighurs, but there has been little action taken against the Chinese government. China's economic power has helped it avoid a severe moral censure. The Chinese government has rebuffed any international criticism of the situation in Xinjiang by claiming that the internment camps are part of a counter-terrorism strategy. They characterize these camps as job-training centers that are needed to curtail Islamic extremism. Their efforts are described as "transformation through education." But former detainees have described a "ruthless and coercive environment" that is laced with "physical and verbal abuse." Human rights activists have referred to the camps as "the worst collective human rights abuse in China in decades."[56]

The earliest documented case of these internment camps was in 2013 in the area of Turpan where the landscape is especially rugged. In 2016, a former deputy party secretary in Xinjiang inspected the "centralized re-education de-extremefication work" being done in one large camp. His approval of this "prototype" camp set the stage for the government's expanded crackdown of the Uighurs in 2017, when it opened many more detention camps in the Turpan region.[57]

Production for *Mulan* began in 2018, a year after the expansion of the detention camps. In the movie's credits, Disney thanked multiple government entities in Xinjiang, including the Turpan Public Security Bureau. This bureau consists of Chinese policemen (and women) who were primarily responsible for displacing the Uighurs from their homes into the "re-education" camps. The credits imply Disney's partnership or collaboration with the authorities in Xinjiang, but the details of that collaboration are unclear.[58]

Mulan was released in September 2020 in China where it topped China's box office for several weeks. However, it was immediately criticized by human rights advocates and exiled Uighur activists. There were calls for a boycott of the film, which grew louder once the credits offering "special thanks" to the eight government agencies in Xingiang were publicized on social media. One congressman tweeted, "while the CCP [Chinese Communist Party] is committing crimes against humanity in Xinjiang, Disney thanked four of the propaganda departments that are lying to the world about these crimes. It also thanked the Turpan Public Security Bureau, which is on the entity list for its role in these atrocities."[59] Disney cancelled plans to release the movie in theaters in many other markets, including the U.S., although it is available through its streaming service.[60]

Study questions

1. Evaluate Disney's behavior in this case. Has the company done anything wrong? Does its collaboration with Xinjiang authorities amount to collusion with a corrupt regime or to "complicity" with the repression going on in this part of China?
2. Is the boycott just and fair, or an overreaction?

Conclusions

Political risks are plentiful in emerging economies, and sometimes multinational corporations are lured into political activism to protect their assets. While some forms of political activism are valid, companies like UFC and ITT had no business promoting regime change. Since these scandals, companies have embraced a non-interference policy, vowing to stay out of a host country's politics. This new ideology of political neutrality helped to allay fears about the abuse of corporate power. A sound non-interference policy, however, must be nuanced and reflect the fact that there is no apolitical way to do business in any country. Also, companies cannot use neutrality as an excuse to ignore the impairment of human rights that is a direct effect or a side effect of their business transactions.

The second issue treated in this chapter was divestment or economic disengagement on moral and social grounds. Under what conditions should companies refuse to do business in a country or liquidate their investment? The condition of business principle stipulates that a multinational should not do business in a country when that country is a systematic violator of fundamental human rights unless certain exceptions apply. This norm is premised on the general principle that moral agents, including corporations, cannot facilitate or cooperate with the objectively immoral actions of others. Such cooperation, especially in cases where human rights are being impeded, cannot serve an authentic common good. Above all, companies should not follow unjust laws in host countries when those laws require the abuse of the rights of workers and other stakeholders. Unjust law has no normative force.

This principle may be a reasonable guideline but it does not end the debate about disinvestment. Where does universalism end and pluralism begin? And how can these universal rights and rational standards be reconciled with the popular notion of strong pluralism or "multiculturalism"? According to Raz, the world's different cultures are all worthy of respect, and the implication is that cultures cannot be ranked in any way.[61] But aren't there circumstances where companies ought to defy cultural standards that endorse the denigration of human rights? The problem with multiculturalism or strong pluralism is that it becomes difficult to judge another culture or polity as morally inferior and an unfit partner for investment or trade.

Notes

1 See Emerson Pugh, *Building IBM: Shaping an Industry and its Technology* (Cambridge, MA: MIT Press, 1995).

2 The "Religion" column on the punch card was to be marked as followed: 1 for Protestant, 2 for Catholic, and 3 for Jew. See Götz Aly and Karl Heinz Roth, *Die reslose Erfassung: Volkszählen, Identifizieren, Aussondern im Nationalsozialismus* (Berlin: Rotbuch Verlag, 1984), 28–30. See also Edwin Black, *IBM and the Holocaust* (Washington, D.C.: Dialog Press, 2001), 52–58.

3 "German Fugitives Tell of Atrocities at Hands of Nazis," *New York Times*, March 20, 1933, 1; and "Reich Post Ministry is Sifting Out Jews," *New York Times*, June 11, 1933, 1.

4 Kevin Maney, *The Maverick and His Machine* (Hoboken, NJ: John Wiley & Sons, 2003), 216.

5 "10,000 Jews Flee Nazi Persecution," *New York Times*, April 15, 1933.

6 William Shirer, *The Rise and Fall of the Third Reich* (New York: Simon & Schuster, 1960), 203, 232–233. For a detailed timeline of events during the growth of Dehomag prior to World War II, consult Shirer's reliable book, especially pages 188–276.

7 "Briefing: The Global Oil Industry," *Economist*, August 3, 2013, 20–22.

8 Heidi Deringer and Jennifer Wang, "Note on Political Risk Analysis" (Boston, MA: Harvard Business School Publications, 1991). See also Schumpeter, "Beyond Economics," *Economist*, February 12, 2011, 75.

9 Schumpeter, "Beware of Sandstorms," *Economist*, June 20, 2015, 66. See also "Beyond Economics."

10 Andrew Stuttaford, "Tsar Power," *Wall Street Journal*, February 12, 2015, A13.

11 Anatoly Kurmanaev, "GM Quits Venezuela after Seizure," *Wall Street Journal*, April 21, 2017, B1, B11.

12 Dan Koeppel, *Banana: The Fate of the Fruit that Changed the World* (New York: Penguin Group, 2008), 74–76.

13 Koeppel, *Banana*, 75.

14 Cole Blasier, *The Hovering Giant: U.S. Responses to Revolutionary Change in Latin America* (Pittsburgh, PA: University of Pittsburgh Press, 1976), 56.

15 Stephen Schlesinger and Stephen Kinzer, *Bitter Fruit: The Untold Story of the America Coup in Guatemala* (New York: Anchor Books, 1983), 65–77.

16 Ibid., 75–76.

17 Koeppel, *Banana*, 127–128

18 Ibid.

19 Schlesinger and Kinzer, *Bitter Fruit*, 60–61. See also Thomas McCann, *An American Company: The Tragedy of United Fruit* (New York: Crown, 1976), 44.

20 Quoted in Schlesinger and Kinzer, *Bitter Fruit*, 199.

21 Daniel Litvin, *Empires of Profit* (New York: Texere, 2003), 159–169.

22 Caroline Elkins, "Who Killed Patrice Lumumba," *Wall Street Journal*, April 4, 2015, C6.

23 Litvin, *Empires of Profit*, 159–169.

24 Emmanuel Gerard and Bruce Kuklick, *Death in the Congo* (Cambridge, MA: Harvard University press, 2015), 33–45. See also Litvin, *Empires of Profit*, 166–168.

25 Crawford Young, *Politics in the Congo* (Princeton, NJ: Princeton University Press, 1965), 503.

26 Steven Wartick and Donnas Wood, *International Business and Society* (Oxford: Blackwell Publishers, 1998), 132–133.

27 "The International Telephone and Telegraph Company and Chile, 1970–1971," Committee on Foreign Relations, United States Senate by the Subcommittee on Multinational Corporations, June 21, 1973. See also John Prados, *Safe for Democracy: The Secret Wars of the CIA* (Chicago, IL: Ivan R. Dee, 2006), 407.

28 Central Intelligence Agency, "CIA Activities in Chile," released September 18, 2000. Available at www.cia.gov/library/reports/generalreports-1/chile.

29 The influential Harvard economist, John Kenneth Galbraith, had just published *The New Industrial State*, an admonition of excess corporate influence that called for the countervailing power of unions and government. See John Kenneth Galbraith, *The New Industrial State* (New York: Simon & Schuster, 1967).

30 Aristotle, *Politics*, 1278b.

31 Thomas Donaldson, *The Ethics of International Business* (Oxford: Oxford University Press, 1989), 129–132.

32 Richard De George, *Competing with Integrity in International Business* (New York: Oxford University Press, 1993), 121–125.

33 Matt Wirz and Carolyn Cui, "Venezuelan Bonds vs. Conscience," *Wall Street Journal*, June 19, 2017, B2.

34 Asa Fitch and Benoit Faucon, "Iran Lures Foreign Investors," *Wall Street Journal,* March 28, 2017, A1, A8. See also Robert Wall, Asa Fitch, and Doug Cameron, "Boeing Homes In on Iran Orders Despite Static," *Wall Street Journal,* April 5, 2017, B1–2.
35 John Schermerhorn, "Terms of Global Business Engagement in Ethically Challenging Environments," *Business Ethics Quarterly* 9 (3) (1999), 486–487.
36 Ibid.
37 Ibid.
38 Kenneth Vogel and Lara Jakes, "Lobbying Drive Started by Chevron to Head Off Sanctions on Myanmar," *New York Times,* April 23, 2021, A15. See also John Kline, *Ethics for International Business,* 2nd ed. (New York: Routledge, 2010), 65–68.
39 Thant Myint-U, *The Hidden History of Burma* (New York: W.W. Norton 2020), 43–44.
40 "Myanmar: Trouble in the Pipeline," *Economist,* January 18, 1997, 39.
41 Kline, *Ethics for International Business,* 66.
42 Schermerhorn, "Terms of Global Business Engagement," 488–490.
43 Debora Spar makes some of these observations in her notes to "The Burma Pipeline" (Boston, MA: Harvard Business School Publications, 1998).
44 "Special Report: Myanmar," *Economist,* May 25, 2013, 3–4.
45 Shibani Mahtani, "Democracy Champion's Rocky Political Path," *Wall Street Journal,* November 6, 2015, A1, A10.
46 Myint-U, *The Hidden History of Burma,* 240–250.
47 Jennifer Szalai, "A Country's Convulsions and Hopes," *New York Times,* November 20, 2019, D4.
48 Hannah Beech, "Was Myanmar's Leader a Hero, a Dupe? Neither It Turns Out," *New York Times,* February 2, 2021, A1, A10.
49 "Myanmar's Coup: Reversion to Type," *Economist,* February 6, 2021, 15–17. See also Niharika Mandhama, "Coup Draws Myanmar into U.S.-China Contest," *Wall Street Journal,* February 3, 2021, A1, A10.
50 Ibid. See also Szalai, "A Country's Convulsions and Hopes."
51 Jon Emont, "Myanmar Coup Hits Foreign Business," *Wall Street Journal,* March 22, 2021, A9. See also Vogel and Lara Jakes, "Lobbying Drive."
52 Thomas Donaldson, *The Ethics of International Business* (Oxford: Oxford University Press, 1989), 131–135. I am indebted to Donaldson's entire discussion of disinvestment in Chapter 8 of his book, 129–144.
53 Emont, "Myanmar Coup Hits Foreign Business," A9. See also Vogel and Lara Jakes, "Lobbying Drive."
54 "The Controversial Origins of the Story behind Mulan," *Time.* Available at time.com/5881064/muln-real-history.
55 "Torment of the Uyghurs," *Economist,* October 17, 2020, 9–10. See also "Human Rights in Xinjiang: Walk on By," *Economist,* June 27, 2020, 30–31.
56 Amy Qin and Edward Wong, "Calls Grow to Boycott Mulan over China's Treatment of Uighur Muslims," *New York Times,* September 9, 2020, A10. See also "Human Rights in Xinjiang," 31.
57 Qin and Wong, "Calls Grow to Boycott Mulan."
58 Ibid.
59 Quoted in Qin and Wong, "Calls Grow to Boycott Mulan."
60 R.T. Watson, "'Mulan' Tops China's Box Office," *Wall Street Journal,* September 14, 2020, B2. See also Chun Han Wong and R.T. Watson, "Disney Sparks Rights Groups' Ire over Xinjiang's 'Mulan' Role," *Wall Street Journal,* September 9, 2020, B1.
61 Joseph Raz, *Ethics in the Public Domain* (Oxford: Oxford University Press, 1995), 120.

Chapter 8

Patents, Big Pharma, and emerging markets

The reputation of the pharmaceutical industry has been badly tarnished over the past several decades. There has been a surge of public disapproval over high prices and excessive industry profits. The industry's regrettable image problems have not been helped by Hollywood. In a movie called *The Constant Gardener*, a rapacious multinational pharmaceutical company is conducting clinical trials of a dangerous drug in Kenya, where human life is expendable and hefty payoffs keep local officials subdued. This is fiction, of course, but some audiences and movie reviewers believed that the movie accurately reflected the dark side of the pharmaceutical industry. One prominent reviewer even praised this fictitious story as a "timely indictment of Big Pharma." The fact is that many drug trials are conducted in Africa. But this is where certain diseases tend to spread rapidly, so drug companies can get a better understanding of the drug's safety and efficacy when the product is tested there.[1]

To be sure, the pharmaceutical industry is constrained by crippling problems that include the withdrawal from the market of several high-profile drugs. There have been highly publicized safety crises such as Merck's arthritis drug, Vioxx, and the popular diabetes drug Avandia. Avandia, which allegedly contributes to cardiovascular problems, has been called "the worst drug safety crisis in our lifetime."[2] Drug companies have also been accused of concentrating on "me-too" drugs that provide little clinical benefit over existing medicine and of relying on acquisitions to compensate for the lack of innovation.[3]

The industry's image has been renewed in some measure due to its collaborative efforts to develop a coronavirus vaccine for the deadly pandemic. The successful quest for a vaccine has renewed the public's faith in the industry's capacity to innovate. In a race against the contagious virus, Pfizer and the biotech firm, Moderna, introduced vaccines in record time that were 90% effective. It helped that researchers already had a vaccine platform that was safe and effective against similar viruses.

DOI: 10.4324/9781003058427-8

As one Big Pharma executive said, "This is what a successful pharmaceutical industry can do."[4]

Yet, despite this heroic effort, the industry cannot escape controversy over its prices and profits. The problem of accessibility remains particularly acute in developing countries. Pharmaceutical products to treat chronic diseases like tuberculosis, cancer, and heart ailments are priced beyond the means of those populations. The problem is compounded to some degree by Trade Related Aspects of Intellectual Property Rights (TRIPS), which symbolizes the globalization of intellectual property rights. This regulation mandates the enforcement of intellectual property rights, including twenty-year patents, for all member nations of the World Trade Organization (WTO). Most developing countries have signed on to TRIPS to preserve their standing in the WTO, but critics claim that it undermines national sovereignty over the rules that regulate and stimulate innovation.

Countries in Africa as well as Brazil and India struggle to enhance the welfare of their citizens by making drugs affordable, safe, and effective. These countries also want to stimulate innovation and research for their respective disease profiles, which differ from the West. Malaria, Chagas disease, and dengue fever are not a high priority for Western drug companies. These two objectives are in tension, and patents are the primary source of that tension. But the story of drug patents is complex, full of paradoxes and conundrums.

A big part of that story is the ethical rationale for patents, the scope of patent protection, and the social justice issue of distributive equity. These interrelated issues are the main axis of discussion in this chapter. Life-preserving pharmaceutical products are a socially important good, but markets do not always distribute that good equitably. But should pharmaceutical companies try to resolve this inequitable distribution that occurs when poor patients cannot afford life-preserving drugs – because patents drive up the price? Also, should companies devote scarce R&D resources to neglected tropical diseases like malaria that affect impoverished populations? But before we consider these questions we begin with an overview of Big Pharma.

The global pharmaceutical industry

The term "Big Pharma" refers to the major Western pharmaceutical companies such as Pfizer and Merck in the United States, GlaxoSmithKline (GSK) in the UK, Novartis and Roche Holding Co. in Switzerland, Bayer in Germany, and Sanofi-Aventis in France. Johnson & Johnson is the largest global pharmaceutical corporation, with revenues of over $56 billion in 2020, followed by Pfizer, with revenues of $52 billion.

The industry has been consistently profitable during its long and sinuous history, which dates back to the end of the 19th century when "ethical" drugs of a fixed chemical constitution first appeared. Drug companies have strong profit margins: gross profit on branded drugs averages about 76%.[5] While past return on equity (ROE) has averaged over 25%, in recent years, average ROE has dropped to around

15%. But in 2019 several firms had an ROE well in excess of that number. Pfizer's ROE was 26% and Merck's around 21%.[6] The global pharmaceutical market is in excess of $1 trillion, with the United States accounting for almost $350 billion in annual sales, followed by Europe and Japan. These countries account for 85% of the world's pharmaceutical market. However, thanks to stagnant demand and mature markets, companies like Pfizer and GlaxoSmithKline are looking to emerging markets for growth.

Pharmaceutical companies have usually depended on a few "blockbuster" drugs (those with over $1 billion in global annual sales) like Lipitor, Cialis, and Viagra to drive profits and revenues. In order to contain costs and prevent holdup in supply chains or distribution channels, these companies have been vertically integrated, performing all value chain activities in house from research and development to manufacturing and marketing. This trend has begun to change in recent years, however, as companies now outsource some of their manufacturing and sales operations.

The biggest threat to Big Pharma continues to be the "patent cliff" and the proliferation of generic or off-patent products. Patents have expired on many blockbuster drugs, and this opens the way for generics to capture a big piece of the market. In response to the expiration of patents, drug companies sometimes resort to the problematic strategy of "evergreening," by making slight modifications in a drug's delivery means of dosage in an effort to make the drug eligible for a new patent.[7]

As companies like Pfizer and Merck face generic competition, their sales have declined. With fewer drugs in the pipeline, there is minimal opportunity to offset patent losses. Although billions have been spent on research, only a few blockbuster drugs have successfully come to market within the last decade. Some companies like GlaxoSmithKline have been hobbled by lackluster R&D. GSK's annualized economic return to R&D spending from 2007–2016 was a mere 3%.[8] However, global demand for the coronavirus vaccine will generate about $26 billion for Pfizer in 2021, and that demand will remain in force for at least several years to sustain protection as the virus circulates.[9]

To deal with industry threats and a dynamic marketplace, the pharmaceutical industry has consolidated and become more concentrated. Pharmaceutical companies continue to spend billions to buy biotech companies that concentrate on specialized areas of medicine. But companies are also more focused. Pfizer, for example, has spun off its off-patent or generic division, Upjohn, which merged with Mylan to become Viatris, one of the biggest global producers of generic drugs. Pfizer will refocus on high-margin prescription drugs instead of generics.[10]

This research-based industry is heavily regulated in virtually every country where drugs are developed, manufactured, and sold. The United States system has come to represent a regulatory paradigm for the industry that has been imitated and refined by other countries. China, for example, has closely aligned its regulatory system with the U.S. system. The first regulation on the books in America was the 1906 Wiley Act, which prohibited the mislabeling or misbranding of drugs by means of false or misleading information. Subsequent regulations have mandated safety and efficacy tests for all products before they can be released to the public. After preclinical tests there must be extensive clinical trials to verify safety, determine the right dosage, evaluate the drug's efficacy, and uncover side effects that might result from short- or long-term usage. The Food and Drug Administration (FDA) reviews these finding and gives final approval before a drug can be marketed and sold to the public.[11] It usually takes twelve or thirteen years for drugs to go through the cycle of testing and FDA approval. Thanks to heightened safety concerns raised by drugs like Vioxx and Avandia, drug trials are longer and larger, and hence more expensive. This higher economic risk makes a pharmaceutical company reluctant to start down the road of safety tests and clinical trials unless it is reasonably assured of success.[12]

While the industry has been dominated by American and European firms, there has been tremendous growth for firms in mature emerging markets such as China and India. The China drug market is $140 billion and industry experts predict that domestic pharmaceutical and biotech firms such as BeoGene will capture most of those sales.[13] India is the largest provider of generic drugs globally. The Indian pharmaceutical sector supplies over 50% of global demand for various vaccines, 40% of generic demand in the U.S., and 25% of all medicine in the UK. As a result, India enjoys a highly favorable position in the global pharmaceuticals sector. The country also has a large number of capable scientists and researchers, and this augurs well for future innovation.[14]

Sun Pharmaceuticals, with over $4 billion in revenues in fiscal 2019, is India's largest pharmaceutical company and the fifth largest supplier of specialty generic products in the world. Sun acquired the pharma giant Ranbaxy in 2014. Other major players include Cipla, established in 1935, Lupin, and Dr. Reddy's. Like Sun, Cipla is a major supplier of generics to global markets. It generated revenues of about $2.5 billion in fiscal 2020. The change in Indian patent law has made the environment more conducive for innovation and increased the growth prospects for these leading firms.[15]

Economics of pharmaceutical pricing and patents

A critical challenge for this industry is the escalating costs for research and development. The Center for Drug Development at Tufts University estimates that the average cost for developing a new drug is $2.6 billion. This sum includes $1.2 billion for the cost of capital required for R&D. The remaining $1.4 billion is the average R&D cost for a random selection of drugs multiplied by the risk factors for failure at any stage in the development process. This cost estimate takes into account the money spent by drug firms on many failed research efforts. The humanitarian organization, Doctors Without Borders, and several consumer groups, have criticized the Center's methodology for including the cost of failures. But the study's main author, Joseph DeMasi, defends the inclusion of costly drug failures "since real money is spent." He pointed out that fewer failures will lower the cost of drug development.[16]

Innovations are reducible to chemical formulae so they are information-based and public goods. This means that they can be copied through reverse engineering. Without protection, free riders would enter the market and, unburdened by any of their own research costs, force the price down close to the marginal cost of production, making it exceedingly difficult for the innovating firm to recover its investment. The prospect that another company could easily copy the drug after all of the innovators' efforts and investment would dissuade any firm from making the initial investment. Thus, some market intervention is necessary to prevent firms "from reaping where they have not sown."[17]

Therefore, from an economic perspective, patents are necessary to solve a market failure: the underproduction of public goods. Due to the substantial investment and risks, little medical innovation would occur in a free market system. Innovators would bear the costs of its failures, but they would not be able to profit from their product successes since they would be copied by free riders. The standard solution corrects this market failure through patents that give innovators a temporary monopoly on their innovation.[18] The patent allows companies to gain monopoly rents that motivate them to secure the capital necessary to commercialize innovations and bring them to the marketplace.[19]

Arguably, patents promote aggregate social welfare by encouraging ingenuity and investments in new technologies. But the introduction of patents for pharmaceutical products creates two market failures that arise because of lost mutually beneficial transactions between sellers and buyers. Since a patent is a limited monopoly, the patent holder can charge the profit-maximizing price, well above the marginal cost of production. In competitive markets, companies can enter the market and force down the price to where the marginal cost (or supply) curve intersects the demand curve, and this price is much lower than the profit maximizing price. Without competition, the patent holder can sell its products at the monopoly price and recover R&D and overhead expenses. But at that high price there is a reduction in the quantity purchased. Many people who cannot afford the drug are squeezed out of the market at the higher price. This expulsion of potential buyers creates the "exclusion problem" or "access problem." This is a serious situation when life-saving drugs are involved.[20]

Second, patents create an "availability problem." In this industry where marginal production costs are so low, expensive drugs generate fat profits. Since there is a direct correlation between the incentive to innovate and the price of the innovative product, the higher the price for a product the more incentive to invest R&D resources. Hence, there is little incentive to invest those resources for diseases that primarily affect people in low-income countries. The vast majority of people in those countries cannot afford to pay for the patented drugs that will cure or treat those diseases. As a result, pharmaceutical companies do not invest R&D in products that are "socially valuable" to poor or small populations. The long list of neglected diseases includes malaria, tuberculosis, Chagas disease, and dengue fever.[21]

There are also secondary costs associated with the patent system, including impediments to cumulative innovation along with foregone consumer surplus associated with economic rents. Patents can also encourage rent-seeking, if companies dissipate scarce resources in their quest for "buried treasure," such as a big research breakthrough and a blockbuster drug.[22] Given these costs, the objective of policy makers should be a balanced patent policy that prudently rewards technological innovation only when necessary.

Thus, patents are controversial, particularly in the health sector, because they are limited monopolies that generate economic rents, higher prices, and lower output. In the case of pharmaceutical products, lower output and high prices often means that life-preserving drugs will not be available to everyone who needs them. From a policy perspective, the goal of the patent system's exclusionary, output-restricting monopolies is to maximize the creation of innovations, including pharmaceutical products, by marginalizing free riders. The presumption is that "thick" property protection will give the innovator the incentive to invent, and provide a favorable environment for the acquisition of the complementary assets, capital, manufacturing, marketing and sales support, which are necessary in order to bring that invention to the marketplace.[23] But the social and economic costs of the patent system are quite high, especially for emerging economies.

The WTO's TRIPS accord

Western society's highly positive vision of thick and durable patents for pharmaceutical products is not in harmony with the experience of most developing countries, which have been quite skeptical of this policy tool. After India was given its independence from the British Empire, it conducted a review of the patent system it had inherited from the British and concluded that this system had failed "to stimulate inventions among Indians and to encourage the development and exploitation of new inventions."[24] Many other countries, including Brazil, Mexico, and Argentina, came to the same conclusion. Like India, they weakened their patent laws to make drugs more affordable and accessible. India's reconfigured patent system, passed in 1970, limited patent length to 5–7 years and allowed for the patenting of manufacturing processes but not the substance itself. The new patent law did not permit patents on imports – only locally manufactured products were patent-eligible. At the same time, it instituted a Drug Price Control Order (DPCO) that put a cap on prices for life-saving and essential drugs.

Big Pharma was dismayed over these developments and so was the U.S. government. At its insistence, intellectual property rights became a chief concern during the negotiations for the establishment of the World Trade Organization (WTO). In an effort to harmonize patent protection, the World Trade Organization introduced its Agreement on Trade Related Aspects of Intellectual Property Rights (TRIPS). The TRIPS accord is ostensibly designed to reduce distortions in international trade that often occur when property rights conflict between two trading nations. TRIPS consists of provisions protecting copyrights, trademarks, geographical indications, industrial designs, patents, and trade secrets. Since TRIPS went into effect in January 1995, some of the most controversial provisions of TRIPS have been those regarding patent protection. A central provision of this multilateral regulation requires that products and manufacturing processes be patentable for twenty years in all countries belonging to the WTO. According to Article 27, "patent rights shall be enjoyable without discrimination ... whether the products are imported or locally produced." Article 31 of TRIPS authorizes compulsory licensing under certain conditions. This means that with government approval a third party can copy a patented product without the consent of the patent holder. The conditions include cases of national emergency or "extreme urgency."[25]

TRIPS may be beneficial for the United States and Europe, but is it beneficial for countries like India and Brazil? Prior to TRIPS many developing countries had exempted pharmaceutical products from patentability, or, like India, offered only weak patent protection. Putting in place this "one-size-fits-all" system seems to make little sense since these countries are at different stages of economic development. Many argue that the case for a global intellectual property system is thin. As Drahos points out, there is a certain hypocrisy involved in obliging both the United States and Rwanda, the least-developed member of the WTO, to have the same patent protection for pharmaceutical products when Rwanda doesn't even have a research-based pharmaceutical industry.[26] In addition, countries cannot follow the model of Switzerland, which had no patent laws for a long time. The Swiss were able to copy foreign inventions and only when it had developed an indigenous base of innovation and research did it put patent laws into place. Yet, thanks to TRIPS, developing countries cannot take the same path as these developed economies, since they cannot take advantage of loose protections that speed the dissemination and assimilation of knowledge.[27] TRIPS raises many questions, but perhaps the most pressing is whether or not developing countries must be able to exclude life-preserving and essential medicines from patentability for the welfare of their citizens.

Some countries such as India seem quite ambivalent about their commitment to these globalized intellectual property rights. In 2005 the Indian Parliament ratified The Patents Amendment Act, which put the country's patent system in compliance with TRIPS. However, the country has broad criteria for compulsory licensing. Also, little noticed at the time was a provision that sets a higher bar for the approval of patents because it stipulates that patents will only be granted when products are more efficacious. According to Section 3(d) of the Indian patent law:

> Mere discovery of a new form of a known substance which does not result in the enhancement of the known efficacy of that substance or the mere discovery of any new property or new use for a known substance or of the mere use of a known process ... is not patentable.

Thus, you cannot patent new forms of a known substance or get a patent for new uses of a known substance that already has a patent or exists in the public domain.

These types of patents are routine in other countries, But, in India, companies can only patent new compounds or ones appreciably different (i.e., with more therapeutic benefits) from the original substance.

Accordingly, the Indian patent office has denied patents for products that are accepted in most other countries. For example, Novartis' application for Glivec was denied on grounds that the company did not demonstrate improved efficacy over earlier versions of this medicine. The company was accused of "evergreening," despite considerable evidence to the contrary.[28] Moreover, a number of patent rulings in India have backed generic producers. For example, in 2008, Bayer was awarded a patent for Nexavar, a kidney cancer drug. But in March 2012, India's patent controller concluded that Bayer had not made Nexavar "reasonably affordable" (the drug's cost was $5,000 per month), and had failed to provide enough of the drug to afflicted Indian citizens. The controller ordered an Indian company, Natco, to sell Nexavar for one-thirtieth of Bayer's price. Bayer will receive a 6% royalty. The controller also allowed Cipla to sell and market its generic version of Nexavar.[29]

A short time later, India's Intellectual Property Appellate Board revoked Roche's patent on Pegasys (a drug for Hepatitis C) after it was challenged by generic drug maker Wockhardt, Ltd. The Board claimed that the drug's invention was "obvious" and could be easily replicated. And in 2018 Novartis was engaged in another patent conflict, this time with Wockhardt, Ltd., which sought to launch a generic version of its blockbuster diabetes drug, Galvus. These cases and rulings underscore the country's lingering suspicions about TRIPS along with the obstacles multinationals still face in penetrating India's fast-growing market with their patented products.[30]

India's conflicts with Big Pharma raise some important questions. Has the country implemented TRIPS in a socially responsible way? Do its practices violate the spirit of TRIPS? And what will be the consequences for multinationals and foreign investment in India if the country continues on its current path?

Normative justifications for patents and intellectual property rights

How can pharmaceutical patents and other intellectual property rights be defended on purely normative grounds? The core of this defense is that these rights, like all property rights, are essential for a fair and just society. There is a strong rationale for rewarding innovative and creative work with substantive legal rights, which converts that work into a useful economic asset. At the same time, these exclusionary rights are permeated with limits and constraints. These limits mean that intellectual property rights, like patents, are subject to redistributive policies aimed at correcting any injustice caused by the granting of these exclusive rights.[31]

There are several normative theories suitable for the justification of intellectual property rights, but we will consider here only the two most prominent theoretical frameworks. First, according to the utilitarian paradigm, intellectual property rights are justified because they yield net gains in aggregate social welfare.[32] Those rights are necessary in order to maximize the production of innovative products and literary expression by providing authors, inventors, and other creators with the reward of an exclusive property right for their work. Without such a reward, which takes the form of the owner's right to exclude others from the use of the subject matter of that right, there will be fewer such creations or inventions. Absent this intellectual property protection, people will be more inclined to copy what has already been created rather than investing in the creation of new ideas or products.[33]

This version of utilitarianism known as "incentive theory" represents a classic *ex ante* justification of property rights that parallels the economic rationale for these rights. U.S. patent and copyright jurisprudence is based primarily on the conceptual foundation of utilitarian reasoning. According to one U.S. Supreme Court opinion, "the patent monopoly was not designated to secure to the inventor his natural right in his discoveries. Rather, it was a reward, an inducement to bring forth new knowledge."[34] The persistence of this incentive paradigm can also be attributed to the language of the U.S. Constitution, which suggests a causal relationship between an "exclusive Right" for an inventor's discoveries and the promotion of "the Progress of Science and the useful Arts."[35]

The philosopher, John Locke, on the other hand, claimed that property is a natural right and not a matter of economic pragmatism. According to the Lockean perspective, a person has a property right, that is, the right to exclude others, in his person, in his creative activity and labor, and therefore in the products of that labor. Thus, Locke relies on a labor theory of property justified by this thesis of self-ownership to demonstrate why these rights are warranted when someone adds value to something that was originally held in common. As Locke explains:

> Man has a Property in his own person. This no Body has any right to but himself. The Labor of his Body and the Work of his Hands we may say are properly his … Whatsoever then he removes out of the State that Nature had provided … he hath mixed his Labor with and joined to it something that is his own, and makes it his Property (II: §27).[36]

It logically follows that Locke's theory applies both to physical and intellectual property, creative works, and inventions, since production of those non-tangible goods also involves creative effort and labor.[37]

Through labor, someone privatizes and appropriates what was once held in common, since labor puts a distinction between an appropriated object and the commons by its transformation of that object into something useful. For example, if someone takes a piece of common, unusable land and through the sweat of his brow cultivates that land and converts it into something valuable and useful, that person has appropriated this land through his labor and deserves exclusive ownership. According to Locke, "As much land as a man tills, plants, improves, cultivates, and can use the product of, so much is his property. He, by his labor does, as it were, *enclose it from the common*" (II: §27; my emphasis). Private property, therefore, is a fusion of labor mingled with preexisting resources. According to Waldron, the "acquisitive action … is the act of laboring on the resource," by transforming it or improving it in some way to make it new and useful.[38]

Implicit in Locke's theory is the notion that property is deserved as a just return for the laborers' efforts, and taking the product of that labor would be an unjust enrichment. As Locke stipulates, one who takes the laborer's property desires the benefits of another's hard work, to which he has no right. While this notion of just deserts for one's efforts is reflected in Locke's general theory, it is important to underscore that a person is entitled to what he or she has worked on primarily because labor belongs to that person. The foundation of property is within the human person. I am justly entitled to the fruits of my labor because my labor has been "annexed" to those transformed common resources, and only secondarily because that labor is often difficult, time-consuming, and onerous (II: §32).

However, people should only appropriate property sufficient for their needs, so there are moral limits on what man can acquire through labor. Locke formulates this sufficiency proviso as follows: "Labor being the unquestionable Property of the Laborer, no man but he can have a right to what that is once joined to, *at least where there is enough and as good left in common for others*" (II: §27). Thus an intellectual property right is by no means absolute and cannot be compared with that subset of natural rights (such as the right to life or the right not to be tortured), which are absolute. On the contrary, property rights are subject to several limitations implied by the proviso to appropriate property while leaving "enough and as good' for others. As long as this proviso is satisfied, then the appropriation "does as good as take nothing at all" (II: §33). For intellectual property, this proviso implies that a property right apply only to the expression of ideas, and not the ideas themselves, so they can be used by others.

In contrast to Locke, some philosophers, like John Rawls, give less emphasis to individual property rights and more to the fair and equitable distribution of assets. Rawls argued that a just society will ensure that each citizen will "have an equal right to the most extensive system of basic liberties compatible with a similar system of liberty for all." Such a society will also arrange social and economic inequalities so that they work "to the greatest benefit of the least advantaged."[39] However, a broad property right is not among these basic liberties. Those liberties include the right to possess certain items of "private personal property," but not the right of "private property in productive assets."[40] According to Merges, "Rawls starts with egalitarian fairness and adjusts for property rights, in contrast to Locke …, who (roughly speaking) begins with property and then adjusts for collective fairness."[41] Unlike Locke, Rawls does not regard thick but limited property rights as essential for a just and fair society.

In summary, Locke's philosophy is a reminder that private property is a means to human well-being and that the person as laborer or entrepreneur has a right to exclude others from the unowned resources he has transformed through work and thereby appropriated. Of course, he also has a duty to the community to be prudent in what he appropriates and respect the needs of others. Despite the moral logic of limited property rights, they are frequently condemned as the source of injustice and inequities. In addition to the moderate criticism of philosophers like Rawls, they have been subject to more substantial critiques by Marxist philosophers who argue that intellectual property rights are a new form of feudalism that foster relationships of great inequality.[42]

A just society rewards innovators and creators with an exclusive property right as a matter of fairness, but it also limits those rights for the sake of distributive equity. The problem with the pharmaceutical industry has been a systemic failure to perceive the moral limits on its patents, even if those limits are not recognized by patent laws and policies.

Neglected diseases

This category of neglected diseases refers to those diseases that have been overlooked by Big Pharma because they chiefly affect the poorest countries of the world. Fortunately, there has also been an increased research emphasis on AIDS, and more attention has been paid to two of the most notorious neglected diseases: tuberculosis and malaria. More resources have been dedicated to these "big three" diseases, especially by private foundations, because of their higher mortality rate and public profile.[43] Tuberculosis is the world's most lethal infectious disease and a new vaccine developed by GSK represents a watershed moment in the fight against this disease. However, the vaccine has only a 50% efficacy rate, so there is still a need for something more effective.[44] Unlike the big three, most other neglected diseases have no one to champion their cause, and they are barely noticed by Western society and the pharmaceutical industry.

The most ignored diseases are found in tropical climates and so they are classified as neglected tropical diseases (NTDs). These NTDs have low mortality but high morbidity rates. NTDs include Buruli ulcer, Chagas disease (sleeping sickness), Chromoblastomycosis, Cysticercosis, dengue fever, dracunculiasis (Guinea worm disease), echinococcosis, and fascioliasis. Dengue, onchocerciasis (river blindness), and sleeping sickness are among those diseases that are transmitted by mosquitoes or flies and that easily spread from rural areas to urban slums. Dengue fever is now the leading cause of serious illness and death among children and adults in some Asian and Latin American countries. There is no specific treatment of dengue, but early detection and access to proper medical care lowers the fatality rate dramatically.[45]

These NTDs are found in 150 countries, and the primary NTD burden is concentrated in low income countries such as those in Africa, Asia, and Latin America. More than a billion people are infected with one of these diseases, and an additional two billion people are at risk from infection. Each year, about 185,000 people die as a result. Infections can cause severe disability, disfigurement, blindness, and malnutrition, and some unfortunate people are infected with multiple NTDs simultaneously. People living in rural areas as well as urban slums are most at risk since they lack access to clean water, decent housing, and good sanitation, which contribute to NTDs' prevalence and impact. Women and children are especially at risk of infection, since they often face impediments to accessing treatment. NTDs adversely impact economic development, hamper educational achievement and cognitive development, and reduce agricultural productivity and food security.

Progress has been made in tackling some of these catastrophic diseases, but according to the World Health Organization (WHO) drug companies need to do more to prevent and treat these diseases. GlaxoSmithKline, Novartis, and Sanofi are among the major drug companies that contribute medicine for these diseases. Merck, famous for its Mectizan drug for river blindness, is developing a children's formula of its drug to treat schistosomiasis, a parasitic worm disease which kills 280,000 per year in Africa. However, some diseases are still completely neglected, and there remains many obstacles in distributing the medicine and therapies that have already been developed. [46]

The gap between the health research and development (R&D) that is needed for neglected diseases and that which is undertaken was revealed twenty years ago. At that time, researchers at the Global Forum for Health Research (GFHR) convincingly demonstrated that less than 10% of global health research expenditure was spent on the health problems of developing countries, which then represented more than 90% of the world's burden of preventable mortality. This disparity became known as the "10/90-gap." Researchers at the GFHR determined that malaria, pneumonia, diarrhea, and tuberculosis, which together account for 21% of the global disease burden, received less than 1% of all public and private funding dedicated to health care research.[47] The nature of the 10/90-gap has changed in the last two decades. Fortunately, the overall global funding for health R&D has increased and there are many more and new types of actors involved in health R&D. However, even though the contours of the 10/90-gap have been modified, the gap itself has certainly not disappeared.[48]

This gap is a manifestation of the availability problem, the second distortion that results from the patent solution to the public goods problem. Drug companies have no incentive to work on treatments and therapies that people are unable to afford. However, it is morally unacceptable that so little funding is directed to drugs for medical conditions suffered by those with NTDs.[49] The more difficult question centers on the obligations of Big Pharma to rectify this problem and close the infamous gap. Do companies like Merck and Novartis have a moral obligation to invest a more than nominal proportion of their scarce R&D funds in neglected diseases of NTDs? Is such a commitment morally necessary, and categorically required of these organizations? Or would such an initiative be better classified as an "aspiration," something that is a supererogatory moral action, above and beyond moral duty?

It is always difficult to establish the demarcation between morally obligatory actions (the omission of which creates culpability) and morally good elective actions or policies. A full review of this question is beyond the scope of this chapter, but a few observations are in order. First, most Big Pharma firms have a modest social agenda and donate some funds and medicines for this cause. Sanofi Genzyme's HAND program (now discontinued) donated research resources to neglected diseases like Chagas and malaria. Because of their unique capabilities pharma corporations should concentrate their philanthropic efforts on NTDs even if other causes give them more publicity or engender more immediate good will. Second, given that human life and serious health issues are at stake and given the unique capabilities of Big Pharma, the plight of those who suffer and die from NTDs creates a moral demand for some type of response (that goes beyond token efforts) and should appeal, in its indisputable seriousness, to the conscience of these firms. These private property holders have a duty to help achieve distributive justice, and that duty becomes more compelling if no one else can conduct this research and there is real probability of success. However, companies must also consider the proportionality between the harm these victims of NTDs are likely to suffer and the impairment of future research that will result from uncompensated access to the medicines they develop.[50]

AIDS in Africa

The African AIDS crisis represents the classic case of the exclusion or access problem that is a side effect of patent protection. The Acquired Immune Deficiency Syndrome disease known as AIDS ravaged segments of the United States population in the 1980s. AIDS was a mystery disease for some time but it was eventually linked to a deadly virus called the human immunodeficiency virus or HIV. Once the invasive HIV virus enters the blood stream it slowly destroys white blood cells and undermines the body's immune system. This virus is not spread through casual contact but requires the direct interaction of bodily fluids. The first treatment for the disease, a drug known as AZT, was approved by the FDA in 1987. Several years later, researchers developed protease inhibitors that halted the infected cells from spreading the virus. Thanks to these drugs and other preventative measures, the AIDS epidemic began to subside in the United States and other Western countries.

However, the AIDS epidemic quickly spread to sub-Saharan Africa with a particular virulence and ferocity. According to the WHO, twenty-five million Africans were infected with AIDS by 2001, with the number growing steadily each day. In South Africa, 4.7 million people were infected with this lethal disease. AIDS also swept through the vulnerable populations of Botswana and Zimbabwe. In Zimbabwe, there were 2.3 million people living with AIDS in 2001, including 240,000 children.[51] There were ominous predictions about Africa's bleak future as it fought this losing battle with AIDS.

Although treatments for AIDS were becoming more efficacious, they were also quite expensive. The drugs on the market didn't cure AIDS, but kept the disease under control and prolonged the patient's life for many years. Major companies marketed an effective drug cocktail of protease inhibitors. Merck sold a drug called Crixivan, and Glaxco Wellcome PLC marketed Combivir, a mixture of AZT and two other drugs that formed the core of its AIDS therapy. An annual dose of Combivir sold for over $10,000 in the United States. Most African nations were too poor to afford this medicine even at much lower prices. Also, making the drug accessible was not just a matter of lowering prices. Most African countries lacked the necessary health care infrastructure to deliver and administer the drugs, monitor their use, and educate people about how to use them.

The governments of these sub-Saharan African countries lacked the resources to buy these drugs from Western companies in order to treat their afflicted citizens, and they did not have the funds to invest in manufacturing plants to make generic drugs. These countries were too poor to afford much funding for any sort of health care. Without follow-up systems and medical assistance the drugs could easily be misused. Nevertheless, Doctors Without Borders and other international agencies were determined to remedy this crisis, and the first step was to acquire enough anti-viral medication to treat as many inflicted Africans as possible.

However, there was no cooperation from Big Pharma. When the United Nations and the WHO set up a pilot program called UNAIDS to provide AIDS drugs at low prices, they asked U.S. companies like Merck Glaxo for steep discounts for their drug cocktails. But these firms initially refused to participate in that program and did not agree to drug discounts. The industry was worried about precedent, threats to its patents for these drugs, and increasing pressure to lower the prices of their other life-saving drugs.[52]

In desperation, the South African government passed the Medicine and Related Substances Control Act. The law authorized the use of compulsory licensing and "parallel importing," so that South Africa could import pharmaceuticals from any source, including generic manufacturers, without the patent holder's permission. The emergency measure also authorized the production of these patented drugs within South Africa without the patent holder's permission. But Western drug companies quickly filed a lawsuit, claiming that the law infringed on their patents by allowing the importation and manufacture of generic drugs.[53] They seemed determined to fight every effort to lower the price of HIV/AIDS drugs or allow for generics.

Thanks to mounting international pressure, however, the industry finally retreated from its recalcitrance and agreed to a decrease in the prices for its HIV/AIDS therapies. Merck agreed to sell Crixivan for $600 a year per patient, and Stocrin for $500; both are critical components of its cocktail therapy. These figures, Merck claimed, represented "no profit" for the company. The total wholesale price of Crixivan and Stocrin was $11,700. Glaxo offered to sell an annual dose of the Combivir cocktail for $1,330, well below its $10,880 price tag in the United States. Merck President Raymond Gilmartin spoke at the time about his company's "evolving stance:" a refusal to discount prices, initial price reductions with strings attached, and then steeper price reductions. This is all part of "gaining experience" for how to handle such complex issues.[54]

These dramatic price reductions, however, failed to bring the crisis to closure or to mute the criticisms of activists and African country officials. Observers complained that the drug manufacturers were still making money. The Indian generic manufacturer Cipla, which had reverse-engineered these drugs, revealed that the active ingredients for making an annual dose of Combivir could be purchased on the international generic market for only $240.[55] Also, despite the apparent magnanimity of providing these "break-even" prices, many Africans still could not afford the product. AIDS activists continued to demand lower prices, but over time a concerted world effort, spearheaded by charitable organizations such as the Gates Foundation, began to make progress in getting these drugs to the poorest Africans. In 2018, a new "gold-standard," an inexpensive triple treatment for HIV/AIDS, was introduced into Africa at an annual cost of $75.[56]

In the wake of the African AIDS crisis, the "Doha Declaration" was signed by WTO signatories in 2001, limiting the rights granted under TRIPS. The Declaration clarified the TRIPS provision on compulsory licensing. "The TRIPS agreement does not and should not prevent members from taking measures to protect public health. We affirm … WTO members' right to protect public health, and, in particular, to promote access to medicine for all."[57] In cases of national emergencies, countries have the latitude to manufacture their own generic version of medicine or import generic copies from other countries.

The story of the fight against AIDS has not been one of the more inspiring chapters in the history of Big Pharma. The industry gets high marks for developing efficacious and safe therapies like AZT and Crixivan so quickly, but low marks for how they handled the AIDS catastrophe in Africa. Companies finally did what was right but only in response to intense public pressure. The industry was squeezed by an indignant public and generic companies like Cipla that were perceived as heroic for their willingness to break patents and supply generic versions of AZT and Crixivan. The industry itself concedes that mistakes were made. One Bristol Myers executive attributes the failure to bureaucracy: "The challenge in the big company is to do the right thing more quickly than inertia and momentum and bureaucracy allows."[58]

But this story is not just about inertia or corporate bureaucracy. The pharmaceutical industry is always worried about the slippery slope and whether or not giving in to demands for compulsory licensing or discounting will affect other products and lead to a calamitous "rippling effect" throughout the whole industry. This fear is not completely unfounded, and it underscores the complexity of these issues for a responsible company seeking to find a compromise between preserving patents and taking care of poor AIDS patients. We review the ethical implications of Big Pharma's behavior in the final section of this chapter.

The case for and against pharmaceutical patents

Some economists argue that intellectual property rights do not adequately resolve the market failure of the underproduction of public goods (i.e., goods that are non-excludable and can be easily copied) because they do not optimize social welfare. These rights lead to excessive monopoly rents and distributional inequities that should not be tolerated in a just society. Yet there is little evidence that IP rights lead to an increase in subsequent innovation. According to Boldrin and Levine, "an intellectual monopoly cannot be justified on the grounds of an economic calculus since benefits do not exceed the costs."[59]

Boldrin and Levine also claim that the pharmaceutical industry is no exception, despite the fact that IP rights seem to be an essential inducement for innovation. They point out that many drugs are discovered by government-sponsored research, especially the National Institutes of Health (NIH), and that "Big Pharma" is more focused on redundant research that yields trivial rather than substantive innovation. Moreover, other rewards for innovation, such as big financial payouts, might yield more breakthrough drug innovations at a much lower cost.[60]

David Herzberg, who blames the industry for the opioid crisis, goes a step further. In profit-driven markets companies hype new products as safe and effective and sell those products with insufficient attention to consumer safety. This is a particular problem for addictive drugs. He proposes that the current system, for-profit drug companies and their patents, be replaced by state monopolies following the public utility model. We must "dramatically minimize" or even eliminate the profits and the profit motive from "psychoactive capitalism."[61]

Werhane and Gorman critique the current patent system based on the obvious asymmetry between intellectual property and material property. Unlike material property, it is difficult to conclude that intellectual property can be "owned" by an individual or a company. Intellectual property protection is allegedly bestowed upon the source of an innovation, but it is difficult to identify that "source." Is it the one who creates or discovers a new idea or formula, or the one who develops the idea into a viable commercial product? The development of new ideas, inventions, and creations is the result of a "network of interrelationships, discoveries, research and development, and exchanges of ideas, some passed down over time." Some credit and attribution is definitely due to the person or group of persons who ultimately "discovers" that idea and brings it to fruition. But we must acknowledge that this breakthrough discovery such as a new cancer therapy or a vaccine has many "ancestral roots." Therefore, a patent assigned exclusively to an individual or company is probably not the proper vehicle for rewarding the "discoverer," since the property has many owners. Werhane and Gorman reject the Lockean-inspired notion that IP rights, like other property rights, are natural rights. Rather, they are *prima facie* rights that are sometimes necessary to stimulate innovation. In their view, the "communal qualities" of intellectual property implies the need to reconceive the present IP rights system predicated on exclusive ownership in favor of one based on "shared rights." When rights are appropriately "shared" the putative discoverer will not have the full proprietary controls associated with the current patent system.[62]

On the other hand, there is certainly some empirical evidence that the pharmaceutical industry, perhaps more than any other, needs those exclusive IP rights in the form of patents for its survival, since there is a positive correlation between patents and research investment.[63] Consider the case of India. After its weak 1970 patent law went into effect, R&D budgets fell to 0.2% of sales in companies like Cipla, compared to 17% for Western companies. Indian drug companies had little incentive to conduct expensive research on malaria or other diseases that afflicted the Indian population. The case of India and other developing countries indicates that without thick patents, research and development will be appreciably reduced and so will the volume of new medicines. Given the experience of these countries, it is difficult to deny that the profit motivation is the principal driver of drug research and medical breakthroughs. Can a "public utility" have the resources and motivation to develop the next "miracle" vaccine or therapy?[64] Moreover, the "shared rights" system proposed by Werhane and Gorman is not without some theoretical warrant but appears to be impractical in an industry where companies must bear high development and commercialization costs and contend with many drug failures.

Claims about the preponderance of government-sponsored research can also be plausibly challenged. A comprehensive research study reviewing how many new drugs benefited from publicly funded research affirms the predominance of the private sector. The study examined 248 drugs that contained one or more molecular entities and that were approved by the FDA from 2008 to the end of 2017. It found that only forty-eight of those drugs, or 19%, originated in publicly supported research and development. In response to the study a Big Pharma spokesperson pointed out that the biopharmaceutical industry invested $97 billion in R&D in 2017, triple the NIH budget of $32.6 billion in that same year.[65] Based on this data, it is reasonable to conclude that without the innovations coming from the private sector most new drugs would never come to market.

However, even if patents are justified on moral and utilitarian grounds, it seems beyond dispute that the pharmaceutical industry was at fault for the mishandling of the AIDS crisis in sub-Sahara Africa. In its zeal to protect its patents, the company failed to consider the scope of its social responsibility when a medical crisis is precipitated by the inaccessibility of patented pharmaceuticals. The crisis was a challenge to the fairness of an intellectual property rights system and even to liberal capitalism, which gives priority to private economic freedoms over distributive equity and social justice. In this chapter we have argued that the most promising normative justification for intellectual property rights can be found within Locke's political philosophy. But is there a way to reconcile Locke's paradigm with a more ethically responsive approach to the African AIDS epidemic? As we have observed, Locke's exclusionary rights are permeated with limits and boundaries. While Locke's theory sanctions strong property rights based on self-ownership, labor, and effort, those rights are constrained by the sufficiency proviso, which mandates that everyone leave "enough and as good for others," after they appropriate what they need. But there is another limitation stipulated by Locke that is not so well known, called the charity proviso, which we briefly discussed in Chapter 2. According to Locke,

> And therefore no Man could ever have a just Power over the life of another, by right of property in Land or Possessions, since 'twould always be a Sin in any Man of Estate, to let his Brother perish for want of affording him Relief out of his Plenty. As Justice gives every Man a Title to the product of his honest industry, and the fair Acquisitions of his Ancestors descended to him; so Charity gives every man a Title to so much out of another's Plenty, as will keep him from extreme want, where he has no means to subsist otherwise (I: §42).[66]

Locke is insisting that people in "extreme want" have a right or a "Title" to another's presumptive property in order to ensure their subsistence or survival when there are no other means available.

The charity proviso strongly suggests that Locke would take quite seriously the distributive inequity that besets the problem of a socially important product like life-saving drugs. The proviso implies that in some cases there should be an attenuation of patent rights over these life-preserving pharmaceuticals in order to ensure their optimal distribution so that the destitute have access. In these situations of dire need, pharmaceutical companies are morally required to accept a lower reward for the work and efforts that led to their innovation.[67]

We have been arguing throughout this book that multinationals have a minimal obligation to avoid depriving people of their rights and sometimes to help protect people from the deprivation of their rights. People have a right not to be deprived of the intrinsic goods of life, health, and bodily integrity by acts contrary to those goods. It follows that they also have a right not to be deprived of essential health care and life-saving medicines, which are instrumental goods necessary for preserving life and sound health. Given their importance for human flourishing, the provision of these socially valuable goods is required of others in justice.

The state and local political community have the joint obligation to ensure that the conditions are met for sustaining the health and well-being of their citizens, who need access to doctors and hospitals, along with safe and effective therapies to treat their illnesses. But sometimes a sovereign state is too poor to provide the conditions for adequate health care. It must then seek out the help of the international community which has a moral duty to provide that assistance within reason based on every person's right to the means to preserve his or her health. Delivering such aid and medicine, however, can sometimes be a complicated business (as we saw in the AIDS crisis), and it requires the goodwill and cooperation of many parties. When life-preserving drugs are needed in these situations, pharmaceutical companies have a duty to cooperate. More specifically, they have a duty to protect this right to essential medicines from deprivation, when that deprivation is occurring primarily because of the enforcement of their patents. Thanks to insurance coverage, price controls, and consumer wealth, patents under normal conditions do not typically interfere with a person's access to life-preserving medicine. But in situations like the African AIDS crisis, where patents block fair access to these medicines, patent rights must be waived. Under these exigent conditions of "extreme want," pharmaceutical companies fail to protect from deprivation a person's right to life-preserving medicine unless they are willing to compromise or surrender their own *bona fide* property rights and cooperate with other institutions in order to ensure equitable access. The application of Locke's charity proviso leads to the same conclusion, and it also helps us to appreciate how rights like property are limited by each other and by the common good.[68]

We must tread carefully, however, because a pharmaceutical company is not a charity. It has an economic mission and its primary obligation is to create value for society by developing, manufacturing, and selling pharmaceutical products. A large part of its value-creating activities involves bringing new innovations to market. In determining the specifics of how far these companies should go in their obligations to make medicine accessible, there are a number of key considerations. Overriding patents will have some detrimental effects on other stakeholders. Given the nature and complexity of pharmaceutical research, one stakeholder group that cannot be neglected are those who will suffer from potentially treatable or curable diseases in the future. If overriding patents will diminish investment for vaccines and cures aimed at treating those diseases, this group will be potentially disadvantaged by Big Pharma's generosity. In calling for the relinquishing or loosening of patent rights, we cannot neglect this critical dimension of intergenerational justice. How will waiving a patent right today affect future generations of disease sufferers? Will weakening of patents for some segments of the world population lead to compromised R&D capabilities because of diminished revenue streams and lower profits? The salient issue of intergenerational equity must be properly balanced with the demands of distributive equity. Charity today must be tempered by concern for the benefits research and innovation will yield for tomorrow.[69]

One implication of these intergenerational justice issues is that the burden of providing affordable medicine to the disenfranchised should not fall disproportionately on the pharmaceutical industry. NGOs, charitable foundations (such as the Gates Foundation), local governments, and multilateral institutions like the WHO and the United Nations should collaborate to ensure an adequate supply of life-saving drugs to those in need. A moral attitude of solidarity, which has not always been evident in the rhetoric or actions of pharmaceutical companies, is necessary for a long-term solution to the problem of access to life-saving medicines.

Case study: Novartis and the Glivec patent controversy

The formation of the Swiss pharmaceutical company Novartis AG in 1996 represented the largest company merger in the pharmaceutical industry's history at the time. The merger of Ciba-Geigy and Sandoz created a giant company that took a name inspired by the Latin phrase *novae artis* or "new skills." The new company immediately dedicated itself to three business areas: health care, agribusiness, and nutrition. Its core business is health care and pharmaceutical products. Some of the company's blockbuster drugs have included Diovan (for hypertension), Glivec, and the innovative vaccine Bexsero.[70]

The Glivec patent became a source of controversy and contention in India after the country changed its patent laws in 2005 to comply with TRIPS. Glivec is a highly effective treatment for chronic myeloid leukemia (CML). For a person with CML, his or her bone marrow produces too many white blood cells that alter the composition of the blood. As the disease progresses, it causes fatigue, spleen enlargement, and a weakening of the immune system. CML is fatal if it is not treated. Researchers looking for a cure discovered that the cause of this disease was a genetic mutation called the "Philadelphia chromosome": chromosome 22 was missing a sequence that appeared on chromosome 9. This genetic defect was the trigger for producing excess white blood cells. In 1993 a Ciba-Geigy scientist developed a substance that blocks the protein that generates CML. A patent was awarded for this medical breakthrough, and the drug became known as Glivec. It is very effective in stopping the propagation of white cells without causing damage to normal cells.[71]

Glivec, with recent revenues in excess of $1 billion, has been a major success story for Novartis. Before its patent expired, Glivec was a global blockbuster drug. In 2003, Novartis introduced this drug into India on an experimental basis with a price tag of $2,666 per month. Thanks to its Glivec International Patient Assistance Program (GIPAP), Novartis provided the drug to impoverished Indian citizens free of charge. This initiative was done in collaboration with the Max Foundation in a "shared value partnership."[72]

Novartis applied for a patent for the drug, but it was rejected by the Indian Patent Office (IPO) in 2006. Citing section 3(d) of the Indian Patent Act, it claimed that Glivec (or Imatinib) was only a modified version of an existing drug that had already been awarded a patent in the U.S. and Europe. It was not a new product that qualified for a patent under the law. The IPO insisted that the modified substance was not more efficacious than the original substance so it was not patent-eligible.[73]

In 2009, Novartis appealed the IPO's decision to the Indian Intellectual Property Appellate Board (IPAB). According to Novartis, the original substance, for which it was given a patent, called Imatinib, was not completely safe nor was it sufficiently efficacious. The development of Imatinib was only the first step in preparing Glivec to become a viable cancer treatment. To complete the process, researchers developed the beta crystalline version of this substance known as Imatinib mesylate, a beta crystal form of the imatinib molecule. This improved product had a better delivery mechanism since it could now be taken in pill form. It was safer and more bio-available than the original Imatinib. Bio-availability refers to the extent to which a drug becomes "available" in the body and reaches its intended biological destination. [74]

IPAB, however, rejected Novartis' patent application because in their view the new substance was not more efficacious than the older one according to Section 3(d) of Indian patent law. Both substances had the same functionality: they reduced the white blood cell count. Increased bio-availability did not qualify as enhanced efficacy. For the court, this was an example of the "evergreening" that this law was designed to prevent. The patent was also denied on the grounds that the drug was too expensive and inaccessible for many Indian citizens.

In 2011, Novartis appealed to the Indian Supreme Court, which handed down its decision two years later. The Court sided with IPAB and dismissed Novartis' patent application. Despite the fact that Glivec is patented in forty other countries, the Court concluded that "Novartis did not convincingly show that the drug offered 'enhanced or superior efficacy' as Indian law requires."[75]

Study questions

1. Do you agree with the Indian Supreme Court's decision in this case? Does enhanced bioavailability constitute a more efficacious drug?
2. Should patents be denied in countries like India based on the criteria of price and affordability?

Conclusions

In spite of its notable success in developing cures and therapies for diseases like HIV/AIDS and vaccines for menaces like Covid-19, Big Pharma enjoys little public approbation. Industry criticism is often laced with hyperbole, but some of this disparagement is justified. Big Pharma has won some reprieve because of its swift development of the coronavirus vaccine, but it still faces the wrath of governments over its patents and high prices.

Patents are limited monopolies that generate monopoly rents as a reward for the risk and expense of developing new innovations. The pharmaceutical industry, where new drugs cost over \$2 billion and take on average thirteen years to come to market, depends on patents to protect itself from free riders. But patents create two severe market distortions: the access problem and the availability problem. The lack of competition keeps prices high and drugs out of reach for the poor and uninsured. In addition, the industry neglects diseases in impoverished countries where most citizens cannot afford the cost of prescription drugs. Nonetheless patent laws have been strengthened throughout the world thanks to TRIPS. On the other hand, countries like India have arguably violated the spirit of this international agreement by elevating the bar for the granting of patents in that country.

Despite their deficiencies, patents still create value for society. Patents are theoretically justified as an incentive to encourage innovation, but most especially on non-economic grounds as a just appropriation of the fruit of one's labor and investment. This Lockean argument is predicated on the thesis of self-ownership: a man has exclusive property in his embodied personhood and in his labor, and hence is entitled to unowned resources transformed by that labor. But Locke recognized their intrinsic limitations of these rights, which were expressed in terms of the sufficiency and charity provisos.

Critics of the patent system claim that these limited monopolies interfere with achieving distributional equity, since the destitute who need medicine are deprived because they cannot afford it. They cite the African AIDS crisis as a prime example of the enormous human toll of this flawed patent system. Lack of access to essential patent-protected medicines, especially for life-threatening diseases like malaria and tuberculosis, persists as a major challenge for the governments and the global health care industry. However, in cases of "extreme want," destitute people have a right to life-preserving medicine even if they are protected by a patent. Locke's balanced approach to property rights implies a duty on the part of pharmaceutical companies to help ensure the distribution of life-saving medicines. This duty might require waiving patent rights when those rights block fair access to that medicine and when there is no other recourse. The entire burden for just distribution of these socially valuable goods should not fall on Big Pharma, however, since uncompensated access to medicine will impair its research base. Hence this moral obligation to assist the poor in this way must be balanced with a commitment to future research for the sake of intergenerational equity.

Notes

1 Roger Bate, "The Companies Everyone Loves to Hate," *Wall Street Journal*, September 16, 2005, W13.
2 Andrew Jack, "Perils for Pill Pushers," *Financial Times*, September 22, 2010, 9.
3 "An Overdose of Bad News – the Drug Industry," *Economist*, March 19, 2005, 89.
4 Scumpeter, "Boffins v the Bug," *Economist*, June 6, 2020.
5 Liyan Chen, "The Most Profitable Industries in 2016," *Forbes*, December 21, 2016. Available at www.forbes.com/sites/liyanchen/2016/12/21/the-most-profitable-industries-in-2016.
6 Statista, "Global Leading Pharmaceutical Companies ROE 2019," March 2020. Available at statista.com/statistics/1093262/global-pharmaceutical-companies-roe

7 Robin Feldman and Evan Frondorf, *Drug Wars* (New York: Cambridge University Press, 2017), 69.

8 Noemie Bisserbe, "Glaxo's Chief Dispenses a Bitter Pill to Fix R&D," *Wall Street Journal*, March 26, 2018, B3.

9 Jared Hopkins and Matt Grossman. "Pfizer Raises Vaccine Forecast," *Wall Street Journal*, May 5, 2020, B1–2.

10 Josh Nathan-Kazis, "Pfizer Refocuses," *Barron's*, November 25, 2019.

11 For a more thorough review of these regulations see Peter Termin, *Taking Your Medicine: Drug Regulation in the United States* (Cambridge, MA: Harvard University Press, 1980).

12 Jack, "Perils for Pill Pushers," 9.

13 "China's Pharmaceutical Industry Is Growing Up," *Economist*, September 28, 2019, 35–36.

14 "Indian Pharmaceutical Industry," IBEF, June 2020. Available at www.ibef.org/industry/pharmaceuticals-india.aspx.

15 Ibid.

16 Ed Silverman, "Can It Really Cost $2.6 Billion to Develop a Drug," *Wall Street Journal*, November 21, 2014, B3.

17 Kenneth Dam, "The Economic Underpinnings of Patent Law," *Journal of Legal Studies* 23 (1994), 247–271. I have relied on Dam's analysis in this discussion on the economic justification for patents.

18 Thomas Pogge, "Human Rights and Global Health: A Research Program," *Metaphilosophy* 36 (1/2) (2005), 186.

19 "A Patent Cure-All," *Economist*, June 15, 1996, 75. See also F.S. Kieff, "Property Rights and Property Rules for Commercializing Inventions," *Minnesota Law Review* 85 (2000), 697.

20 Jorn Sonderheim, "Ethical Issues Surrounding Intellectual Property Rights," in *New Frontiers in the Philosophy of Intellectual Property* ed. Annabelle Lever (Cambridge, UK: Cambridge University Press, 2012), 110–112. See also Pogge, "Human Rights and Global Health," 186.

21 Ibid.

22 Dam, "The Economic Underpinnings of Patent Law," 251–252.

23 Kieff, "Property Rights and Property Rules for Commercializing Inventions," 697. See also Robin Feldman, *Rethinking Patent Law* (Cambridge, MA: Harvard University Press, 2012), 77.

24 S. Vedaraman, "The New Indian Patent Law," *International Review of Industrial Property and Copyright Law* 3 (1972), 39. See also Peter Drahos, "Negotiating Intellectual Property Rights: Between Coercion and Dialogue," in *Global Intellectual Property Rights* ed. Peter Drahos and Ruth Mayne (New York: Palgrave MacMillan, 2002), 165.

25 Carlos Correa, "Pro-competitive Measures under TRIPS to Promote Technology Diffusion in Developing Countries," in *Global Intellectual Property Rights*, 49–50.

26 Peter Drahos, "Introduction," to *Global Intellectual Property Rights*, 1–9.

27 Martin Khor, "Rethinking Intellectual Property Rights and TRIPS," in *Global Intellectual Property Rights*, 205–206.

28 Geeta Anand, "Drug Makers Decry Indian Patent Law," *Wall Street Journal*, February 12, 2010, B1–2.

29 "Indian Drug Patents: Taking Pains," *Economist*, September 8, 2012, 47.

30 R. Jai Krishna and Jeanne Whalen, "A Bumpy Road in India," *Wall Street Journal*, April 2, 2013, A1–2.

31 Robert Merges, *Justifying Intellectual Property* (Cambridge, MA: Harvard University Press, 2011), 12–26. I have relied on Merges' discussion on foundations of intellectual property law throughout the Introduction of his book.

32 Social welfare is understood as the maximization of aggregate wealth society gets from its scarce resources.

33 Edmund Kitch, "Taking Stock: The Law and Economics of Intellectual Property Rights," *Vanderbilt Law Review* 53 (2000), 1727.

34 *Graham v. John Deere of Kan. City* 383 U.S. 9 (1966).

35 U. S. Constitution, art 1, §8, cl. 8.

36 John Locke, *Second Treatise of Government* ed. P. Laslett (Cambridge, UK: Cambridge University Press, 1988). References in the text are to paragraph numbers in this edition.

37 David McGowan, "Copyright Non-Consequentialism," *Missouri Law Review* 69 (1) (2004), 36–40.

38 Jeremy Waldron, *The Right to Private Property* (Oxford: Oxford University Press, 1988), 263–264.

39 John Rawls, *A Theory of Justice* (Cambridge, MA: Harvard University Press, 1971), 302. According to Rawls' theory of "justice as fairness," the first principle of equal liberties has "lexical priority" over the second principle, which stipulates that social and economic inequalities are justified only if they are to everyone's advantage. The latter principle cannot be satisfied at the expense of abrogating basic rights.

40 John Rawls, *Justice as Fairness: A Restatement* (Cambridge, MA: Harvard University Press, 2001), 138.

41 Merges, *Justifying Intellectual Property*, 107.

42 Peter Drahos and John Braithwaite, *Information Feudalism: Who Owns the Knowledge Economy* (New York: The New Press, 2002), 2–3.

43 KFF, "The U.S. Government and Global Neglected Tropical Disease Efforts," *Global Health Policy*, January 2020. Available at kff.org/global-health-policy/fact-sheet/the-u-s-government-and-global-neglected-tropical-disease-efforts.

44 Donald McNeil, "New Tuberculosis Vaccine Could Save Millions of Lives, Study Suggests, *New York Times*, October 30, 2019, A12.

45 World Health Organization, "Dengue and Severe Dengue," November 2019. Available at www.who.int/news-room/fact-sheets/detail/dengue-and-severe-dengue.

46 "Fight against Neglected Tropical Diseases Needs Big Pharma Push," *Reuters*, April 12, 2017, 6.

47 Pogge, "Human Rights and Global Health," 190.

48 Roderick Viergever, "The Mismatch between Health R&D that Is Needed and the R&D that Is Undertaken," *Global Health Action* 6 (10) (2013), 22–45.

49 Pogge, "Human Rights and Global Health," 189–190.

50 For more about moral obligation and issues discussed here see Josef Seifert, *The Moral Action* (Irving, TX: International of Academy Press, 2017), 20–21, 54. See also Eric Darcy, *Human Acts: An Essay in Their Moral Evaluation* (Oxford: Oxford University Press, 1963), 56–57.

51 University of California at San Francisco, AIDS Policy Research Center, "HIV/AIDS in Zimbabwe," December 2003.

52 Gardiner Harris, "AIDS Gaffes in Africa Come Back to Haunt Drug Industry at Home," *Wall Street Journal*, April 23, 2001, A1, A6.

53 James Gathi, "Third World Perspectives on Global Pharmaceutical Access," in *Ethics and the Pharmaceutical Industry* ed. Michael Santoro and Thomas Gorrie (New York: Cambridge University Press, 2015), 339.

54 Mark Schoops and Michael Waldholz, "AIDS Drug Price War Breaks Out in Africa, Goaded by Generics," *Wall Street Journal*, March 7, 2001, A1, A14.

55 Melody Petersen, "Lifting the Curtain on the Real Costs of Making AIDS Drugs," *New York Times*, April 24, 2001, C1, C10.

56 Tina Rosenberg, "HIV Drugs Cost $75 in Africa," *New York Times*, September 18, 2018, A22.

57 World Trade Organization, "Declaration on the TRIPS Agreement and Public Health," Doha Ministerial Declaration, November 20, 2001, www.wto.org. In later years clauses have been added to TRIPS that clarify even further the steps to be taken by a country to issue a compulsory license and, if necessary, to obtain generic drugs if the country is unable to manufacture that drug on its own. See Arthur Daemmrich, "Stalemate at the WTO: TRIPS, Agricultural Subsidies, and the Doha Round," (Boston, MA: Harvard Business School Publications, 2012).

58 Schoops and Michael Waldholz, "AIDS Drug Price War Breaks Out," A1.

59 Michele Boldrin and David Levine, *Against Intellectual Monopoly* (Cambridge, UK: Cambridge University Press, 2008), 223. See also "Protection Racket," *Economist*, April 24, 2021, 66.

60 Ibid.

61 David Herzberg, *White Market Drugs* (Chicago, IL: Chicago University Press, 2020), 286–288.

62 Patricia Werhane and Michael Gorman, "Intellectual Property Rights: Access to Life-Enhancing Drugs and Corporate Moral Responsibilities," in *Ethics and the Pharmaceutical Industry* eds. Michael Santoro and Thomas Gorrie (New York: Cambridge University Press, 2005), 269–271.

63 See for example J.H. Stuart Graham, Robert Merges, and Pamela Samuelson, "High Technology Entrepreneurs and the Patent System: Results of the 208 Berkeley Patent Survey," *Berkeley Law Journal* 24 (2010), 1256. This survey determined that patents were much more important in the biotechnology industry than in other industries such as computer software. See also Merges, *Justifying Intellectual Property*, 281–282.

64 Sally Satel, "Addiction by Prescription," *Wall Street Journal*, October 21, 2020, A17.

65 Ed Silverman, "How Many Taxpayer Dollars Should Fund Drug Research," *Boston Globe*, November 13, 2019, B6, B8.

66 Elsewhere Locke writes, "common Charity teaches, that those should be taken care of by the Law, who are least capable of taking care for themselves." John Locke, "Some Considerations of the Consequences of the Lowering of Interest and the Raising the Value of Money." Available at http://socserv.mcmaster.ca/econ/ugcm/3113/locke/consid.txt. This text was quoted in John Tomasi, *Free Market Fairness* (Princeton, NJ: Princeton University Press, 2012), 128.

67 St. Thomas Aquinas holds a similar position on the moral limits of property rights. He endorses such personal property rights as essential for the proper management and distribution of resources. But in exigent circumstances when people are in dire need, "all resources become common resources." *Scriptum super Libros Sententiarum Petri Lombard* (Commentary on the Sentences of Peter Lombard), IV, d. 15, q. 2, a. 1 sol. 4 ad 2. in Latin ed: *Sancti Thomae Aquinatis Doctoris Angelici, Opera Omnia* vols, VII–XI, eds. S.E. Frette and P. Mare (Paris: L. Vives, 1889–1890).

68 See Richard DeGeorge, "Intellectual Property and Pharmaceutical Drugs: An Ethical Analysis," *Business Ethics Quarterly* 15 (4) (2005), 549–576. Following DeGeorge, these arguments apply to drugs that are essential for the preservation of life (life-preserving

drugs) but not necessarily life-enhancing drugs like Viagra. Also, others such as Merges have used the charity proviso in this context. See *Justifying Intellectual Property*, 270–287.

69 Merges, *Justifying Intellectual Property*, 281–286. According to Merges, we must "weigh the intergenerational effects against the immediate benefits of expanded access," 282.

70 Walter Dettwiler, *Novartis: How a Leader in Healthcare Was Created Out of Ciba Geigy and Sandoz* (New York: Profile Books, 2014), 146–149.

71 Ibid., 162.

72 "Glivec: Treatment Access Solution," The Max Foundation. Available at themaxfoundation.org/our-work/treatment/glivec. See also Mridula Anand, "Novartis in India: Innovation versus Affordability" (Ontario, Canada: Ivey Publishing, Richard Ivey School of Business, 2013).

73 "Why Was Novartis Denied a Patent for Glivec in India," *Economic Times*, April 2, 2013.

74 Novartis, "FAQ on the India Glivec Patent Case." Available at www.novartis.com.

75 Editorial Board, "India's Novartis Decision," *New York Times*, April 4, 2013, A17.

Chapter 9

Big Tech, censorship, and geopolitics

Digital technologies were supposed to create a pathway to a more democratic future through open discourse and spontaneous organization. But authoritarian regimes have successfully harnessed digital tools to counteract this trend and they have deployed those tools to monitor text messages, to restrict website downloads, and to track the movements of their citizens. These regimes exercise despotic control over the Internet whenever possible. As a result, potentially freedom-enhancing technologies have been successfully manipulated to preserve power and repress the rights of ordinary citizens.[1]

Digital autocracies want to insulate their citizens from the "invasion" of Western ideas and culture and to monitor the activities of dissidents. Some countries have undertaken herculean efforts to close off parts of cyberspace and the World Wide Web from their citizens. After a military coup, Myanmar shut down the Internet in nine townships because it was allegedly being used to "coordinate illegal activities." Pakistan has employed similar tactics to quell protests and incipient unrest that might spiral out of control. Venezuela has blocked social media platforms, including Facebook and Twitter. Both Iran and Iraq have taken the whole country offline on occasion in order to put a stop to anti-government protesters.[2] Of particular importance is the suppression of social media platforms for grassroots organization or mobilization that occurs outside the one-party structure, since these activities might endanger the durability of the regime. Censorship and surveillance narrow the space for protest and civil unrest and provide security from the turmoil and perils of an unfiltered Web.[3]

Western democracies should be opposed to such tactics, but United States and European multinationals have played a substantial role as the purveyors and architects of censorship and surveillance technologies. Many companies, including Cisco, Google, Skype, and LinkedIn, ostensibly committed to promoting free expression

DOI: 10.4324/9781003058427-9

and open communication, have been implicated in efforts to censor the Internet in China. Cisco equipped China's Great Firewall. Siemens' joint venture with Nokia, known as NSN, provided Iran's largest telecom company with a monitoring center that can intercept and record calls made over mobile networks.[4] Microsoft has censored its blog services in China, and Skype has permitted its Chinese version, TOM-Skype, to censor user conversations based on keywords.[5]

The biggest and most elaborate censorship apparatus can be found in China, which has transformed the Internet into a "giant cage." The cage metaphor suggests the extent to which the Chinese government has infused regulatory controls into the Internet's architectures and processes. With hundreds of millions of Internet users, China represents an attractive investment opportunity for multinational high-tech companies like Google, Facebook, and LinkedIn. But the Chinese government demands that companies investing in China play by their rules, and their rules include cooperating with its strict censorship and surveillance laws. As a result, multinationals like Yahoo and Google have had to navigate an ethical minefield in China, and many would argue that their navigation has been quite poor. Both companies have exited China after scandals erupted in the West over their compliance with China's censorship regime. LinkedIn, on the other hand, is still willing to censor content on its China site to placate Chinese officials. Still other companies like Twitter have refused to comply with China's censorship laws. "We are not going to make the kinds of sacrifices … [necessary] to be unblocked in China," declared Twitter's then-CEO Dick Costolo.[6]

The primary theme of this chapter is the ethical risk that Internet companies must assume when they invest in countries like China or Iran, which are committed to the censorship and surveillance of Internet activities. The principal ethical question is straightforward: to what degree can these companies cooperate with a government's Internet-monitoring efforts or online censorship policies that deny people the right to protest or to criticize their own government? A larger philosophical question overshadows this issue. Is free political speech a universal right or is it one conditioned by culture? If this right is relative to culture, multinationals should enjoy extensive free moral space.

We explore this issue by focusing on the actions and policies of several Western firms that have either helped build the foundations of China's censorship system or provided assistance in their role as intermediary actors. Cisco sold routers to China that became equipped with filtering software to block an array of unwanted speech. Is Cisco accountable if its product is used in a way that suppresses free speech? Intermediaries like Google and LinkedIn have also played an essential role through their self-censorship efforts that implement the state's directives against "offensive" online content.

The Cisco discussion suggests how deeply political considerations have affected the deployment of Internet architectures that connect a country and its citizens to the rest of the world. Hence, the politicization of networking and social media technologies is a secondary theme of the chapter. The Chinese company Huawei, a major competitor of Cisco, has faced formidable challenges in distributing its products overseas. The United States has virtually banned Huawei products out of fear that they will be used to spy on Americans. A case study will present those allegations and the U.S. response to this presumptive threat. Since most of the geopolitical issues involve the U.S. and China, we begin with an overview of China's Internet giants.

China's "Big Tech" landscape

The use of computer technology in China has grown exponentially over the last two decades. According to recent estimates, by 2021 China had approximately 990 million Internet users, which amounts to 55% of the population. China is the fastest growing market for mobile apps and the largest online community. Penetration remains particularly strong in eastern cities like Shanghai and Beijing.

Digital technology has given rise to many business opportunities for qualified Chinese companies, and many companies have seized that opportunity. As a result, the U.S. and China are in the midst of a great struggle for technological supremacy. At the forefront of this battle is the telecom firm, Huawei Technologies, Inc. Huawei is one of only four cellular equipment makers thanks to a series of mergers. The other three are Nokia, which acquired Alcatel-Lucent in 2016, Ericsson, and another Chinese firm, ZTE. Nokia's acquisition has transformed the Finnish company into a major provider of routers and other infrastructure to cable and Internet providers. Only Huawei is bigger, and no U.S. companies have a sizable presence in the wireless market. Some U.S. officials worry that in the future Huawei and ZTE will be the world's only telecom suppliers.[7]

Huawei has played a critical role in shaping China's information infrastructure, which is highly centralized. This company is the world's largest producer of telecommunications equipment and the number two provider of smartphones. It began to expand beyond China about two decades ago and won contracts in developing countries by offering quality products at a discount. As the world transitions from 4G to 5G networks, which provides enhanced speed for cellular devices, Huawei is leveraging its supremacy to push the global adoption of its 5G standards.

Unlike the fragmented European market, America has three network operators for its mobile phone customers (Verizon, AT&T, and T-Mobile), and so does China. China Mobile, Ltd., is the biggest mobile carrier by subscriber, with a 68% share of the Chinese market. China Unicorn and China Telecom are the other two major players in this market. These companies are investing massively in 5G technology.

Aside from network suppliers and network operators, three other big Chinese Internet companies shape the Big Tech landscape. All of them have become powerful thanks to their huge home market and the light touch of Chinese regulators. The online commerce space is dominated by Alibaba, China's largest e-commerce firm that handles more transactions per year than eBay and Amazon combined. In 2001 a Chinese search engine, Baidu.com, was introduced throughout the country to compete with Yahoo. After Google departed from China, Baidu became the dominant search engine in the Chinese market.[8]

The third Internet giant is Tencent Holdings, which specializes in online gaming and social media. Tencent's chairman has said that he wants to preside over a "global tech revolution of the future."[9] Tencent is the owner of WeChat, an immensely popular mobile app with 1.2 billion users worldwide. WeChat allows users to send messages, make phone calls, and transfer money. It also operates as a social media platform and it is widely used by Chinese companies. Both apps have been the source of controversy. President Trump issued an executive order curbing Americans' use of WeChat, but the order was blocked by a federal court. The Trump Administration claims that the data collected by WeChat could be shared with the Chinese government.[10]

Another Internet force in China is ByteDance. This 30-billion-dollar company's most popular product is TikTok, a short video app that quickly became a worldwide sensation. The company has 70 million American users and has been downloaded over 2 billion times. TikTok competes with Facebook and SnapChat. Despite its popularity and its benign functionality, TikTok found itself in the middle of several political firestorms in 2020. India banned the app on national security grounds. And American officials have voiced two concerns: the company's censorship of sensitive political topics such as repression of Muslims in Xinjiang and the need for compliance with Chinese laws that would require handing over user data to the Chinese government. TikTok, like other social media apps, records GPS location, Internet address, and browsing and search history on the app. As a result of these concerns, President Trump sought to force the sale of TikTok's American operations to a domestic buyer. The Trump Administration chose the software giant Oracle for this deal but ByteDance ended negotiations in 2021 after Trump lost the presidential election. [11]

As the United States and China vie for technological supremacy, there is growing disquiet over China's technological progress and the threat it poses for American security. If the U.S. continues to target Chinese firms over concerns about propaganda and cyber-snooping, it will be more difficult for those firms to expand their international presence. While some of these concerns are valid, the tactics, which border on virtual expropriation, are highly questionable.

Censorship and digital technologies

It was once presumed that the Internet's distributed and anarchic architecture would make it strongly resistant to government regulation, including traditional types of censorship. Conventional wisdom was that this international network would eventually erode the state's sovereignty and regulatory powers. The virtues of this distributed network were resiliency, contingency, interoperability, flexibility, and heterogeneity, along with a capacity to operate according to the simple principle,

"Accept everything, no matter what source, sender, or destination."[12] Nonetheless, governments have found ways to control and censor the network, often under the pretense that regulated access will "protect" their citizens from corrupting foreign influences located in cyberspace. These governments justify censorship by claiming that they must safeguard vulnerable citizens from alien and corrupting cultural influences, but most often their main goal is to cut off dissenting political discourse and to deter anti-government protests.

Censorship is defined as restriction on the public expression of information or on public access to information by authorities who believe that the information in question has the potential to undermine their authority and make them accountable to the public. Thus, two types of action are restricted by means of censorship: the expression of certain information and access to information.[13]

Censorship can be accomplished by many means, including fear and intimidation. But in the digital era, the primary mechanism of censorship is a combination of software code and legal rules. Code creates new opportunities for the censor, who can inscribe restrictions on speech into technologies by means of software filters, firewalls, and similar architectures. Code also creates unprecedented opportunities for online surveillance. Ordinary users have little recourse and usually offer no resistance to this extension of surveillance and content controls into their networked space. Thanks to the proliferation of filtering and monitoring technologies, the Internet in some countries has been transformed from a networked information community into a "society of control."[14]

The problem of censorship extends well beyond authoritarian regimes, which have proven themselves to be quite resilient in the face of the Internet's democratizing potential. In Western countries, like the United States, where free speech rights are better protected, censorship comes from private actors such as Facebook and Twitter. Social networks are no longer neutral platforms but more like publishers who vet and control the content appearing on those platforms. Social networks decide what speech is acceptable. As private companies, they can set their own rules about what to publish, and sometimes those rules are arbitrary or politically biased. But if these trends continue, social media's role in public life is likely to be greatly diminished.[15] While private censorship is not our main axis of discussion, this trend should provoke as much concern as the actions of authoritarian states. In both cases, there is an attempt to seize "guardianship of the public mind" through the regulation of speech.[16] The pervasiveness of digital censorship suggests how profoundly we are governed by the dynamic exigencies of technology that supersede the order of liberal democracy and even the rule of law.[17]

Any suppression of political speech is antithetical to the philosophy of the Internet's original design. Cyberspace was supposed to be an open environment where anyone could express their opinions, protest corruption, or engage in digital activism without reprisals from the state. Its end-to-end design created an environment conducive to liberty and democracy, with unfettered access to all types of information in different digital formats. As the U.S. Supreme Court eloquently wrote in its *Reno v. ACLU* decision, the Internet enables an ordinary citizen to become "a pamphleteer, … a town crier with a voice that resonates farther than it could from any soapbox."[18] But this potent combination of law and software code has enabled authoritarian societies as well as private enterprises to effectively thwart the Internet's libertarian ethos.

The "Great Firewall" of China

China is a prime example of state capitalism with the economy firmly in the grip of the Communist Party. This Party, which controls the Chinese legislature, is known for its intolerance of internal political dissent. The country has vigorously suppressed spiritual cults like Falun Gong, and it has clamped down on citizens seeking independence for Tibet. Any internal criticism of China's despotic government is regarded as "subversive" speech. These restrictive policies are consistent with a nationalistic sentiment that regards social order and political stability as necessary for the restoration of the country's lost wealth and power.

China's Ministry of Information Industry (MII) controls several state-owned government companies that operate networks that connect to the global Internet. These are the backbones or hubs through which all Internet traffic must pass, including all data files and communications such as email. Chinese users access the Internet through the services provided by these state-licensed Internet Access Providers (IAPs), including China Telcom and China Netcom. Thanks to this system, the Chinese government controls the whole physical infrastructure that permits connectivity to the outside world.

While TikTok and WeChat face opposition abroad, China blocks many European and U.S. Internet platforms. China began blocking Internet content in August 1996, only a year after it made Internet service available to its citizens. Among the first websites to be blocked was Voice of America. China's comprehensive censorship standards are now among the most restrictive in the entire world. The Net's distributed and anarchic architecture appeared to make it resistant to most forms of government regulation. Nonetheless, despite the initial difficulties involved with censoring digital technology, China has been quite successful at directing and regulating its citizens' use of the Internet.

China believes that the Internet must be tightly controlled in order to ensure social harmony and economic stability. It makes no secret of its commitment to active censorship and shows no reluctance to aggressively enforce its Draconian censorship laws. But China relies even more heavily on simple digital technologies. In the late 1990s, the Chinese Government put in place an impressive security infrastructure, known as the Golden Shield. It includes a surveillance and security management information system along with a criminal information system. A big piece of the Golden Shield is the "Great Firewall of China," by which the country blocks hundreds of thousands of websites from the view of Chinese citizens.[19]

The firewall blocks any forms of speech or political content that the Chinese government finds objectionable. It blocks references to the Tiananmen Square incident in 1989 when young Chinese citizens sought to defy the government by demanding a more open political society. The famous image of a young woman confronting a tank in the square can be downloaded almost anywhere in the world except China. Information on Tibet's political autonomy, Taiwanese independence, or the repression of the Uighurs in Xinjiang is also filtered by the firewall.

Many media and news websites are also subject to government censorship. For example, the web site of the British Broadcasting Corporation (BBC) is blocked (www.bbc.co.uk), and the international news website of Voice of America (www.voa. go)] remains off limit. Other major Internet content providers such the *New York Times* and Bloomberg News are no longer available. If Chinese users try to access popular and influential human rights sites like Amnesty International or Human Rights Watch (http://hrw.org) they will be disappointed.

In addition to filtering objectionable websites, the Chinese government also monitors all email and text messaging, and it keeps a close eye on blogs. It has demanded removal of any blog posts about things like Tiananmen Square, Uighur repression, or government corruption. China also forbids any access to global social media platforms such as Facebook, Twitter, and Instagram. In many countries these platforms have been used as organizing tools for protesters. But in China Facebook and Twitter were permanently blocked in 2009 after riots in Xinjiang. These sites feed the natural impulse to share and disseminate information, not all of which is benign (at least from the Chinese government's perspective). YouTube was permanently blocked in 2008 after videos of unrest in Tibet created a stir in the country. Each one of these platforms hosts too much uncensored content about human rights, politics, and religion. There are social networking platforms like RenRen that substitute for Facebook, but they are carefully monitored by the Chinese censors.

China's Great Firewall has ramifications that go well beyond China. The country's "giant cage" has undoubtedly contributed to a more balkanized and fragmented Internet. Thanks to China and other autocratic governments, the Internet is no longer a borderless global technology with few restrictions on information flows but a collection of nation state networks that heavily restrict content. While information may move more freely within a country, there is far less mobility across cultural borders.[20]

Cisco in China

The Chinese authorities could not build or sustain their "Great Firewall" without the technological assistance of giant high-tech Chinese companies like Huawei and ZTE. It has also had the assistance of some U.S. companies such as Cisco. Cisco was founded in 1984 at the height of the personal computer revolution, when opportunities abounded for companies developing network technologies. Known for its customer service mentality and superior product line, Cisco took full advantage of the surge in private organizations that wanted Internet connectivity. Cisco also provided local area networks and many other network solutions to a wide variety of corporate clients.

The company's core products, including switching equipment and routers, are manufactured primarily for the telecommunications industry. Competitors in this segment of Cisco's business include Sweden's Ericsson, China's Huawei, and France's Alcatel-Lucent. The router is a synthesis of hardware and software that provides data routing capability central to the Internet infrastructure. Routing is the process by which a path or route is selected for transmitting packets of data across the Internet in accordance with the TCP/IP protocols, which break that data (such as an email message or website content) into packets. This flexible routing system is achieved through a "hopping" process whereby these packets of data are passed from one computer to another until they reach their destination where they are reassembled.[21] By 1999, Cisco had an 80% share of the global market for routers, and it remains a major player. In later years Cisco has expanded into a whole range of application software in order to provide more seamless and comprehensive solutions to its customers.

Cisco began selling routers and other networking technologies to China in 1998, about two years before the Golden Shield program was initiated. How do its products factor into this country's technologies of control? There are eight large gateways coming into China from the global network that provide Internet access for Chinese citizens. They are managed by telecom companies, such as China Telcom. Those gateways used Cisco routers, which became the "backbone" of the Chinese network. After they were purchased from Cisco, those routers were equipped with packet filtering capability that enabled the filtering out of unwanted content. While the primary purpose of routers is to direct or "route" Internet traffic to its correct destination, they can also be easily configured to block content and thereby *prevent* information from getting to its destination. These specially modified gateway routers blocked websites based on an access control list. Any website on the list, which is managed by the Ministry of Information, will be blocked. The router itself, therefore, becomes the censor.[22]

Cisco certainly knew that its routers would be transformed into censorship systems. Internal memos reveal that its engineers regarded the Chinese government's severe internet censorship program as an opportunity to do more business with China. Under the category "Cisco Opportunities," a ninety-page document on new opportunities outlined how the company might benefit economically from the enhancement of China's Golden Shield censorship system. Cisco executives repudiated this document, but, for some, it was evidence that the networking giant marketed its routers to China specifically as a censorship tool.[23]

In 2004 China began its CN2 project, which was an upgrade of its networking technologies. Two companies, Juniper and Cisco, provided routing equipment for the regional backbones. The Cisco routers were technologically superior to the ones it had sold in 1998. They could be equipped with 750,000 sophisticated filters. The more state-of-the art the router, the more "granular" its filtering mechanisms become. Thus, these new network technologies allowed the Chinese government to control and monitor online speech even more tightly. Web content or sub-pages could be filtered through "deep packet inspection." With this software, the router can filter out pages within a website by examining the specific content of those pages. While some of the website is passed along to the user, any sub-pages within that site containing forbidden key words would be blocked.[24]

Some reports have indicated that in the CN2 project Cisco played a more active role in helping the Chinese censor content. According to the *International Herald Tribune*, not only has Cisco sold thousands of routers with sophisticated filtering capabilities to China, "the firm's engineers have helped set [those routers] to spot 'subversive' key words in a message."[25] Cisco has denied allegations that it directly assisted Chinese technocrats to censor the Internet, but one major investment firm sold its sizable stake in Cisco because the company lacked transparency and has been too reticent about its business practices in China.[26]

Of course, these routers and filtering mechanisms used for the purpose of censorship are far from foolproof. Like all firewalls, China's has a certain level of porosity. Circumvention technologies like proxy servers located outside of China can help sophisticated Internet users to bypass the firewall. There are also anti-censorship software tools. Yet the best estimate of researchers is that only 1% of Chinese Internet users take advantage of such tools to access forbidden content or social networks like Twitter and Facebook. This may be due to fear of getting caught, a lack of awareness that such tools exist, or perhaps a lack of interest in what lies beyond this formidable "fire wall."[27]

Cisco has come under harsh criticism for supplying China with networking equipment, and also for selling the country surveillance software. There were two lawsuits that accused Cisco of helping the Chinese government censor the Internet. But is this criticism fair? In Congressional Hearings in 2006 and 2008, Senior Vice President Mark Chandler acknowledged that its networking equipment included filtering capabilities. But he protested that Cisco sells the exact same standard, unmodified networking equipment to all countries seeking its services. Moreover, he added, Cisco "does not customize, or develop specialized or unique filtering capabilities in order to enable different regimes to block access to information."[28] Nonetheless, Cisco routers, specially configured by Chinese experts to stand guard over the virtual borders of China, have been transformed into a censorship tool.

Should Cisco have sold to China its routing equipment, equipped with generic packet filtering capability, knowing in advance that they will become a principal component in China's Great Firewall? Should companies be held accountable for how their products are configured by an authoritarian state? It seems unreasonable to hold this networking company responsible for everything its customers do with generic switching equipment and routing technologies. Cisco sells routers to China for the ethically suitable purpose of enabling Internet connectivity, and a side effect of that transaction is the modification of those routers by its customer with censoring architectures. The "Cisco Opportunities" memo is disturbing, however, because it implies that Cisco shared in China's intentions to block entire websites and filter web content such as Western media platforms that are seen by most of the world. If the company intentionally sought to profit from China's active filtering of political speech, there is some complicity and hence blameworthiness on Cisco's part. Also, if allegations are true that Cisco engineers helped to configure the routers to detect sensitive key words and block websites or sub-pages with those key words, Cisco is culpable of materially cooperating with the Chinese government in depriving its people of free speech rights.

Custodian of the Internet in China

Google

Google was founded in 1998 by two Stanford graduate students, Sergey Brin and Larry Page. The company's original mission was "to organize the world's information, and make it universally acceptable and useful." Their specific goal was to create software that facilitated the searching of the Internet's vast pools of data and information. Thanks to its PageRank algorithm, it pioneered the delivery of reliable organic search results by giving priority to web pages that were referenced or "linked to" by other web pages. Google monetized its technology by licensing its search engine, by ads linked to user searches, and by paid listings, or "sponsored links," positioned next to web search results. Thus, Google is able to provide users with both organic search results that preserve its impartiality and paid content that generates revenue.[29]

Google is a virtual monopoly in search, with a 70% share of the global search engine market. Google owns YouTube, and has expanded into many different directions with products like Google Maps, Gmail, Google Docs, and a leading Internet browser called Google Chrome. Google entered the cell phone market with its Android operating system that powers many mobile phones made by companies like Xiaomi, Motorola, and Samsung.

Google and its workers are guided by a set of principles or "golden rules." These rules or values include "Encourage creativity," "Communicate effectively," and "Don't be evil."[30] The "Don't be evil" principle primarily reflects the company's commitment to search neutrality. Despite the opaqueness of its algorithms, the company vows not to compromise the integrity of its search results, and to allow ads to appear with those results if they are relevant. Google has set high ethical expectations for itself and is often criticized when it deviates from its core values.

Google introduced a Chinese version of its search engine in early 2006, google. cn.[31] Its main rival in China was Baidu.com, Inc., which had a 60% share of the China Internet search engine market. Given the size of the market and its future potential, the company admitted that it was motivated to enter China because it was "strategically important."[32] But Google remained a distant second to Baidu, which had dominated its home market since its founding. Baidu claimed that its success came from its emphasis on service rather than "innovation for innovation's sake." But the company also got special favorable treatment from the Chinese government.[33]

In order to comply with China's austere censorship laws, Google agreed to self-censor, that is, to purge its search engine results of any links to websites or other content not approved by the Chinese government. These included Western media sites along with the websites of NGOs critical of China, such as like Human Rights Watch or China Labor Watch. Any web pages with politically sensitive key words would not be accessible through a Google search. As one reporter indicated:

> If you search for "Tibet" or "Falun Gong" most anywhere in the world on google.com, you'll find thousands of blog entries, news items and chat rooms on Chinese repression. Do the same search inside China on google.cn and most, if not all, of these links will be gone. Google will have erased them completely.[34]

China's strategy for co-opting companies like Google was to use these information intermediaries to make its censorship less transparent by erasing traces of censored websites so that people wouldn't even realize the specific websites or blogs being blocked by the firewall. Even without this form of censorship, the "technical opacity" of search engines threatens the ideal of equal access to information, but Google makes things far worse by showing Chinese users only the links the government wants them to see.[35]

Human rights groups and the Western media accused Google of hypocrisy and of violating its principled approach to doing business as expressed in its "golden rules." But Google argued that its presence in China had net benefits, since they provided Chinese citizens with greater access to information. According to a Google spokesperson, "While removing search results is inconsistent with Google's mission, providing no information (or a heavily degraded user experience that amounts to no information) is more inconsistent with our mission."[36] Google firmly believed that its presence in China would contribute to the country's economic reform and modernization, and that this consideration must be balanced with the censorship requirements imposed by the Chinese government.

Nonetheless, after four years of complying with China's censorship regime, Google suddenly decided to reverse course. The catalyst for this decision was a cyber-attack on Google.com that clearly targeted the Gmail accounts of human rights activists. As a result, on January 12, 2010, Google announced that it would no longer "self-censor" its China search engine. As the conflict with China intensified, Google began redirecting its Chinese users to google.com.hk, its unfiltered Hong Kong site. In response, the Chinese government began blocking the Hong Kong search site.[37] Sergey Brin was the driving force behind this decision, while others, like CEO Eric Schmidt, believed that Google should persevere with its current China policy. Brin's change of heart came about because of his own negative experience with the information censorship that he experienced as a child growing up in the Soviet Union.[38]

LinkedIn

While most social media companies are banned from China, LinkedIn is a notable exception. LinkedIn, owned by Microsoft, is a social media platform for business people and professionals. Social media platforms help to shape public discourse and LinkedIn is no exception. Like all social media platforms, it moderated content according to community guidelines. For example, participants must use their real names and any inaccurate information in user profiles is prohibited. In China, of course, content moderation takes on a whole new meaning.[39]

LinkedIn allows its users, both workers and employers, to create profiles and "connections" to each other in an online social network. The company's ambitious global mission is simple: "To connect the world's professionals to make them more productive and successful." And the company's vision is to create opportunities for every member of the global workplace so that he or she can "work smarter."[40]

When a person joins the LinkedIn platform, he or she gets access to people, jobs, news, updates, and advice that will help them in their professional lives. Members can search for business contacts and join industry groups or professional organizations relevant to their careers. Anyone can join LinkedIn, but most people sign up when they receive an invitation from a LinkedIn member to become one of the connections in their network. Upon joining LinkedIn, the new member creates a profile that includes his or her educational background, work history, and any professional affiliations. Once this person becomes a LinkedIn member, she can invite others to become part of her network of connections. That network, which consists of direct connections along with secondary and tertiary ones (that is, connections of a user's connections, etc.), will most likely reflect and imitate professional relationships in the real world. Thus, a doctor will have connections with other doctors, nurses, and medical professionals.[41]

In 2014, LinkedIn launched its local Chinese website called Ling Ying and established official operations in China. From its founding, LinkedIn executives aspired to make the company a major player in China to fulfill its mission of linking together the global workforce. But they also knew that this was fraught terrain for Western social media companies because of the country's strict rules for content moderation and its favoritism toward local competition. However, LinkedIn has found the formula for success. Unlike Facebook, Twitter, and Instagram, the Chinese government has never blocked access to the website. The secret of LinkedIn's good fortune is its disposition to self-censor, to filter objectionable content from view of its Chinese users. In an interview with the *Wall Street Journal*, LinkedIn CEO Jeff Weiner said the company expected "there will be requests to filter content," adding, "we are strongly in support of freedom of expression and we are opposed to censorship ...

[but] that's going to be necessary for us to achieve the kind of scale that we'd like to be able to deliver to our membership."[42]

Thus, on both the Chinese and English language sites in China, LinkedIn censors any offensive content, including web pages with certain key words and phrases along with links to all blacklisted websites. Like its social media counterparts in the U.S., LinkedIn relies primarily on software algorithms to determine which content will be blocked. When a user engages in political criticism of China or posts content with forbidden language, he or she receives an email message stating that what they have written is prohibited expression in China and "will not be seen by LinkedIn members located in China." Any subject matter or content on the "access control list" of China's Ministry of Information will be blocked by LinkedIn's efficient algorithms.[43]

In addition to censorship, LinkedIn imposes other restrictions on its Chinese users. They are denied access to important social media tools. For example, users cannot create and join groups and they cannot post long essays. This digital repression is designed to limit in-depth online discussions (that might have criticism of the government woven into the text) and to prevent the formation of virtual communities that could mobilize protests against the government.[44] LinkedIn has also agreed to store all data about its Chinese users on servers located within China and consent to allow Chinese authorities access to that data upon request.[45]

The LinkedIn story demonstrates the high ethical risks of doing business in a country like China that does not respect certain rights like free political speech. By entering the Chinese market, the company puts itself at great risk of violating universal rights along with its own core values. Those values emphasize building trust with their customers and "doing what is right." But it is difficult to see how the onerous restrictions imposed on its Chinese user base builds trust or how censorship of important political speech is consistent with doing what is right and just.[46]

The right to free speech and intellectual freedom

How do we assess the moral implications of the policies of these Internet custodians like LinkedIn and Google? To address this matter we must begin with another question about China: is the country guilty of malfeasance for its suppression of political speech? Its rigid censorship regime seems intuitively wrong to those in liberal democracies, but should critics in those democracies be more tolerant of China's different standard for free speech? Should they avoid the temptation to universalize a "Western" idea? Chinese authorities have maintained that the country's Internet regulations are not oppressive and on the contrary are compatible with its nationalistic pride and its cultural traditions.

Some ethicists have defended the obligation to abide by different moral belief systems when doing business abroad, however discordant those systems may be with traditional Western norms. Echoing Rawls, who supports a thin theory of universal rights, these philosophers have argued that we must be more sensitive to the reality of ethical pluralism, which presumes that there are a broad range of ethical viewpoints that can be validly chosen by different communities. Pluralists may find some extreme moral positions to be invalid, but believe that cultures deserve copious moral free space and so their values must be presumptively authoritative.

Defenders of China's policy also observe that it has a different conception of the person's role and status within the state. China gives priority to the social whole, the political community, over the individual. It prioritizes collective national dignity over individual dignity. Therefore, the country promotes a more collectivist view of human rights that justifies its overall approach to censorship. The nation's self-assertion is far more important than individual expression. While free speech is a universal right, there are different cultural expressions of that right. The Chinese government respects in broad terms the value of free expression, but interprets that value differently than its counterparts in the West. It chooses a different equilibrium between freedom and social order than what is typical of countries like the United States.[47]

The Confucian tradition supports this viewpoint. This ancient and revered system emphasizes respect for authority and sees the primary purpose of law as the protection of social harmony, which is inconsistent with the normative individualism of the Western liberal democracy. Confucianism embodies a social vision of family and society where "all key relationships were those of superior to inferior with a general duty of obedience owed by the inferior to the superior and a reciprocal duty of caring, support, and guidance owed by the superior to the inferior."[48] The regime provides durable political order resting on the rule of law, and in turn its citizens must be loyal to the state and obey that law. Thus, deference to authority and unwavering loyalty are traditional Confucian values that have shaped Chinese culture and provide some warrant for the country's constraints on defiant forms of political speech.

Since the time of Chairman Mao's "Cultural Revolution," the country has sought to control the knowledge of its citizens and to restrict democratic self-expression so there is no challenge to the state's uniform message or its exercise of power, however arbitrary it may be. This restriction is consistent with China's nationalism and pragmatic authoritarianism, which sees unequivocal support for the party as the only way for China to gain greater respect from other countries. According to Vincent, "The fundamental rights and duties of citizens are to support the leadership of the Communist Party of China, support the Socialist system, and abide by the Constitution and the laws of the People's Republic of China."[49]

Given these cultural anomalies and different value structures, it is no surprise that China adopts such a narrow conception of intellectual freedom and free speech "rights." The Chinese model, which heavily limits democratic self-expression for the sake of the collective good, represents the concrete reality of ethical pluralism, which must be factored into moral decision making by those doing business in China This pluralistic understanding of ethics and rights underlies the public responses of companies like Google and LinkedIn to criticism about their policies. These and other companies caught up in free speech controversies have argued at one point that their policies reflect the moral flexibility mandated by respect for cultural diversity. The social norms and civil liberties in a country like China are simply different from the norms and liberties enjoyed by U.S. citizens, and it's imperialistic to maintain that U.S. norms are superior. From a pluralist perspective, companies like Google or Cisco are doing nothing wrong when they cooperate in China's extensive censorship regime.

Instead of pluralism, we have defended the position of a moderate universalism, a comparatively thick set of universal human rights that limits the free moral space of every culture. Those rights proceed from intrinsic human goods valued for their own sake as constitutive aspects of human flourishing. These substantive goods, such as life and health, knowledge, and sociability (including friendship) constitute the foundation of normativity and provide a secure grounding for moral judgments about justice and human rights. Free expression is not an intrinsic good, since it does not directly contribute to human flourishing. Free speech doesn't really fulfill or perfect us, but it does allow us to pursue certain intrinsic goods. Thus, it is desired as a means to other important ends essential for human flourishing. For example, free expression is of fundamental importance for the pursuing the good of sociability, which "ranges through the forms of human community to its strongest form in the flowering of full friendship."[50] Free speech helps to bring about the harmonious cooperation that fortifies community and bonds of fellowship. Miscommunication or misunderstanding among people is common, but this reality means that communication efforts must be refined or revised, but certainly not suppressed. Dissenting political speech often brings to light problems and conflicts that must be resolved if a political community is to overcome differences and evolve into a more authentic communion of persons based on the common good.[51] A persuasive case can be advanced that because free speech fosters the intrinsic goods of social harmony and community, it is an instrumental good, necessary in some ways for human flourishing. Hence there is a requirement imposed upon others not to interfere with a person's enjoyment of this form of good we call free speech, and this requirement can be expressed in terms of a right to free speech.

Free expression is also a pillar undergirding the intrinsic good of knowledge and reflective understanding. Knowledge of truth is a basic good – it is far better to be well-informed and "clear-headed" than to be ignorant and befuddled. Disinformation or the unwarranted withholding of valuable information interferes with the acquisition of knowledge. The communication of objective knowledge is contingent on the ability of educators and others in positions of authority to disseminate that knowledge without fear of retribution or punishment. Government censorship and suppression of certain information is typically motivated by an impulse to keep the truth from citizens. As a result, they remain in the dark about important affairs of state or historical events. The restriction of free expression aims to achieve conformity of thought, rather than promote the discovery and dissemination of knowledge that is fundamental for human flourishing.[52]

From this analysis we can deduce that there is at least a moral presumption in favor of broad (but not absolute) free speech rights because free speech is an essential instrumental good. The right to free expression protects a person's ability to participate in several intrinsic human goods that constitute the basis of human flourishing. These self-evident goods, knowledge and sociability, are aspects of human flourishing, and so are sought after by all rational human persons. Every society exhibits concern for these goods. A decent society recognizes the value of knowledge and educates its young people in practical and theoretical matters. Therefore, it is plausible to argue for the universality of this right to free expression. Basic human rights are grounded in the necessity of these goods, in what human persons need and rationally desire for their well-being and well-being of communities to which they belong.[53]

Additional support for the universality and intrinsic value of this right to free expression is its endorsement by the United Nations in its Declaration of Human Rights: "Everyone has the right to freedom of opinion and expression; this right includes freedom to hold opinions without interference and to seek, receive and impart information and ideas through any media and regardless of frontiers."[54] The United Nations is certainly sensitive to cultural issues and to the need for flexibility in implementing rights. But rights like free speech cannot be ignored or subordinated to the preferences of the state. As the UNDHR stipulates, "All human rights are universal, indivisible, interdependent, and interrelated."[55]

If we conclude that there is such a natural, universal right to free speech, properly configured to protect morally justified privacy, secrecy, and security concerns, the Chinese government violates this right by prohibiting legitimate dissent, good faith disagreement with government policies, or attempts to correct a historical record that obscures the truth. As we have observed, China relies on its cultural tradition and its history as an oppressed state as a rationalization to support its nationalistic and authoritarian impulses. Loyalty and deference to authority have a grounding in Confucianism. However, there is a difference between the virtue of loyalty and blind obedience to the state and its arbitrary exercise of power. The Chinese state is not above committing injustice and when it does citizens must be free to call attention to that injustice and demand its correction. Yet China's laws and social structures do not allow for this type of critical political speech. China is guilty of a moral failing by not respecting this limited right to democratic self-expression, which many of its citizens have demanded for decades.

Given this moral analysis, the culpability of Google and LinkedIn logically follows. Both Big Tech players have actively cooperated in depriving the Chinese people of their free speech rights. All moral agents, including corporations, have a duty to avoid depriving people of their rights, and the responsibility for rights deprivation does not just fall on the principal actor (China), but on those who provide material assistance. These Internet platforms have assisted the Chinese government in perpetuating and implementing its censorship regime that deprives people of their right to free expression. If China is willfully violating this right by blocking certain content and restricting access to information, the policies of LinkedIn and Google are unjust and immoral.

These cases bring to light an axiomatic principle: a moral agent should not actively participate or cooperate in another's wrongdoing. The apposite ethical concept is cooperation, which is defined as "material assistance afforded to another … to carry out his purpose of doing wrong."[56] A moral agent can become implicated in the primary act of wrongdoing, such as censorship, by being an assistant or cooperator in that act. As Oderberg explains, being a cooperator is subsidiary to being the primary agent who performs the wrongful act, but it is a "partnership in that act that receives … some of its moral taint."[57] Google and LinkedIn are culpable of formal cooperation, since they used their technological capabilities to "materially assist" the Chinese Ministry of Information's censorship mechanisms and so they have deliberately participated in its wrongdoing (human rights abuses). For both companies, there was an explicit intent to share in the responsibility of the primary agent's objective of censoring content and limiting access to information. Such formal cooperation is always wrong, and there are no mitigating factors that attenuate the moral imprudence and complicity of both companies.

There is room, of course, for some flexibility when universal rights are expressed in a particular cultural context. The tradition of Confucianism may mean that the Chinese do not favor the same high level of intellectual freedom found in the West. However, flexibility for putting rights into practice does not mean unbounded pluralism. There must be freedom to criticize the government when it is corrupt or unjust in order to strengthen political community. To remove that freedom is too extreme because it completely negates the right to democratic self-expression. A strong, albeit limited and culturally conditioned, right to free speech qualifies as a hypernorm that is endorsed by many international agencies, including the United Nations.[58]

Case study: banning Huawei

Huawei was founded in 1987 by Ren Zhengfei with $3,000 of borrowed funds. From its earliest days, there have been suspicions that Huawei was loosely connected to the Chinese government, at least covertly. But Ren has repeatedly insisted that Huawei is an independent private enterprise with no government ties. However, the company's management structure closely resembles the structure of the Communist Party. Huawei admits that it carries certain "deep imprints" of the Party. In a country with little business expertise or capitalist traditions, China's entrepreneurs like Ren had to depend on the Communist Party culture as a managerial role model.[59]

Huawei is not publicly owned and has never sold shares to the public. The firm claims that it is entirely owned by its employees. Some critics of

Huawei worry that the company is still susceptible to interference by the Chinese government. They also point out the ambiguities surrounding this scheme of employee ownership. According to Huawei, employees own virtual Huawei stock so they can share in the company's financial success. This "ownership" is separate from the union that is the company's legal and registered owner. Employees cannot transfer shares and if an employee leaves, the company buys back his or her shares.[60]

Huawei began as a competitor of Internet pioneers, like Cisco and Juniper, selling routers and telephone equipment. With 180,000 employees, Huawei is now the world's largest manufacturer of telecommunications equipment, with revenues of $123 billion. The company is also the number two global smartphone vendor, behind Samsung Electronics.[61] Huawei began to expand outside of China around the turn of the century. It won big accounts in many Western countries with its low prices and quality networking products. Besides being competitive in its pricing, Huawei is also innovative. After a series of mergers only four major cellular equipment producers remain: Nokia, Ericsson, Huawei, and ZTE.

Huawei is one of the leading suppliers of the network infrastructure components that are necessary for building 5G networks. Huawei's 5G system allows wireless carriers to deliver high-speed WiFi directly to homes (without the need for installation of any equipment). The transition from 4G to 5G will markedly increase data speeds on mobile devices, making possible the coming Internet of Things and other innovations. Ren's ambitious company now wants to help shape the world's technological future by pushing the global adoption of its 5G standards. Those standards include frequencies to be used, and Huawei uses frequencies close to those reserved for the U.S. military.[62]

U.S. officials have expressed concerns about Huawei not only because of its opaque ownership structure but also because of Chinese laws. China's 2017 National Intelligence Law requires all Chinese companies to supply data to the government whenever it is requested. U.S. government officials also contend that Huawei has constructed network equipment that allows the company to access mobile phone networks without the carriers' knowledge. This is made possible by a system of back doors built into the equipment.[63]

As a result of these concerns, the United States government has effectively barred Huawei from selling its cellular equipment to U.S. companies. It is also illegal to sell American-made components to Huawei. This includes the advanced computer chips necessary for its networking products. When the Trump Administration realized that Huawei was still getting these chips from factories outside the United States, it extended its ban to include American-made semiconductor equipment. Thus, if a company like Taiwan

Semiconductor were using American technology it could no longer develop Huawei-designed chips.[64]

The United States has also tried to convince other countries not to use Huawei equipment for its 5G projects. Australia has imposed a ban on Huawei products and Japan has placed tight restrictions on the company's gear for government use. But the U.S.'s plea to ban Huawei has been met with some skepticism in Europe. The UK, for example, gave Huawei permission to construct noncritical parts of its 5G network. The global telecom equipment maker will be banned from the centralized parts of the 5G infrastructure that route data across the network as well as from locations near military or nuclear installations. Instead Huawei will be confined to providing only peripheral equipment, such as base stations and antennae, that connect the network core to customers' devices.[65]

Will the U.S. succeed in keeping Huawei out of the 5G networks of Europe and other countries? The logic of the U.S. Huawei strategy, crafted by the Trump Administration, is rooted in economic disengagement that will restrict Huawei as much as possible to its domestic market. As an alternative, countries can attempt to do business with Huawei in a way that is consistent with their strategic security. Perhaps adoption of some type of international security certification can be a reasonable compromise.[66]

Study questions

1. Was the U.S. right to ban Huawei from its 5G networks?
2. What strategy would you recommend for dealing with this company?

Conclusions

The freedom-enhancing potential of networked information technologies has not become a reality thanks to autocratic regimes and private censors. This "technology of freedom" was supposed to be a servant of truth and justice.[67] However, Internet architectures have been converted into another mechanism for exercising the state's authority. The Chinese government, for example, has discovered the hegemonic nature of Internet protocols and exploited them to its advantage. In its quest for state control of information flows it has erected a "giant cage" around its Internet. To accomplish this task China has depended on domestic companies like Huawei along with the assistance and technological expertise of Western Big Tech firms. Chinese authorities have used these companies to help build and maintain its censorship regime centered around the Great Firewall. Manufacturers like Cisco have supplied it with filtering-capable routers and networking equipment to build this infrastructure. At the same time, China has demanded that search engines and social media platforms self-censor in order to do business in China.

The conflicts faced by these companies exemplify the tensions between respect for local law and culture and the protection of universal rights. While China is an extreme case where virtually all forms of dissenting political speech are subject to censorship, there are borderline cases in other countries, which restrict speech in more limited ways. Some may argue that free expression is not a universal right but one that is culturally conditioned. Rawls did not believe that this right had any "urgency," and so presumably it could be marginalized. China's Confucian tradition might also support the country's collectivist view of human rights, which hollows out the essential meaning of the right to free political speech. But if an analysis of rights proceeds from an understanding of those intrinsically valuable human goods we all share in common, the necessity of a strong but limited right to free expression and intellectual freedom becomes readily apparent. Lending support to this viewpoint is the unequivocal affirmation of this universal right within the United Nation Declaration of Human Rights.

A secondary theme of the chapter has been the political consequences of the battle for technological supremacy now unfolding between the United States and China. Huawei has come to symbolize China's technological prowess and economic ascent. The rise of these China tech giants stokes fears in the West that its days of technological superiority are close to an end. Technological platforms have become both a military and economic necessity so the repercussions of this high-stakes battle could not be more profound.

Notes

1   Andreas Kendall-Taylor, Erica Frantz, and Joseph Wright, "The Digital Dictators," *Foreign Affairs*, March/April (2020), 14–21.
2   Feliz Solomon, "Governments Embrace Web Shutdowns," *Wall Street Journal*, February 26, 2020, A1, A10.
3   James Griffiths, *The Great Firewall of China* (London: ZED Books, 2019), 8–10. See also Kendall-Taylor, Frantz, and Wright, "The Digital Dictators."
4   Steven Secklow, Farnaz Fassihi, and Loretta Chao, "Chinese Tech Giant Aids Iran," *Wall Street Journal*, October 27, 2011, A16.
5   Rongbin Han, *Contesting Cyberspace in China* (New York: Columbia University Press, 2018), 57.
6   Shira Ovide, "Free Speech a Test for Twitter," *The Wall Street Journal*, August 5, 2013, B1–2.
7   Stu Woo, "Nokia Revives at Huawei's Expense," *Wall Street Journal*, April 7, 2019, A1, A8.
8   "Three Kingdoms, Two Empires," *Economist*, April 22, 2017, 55–56.
9   Ibid., 55.
10 Sebastain Herrera and Katy Ferer, "U.S. Bid to Block WeChat is Halted," *Wall Street Journal*, September 21, 2020, A1, A8.

11 Raymond Zhong, "ByteDance Looks Outward for Future Growth," *New York Times*, September 15, 2020, B1, B6. See also "Internet: Sixty Seconds of Fame," *Economist*, July 25, 2020, 49–50.

12 Alexander Galloway, *Protocol* (Cambridge, MA: MIT Press, 2004), 42.

13 Margaret Roberts, *Censored* (Princeton, NJ: Princeton University Press, 2018), 37.

14 Gilles Deleuze, "Control and Becoming," in *Negotiations* trans. Martin Joughin (New York: Columbia University Press, 1990), 175.

15 "Who Controls the Conversation: Social Media and Free Speech," *Economist*, October 24, 2020, 18–20.

16 Floyd Abrams, *The Soul of the First Amendment* (New Haven, CT: Yale University Press, 2017), 11.

17 Michael Hanby, "A More Perfect Absolutism," *First Things*, October 2016, 25–31.

18 *Reno v. ACLU*, 521 U.S. 844 (1997).

19 "China and the Internet: A Giant Cage," *Economist*, April 6, 2013, 5–7.

20 Eric Schmidt and Jared Cohen, *The New Digital Age* (New York: Knopf, 2013), 85.

21 Galloway, *Protocol*, 44–45.

22 Jack Goldsmith and Tim Wu, *Who Controls the Internet* (Oxford: Oxford University Press, 2006), 93–94. See also Schmidt and Cohen, *The New Digital Age*, 84.

23 Sarah Stirland, "Cisco Leak: 'Great Firewall' of China was a Chance to Sell More Routers," *Wired*, May 2008, 33.

24 Rebecca MacKinnon, "China's Internet: Let a Thousand Filters Bloom," *YaleGlobal Online*, June 28, 2005.

25 Jonathan Hurshy, "China's Tyranny Has Best High Tech Help," *International Herald Tribune*, January 15, 2006, 1, 14.

26 Robert McMahon and Isabella Bennet, "U.S. Internet Providers and the 'Great Firewall' of China," Council on Foreign Relations, February 23, 2011.

27 Rebecca MacKinnon, *Consent of the Networked* (New York: Basic Books, 2012), 35.

28 Mark Chandler, Cisco Testimony before House International Committee, February 16, 2006. Available at http://blogs.cisco.com/gov/cico_testimony_before_house_international_relations_subcommittee.

29 Scott Galloway, *The Four: The Hidden DNA of Amazon, Apple, Facebook, and Google* (New York: Penguin, 2017), 131.

30 Eric Schmidt and Hal Varian, "Google's Ten Golden Rules," *Newsweek*, December 2, 2005, 38.

31 In 2000 Google began providing a Chinese language version of its search engine from the U.S., but it had to deal with sluggish performance thanks to the firewall along with occasional blockades by the Chinese government. By moving its servers to China, Google could provide faster service, since it wasn't subject to the firewall, but it would have to deal with China's censorship law.

32 Declared in a 2004 company presentation. Quoted in Jason Dean, "As Google Pushes into China, It Faces Clashes with Censors," *Wall Street Journal*, December 16, 2005, A1, A12.

33 Loreta Chao and Ethan Smith, "Google Aims to Crack China with Music Push," *Wall Street Journal*, February 6, 2008, A1, A16.

34 Clive Thompson, "China's Google Problem," *New York Times Magazine*, April 23, 2006, 51.

35 For a discussion on the politics of search engines see Julie Cohen, *Configuring the Networked Self* (New Haven, CT: Yale University Press, 2011), 193–199.

36 Quoted in "Google in China," *Wall Street Journal*, January 30, 2006, A 18.

37 Roberts, *Censored*, 56–57.

38 Jessica Vascellaro, "Brin Drove Google's Pullback," *Wall Street Journal*, March 25, 2010, A1, A18.

39 Tarleton Gillespie, *Custodians of the Internet* (New Haven, CT: Yale University Press, 2018), 23, 62.

40 See company web site: www.linkedin.com/about.

41 "Workers of the World, Log In," *Economist*, August 16, 2014, 51–53. See also David Yoffie and Liz Kind, LinkedIn Corporation 2012 (Boston, MA: Harvard Business School Publishing, 2015), 5–6.

42 Reed Albergotti, "LinkedIn's CEO: We're Going to Expand in China; Goals 'Aligned' with Government," February 24, 2014. Available at https://www.wsj.com/articles/BL-DGB-33100.

43 Paul Mozur and Vindu Goel, "To Reach China, LinkedIn Plays by Local Rules," *New York Times*, October 6, 2014, B1, B5.

44 Ibid.

45 Charlie Smith, "LinkedIn: Technological and Financial Giants but Moral Pygmies," *Huffington Post*, July 15, 2016. Available at https://www.huffingtonpost.com/charlie-smith/linkedin-in-china-technol_b_7791126.html.

46 For a list of the company's values see LinkedIn 10-K Report, Securities and Exchange Commission, 2016.

47 David Runciman, "China's Challenge to Democracy," *Wall Street Journal*, April 28, 2018, C1–2.

48 Daniel Chow, *The Legal System of the People's Republic of China in a Nutshell* (St. Paul, MN: West, 2009), 42–43.

49 R.J. Vincent, *Human Rights and International Relations* (New York: Cambridge University Press, 1998), 56. See also Runciman, "China's Challenge to Democracy," C1–2.

50 John Finnis, *Natural Law and Natural Rights* (Oxford: Oxford University Press, 1980), 88.

51 Germain Grisez, *Living a Christian Life* (Chicago, IL: Franciscan Herald Press, 1993), 397–398.

52 Finnis, *Natural Law and Natural Rights*, 82–83.

53 Ibid.

54 United Nations Charter, "The Universal Declaration of Human Rights," in *Moral Philosophy for Managers*, 5th ed., ed. Richard Spinello (New York: McGraw-Hill, 2008), 293–297.

55 Ibid., art. 15

56 David Oderberg, "The Ethics of Co-operation in Wrongdoing," *Royal Institute of Philosophy Supplement* 54 (March 2004), 205.

57 David Oderberg, *Opting Out: Conscience and Cooperation in a Pluralistic Society* (London: IEA, 2018), 40–41.

58 Mary Ann Glendon, "The Universal Declaration of Human Rights at 70," in *Fundamental Rights and Conflicts among Rights* (Steubenville, OH: Franciscan University Press, 2020), 235.

59 Li Yuan, "Huawei's Identity Problem," *New York Times*, May 1, 2019, B1, B7.

60 Raymond Zhong, "So Who Owns Huawei? Answer is Complicated," *New York Times*, April 26, 2019, B1, B4.

61 Dan Strumpf, "Huawei Founder Defends Firm in Public Address," *Wall Street Journal*, January 16, 2029, A7.

62 Bojan Pancevski, "Europe Resists U.S. Effort to Bar Huawei from Market," *Wall Street Journal*, February 20, 2019, A1, A7. See also Thomas Ayres, "How to Pre-Empt the Huawei Threat," *Wall Street Journal*, November 18, 2019, A7.
63 Bojan Pancevski, "U.S. Says Huawei Can Secretly Tap Networks," *Wall Street Journal*, February 12, 2020, A1, A10.
64 "Chip Wars: Immaculate Misconception," *Economist*, May 23, 2020, 51–52.
65 Max Colchester, "U.K. Backs Huawei, A Setback for U.S.," *Wall Street Journal*, January 29, 2020, A1–2.
66 "Trade without Trust," *Economist*, July 18, 2020, 7.
67 Julie Cohen, "Between Truth and Power," in *Information, Freedom, Property* ed. Mireille Hildebrandt (London: Routledge, 2016), 59.

Chapter 10

Multinationals and environmental integrity

Centuries of industrial development have taken an immense toll on our natural environment. Some of this is due to carelessness but also to "the disordered desire to consume more than what is really necessary."[1] Multinationals have surely contributed to this situation, although attitudes are changing. In corporate boardrooms throughout the world there is a more acute awareness of the natural environment's vulnerabilities and the urgent need for its protection.

Despite this heightened consciousness about the dangers of environmental degradation, some multinational corporations are still not sufficiently assiduous in their handling of environmental issues. They are remiss in assuming their stewardship obligations, and they have failed to invest the necessary funds in order to prevent damaging externalities such as oil spills and excessive carbon dioxide emissions. Others like Volkswagen have deliberately polluted the environment rather than pay for the environmental protection required by law. When VW discovered that its new diesel engine, the EA-189, had failed to meet the U.S. Environmental Protection Agency's standards for emissions, it decided to solve the problem with software designed to cheat on emissions tests. This "acoustic function" software, also known as a defeat device, could recognize when a car was undergoing an emissions test. Under those conditions, it would set in place temporary pollution controls to reduce emissions so that the car would pass the test. However, during normal day-to-day operations an automobile with this diesel engine could emit up to forty times the legally permissible amount of nitrogen oxide, one of the most harmful pollutants. Cars from the 2009 model year with the EA-189 were sold in the United States to unsuspecting customers. Over the years that device was installed on 11 million vehicles worldwide, including 2 million in Germany.[2]

Nonetheless, apart from these exceptions, as environmental issues like global warming attract more attention companies are changing their attitude. Nike, for

DOI: 10.4324/9781003058427-10

example, has committed itself to "Move to Zero," a comprehensive sustainability plan designed to "help protect the future of sport." The program builds upon previous sustainability programs that sought water reduction from its disparate suppliers. Nike's ambitious goal is to power all its facilities with 100% renewable energy by 2025 and operate with net-zero carbon emissions.[3] It might be possible to recover some of the costs associated with "Move to Zero" by differentiating its products along environmental lines.

The global oil industry dominated by multinationals like British Petroleum (BP), Royal Dutch Shell, ExxonMobil, and Chevron has a mixed record on environmental issues. More recently, BP's Deepwater Horizon accident in the Gulf of Mexico left the industry reeling for many years. The massive oil spill caused great damage to the Gulf region's ecosystem and generated severe economic losses for many Gulf-area businesses and individuals. BP was guilty of gross negligence for its multiple safety compromises linked to its myopic focus on cost containment.

But BP has reformed its ways as it pivots to green energy. At the center of BP's enlightened energy strategy, introduced in 2020, is the "green plan," which prescribes a 40% reduction in oil and gas production over the next decade. It includes major investments in low carbon energy along with wind and solar technologies. The company believes that demand for oil has peaked, while demand for renewable energy is poised to soar. Although BP's plan was lauded by some environmentalists, oil industry analysts expressed skepticism about the company's future. BP has not explained how these new operations will compensate for its decline in the oil business.[4]

Royal Dutch Shell (RDS), on the other hand, has tied its future to natural gas, which it believes is the energy source of the future. Gas is a cleaner source of energy than oil or coal. Burning gas emits less greenhouse gases than those carbons. However, gas is susceptible to leakages of methane, another dangerous greenhouse gas. Methane causes more warming that carbon dioxide, though it does not linger in the atmosphere the way CO_2 does. RDS presumes that natural gas is a viable bridge between fossil fuels like coal and renewables such as wind and solar. But this is a risky strategy for RDS, with the economic outlook for global gas demand projected to peak in the 2030s.[5]

U.S. oil companies have followed the example of RDS and taken a different path from most other European majors like BP. The leading US supermajors, Chevron and ExxonMobil, have placed their bets on a long-term future for gas and oil. ExxonMobil has increased spending to boost oil and gas production. Both companies continue extensive shale drilling in Texas and New Mexico along with deep-water offshore production. Chevron, however, is increasing its own use of renewable energy, and has a long-term plan to transition away from fossil fuels. But most U.S. energy firms like Chevron and ExxonMobil do not want to sacrifice economic returns for their investors during this transition period.[6]

There are certainly other issues besides climate change and sustainable development. Multinationals have struggled with the question of whether there should be universal environmental standards that do not differ from country to country, or whether standards can be varied depending upon local customs and regulations.

The oil industry has a long and troubling history of problems in developing economies where, unlike the United States or Western Europe, regulations are feeble and enforcement virtually non-existent. In these more remote locations, where the rule of law is so casual, victims often have a difficult time vindicating their rights. Also, companies contribute to corruption in some countries by allowing venal sovereigns to amass big sums of money at the expense of their citizens. This is part of the resource curse: a fight for rents over oil profits that destabilizes a government. Thus, behavior of oil companies in countries like Nigeria or Equatorial Guinea deserve scrutiny and some ethical analysis.

This chapter will explore these demanding environmental issues confronting multinationals that are pressured toward the goals of sustainable development and high environmental performance. Their strategic decisions require tough tradeoffs. For now, the most difficult tradeoff is between economic development and the integrity of public goods. Companies like ChevronTexaco (now just "Chevron") and BP must produce private goods while preserving public goods. This leads to a fundamental tension because corporations are compensated for the private goods (oil) they produce, but not for the public goods (a sound ecosystem) they might strive to protect.[7] Compounding the issue for multinational corporations is the matter of regulatory arbitrage: energy companies like RDS are often subject to loose regulations and low standards in their emerging economies (like Nigeria) that differ from the higher standards in developed economies. To what extent can these corporations take advantage of this discrepancy? While we consider such issues, the major portion of this chapter is devoted to an analysis of the ethical basis for environmental protection and some treatment of how companies can balance responsible stewardship with economic efficiency. As preparation for that analysis the chapter presents a brief overview of the types of environmental damage that continue to cause unrelenting pressures on the ecology.

Environmental degradation

In the past, corporations throughout the world were able to largely ignore environmental issues. The reason for this indifference is that water, air, and the earth are free goods or public goods. The physical environment was conceived as a common good or common property that no one owns. Hence, this "property" could be used with impunity to emit waste or air pollutants without taking into account the damage that might be done. A DuPont plant in West Virginia, for example, dumped 10,000 tons of waste into the Gulf of Mexico until it was finally stopped in 1974.[8] In the 1980s it was discovered that the Pine River in Michigan had been heavily polluted by poisonous chemical dumped into the river by Michigan Chemical Company. And in 1969 the Cuyahoga river in Ohio became so polluted with industrial waste that it caught on fire. The list of such environmental abuses is virtually endless. These are classic cases of market failure, where a negative externality imposes costs on those powerless to affect the outcome.

This ethically naive view of the environment as a "free" good came to an abrupt halt when the cumulative effects of all this pollution and environmental pillaging became obvious. Constant air pollution along with the careless dumping of toxic wastes by so many companies was slowly creating a "tragedy of the commons."[9] As a result, governments, businesses, and other institutions became more attentive to environmental externalities. This tragedy of the commons came into more discrete focus with the intellectual help of environmentalists like Aldo Leopold who passionately argued that ethics rather than economic self-interest must be the guiding norm for the use of environmental resources. According to Leopold, "A thing is right when it tends to preserve the integrity, stability, and beauty of the biotic community; it is wrong when it tends otherwise."[10]

Leopold's principle may be an oversimplification of complicated issues, but it captures the importance of taking into account ecological integrity when investment and production decisions are made. The environmental question must be addressed as a moral issue – not just an economic one – and risks to the environment must be prudently managed. Taking this moral imperative seriously, however, does not necessarily imply an incompatibility between economic development and environmental integrity. It does mean that economic growth should not come at the expense of environmental quality, especially when alternatives are available to use fewer resources and emit less pollution. Some of those alternatives may even create opportunities for corporations to increase profits by enhancing their environmental performance.

Thanks to the work of Leopold and other environmentalists such as Rachel Carson, improvements have been made and the physical environment is in far better shape than it was several decades ago. In the United States legislation such as the Clean Air Act and the Clean Water Act has begun to reverse years of damage caused by the careless pollution practices of corporations. However, the decline in pollution and other forms of environmental destruction that has taken place in advanced economies during this period has not been matched in developing economies. Millions of children still die each year because of adulterated drinking water. Similarly, urban smog, which has receded in major Western cities, continues to be a serious problem in urban areas in developing economies. Part of the problem is that these countries cannot afford pollution abatement or other mechanisms. As these economies mature, there is hope that there will be more substantial investments in environmental controls.[11] In some of these countries like Mexico sound environmental restrictions are in place, but, in the past, enforcement has been suboptimal.

In China, accelerated economic growth linked with a history of inertia regarding environmental regulations have taken a heavy toll on this country's ecosystem. Studies blame heavy air pollution caused by coal combustion for reducing life expectancy by five years in parts of the country. Toxic and rancid smog, contaminated soil, and heavily polluted waterways are among the country's biggest problems. The primary cause for all of this pollution is the voracious need for material resources required by China's expanding economy. While China accounts for only 16% of the world's output, it consumes between 40% and 50% of the world's coal, copper, steel, aluminum, and zinc.[12] China has made commendable progress addressing the problem of air pollution but soil pollution remains another grave problem that also needs attention. The country is filled with "brownfield sites," areas once used for industrial waste, along with polluted farmland; 16.1% of all soil and almost 20% of farmland has been contaminated by chemicals. The problem stems from poor regulations of the chemical and fertilizer industries for many decades. There has been a recent crackdown on the dumping of chemical waste, yet Greenpeace has still discovered heavily tainted soil in the countries' chemical-industrial parks.[13]

In addition, to meet its massive energy needs, China still relies heavily on coal. It generates 49% of the world's coal-fired electricity. China expanded its electricity-generating coal capacity to meet its growing economy, which saw GDP increase by 200% between 2000 and 2012. But the use of coal has tripled the country's carbon dioxide emissions, making China the largest emitter of CO_2 in the world. The country has plans to reduce coal capacity, but the transition to other energy sources will take a long time.[14]

The ongoing environmental degradation in China demonstrates that there are still pressures on the world's vulnerable ecological systems and threats to human welfare. Among the most severe and troubling global environmental problems are the following: ozone depletion, global warming, continuing water and air pollution, and toxic waste disposal into the earth. Wetlands and coastal erosion is also a prime concern. Many of these problems may seem to be localized but actually have a broad reach – failure to contain air pollution in a small city affects not just the citizens of that city, but neighboring communities and at some level the whole ecological system. Pollution in the border areas of Mexico, for example, will have an impact on southwestern areas of the U.S.

Some of these environmental problems are aggravated by deforestation trends. Denuded forests erode more easily and allow for more sediment to flow into waterways. Forests and wetlands filter and purify water and they act as reservoirs to capture rain and melting snow. Forests also act as "sinks" for carbon dioxide gases. The rainforests of the Amazon soak up and store a considerable proportion of the global CO_2, so they serve as a critical brake on the forces of climate change. Deforestation has intensified in countries like Brazil. Looser regulations allow more logging, mining, and farming activities in the Brazilian Amazon. Illegal logging has also plagued the country. Brazil's President, Jair Bolsonaro, has expressed his affinity with wildcat loggers, who are among the Amazon's poorest residents, along with wildcat cattle ranchers and gold miners. There is "plenty of forest to exploit," he declares. As a result, deforestation in Brazil grew by about 55% from 2019 to 2020.[15]

Global warming and climate change

The environment suffers from many problems, but the gravest long-term environmental danger is global warming and climate change. The risk of appreciable climate change is not only an issue for policy makers. It also matters to the private sector. Climate change can pose a threat to the way companies operate, though it can also be a competitive opportunity. By improving environmental performance companies might discover offsetting cost savings or they may find that consumers are willing to pay a premium for the preservation of public goods.

What is climate change and why is this such an urgent issue? Certain gases such as carbon dioxide (CO_2) and nitrous oxide (NO_2) trap solar heat in the earth's atmosphere, preventing it from radiating back into space. This trapping of energy insulates the earth's surface and thereby causes the earth's temperature to rise. Since these gases trap heat, they are known as "greenhouse gases" and the rising temperature is known as the "greenhouse effect." Carbon dioxide, which is emitted by burning gas and other fossil fuels, is the chief greenhouse gas. Scientists estimate that about 26 billion metric tons of CO_2 are emitted annually into the atmosphere.[16] A third greenhouse gas is methane (CH_4), which can leak into the atmosphere from natural gas. More than 300 million tons of methane is emitted each year into the atmosphere, and a ton of methane causes eighty-six times more warming than a ton of CO_2.[17] The fossil fuels that emit these three gases account for 82% of the world's current energy consumption.

The higher the level of these gases in the environment, the more radiation is trapped by the atmosphere and is redirected back to the surface. This process is known as radiative forcing. There is no doubt that global average temperatures have increased over the past two centuries. The Intergovernmental Panel on Climate Change (IPCC) has predicted that the global mean surface air temperature will rise by at least 2.0° C over pre-industrial levels by 2100. But without concerted efforts to decarbonize and curtail CO_2 in the atmosphere, the temperature increase could even be as high as 3.0° C.[18]

Many scientists remain convinced that global warming trends, if left unchecked, will have cataclysmic effects on the surface of the planet. When the earth's surface gets warmer, sea levels rise. As the ocean warms, it expands. Cities and other populations in low-lying areas will be threatened by these rising sea levels. Global warming will also cause ice fields to melt, including the polar ice caps. That melting combined with thermal expansion of the oceans will lead to a rise in sea levels that will cause flooding in coastal areas. The best estimate of the IPCC is an inordinate 50 cm increase in average sea level by 2100. Some scientists are persuaded of this dire prognosis while others argue that warming of the earth's atmosphere by 2° or so will be insufficient to cause such a drastic chain of events.[19]

Other effects of global warming include more severe storms and weather events (such as floods or extended droughts), disruptions to agriculture, and an increase in tropical disease. Current climate models, however, cannot accurately confirm the likelihood of these events. The uncertainty of the science behind global warming and the difficulty of establishing causal connections has clouded the policy debates over this issue. One thing is certain, however. If this massive public goods problem is to be dealt with effectively it will require a high level of global cooperation. It will also require that multinational corporations be more conscientious about integrating environmental concerns into their corporate strategies and policies.

What obscures the resolution of environmental issues like global warming is the inevitable tradeoff between economic development and conservation of the environment. Shifting economies away from heavy reliance on fossil fuels will be quite expensive. Policy makers and multinationals must come to terms with what level of economic cost is acceptable for preserving environmental assets. In addition, few areas of science are as complicated and "multidisciplinary" as the planet's climate. While scientists concur that the globe is warmer, there is legitimate disagreement about the magnitude of human contribution to climate change and the speed at which the process is occurring.[20] Physicist Steve Koonin, for example, presents a reasonable case that "the net economic impact of human-induced climate change will be minimal through at least the end of this century."[21]

International environmental policy

Environmental problems like global warming affect the entire world and so demand multilateral solutions. A precedent for effective multilateralism was the international community's engagement over the issue of chlorofluorocarbons (CFCs). This refrigerant, used in air conditioners and refrigerators, emits chlorine when it is released into the air, which assaults the ozone layer that protects the earth's surface from harmful solar waves. Industrialized nations realized the danger and agreed to a ban on this ozone-depleting substance. These nations reached consensus on this ban in the Montreal Protocol on Substances that Deplete the Ozone Layer signed in 1987. DuPont, the world's largest producer, initially opposed the ban but eventually relented when the scientific picture about CFC damage became clearer. The company refrained from exporting its technology to developing countries even during the period when they were permitted to do so according to the terms of the Protocol. Recognizing the negative environmental impact of the continued use of CFCs, DuPont correctly exercised corporate leadership to drop CFCs despite the economic cost and to search for a replacement. CFCs have been replaced by hydroflourocarbons (HCFCs), which also contain ozone-depleting chlorine but at a much lower level than CFCs. Environmentalists continue to press for the adoption of a viable alternative to HCFCs.[22]

Even as early as the 1990s, evidence of global warming induced government officials across the globe to attempt concerted action to avoid impending catastrophe. A global treaty on global warming seemed to be the most sensible way to deal with this pressing environmental problem. The 1992 Earth Summit in Rio de Janeiro laid the groundwork by affirming the notion of "common but differentiated" responsibilities so that the burden of dealing with these problems falls on rich countries rather than poor ones.[23] Subsequent to the Rio treaty, the Kyoto Protocol was signed by the industrialized nations in 1997 and went into effect in 2004. By signing this

Protocol 150 nations agreed to reduce their emissions of greenhouse gases. The Protocol required industrialized nations to reduce carbon dioxide emissions during the first commitment period by an average of 5.2% below 1990 levels. The United States agreed to reduce its emissions to 7% below 1990 levels. Developing countries like India and China were not required to cut their emissions during this period. In keeping with the Rio treaty rich countries agreed to take the lead and act first.[24]

The United States, however, never ratified the treaty thanks to opposition of the Bush Administration, which cited the uncertainties of climate science and the prohibitively high economic cost of reducing greenhouse gas consumption. In 2015, 195 countries signed an agreement at the Paris Climate Conference. The signatories agreed once again to curtail greenhouse gas emissions in an effort to keep the earth's temperature increase "well below" 2° C of pre-industrial levels. The stretch goal is to keep global warming below 1.5° C.[25] President Trump pulled the U.S. out of the Paris Accord, but that decision was overruled when President Biden took office in 2021.

Reaching the Paris Accord goal will require a difficult energy transition from fossil fuels to renewable energy sources. About 90% of the world's energy that is now derived from fossil fuels will need to be replaced by renewable energy such as wind and solar. While this is a formidable challenge, there is room for optimism. Many governments are committed to this effort and the world has more renewable energy generation capacity. Solar power is a particularly promising technology. But if the political status quo remains unchanged and countries do not take decisive action, the temperature rise by the end of the century could be as high as 3° C.[26]

What are the implications of the Paris Accord's ambitious goals for multinationals and the private sector? Companies must obviously play a significant role in decarbonizing the economy. They face many "climate risks," such as falling sea levels that affect maritime trade "pinch points" such as the Suez and Panama canals. These risks will be amplified if the Paris goals are not attained. Thus, it is in their enlightened self-interest to take steps to help improve the climate. Also, regulations will force firms to act, so it is expedient to adopt a proactive rather than reactive strategy. Above all, companies can commit to the purchase of cleaner, renewable energy. Many firms have already vowed to reach zero carbon by 2050 or earlier. Green cars are part of this solution. Amazon, for example, is committed to add electric vehicles to their extensive fleet of delivery trucks. Companies can also attempt to decarbonize its supply chains by putting pressure on supplies to reduce carbon as much as possible.[27]

The general question is the scope of a multinational corporation's obligation to sustainability and to environmental integrity. Is it enough to follow current regulatory guidelines, especially in democratic societies where those guidelines really reflect the will of the people? Or is it imperative to exercise corporate leadership by proactively investing in more environmental quality protections than what is required by law? We argue in the next section that there are strong reasons for a resolute commitment to sustainable development when this whole issue is examined through the lens of basic human rights and other moral considerations.

Ethics and the environment

Some multinational companies that have adopted sustainability practices seek to use the environment as a lever to achieve competitive advantage. Improving environmental performance can become a source of strategic opportunity rather than a costly burden. For example, a corporation which enhances its environmental performance might then seek to recover the cost increase by differentiating that product by highlighting its environmental quality. An apparel manufacturer, for example, that conserves water throughout its supply chain could seek a premium price for its conservation efforts and differentiated product line. Sustainability can also be a driver of innovation within an organization and a means to enhance efficiency.[28]

Environmental concern as a source of strategic opportunity, however, may obscure the ethical issues at stake in these debates along with the need to sometimes subordinate economic objectives to environmental goals. While the sustainable use of natural resources, protecting the biosphere, and risk reduction are undoubtedly sound business practices, there is a general moral responsibility to the natural environment. The deeper question is whether the natural environment has intrinsic moral value or just instrumental value; if the latter is true, the obligation to protect the environment emanates primarily from effects on human health and welfare that come to pass through environmental degradation.

An ethical appreciation of environmental issues should begin with a proper understanding of the role of the natural environment in human affairs. In the past, there has been an unfortunate tendency to commodify nature and to regard it as material for human exploitation. This attitude assumes that sub-personal realities are devoid of intelligibility and natural worth, and are merely at humanity's disposal. Technology becomes a vehicle to serve humanity's insatiable desires, no matter how extravagant or excessive they may be. There are no limits on such exploitation except self-interest. This reckless view of nature, if taken to its extreme, can easily lead to irreversible changes in the ecosystem and a steady depletion of the world's natural resources.[29]

This tendency toward the objectification and exploitation of nature has its roots in the same philosophical soil that has nurtured the Cartesian tradition of subjectivism which, conceived all extended matter as objects to be controlled by the thinking subject. The natural world is thereby stripped of its marvelous depth, beauty, and complexity, and it comes to be seen merely as an instrument for technological manipulation. As Spengler observed, "One no longer sees a waterfall without transforming it into the thought of electric power."[30]

According to Heidegger, this form of subjectivism manifests itself in modernity's prevalent attitude of *technicity* (*die Technik*). Heidegger's term expresses how all beings, even the person and his or her body, are raw material for humanity's use and disposal. All natural beings are submitted to man's tight control, objectified by his calculations, planning, and cultivation. Everything in the world is a pawn, an "empty shell" devoid of any independent value, that man can manipulate the way he might manipulate scientific experiments.[31] Within this worldview, which drives modern technology, it is not surprising that the value of nature is reduced to its utility for the purpose of scientific and economic progress.[32]

Any sound view of the environment must overcome this pernicious attitude of technicity, which regards the earth merely as an object of utility that is to be mastered and transformed. Influenced by this paradigm, those who dwell on the earth submit nature to their own dispositions rather than "tend to" nature as a "watchman" or "shepherd."[33] On the contrary, humanity must safeguard and preserve sub-personal things in accordance with their true value rather than dominate and exploit them. We can use these sub-personal entities when necessary to promote our own human flourishing, but we cannot misuse them.

Once we can appreciate the inauthenticity of the attitude of *Technik* and its instrumental view of reality, we are in a better position to address the limits of technology and the dangers of the technological imperative, which has set in motion a war against nature's limitations. We can also isolate the fundamental moral obligations of corporations and other moral agents whose actions have an impact on the environment. Given the environment's natural beauty and value, and especially its indispensable role in promoting human flourishing, human action and technological intervention need to take into account three fundamental ecological considerations: each thing's nature and its place within the cosmos, the limits and non-renewability of natural resources, and the impact of economic development on the quality of human life, especially in industrialized areas. A good faith regard for these three factors represents an ethically responsive rather than exploitative approach to nature, which calls for using natural things reasonably and with restraint.[34]

With these general standards in mind, we can articulate several concrete and specific moral norms for multinational corporations and other international moral agents. First, nature should be respected and left undisturbed whenever possible, out of respect for the relative value immanent in nature and recognition of how everything in nature is interconnected. This principle implies that people and corporations should not disrupt natural things except to serve the common good or satisfy a valid human need that cannot be satisfied any other way. Humanity needs sources of energy to provide a means for transportation and protection from the cold. Past generations, who were not cognizant of global warming, were not irresponsible for developing sources of energy found within the earth, so long as they did so in a reasonable and restrained manner that deployed resources prudently to prevent waste and minimize any environmental harm.[35]

A correlative principle of this norm is the ethical demand to respect indigenous rights by consulting and compensating the inhabitants of tribal territories before exploiting resources on their land. Respect for native rights cannot be segregated from environmental issues, since indigenous people are rightly worried about the social problems generated by technological progress and the commodification of their lands.

Second, a multinational corporation must not unfairly accept bad side effects to other persons' health through its neglect of environmental concerns, even if the law of a certain country allows it to do so. According to Frederick and Hoffman, solutions to environmental challenges must be economically and technically feasible, environmentally manageable (i.e., not cause irreversible environmental harm), and ethically responsible. A decision is ethically responsible if it "poses no unreasonable threat to human life or health" and does not unjustifiably violate human rights.[36] An oil company's use of inferior equipment, which significantly increases the risk of oil spills or environmental contamination that would adversely affect the health and welfare of people in the area of its pipelines and drilling sites, is a flagrant instance of moral irresponsibility because it unjustly accepts the possibility of these harmful side effects. This is especially true if the risk of health hazards can be reduced by the use of state of the art technology. Similarly, pollution of waterways and land with hazardous material or toxic substances can never be condoned. Such behavior fails to avoid unreasonable risk to human health and welfare. As we saw in previous chapters, health and life are fundamental human goods. Hence intentional acts contrary to health are always wrong, along with the unreasonable acceptance of side effects harmful to others' health due to negligence or moral indifference. The goods of life and health are protected by rights that cannot be set aside merely for utilitarian purposes. Multinational corporations have a duty to protect those rights from deprivation by taking all necessary and reasonable environmental precautions to ensure that any risk to human health is minimized.[37]

Third, in accommodating the real human needs of the present, multinational enterprises must strive to avoid long-term and incremental environmental damage or resource depletion that will be detrimental to the quality of life for future generations. Multinationals must commit to an unequivocal sustainability strategy that gives priority to the use of renewable resources (such as solar energy or hydroelectric power), minimizes waste, and limits the use of non-renewable resources, such as fossil fuels, whenever possible. This commitment is a matter of intergenerational equity and reflects an attitude of stewardship rather than technicity.

In summary, respect for the relative values inherent in nature, the avoidance of unreasonable threats to human health and welfare by minimizing risk, and the sustainable use of natural resources, are matters of justice that reflect a proper respect for the rights and aesthetic interests of human persons.[38]

But what about the claims of the deep ecologists who argue that even this level of moral commitment is inadequate? Deep ecologists believe in the intrinsic value of the natural environment so that the conscious human person is no longer the central reference point. They contend that the environment must be preserved and "tended to" for its own sake, not just because mistreatment of the environment, or environmentally unfriendly policies, harm humanity in some way. What sort of moral standing do sub-human beings have? This is an extremely difficult issue to assess unless one perceives nature through a religious or metaphysical lens. God's creation by virtue of its very existence has an ontological goodness and immanent finality that deserves some measure of acknowledgment and respect. This perspective falls short of the biocentric viewpoint suggested by the deep ecologists that comes close to the divinization of nature and often calls for radical proposals that impede some legitimate uses of natural resources.[39]

The deep ecologist typically sees the cause of the environmental crisis as the anthropocentric character of Western culture. Environmental ethics has been heavily influenced by Lynn White's highly influential 1967 essay that traces our environmental problems to the anthropocentric perspective of the Genesis creation story, which segregates man from the rest of creation and authorizes his dominion over nature.[40] The only answer for this "arrogance" is "biocentric egalitarianism" that would drastically limit humanity's ability to meet its material needs.[41] This is a far more radical solution to the problem than we have proposed, and many will be uncomfortable with its practical implications. Contrary to White's thesis, the Judeo-Christian tradition insists that the universe has been created *for persons*, since without conscious persons in the universe there would be no one aware of nature's beauty and majesty.[42] Yet nature is not just raw material for our exploitation but a gift of the Creator to be conserved wisely and used prudently. According to Pope John Paul II, "The dominion granted to man is not an absolute power, nor can one speak of a freedom to 'use and misuse,' or to dispose of things as one pleases."[43]

This ongoing debate about deep ecology is too dense to be discussed at length in these pages. Rather than defend a secular view of deep ecology or the more moderate religious view, we might simply note that most environmental damage has an adverse impact on people in some way, either directly or indirectly. The integrity of the environment is vital for future generations, and by saving the wilderness and its wildlife from the hands of unscrupulous developers or by reducing global warming, we save ourselves. As Hoffman observes, "in most cases, what is in the best interests of human beings may also be in the best interest of the rest of nature."[44] If multinational enterprises concentrate on protecting their present and future human stakeholders from environmental harm, they will go a long way in living up to their responsibilities to the natural environment itself.

Big oil and the environment

Thanks to a round of mergers in the 1990s the global oil industry is now dominated by a group of "supermajors," including Chevron, Royal Dutch Shell, and Exxon-Mobil. But much of the industry's oil reserves are under the control of national oil companies (NOCs), which are owned (in part) by their respective governments. They include Gazprom, PetroChina, and Pemex. The supermajors spend $100 billion a year on exploration and production. As we have discussed, the industry must manage the "energy transition" away from oil, natural gas, and coal to renewables, but that is most likely still decades away. The oil and gas industry has also entered a new phase of extreme price volatility, which has an enormous global impact, since oil remains a strategic commodity. While advanced economies are less dependent on oil and natural gas to generate growth, oil is essential to sustain the rapidly expanding emerging economies in Asia, Latin America, and Africa.[45]

While all companies and organizations have a general responsibility to the natural environment, oil companies have a special obligation given their substantial economic power and the potential for environmental harm caused by their operations. Oil and natural gas extraction pose great risk to the integrity of the natural environment. The cost of those risks does not completely fall upon the company but is exported to third parties who are victims of oil spills, flaring, or other abuses. Among most U.S. firms, the industry's risky operations are compounded by a lack of commitment to renewable energy investment. Many shareholders, however, have resisted this carbon-heavy strategy, and companies might be forced to reform if those pressures persist. Also relevant is the question of whether fossil fuel companies like those in the oil industry should be held accountable for the global warming trends caused by their products.

In the past, the global oil industry has too often failed to deliver on environmental performance, and externalized the costs of oil spills and waste disposal. Some big companies have moved from one jurisdiction to another, evading accountability for their actions. Particularly in emerging economies, there has been an attitude of moral laxity or complacency about environmental protection. As Scruton points out, it is "this carelessness toward 'other places' that underlies environmental catastrophes."[46] It is instructive to review two of those catastrophes. In both cases supermajor oil firms failed to weigh the environmental consequences of their actions.

Aside from the BP oil spill in the Gulf of Mexico, two of the worst environmental disasters have occurred in Ecuador and Nigeria. Consider first the dreadful behavior of Texaco (now owned by Chevron) in Ecuador. After many years of exploration, Texaco discovered oil in the Lago Agrio region of Amazonian Ecuador. This was a large area occupied by indigenous people. Texaco entered into a partnership with the state oil company, Petroecuador. Although Texaco only owned 37.5% of this joint venture, it was given full operational control. Four hundred drilling sites were constructed along with necessary infrastructure such as roads and pipelines. This infrastructure included the Trans-Ecuadorean pipeline, which transported the oil across Ecuador to shipping ports in other parts of the country. Much of this crude oil was exported to the United States.

Texaco's Lago Agrio oil wells were productive but at an excessive social cost. The end result of Texaco's exploits in Ecuador was a poisoned land. The primary problems were the number and magnitude of oil spills in the region. Over the 18-year period that Texaco operated the 312-mile Trans-Ecuadorean pipeline, there were twenty-seven major pipeline ruptures. The total amount of oil spillage was 17 million gallons, and most of this oil was never properly cleaned up. Some of those oil spills made their way into the border areas of neighboring Peru. It's not known how much oil has spilled from the secondary pipelines. By comparison, the 800-mile Alaskan pipeline spilled about 1.6 million gallons of oil over a twenty-five-year period. Thus, it is reasonable to conclude that Texaco's environmental performance was well below industry norms.[47]

Second, the disposal of toxic waste was not handled with the proper precautionary procedures that would reduce the risk of spillage. During the process of drilling and testing a well for commercial production, toxic "formation water" rises to the surface. This heavily polluted water must be disposed of along with the drilling mud. Texaco dumped over 4 million gallons of this toxic waste into unlined, open pits, and some of that waste (drilling mud, formation water, and oil) eventually leached into rivers, streams, and shallow wells. As a consequence, drinking water in the vicinity of these pits was often contaminated. Rather than follow U.S. industry standards for waste disposal by fencing off the pits and lining them with concrete or metal to prevent leaching, Texaco was satisfied with the perfunctory environmental standards acceptable in Ecuador at the time. There were about 800 of these seven foot deep unprotected pits, and so the amount of waste escaping into the earth and dozens of adjacent streams was substantial.[48]

The company has always vaguely insisted that it abided by "international standards," and that most of the oil spills were the result of natural disasters rather than corporate negligence. But that claim is little consolation for those who have contracted cancer and other ailments thanks to Texaco's behavior. Experts concur that there have been over 1,400 cancer deaths in this region of the Amazon jungle. Geological reports show an excessively high level of toxins in the soil and water in the vicinity of the Texaco production sites.[49]

Texaco spent $40 million to clean up the oil spills and the pits with toxic waste. It received a liability release from the Ecuadorean government in the 1990s. But some residents of Amazonian Ecuador, sickened by the tainted drinking water and air pollution, filed a lawsuit against Texaco. The lawsuit was transferred to Ecuador in 2003, and in 2011 an Ecuadorian court blamed the oil company for the oil pollution and ordered it to pay $9.5 billion in damages. However, Chevron has refused to pay, citing its release from liability. In 2018, an international arbitration panel sided with Chevron and ordered Ecuador to vacate the verdict, but Ecuador has refused. As a result, the lawsuits and counter lawsuits have continued in the oil industry's "longest running legal slugfest."[50]

Far away, on another continent, Royal Dutch Shell caused similar damage in Nigeria. The corporation's regrettable experience in that country in the 1990s epitomizes the ethical and social challenges that oil companies face in developing countries. When oil was discovered in 1956 in the Niger River Delta, Royal Dutch Shell was the first of the major energy companies to initiate oil production operations. In the early 1970s, Royal Dutch Shell and the Nigerian Natural Petroleum Corporation (NNPC) entered into a joint venture, which controlled about 60% of Nigeria's discovered oil reserves. The NNPC was the majority partner with a 55% stake. The consortium produced 930,000 barrels of oil per day from oil wells scattered around the fertile Niger Delta.[51]

Much of the environmental damage and controversy was centered in Ogoniland, a 400-square mile ancestral land of the Ogoni people. Shell built ninety-six oil wells and five pumping stations in this area. Ogoni activists demanded a "fair proportion" of oil revenues and more investment in environmental quality. But the Ogoni received very little remuneration and had to contend with a vast pipeline network that blighted the landscape. Those pipelines periodically leaked oil that ruined the land. The incessant leaks and oil spills destroyed crops and polluted the waterways where the Ogoni fished. Some of the bigger oil spills were due to sabotage, but others were caused by natural disasters or equipment breakdowns. A 1995 World Bank study documented oil leaks into the Delta waters, which indicate "poor or no treatment of effluents" by Shell. In addition, the Ogoni people were subjected to natural gas flaring, the burning of natural gas that is a byproduct of oil production. Flares from tall vents constantly lit the night sky and polluted the air.[52]

Ogoniland was not the only area polluted in the Niger River Delta, where Shell shares operations with four other multinational oil companies. The five oil companies that operated in the Delta were producing about 2 million barrels of oil per day. There were also substantial oil spills at Oruma, Goi, and Ikot Ada Udo between 2004 and 2007. In 2010, an antiquated ExxonMobil pipeline in the Gulf of Guinea, near some Nigerian coastal villages, ruptured and spilled a million gallons of oil into the Niger Delta. According to a 2006 study, an average of 11 million gallons of oil per year (about 550 million gallons) has leaked into the Delta.[53] Hence it is no surprise that the once beautiful Niger Delta has been called an "environmental basket case" or an "ecological catastrophe" by vocal environmental groups.[54]

Shell has conceded that the environmental standards at its oil drilling sites in the Niger Delta were inferior to its standards in Europe and the United States. Part of the problem is that the Nigerian government, the lead partner in its joint venture, refused to pay its share for environmental upgrades. As the majority partner the government must pay 55% of environmental improvements, and, in Shell's estimation, it did not want to sacrifice its oil profits for "costly environmental protection." Without the government's cooperation, Shell refused to unilaterally bear the burden for these costly protections.[55]

After decades of drilling and despite constant complaints about pollution, Shell never did an environmental impact study of the region, which could have become the basis for improving environmental performance. A study was finally commissioned in 1996 in light of the negative publicity of the events in Ogoniland. In an interview at the time, Shell's CEO, Mr. Moody-Stuart, admitted that this was a huge oversight: "What I regret is that we did not launch our Niger River Delta Environmental Survey six or seven years ago."[56]

How do we assess Shell's corporate policies and behavior from a moral point of view in light of our framework for reviewing the ethical implications of environmental issues? First, it is questionable whether there was any need to drill for oil in this region where the production activities would be so disruptive both to the environment and to the vulnerable indigenous population of the Delta area who depended on those waters for their livelihood. Above-ground pipelines in such proximity to Ogoni villages are quite dangerous and exhibit no regard for aesthetic values. There is a valid human need for oil, especially until alternative energy sources are cultivated, but arguably there are more reasonable places available for the extraction of this resource than Ogoniland. There may be conditions in which oil production operations in the Niger Delta region would be acceptable. Those conditions would likely include the consent of the Ogoni tribe along with a large share of revenues returned to the Ogoni people so they could escape the shackles of poverty. Oil companies must also give high priority to expensive, state-of- the-art environmental protection. Of course, none of these conditions were not met in this case.

Shell has an obligation to operate by the highest environmental standards, no matter where it produces oil. Shell's refusal to upgrade its equipment and adopt advanced drilling and pipeline technologies because the Nigerian government refused to pay its share is morally unacceptable. As we have argued, any solution to an environmental risk problem must be economically and technically feasible, but it must also be ethically responsible. A decision is ethically responsible if and only if it does not pose an unreasonable threat to the quality of human life and health. But using inferior and marginally safe equipment does pose such an unreasonable threat to the health and welfare for those who live in the Niger Delta. The use of such second-rate equipment unfairly accepts bad side effects to others' health and welfare. Hence, by failing to take necessary precautions, Shell did not adequately protect the right to health of the people in this region from being deprived. An ethically responsible decision also gives proper consideration to the values, interests, and rights of those affected by that decision. There is no evidence that the Nigerian people's right to a safe, pollution-free environment was given the weight which it deserved. There are certain limits to what state-of-the-art technology can achieve. It cannot stop sabotage and acts of vandalism, but it can prevent those oil spills that happen due to accidents caused by shoddy, aging equipment.

Moreover, Shell cannot fall back on the argument that it could not afford to make these investments without the help of its major partner, the Nigerian government. Royal Dutch Shell is a company with vast economic wealth, and its behavior is not excused by the Nigerian government's insensitivity to environmental concerns. Every company must behave in an ethically reasonable manner even if it has unwilling and uncooperative partners. Either Shell must invest in the proper equipment without the government's help and help protect the rights of the Nigerian people, or exit the country if it concludes that it cannot make a profit there by operating in a responsible way.

Companies like Chevron and Royal Dutch Shell should surely be held accountable for poor environmental performance in emerging economies, but should the oil industry itself be liable for global warming, since their carbon-based products are a major contributing factor? In 2021, a Dutch court ruled that Royal Dutch Shell was partially responsible for climate change and it directed the oil giant to sharply reduce its carbon emissions by 45% compared with 2019 levels. The lawsuit was filed by Friends of the Earth, which alleged that the corporation violated a "duty of care" by its production of oil and natural gas. The environmental group did not seek damages but asked the court in the Hague to compel Royal Dutch Shell to reduce its carbon emissions.[57]

Many cheered this ruling and hoped it would set a precedent for holding energy companies liable for climate change. However, would it really be fair to place a big proportion of the blame for climate change on companies who supplied what consumers still need and demand? About 84% of the world's energy supply still comes from fossil fuels, and no other technology available today can meet the energy needs of everyone on the planet. Thus, these fossil fuels are both lawful and necessary products. Companies should not be held liable for legal products that perform the function they were intended to perform. Renewables make up only 11% of U.S. energy consumption, and without fossil fuels life would be unbearable, since there would be no relief from extreme heat and cold. Also, it is not fair to target a single industry for a complex economic and social problem. This perspective by no means implies that energy companies can afford to be complacent. They must be more committed to safety and to investing in renewable energy as they shift away from fossil fuels.[58]

Case study: the Amazon and deforestation

One of the most pressing environmental problems of the 21st century is rapid deforestation. Despite the calamity of global warming, many countries continue to give priority to economic necessity over environmental sustainability. China, for example, has turned to Russia's far east to supply the massive demand of its construction companies and furniture manufacturers. Russia has sold Chinese companies logging rights at low cost and the result has been the ravaging of Russia's vast forests, especially in Siberia. China's insatiable demand for wood has also stripped once pristine forests in Peru, Papua New Guinea, and Myanmar. In the Solomon Islands the current pace of logging by Chinese companies will totally deplete their rainforests by 2036. There has been some backlash in Russia where protests have erupted in Siberia and the Russian far east. "Stop the barbaric deforestation," was the rallying cry of the protesters.[59]

The deforestation issue captured the world's attention in 2019 over the thousands of fires that had been deliberately set in the Brazilian Amazon rainforest. The fires created a global panic along with calls to boycott Brazilian products. Brazilians for the most part looked upon these fires as a normal part of life in this region, and pointed out that this is how farmers clear the land to make a living. The land is "deforested" for growing crops and for cattle grazing. The farmers and ranchers are supported by President Bolsonaro who prioritizes economic development in these areas over environmental integrity. The Brazilian government maintains that fires and the subsequent deforestation are essential for keeping ranchers and farmers in business. They export large amounts of beef and soy, vital for the Brazilian economy.[60]

The trees of the Amazon rainforest and the forests of Siberia absorb and store a large portion of the carbon emissions that are released around the world. Over 20% of the world's fresh water can be found in the Amazon, which is one of the world's most precious carbon sinks. These carbon sinks serve as a "critical brake" on the momentum of climate change and global warming. Thanks to deforestation, Brazil's own carbon emissions have risen by 10–20% from its 2018 level. Because of its role in preserving the globe's environmental quality, many environmentalists look upon the Amazon as an "invaluable piece of world heritage that must be zealously conserved."[61] Hence, there is powerful opposition to Brazil's policies among environmentalists and a number of world leaders.

But there is also strong resistance in Brazil to this neo-colonial point of view. Why should outsiders, however well-intentioned, dictate Brazil's environmental polices? The restrictions contemplated by environmentalist and other global leaders would threaten Brazil's tenuous and sometimes erratic economic growth. The question is whether the world's environmental needs trump Brazil's economic welfare and national self-determination.

Caught up in the middle of this conflict are several key multinational players, especially JBS and Cargill. Both companies serve as intermediaries for beef and soy, the two commodities that are behind these deforestation trends. Soya-driven deforestation, for example, affects the *cerrado*, a tropical area southeast of the rainforest. In the past most of the soya exported from Brazil was grown on deforested lands, some of it done illegally. But in more recent years, the area of new soya fields planted on deforested lands in the *cerrado* has declined from 215,000 to 79,000 hectares. Nonetheless, Cargill, a giant food conglomerate, still acquires soya from deforested land in the *cerrado* and elsewhere. The company has pledged to source only from land that has not been deforested. It hopes to achieve this goal by 2030, but critics claim that Cargill should move much faster.[62]

Study questions

1. Are demands of other countries that Brazil improve its policies to limit deforestation a form of cultural imperialism?
2. Should food companies like JBS or Cargill acquire soy from farms on deforested land, assuming the deforestation was done legally?

Conclusions

Environmental issues such as polluted waterways, deforestation, and global warming remain a paramount concern. While the world has made progress, countries and multinationals continue to sacrifice ecological integrity for the sake of economic growth. China, for example, still relies heavily on coal to meet its energy needs. Global warming remains the overriding concern because of the broad ramifications of climate change. The earth is getting warmer but the impact of human-induced climate change is a matter of debate, since the planet's climate is such a complicated area of science.

The international community has had a mixed record in its cooperative efforts to deal with environmental problems that have a global impact. While it was successful in curbing CFCs it has not been so successful in reducing the carbon dioxide and methane gas emissions that cause global warming. The Kyoto Protocol achieved only modest gains, and it remains to be seen whether the Paris Accord will be effective. The goal of this agreement signed by 190 countries is to keep the earth's mean temperature less than 2° C above pre-industrial levels.

Social demands for improving environmental quality have put considerable pressure on multinational enterprises to be more environmentally responsible. Some seek to profit from environmentalism by differentiating their products, by discovering offsetting cost savings, or by managing regulatory risks better than the competition. But sometimes taming environmental contamination and decarbonizing operations will conflict with economic objectives. Nonetheless, companies must acknowledge their ethical obligation to the environment even if it means lower returns to shareholders.[63]

The proper ethical attitude for thinking about the environment begins with overcoming the mindset of technicity (*die Technik*) or experimental rationality that enshrines the scientific method as a technique of "possession, mastery, and transformation." Technology is no longer a way of relating to the natural world but instead becomes a challenge to that world.[64] Nature's resources must be extracted from the earth to satisfy valid human needs, but this must be done in a reasonable way and always with suitable restraint. However, the attitude of *Technik* identified by Heidegger induces multinationals to push nature beyond its limits instead of respecting the possibilities it has to offer. At a minimum, companies must acknowledge nature's instrumental value along with basic human goods that are threatened by environmental degradation. They must also take seriously the imperative of intergenerational equity when making decisions about resource use and extraction.[65]

Multinational corporations in the extractive industries, such as oil, must be ethical, responsible, and progressive about their environmental policies, particularly in developing countries. They cannot take advantage of countries with dysfunctional governments or weak institutions to adopt lower safety standards or employ second-rate equipment. A good rule of thumb is the one followed by DuPont in its overseas plants: "If our safety standards are higher, we use ours, if the other country's are higher we use theirs."[66] Oil companies should recognize that there must be uniformly high safety standards and environmental controls no matter where they operate so that the risk of oil spills and other ecological disasters is minimized. These companies must also correct and compensate for the social injuries they cause. The sorry track record of the oil industry, exemplified in the cases of Royal Dutch Shell in Nigeria and Texaco in Ecuador, reveals a pattern of injustice in managing its environmental impacts in emerging economies that must be rectified.

Notes

1 Pope Francis, *Laudatio Si* (Vatican City: Vaticana Editricia, 2015), 123.
2 Jack Ewing, *Faster, Higher, Farther: The Volkswagen Scandal* (New York: W.W. Norton, 2017).
3 Bethaney Biron, "Nike Unveils Big New Sustainability Initiative," *Business Insider*, September 20, 2019.
4 Sarah McFarlane, "Skepticism Greets BP's Green Plan," *Wall Street Journal*, September 30, 2020, B3.
5 Sarah McFarlane, "Shell's Natural Gas Bet is at Risk," *Wall Street Journal*, March 29, 2021, B3.
6 Hiroko Tabuchi, "Oil Giants an Ocean Apart on Adapting to Climate Change," *New York Times*, September 23, 2020, B1, B9.
7 See Forest Reinhardt, "Conceptual Overview: Business and the Environment" (Boston, MA: Harvard Business School Publications, 1999), 3.
8 Manuel Velasquez, *Business Ethics: Concepts and Cases* (Englewood Cliffs, NJ: Prentice-Hall, 1982), 187.
9 Garrit Hardin, "The Tragedy of the Commons," *Science* 162 (3859) (1968), 1243–1248.
10 Aldo Leopold, *A Sand Country Almanac* (New York: Oxford University Press, 1949), 88. Some have relied on Leopold's insights to support a biocentric view of these issues rather than an anthropocentric one. We're generally agnostic on this issue, but our concern is primarily with the ill effects of pollution on the welfare of human persons.
11 Jay Richards, *Environmental Stewardship* (Grand Rapids, MI: Acton Institute, 2007), 80–84.
12 "China and the Environment," *Economist*, August 10, 2013, 18–21. See also Richard Silk, "China Weighs Environmental Costs," *Wall Street Journal*, July 2, 2013, A7.
13 "The Bad Earth," *Economist*, June 10, 2017, 24–26.
14 "Coal's Endgame: Crushing It," *Economist*, December 5, 2020, 25–27.
15 Paulo Trevasani, "Illegal Loggers Undercut Brazil Forest Efforts," *Wall Street Journal*, October 29, 2020, A18. See also "Of Chainsaws and Supply Chains," *Economist*, June 13, 2020, 23–25.
16 World Resource Institute, *World Resources: A Guide to the Environment* (New York: Oxford University Press, 1996), 316.
17 "The Other Greenhouse Gas," *Economist*, April 3, 2021, 63–65.
18 "Summary for Policymakers," Intergovernmental Panel on Climate Change, 2014, 9. See also "Not So Slow Burn," *Economist*, May 23, 2020, 49–50.
19 Singer, for example, presents data to show that while the global sea level has undergone a rising trend for the past century, its cause is unrelated to climate change. See

Frederick Singer, Presentation at 1997 Meeting of the American Geophysical Union. Available at www.sepp.org/scirsrch/slr-agu.html. See also Richards, *Environmental Stewardship*, 90.

20 Mark Mills, "The 'Consensus' on Climate," *Wall Street Journal*, April 26, 2021, A15.

21 Steven Koonin, *Unsettled* (New York: BenBella, 2021), 15.

22 John Holusha, "Ozone Issue: Economics of a Ban," *New York Times*, January 11, 1990, D1, D6.

23 "Global Warming: Oh No, Kyoto," *Economist*, April 7, 2001, 73–75.

24 Ibid. See also Kimberly Packard and Forest Reinhardt, "Global Climate Change" (Boston, MA: Harvard Business School Publications, 1999), 1–7.

25 "Coal's Endgame," 25.

26 "Not So Slow Burn," 49–50.

27 "Business and Climate Change," *Economist*, September 19, 2020, 4–8.

28 Reinhardt, "Conceptual Overview," 5–6.

29 Germain Grisez, *Living a Christian Life* (Quincy, IL: Franciscan University, 1993), 771–772.

30 Oswald Spengler, *The Decline of the West* trans. Charles Atkinson (New York: Alfred A. Knopf, 1928), 178.

31 Martin Heidegger, *Holzwege* (Frankfurt: Klostermann, 1950), 237. See also William J. Richardson, "The Place of the Unconscious in Heidegger," *Review of Existential Psychology and Psychiatry*, 5 (1965), 281–282.

32 For Heidegger's more thorough treatment of these issues see *The Question Concerning Technology* trans. William Lovitt (New York: Harper Colophon, 1977). Deep ecologists who probe the deeper and more elusive meaning of the ecological crisis would be most sympathetic with a Heideggerian analysis of this sort. See Michael Zimmerman, "Implications of Heidegger's Thought for Deep Ecology," *Modern Schoolman* 44 (4) (1986), 19–43.

33 Martin Heidegger, *Vorträge und Aufsätze* (Pfullingen: Neske, 1954), 179.

34 Grisez, *Living a Christian Life*, 775–776. See also Pope John Paul II, *Sollicitudo Rei Socialis* (Boston, MA: Pauline Books and Media), §34. The Pope explains, for example, that using natural resources "as if they were inexhaustible, with *absolute dominion*, seriously endangers their availability not only for the present generation but above all for generations to come."

35 Grisez, *Living a Christian Life*, 780–781.

36 Robert Frederick and W. Michael Hoffman, "Environmental Risk Problems and the Language of Ethics," *Business Ethics Quarterly* 5 (1995), 705. See also W. Michael Hoffman, "Business and Environmental Ethics," *Business Ethics Quarterly* 1 (1991), 169–184.

37 Grisez, *Living a Christian Life*, 532–533.

38 These moral norms are also expressed in the "Valdez Principles" (named after the Valdez oil spill in Alaska), which were published in 1989 by CERES (Coalition for Environmentally Responsible Economies).

39 Some philosophers propose a more radical approach to ecology than biocentrism. Luciano Floridi advocates what he calls an ontocentric, ecological macroethics. The biocentrists maintain that we should not needlessly destroy or harm any living being. The ontocentrist, on the other hand, declares that no being or informational object should be damaged or destroyed without sufficient reason. All beings have the Spinozian right to persist in being and a "constructionist right to flourish." Luciano Floridi, "Foundations of Information Ethics," in *The Handbook of Information and Computer Ethics* eds. Ken Himma and Herman Tavani (Hoboken, NJ: Wiley, 2008), 10–11.

40 Lynn White, "The Historic Roots of our Ecologic Crisis," in *The Environmental Ethics and Policy Book* (Belmont, CA: Wadsworth Publishing, 1994), 43–51.

41 Michael Zimmerman, *Heidegger's Confrontation with Modernity* (Bloomington, IN: Indiana University Press, 1990), 242–243.

42 W. Norris Clarke, *The Universe as Journey* (New York: Fordham University Press, 1983), 80.

43 Pope John Paul II, *Sollicitudo Rei Socialis*, 34.

44 Hoffman, "Business and Environmental Ethics," 838.

45 Robert McNally, *Crude Volatility* (New York: Columbia University Press, 2017), 3. See also "Briefing: The Global Oil Industry," *Economist*, August 3, 2013, 20–22.

46 Roger Scruton, *How to Think Seriously about the Planet* (Oxford: Oxford University Press, 2015), 31–32.

47 William Langeweische, "Jungle Law," *Vanity Fair*, May, 2007. Available at https://www.vanityfair.com/news/2007/05/texaco200705.

48 Langeweische, "Jungle Law." See also Paul Barrett, *Law of the Jungle* (New York: Broadway Books, 2014), 27.

49 Juan Forero, "In Ecuador, High Stakes against Chevron," *The Washington Post*, April 28, 2009, A12.

50 Sara Randazzo, "Lawsuit without End: 28 Years So Far," *Wall Street Journal*, May 3, 2021, A1, A10.

51 Lynn Sharp Paine, *Value Shift* (Boston, MA: Harvard Business School Press, 2003). See also Milan Moldoveanu and Lynn Sharp Paine, "Royal Dutch Shell in Nigeria" (Boston, MA: Harvard Business School Publications, 1999), 1–6.

52 Douglas Farah, "Nigeria's Oil Exploitation Leaves Delta Poisoned, Poor," *Washington Post*, March 18, 2001, A22. See also Paul Lewis, "Nigeria's Deadly Oil War: Beleaguered Shell Defends its Record," *New York Times*, February 13, 1996, A10.

53 Rachel Maddow, *Blowout* (New York: Crown, 2019), 93.

54 Farah, "Nigeria's Oil Exploitation Leaves Delta Poisoned, Poor," A22.

55 Lewis, "Nigeria's Deadly Oil War," A10.

56 Ibid.

57 Sarah McFarlane and Christopher Matthews, "Exxon, Shell Suffer Defeats on Climate," *Wall Street Journal*, May 27, 2021, A1, A6.

58 Linda Kelly, "Should Fossil Fuel Companies Bear Responsibility for the Damage Their Products Do to the Environment?" *Wall Street Journal*, November 20, 2019, R8. See also Philip Broughton, "Go Ahead, Fill 'Er Up," *Wall Street Journal*, December 2, 2014, A15.

59 Steven Lee Myers, "Ravaging Far Away Forests While Protecting Trees at Home," *New York Times*, April 10, 2019, A4.

60 Manuela Andreoni and Ernesto Londono, "Despite World's Outrage, Farmers in Amazon Remain Defiant," *New York Times*, August 27, 2019, A4.

61 Ibid.

62 "Of Chainsaws and Supply Chains."

63 Reinhardt, "Conceptual Overview," 2–3.

64 Heidegger, *The Question Concerning Technology*, 296.

65 Pope Francis, *Laudatio Si*, 106. See also Michael Hanby, "The Gospel of Creation and the Technological Paradigm," *Communio* 42 (2015), 729.

66 Quoted in Thomas Donaldson and Thomas Dunfee, *Ties that Bind* (Boston, MA: Harvard Business School Press, 1999), 175.

Chapter 11

Responsible sourcing and offshoring

H&M Group is the world's second largest retailer. When the company was accused of profiting from the forced labor of the Muslim Uyghurs in the Chinese region of Xinjiang, executives decided that they would no longer purchase cotton from that area. The fertile Xinjiang region is the source of 85% of China's cotton. This variety of cotton is in large demand because it produces whiter and smoother fabrics. Much of that coveted cotton is exported to fourteen countries, including India, Pakistan, Vietnam, and Bangladesh where a large percentage of the world's clothing is produced. But Xinjiang is home to the Uyghurs who have been persecuted by the Chinese government. Many innocent citizens have been detained in camps and forced to do manual labor such as picking cotton. To avoid profiting from these oppressed workers, H&M vowed to eliminate this cotton from its supply chain.[1]

However, H&M's strategic decision was met with a severe backlash in China. Chinese consumers, encouraged by the government, vilified the company and called for a boycott in an intense social media campaign. The Chinese government and many of China's citizens want to deflect attention from what is going on in Xinjiang, and resent H&M's implicit denunciation of Chinese authorities' behavior in this region. Hence H&M faces an intractable dilemma. If they continue to use this tainted cotton picked by forced laborers they will have to contend with the ire of labor activists and possible Congressional intervention in the U.S. On the other hand, if they stick to their plans for forbidding the use of this cotton in the manufacture of their clothing, they risk alienating Chinese consumers who form a very sizable market.[2]

Other clothing retailers such as PVH Group, which includes brands such as Calvin Klein and Tommy Hilfiger, have also said that they will cut ties with Xinjiang and avoid the use of this tainted cotton. But H&M's dilemma shows how complex these decisions can become, especially when dealing with China. First, it is

DOI: 10.4324/9781003058427-11

immensely difficult to verify the source of cotton used to make clothing since cotton from one area is often mixed with other varieties. Second, these sourcing problems are compounded by geopolitics, including the power of the Chinese state and the size of the Chinese economy. Moreover, American support for their efforts is often somewhat equivocal.[3]

Evaluating the treatment of workers in areas of the global marketplace where there is repression and poverty is an ongoing challenge for businesses in many industries. This controversy over supplier working conditions has not gone away and still erupts into the headlines from time to time. The problem is rooted in the economic reality that companies like Walmart, Nike, and H&M rely on a network of suppliers from all parts of the world. They benefit appreciably from the division of labor and the lower production costs in emerging markets. They engage in a game of labor "arbitrage," moving from one country to another to find the lowest wages in order to minimize their cost structure. This strategy may make good economic sense but it has elaborate moral and social implications. It is a demanding task to keep labor costs exceedingly low while also safeguarding the rights of foreign workers. To what extent can companies take advantage of the social and cultural differences in countries where they source inputs or have their products made? Should they allow their contractors to hire workers who are only thirteen or fourteen years old if that is the long-standing local custom? And in what areas (such as safety or environmental protection) should they strive for uniform corporate policies that transcend cultural norms?

The theoretical issue at the focal point of this debate is the degree to which multinationals are responsible for the moral defects of their direct suppliers. And what about the suppliers of those suppliers – where does accountability end in intricate global value chains? Arguably, it's not sufficient for clothing companies like H&M to have garments made in factories with good working conditions. It is also necessary to ensure that their supply chain is not tainted by forced labor or other human rights abuses. But on what moral basis can multinationals interfere with their suppliers' operations, given that they are independent companies rather than wholly owned subsidiaries or even joint ventures? What are the grounds of their moral agency? And how can companies ensure that zealous auditing of the workplaces involved does not make life even more difficult for workers? We will address these vexing matters throughout this chapter, but first we examine the origin and explosive growth of outsourcing and offshoring, which has become so characteristic of this latest phase of globalization's history.

Offshoring and outsourcing

The Nike corporation, well known for its high-performance athletic shoes, pioneered the idea of the virtual or "hollow" corporation. From its inception, the Oregon-based footwear company decided to outsource all but its core value-chain activities: product design and marketing. The company focused solely on those critical functions, with marketing campaigns that relied heavily on celebrity endorsements. At the same time, it outsourced manufacturing and sales. Nike's CEO, Phil Knight, insisted that there would be no in-house production of Nike's athletic footwear. Knight's goal was to keep manufacturing costs low by outsourcing production in order to minimize overhead and labor costs. There was a growing consensus among strategists and consultants that the Nike approach was viable and that business activities should not be performed within the corporate hierarchy unless absolutely necessary.

To pursue its low-cost outsourcing strategy, Nike first sought out independent contractors in South Korea and Taiwan, but then moved to lower-wage countries like China and Indonesia. Contractors in the latter countries could produce shoes for 50% less than shoes produced in Taiwan or South Korea.[4] During the 1980s in Indonesia, the Suharto regime had been accused of flagrant human rights abuses and the country was considered to be a "human rights sinkhole," where the rights of workers were virtually non-existent. Nike's Indonesian contractors paid exceedingly low wages so Nike was able to invest in its core activities and earn substantial rents on its brand. These contractors also relied heavily on underage children to do the work. But Nike paid a price for its unorthodox strategy. It quickly gained a reputation as an opportunistic and callous organization, willing to exploit cheap Asian labor to advance its strategic objectives. Worried about damage to the brand, Nike finally responded to its critics. In 1998, Nike committed itself to ending child labor and to allowing outside auditors to check the working conditions of its suppliers' factories. Employees now had to be sixteen years old to work in its contractors' plants even in countries where it was commonplace for fourteen-year-olds to hold such jobs.[5] Little was done, however, about the meager wages paid by these contractors. Workers in Vietnam factories were making less than $2 day, which is estimated to be well below the subsistence level for this country.

Despite the moderate ethical risk, many other Western companies jumped on the offshoring bandwagon in order to combat high labor costs in their home markets. Offshoring means moving work and jobs beyond the borders of a corporation's home country. It usually involves outsourcing, which means using outside contractors to do the work. China, Thailand, Mexico, and Indonesia were some of the many countries where these contractors could find adequately skilled labor for cheaper wages. Offshoring and outsourcing trends accelerated during the economic boom of the 1990s, as more companies sought to leverage global labor arbitrage. Multinationals learned to seize the advantage of wage differences among countries that competed for their business. As wage rates rose in certain countries thanks to higher demand for labor, companies simply sought out contractors elsewhere. When wages in China rose to $3 per hour, production was shifted to countries like Sri Lanka and Indonesia where the average wage was $1 per hour. Some of this wage differential was offset by China's scale and well-developed supply chains, but not enough to keep manufacturers from fleeing to those lower-wage markets.[6]

Offshoring is unpopular in the West, however, because it has contributed to big job losses in high-wage countries, especially for unskilled labor. Despite the vocal protests, many of these cost-conscious companies have continued to increase foreign investment. Offshoring is the one element of globalization that workers in developed economies fear and loathe the most. In many countries, including the United States, people overwhelmingly blame offshoring as one of the prime sources of low economic development.[7] These job losses at the hands of foreign suppliers were a major impetus for the election of President Donald Trump in 2016.

But if offshoring is disdained in the West it is regarded by emerging economies as a means of jumpstarting stationary and bleak economies. Sweatshops, described as "monstrous" by some NGOs, are regarded even by some heterodox liberal economists as the "essential first step toward modern prosperity in developing countries."[8] What is viewed as exploitation by people in developed economies is regarded in low-wage countries as "opportunity." For example, despite low labor standards and a preponderance of underage workers in Honduras, people there have welcomed the sweatshops. According to one local labor leader, teenagers working at assembly plants are "a million times better off in here than out there on the street, because the *maquila* represents progress."[9] Critics of multinational corporations, however, have remained unconvinced.

Thanks to very low prices, countries like Bangladesh have attracted many foreign clothing companies and retailers as a source for their products. But to keep prices low, clothing factories pay low wages and have little money to invest to ensure safe and decent working conditions. These poor working conditions often put workers at risk. Two garment factory disasters shined a bright spotlight back on the plight of the country's garment workers. In November 2012, 112 workers were killed when a moderate-sized garment factory went up in flames. When the fire alarm went off, workers were told that it was a false alarm and were ordered back to work. As the factory floor filled with black smoke, some workers were able to break windows and jump to safety, but most them perished in the engulfing flames. There have been over 500 people killed in Bangladesh fires since 2006, but this fire in the Tazreen Fashions, Ltd. factory was the worst. The cause of this fire and several others appears to have been unsafe electrical wiring. The Bangladesh government sets fairly low safety standards, but even those are ignored by some local factory owners. Many major Western brands were produced at the Tazreen factory, such as Walmart's Faded Glory and Sean Combs' Enyce brands. Clothing for Sears Holding Corporation was also made at this factory.[10]

The tragic Tazreen factory fire was followed by a factory collapse just outside the capital city of Dhaka in April 2013, which killed 1,127 people. The sudden collapse of the eight-story Rana Plaza building that housed a number of clothing factories is one of the worst industrial disasters in history. Rana Plaza was built with shoddy materials, and the owner was arrested for constructing the building without safety permits. Managers repeatedly ignored signs of trouble. Workers were ordered back to work on the day of the building collapse despite an earlier evacuation after a huge crack was discovered in an outer wall. Shortly after factory workers re-entered the poorly constructed building, the edifice abruptly collapsed and they were crushed to death.

Both of these accidents happening in such close succession have put enormous pressure on the Bangladesh government to establish and enforce more rigorous safety standards. The country's thriving $25 billion a year garment industry has made Bangladesh one of the world's largest clothing exporters. There are 5,000 factories employing over 5 million people. Some of the chief U.S. and European retailers have sourced their clothes from Bangladesh. Included in this group are U.S. companies like Walmart, Sears, the Gap, and J.C. Penney. Designer brands like Giorgio Armani and Ralph Lauren have also outsourced manufacturing to Bangladesh. Both Italy's Benetton and Spain's Mango MNG used factories in the building that collapsed.[11]

Despite the inferior working conditions, there is no shortage of workers. In Bangladesh, about 85% of the population earns less than $2 per day. But in the clothing factories workers earn more than $2 per day. Working in sweatshops in Bangladesh, El Salvador, India, and Indonesia results in wages that are twice the national average. Also, while conditions in sweatshops are bad, the conditions in alternative employment (like agriculture) are often worse.[12]

Although sweatshop employment is the best alternative for workers in many poor countries, Western retailers and fashion houses should still strive to improve working conditions and wages. As long as retailers relentlessly pursue the lowest manufacturing costs, their goods will be made in factories that lack adequate safety safeguards and worker protection. A Bangladesh factory owner described how he can do no better than break even because he must sell his shirts at the going rate of $6.75. The cost of material (such as cotton, buttons, etc.) is $5.75 and the remaining $1 is used for overhead, wages, and other expenses.[13] There is no money left over to invest in safety enhancements. Clothing factories in Myanmar, Pakistan, and Indonesia pose the same safety risks as the factories in Bangladesh. The relentless drive to cut labor costs in all of these countries to satisfy retailers' demands usually creates pressure to skimp on safety, and this means that there are probably more disasters on the horizon. With this in mind, activists have repeatedly called upon these retailers to invest in making factories better and safer, but those proposals have been met with firm resistance.[14]

Moral responsibility in the supply chain

Activists have assigned some blame to Walmart, Carrefour, and other brand owners whose products were being made at the Tazreen factory because they did not attend to its unsafe working conditions. Their argument might proceed along the following lines: the fire was a foreseeable but unintended side effect of doing business with a firm that had such a terrible safety record; by not taking action on worker safety and awarding new contracts to this company, they were carelessly tolerating its unsafe working conditions. But is that a fair assessment?

Companies are responsible for the wages and working conditions at the offshore factories that they own and operate. But what about a corporation's responsibilities for the activities of its suppliers, which are legally independent and operate outside the corporate hierarchy? When these issues about sweatshop working conditions first surfaced, Nike deflected accountability by claiming that it could not realistically be held blameworthy for the inhumane working practices of certain suppliers. "We don't make shoes," was the response of a Nike spokesperson who was queried about poor labor conditions in the Indonesian factories.[15] And Walmart once complained that it lacked the ability to enforce global labor standards. We have policies against child labor, a spokesperson said, but "we can't police every factory 24 hours a day."[16] Before media attention was focused on this issue, it was not common for corporations to screen suppliers for human rights violations because companies assumed that they lacked accountability and moral agency.

The public and the media, however, did not accept these rationalizations, and so, for the most part, companies have retreated from these unpersuasive arguments. Many corporations have begun to assume full responsibility for the activities of their multiple suppliers. The brand owner Levi Strauss & Co developed Global Sourcing Guidelines along with its Business Partner Terms of Engagement. The latter document laid out specific standards for suppliers and contractors abroad. The Terms of Engagement flowed from Levi Strauss's code of ethics, which gave the firm an overarching set of principles to deal with moral problems. These "terms of engagement" required its contractors to provide safe and healthy working conditions, pay employees no less than prevailing local wages, limit the work week to no more than 60 hours, prohibit the use of child and prison labor, and allow for unannounced visits by the firm's auditors.[17]

Even if corporations adopt such high standards, monitoring contractors and suppliers scattered throughout the world can be a costly burden and a demanding undertaking. Most companies rely on independent labor auditors, who are specialists at monitoring these factories and more savvy in identifying fraudulent situations. But supply chain complexity often interferes with the best auditing efforts. For example, thanks to safety audits, Walmart had forbidden work to be done by Tazreen (owned by the Tuba Group), the location of the tragic fire in Bangladesh in 2012. But Walmart signed a contract with Simco to produce its Faded Glory brand of clothing. Without Walmart's knowledge, Simco subcontracted some of this work to the Tuba Group, which in turn passed the work on to Tazreen.

The motivation for most corporations to purge supply chains of abusive labor practices is to protect their corporate reputations. Disney, for example, which is fanatically protective of its brand and image, pulled out of Bangladesh after the fires and building collapse rather than take the chance that its products would be discovered in a burned-out factory. No company wants its branded products associated with sweatshop labor or deathtraps like Tazreen. Also, these abuses can undermine employee morale, especially if a company aspires to high social responsibility standards.

There are also ethical reasons as well as economic ones to reject the "Nike defense" and assume that market participants are responsible to some degree for working conditions within their supply chain. Apparel companies that source from suppliers where there are human rights abuses have no intention to harm those workers. It is difficult to know if retailers like Walmart or brand owners like H&M would take action if it weren't for the media spotlight that shape consumer expectations. Without that attention, they might continue to assert that they have no accountability for what goes on behind the walls of the factories within their supply chain. The foundation of such a claim is the contractual relationship between retailers and brand owners and those suppliers producing their goods. They are simply outsourcing non-essential corporate functions to be more efficient and deliver higher value for shareholders. According to this perspective, the retail chain–supplier relationship is reduced to an arm's-length commercial transaction and nothing else. A Bangladesh business, for example, making apparel for famous Western brands, is an autonomous entity, free to sever the relationship at any time. This is purely a business-to-business relationship that is far removed from an employer–employee relationship.[18]

But as Barerra argues, this conceptual framework is the wrong way to conceive the relationship between retailers or brand owners and their multiple suppliers. This is not a mere contractual relationship, but a principal–agent one where garment factories act as agents on behalf of the principals (retailers and brand owners). Those factories manage and execute the production process on behalf of the principals. In both the legal and philosophical traditions, principals are liable for the actions of their agents even if they do not know about or participate in the wrongdoing. In legal terms, the responsibility of the principals is classified in terms of "vicarious liability." In addition, since these workers are making products for brand owners and retailers they should be considered as indirect employees of those companies because of their critical role in the value added process. Brand owners and retailers have considerable leverage over the employment practices of their contractors. Not only can they demand certain policies such as limited overtime as a condition of doing business, but they can also influence working conditions by offering that contractor a fair price and a profit margin that will leave room for decent wages.[19]

We have also argued that corporations have a duty not to deprive people of their rights and to protect rights from being deprived. The latter duty would apply in this case for two reasons. First, actions to protect rights and avoid harm are required by certain relationships, such as the child–parent relationship, or, in this case the principal–agent relationship. Second, there is a general obligation to others even if they are perfect strangers. According to Bentham, "A man's duty to his neighbor is accordingly partly negative and partly positive: to discharge the negative branch of it, is *probity*; to discharge the positive branch, *beneficence*."[20] Thus, we have a duty to avoid harming our neighbor (probity) and a duty to come to our neighbor's assistance when he or she is being harmed (beneficence). But under what circumstances does this duty of beneficence become morally relevant? According to D'Arcy and others, who have refined the Bentham argument, the duty for a moral agent to help another or intervene when there is wrongdoing applies only when several key conditions prevail. Under these conditions, a moral agent, A, is required to do X in order that Y does not happen to B. First, there is proximity, a closeness to the wrongdoing by virtue of a certain relationship or a knowledge of what is transpiring. Second, the need must be critical; there must be the danger of a significant loss, since there is no moral obligation to intervene for trivial matters. Third, there is the capability to act such that there is a strong probability that A's doing X will prevent Y. Fourth, A's doing X must be necessary to prevent Y, because X is the last resort for a remedy. Fifth, in most situations A is not obligated to assume a disproportionate risk to his own welfare in order to help B.[21] Under these conditions, a moral agent's failure to act in the face of wrongdoing constitutes a "wrongful omission."[22]

In the case of international corporations and their contractors, the duty of beneficence, which takes the form of intervention in order to protect rights from deprivation, seems almost axiomatic. First, there is adequate proximity, since multinationals are aware or have the potential to be aware of what's going on inside these factories. Social expectations and moral reasonableness demand that they be alert to critical need among key stakeholders such as contractors, especially where there is good reason to suspect poor workplace conditions in countries like Pakistan or Bangladesh. There is also a close working relationship between the international buyer and its foreign suppliers, which become important stakeholders. Although there are no formal ties of ownership, a global corporation such as Walmart enters into a partnership with its suppliers, and that gives Walmart the prerogative to investigate the presence of any rights violations or social injury occurring within their suppliers' factories. Second, the need is critical. Flagrant human rights abuses are sometimes at stake; unsafe working conditions, for example, mean that workers could be in danger of severe injury or loss of life. Excessive overtime is a severe threat to a person's physical and mental health. Third, multinationals have the capability to take remedial action by demanding that human rights abuses be stopped as a condition of future contracts because they have substantial leverage over their suppliers. They surely have authority to dictate quality and production standards, so it is logical to assume that they can exercise that same authority by prescribing suitable working conditions. That capability might be compromised somewhat by the difficulty of monitoring so many foreign operations to ensure that human rights abuses are not occurring. But companies that make substantial profits thanks to these low-wage suppliers are obliged to invest the necessary funds to maximize their monitoring capabilities. Fourth, given the impotence and disinterest of local governments in developing countries, multinationals are often the last resort for taking effective action. Fifth, there is minimal risk on their part, while the harm being prevented is substantial. Hence, their failure to act and protect workers from the deprivation of their rights amounts to a wrongful omission.

However, the scope of this ethical obligation to protect the rights of contractors' workers is open to some question and debate. Should companies be held accountable for working conditions throughout their entire, complex supply chains? Asking a company like Walmart to also take responsibility for the activities of its contractors' multiple suppliers might impose an unreasonable burden under ordinary circumstances. Walmart has 100,000 global suppliers and contractors, and all of them have their own suppliers. Beyond direct suppliers or contractors, responsibility for working conditions for companies further up in the value chain is heavily mitigated by the lack of proximity and capability. On the other hand, if companies are alerted to forced labor and other abuses in their supply chains, it would be necessary to take action. Once a brand owner like H&M is informed that Xinjiang cotton is being used by a supplier to the factories that make its dress shirts and that cotton has been picked and processed by forced labor, it is morally incumbent upon them to take action.

This conception of a broad but reasonable scope of corporate accountability for contractors' activities is reinforced by the valid expectations of the public. They assume that these international corporations have certain obligations to the workers of their contractors, since they realize immense economic benefits from having their goods manufactured in low-wage countries. The lower labor costs achieved with the help of these contractors contributes greatly to profitability and sustainable competitive advantage. But no moral agent should benefit from the wrongdoing of another. A person should not take money from a friend who has enriched himself by embezzling corporate funds. And multinationals should not profit from oppressive working conditions or from the unfair wages paid to laborers by their contractors. To profit from the wrongdoing of contractors further aggravates the failure to protect against the deprivation of workers' rights. As a result, international corporations must insist on putting an end to the abusive practices of a particular contractor or move production to one with greater moral integrity.

Fair wages and decent working conditions

Now that we have elaborated the arguments supporting the responsibility of multinationals for the actions of their suppliers in the supply chain we must consider how to define suitable conditions at these factories. How should wages be determined and what constitutes a "fair wage"? What are acceptable working conditions? And should child labor ever be tolerated? In general, what are the proper guidelines for the workplace standards of contractors?

We begin with a review of acceptable workplace conditions. Above all, the work environment must be safe and free of unreasonable workplace hazards. Workers cannot be exposed to unreasonable health dangers, and therefore employers must take into account the potential impact of construction and production decisions on worker safety. As we argued in the preceding pages, life and health are intrinsic goods, sought after and valued for their own sake, and intentional acts contrary to human health are always wrong as well as unreasonably accepting side effects harmful to health. Constructing a factory with inferior electrical equipment, likely to cause a fire, is unfairly accepting the bad side effects to others' life and health that will follow if there is such a fire. Managers must ensure that the workplace environment is properly configured to avoid such foreseeable side effects by taking all reasonable safety precautions. In sum, a person's right to health and safety required of others in justice must not be deprived or jeopardized by employers and it must be protected by multinationals which source from those employers.[23]

In developing countries, where laws like the U.S.'s Occupational Health and Safety Act are either non-existent or unenforced, violations of safety rights are rampant. For example, in Mexico young workers were hired to "smear glue on the soles of sneakers" with their hands despite the warning that inhalation of this toxic substance causes "grave health damage."[24] Similarly, far too many companies in the Yonkang district of China have a terrible track record for worker safety. Yongkang, just south of Shanghai, is called the hardware capital of China where over 7,000 factories produce an endless stream of pots and pans, metal hinges, tools, fans, and hubcaps. But most of the factories do not invest in safe machinery with infrared devices that shut down when hands or limbs are extended past the "safety zone." As a result, Yongkang is also known as the "dismemberment capital" of China, and companies who source from this region that do not demand attention to safety issues share some of the blame for these conditions.[25]

There will always be risks in any workplace, and workers must be duly informed of those risks. But a safe environment implies an acceptable level of risk and a workplace area without recognized hazards that are likely to cause serious or fatal injury. Factories that routinely use machines like mechanical hammers and lathes without proper safety controls cannot be classified as safe environments. The risk of dismemberment is disproportionately high and hence that risk is unacceptable. It follows that international companies that source from Yongkang's factories must protect the right to health and safety of workers by demanding that contactors use safe equipment with the proper controls as a condition of future contracts.

Decent working conditions include more than a safe physical environment. There must also be restrictions on the work week. Most companies impose the limit of a 60-hour work week for their contractors, which seems to be a fairly reasonable standard. Many factories in China now house workers who travel there from all parts of the country. At these factories there is a need for sufficient dormitory space and proper eating facilities. Unfortunately these standards are often not met. Finally, a decent work environment should recognize a worker's right to organize and form a labor union. These are rights recognized in the UN Declaration (art. 23). National laws, however, sometimes forbid unions, and in these situations, international corporations probably need to allow their contractors to comply with the local law or they will be accused of meddling in local politics. Disputably, this is one area where countries should be allowed moral free space.

What about the issue of wages? Some corporate guidelines stipulate that workers be paid the "prevailing wage" in their locale, but there is some debate as to whether the market or even the local law sets a morally adequate standard for labor wages. Should multinationals simply ensure that contractors pay the legally mandated wage or the prevailing market wage in a country or region? Or should they always require that a fair wage be paid no matter what the market conditions are, and, if so, what is a fair wage? These different alternatives need some further elaboration.

One way to deal with the issue of wages is reliance on the free market principle, which allows wages to be determined by the local labor market, that is, by the forces of supply and demand. Wages are set at a level that individual workers are willing to accept and employers are willing to pay. Sometimes this can mean exceptionally low levels of remuneration. In Bangladesh, an average garment worker, who works ten-hour days, has a take home pay of $70–80 per month.[26] This is below the subsistence level for this worker and his or her family. Nevertheless, those who argue for this principle maintain that as long as a multinational's contractors are paying market wages that are never lower than the minimum allowed by law, they are not behaving unjustly. According to the law of supply and demand, wages can never be too low or too high.[27]

This ethical posture on the wage issue might seem acceptable, since it depends on an unprejudiced and impersonal market that sets wages in a way that treats everyone alike. Also, the right to economic liberty appears to be intact, since workers are free to choose their occupation and their employer. But there is an asymmetrical relationship between international companies, which have the mobility to locate their factories anywhere in the world, and workers in low-wage countries, who are anxious for a job and have no alternatives. As a result, they are often willing to accept wages that are below the subsistence level. Implicit consent to a labor contract that pays low wages does not necessarily imply that the contract is a fair one. Markets are blind to social justice issues, and they allow multinationals to take unfair advantage of poor economies and the dismal situation of their workers. Countries like Malaysia, Bangladesh, and Sri Lanka need multinationals and have little leverage or bargaining power to demand that workers be treated fairly.

A more equitable and simple solution seems to be called for, such as "equal pay for equal work," which stipulates that people ought to be paid the same for equal work no matter where they live. But this principle, however attractive, is unrealistic. Paying Malaysians the same as Americans for making clothes makes little sense because there is such a disparity in the cost of living between these two countries.[28] A superior alternative is to insist upon a fair wage or a living wage. Such a wage can be broadly defined as one that is adequate to support a worker and his or her family with the basic necessities of life. Quigley defines a living wage as one that will provide enough income to escape from poverty and become self-sufficient.[29] This fair wage is often referred to as the subsistence level wage, though the definition of "subsistence" is open to some interpretation. A compelling moral case can be put forth that employers owe something more to their workers than the market wage or the local minimum wage when that compensation is not commensurate with the work performed and the value added by the worker.

Everyone has a right to subsistence, but a corporation does not have a duty to aid those who are deprived of this right, when that deprivation is not connected to its business operations. A corporation's failure to provide food, clothing, and housing for the indigent in the host countries where it operates is not a rights violation on its part. On the other hand, if corporations pay below subsistence wages in their own factories they are depriving their workers of an important right. If they tolerate such wages in the factories of their suppliers they are derelict in their duty to protect from deprivation the right to subsistence, since those workers are its "indirect employees" who deserve fair treatment. The right to just compensation proportionate to the worker's contribution is to be reasonably expected by any worker and reflects a corporation's respect for the equivalent humanity of others. But a meager and unjust wage for full-time work prevents people from acquiring the material goods they need in order to survive. In these situations, the corporation is acting more like an unprincipled opportunist rather than a custodian of those human rights that are within its purview to protect.[30]

In the social encyclical *Laborem Exercens*, Pope John Paul II declared that every worker has the right to "just remuneration for work done."[31] The encyclical goes on to explain that payment of a fair wage is the primary means of ensuring a just relationship between workers and their employers. The just wage is also the most concrete and verifiable way of determining the justice of the economic system. While it is impossible to quantify a universal just wage, John Paul II provided a workable definition of a fair wage that is consistent with our point of view: "just remuneration for the work of an adult who is responsible for a family means remuneration which will suffice for establishing and properly maintaining a family and for providing security for its future."[32]

It is also evident that the philosophers of high liberalism, who put so much emphasis on the distributive dimensions of social justice, would be particularly aggrieved by these exceedingly low and unjust wages. As we have seen, high liberalism is more committed to social justice issues than to private economic liberty. According to Rawls, the principles of justice are those which equal, rational, self-interested individuals would choose as the terms of a social contract for themselves and their descendants. One of those principles is called the *difference principle:* "justice requires that we seek to maximize the benefits of the least well-off."[33] This means that disparities in the distribution of wealth and other social goods would be tolerated *only* if they could be shown to benefit the "least advantaged," the lowest on the socio-economic scale.[34] A just society, therefore, is not necessarily an egalitarian one where all goods are distributed equally, but one in which inequalities must work to everyone's advantage, especially the most disadvantaged.

Rawls' theory could be endorsed as a sensible metric for assessing global distributive justice. From that lofty perspective, the institutional and corporate structures that permit the low wages we see in today's global economy are quite difficult to justify since they do not maximally benefit the poor. Advocates of a Rawls theory of justice would probably argue that these low wages are representative of capitalism's excess, a side effect of under-regulated markets that must be corrected by government intervention if necessary. International corporations cannot resolve the gross inequities that cast a shadow over global capitalism. However, they can ensure that a fair wage is paid to their direct and indirect employees. Paying a fair wage and providing other workplace amenities would help to correct this inequitable distribution so it is more consistent with the requirements of social justice. Fair wages are also consistent with an acknowledgment of the corporation's common good. Recall that the common good consists of efficient economic cooperation and fairness to all participants in this cooperative enterprise, including workers, who deserve a fair distribution of a corporation's benefits proportionate to what they contribute.

Child labor: the great dilemma

Finally, we must address the vexing issue of child labor, which persists in countries like Pakistan and India. Anti-globalizers often seize upon this emotional issue as a basis for demanding a contraction of globalization because of its malicious effects on children and other vulnerable workers. As many companies have found out, child labor in the supply chain is another notable strategic risk that can quickly damage a company's brand and reputation.

Child labor is loosely defined as labor performed by children under the age of fourteen. The International Labor Organization (ILO), affiliated with the United Nations, provides a more formal definition: child labor is "work that deprives children of their childhood, their potential, and their dignity, and that is harmful to their physical and mental development."[35] Some child labor, such as work at the family home or farm, is ordinary and acceptable. But work performed outside the household at a young age is often mentally or physically harmful and it deprives children of their ability to receive an education. The ILO estimates that one in six of the world's children between the ages of five and seventeen work in some capacity outside the home with the highest proportions of these laborers in Asia and Africa.[36]

Child labor appears to be endemic to certain labor-intensive industries like hand-woven carpets, where children have proven themselves to be adept at weaving together this material quickly and efficiently. A Harvard University report issued in 2014 documented over 3,200 cases across India of child labor at carpet factories operated by companies that export to U.S. retail stores. Those stores included Macy's, Bloomingdale's, Neiman Marcus, and IKEA. The research team found that child labor was "rampant, chronic, and almost entirely in deeply rural Muslim villages."[37]

One form of child labor that is particularly reprehensible is bonded child labor. In most of these situations, which are rampant in India, children are coerced into certain work places in order to repay a debt owed to the employer by the child's impoverished parents. Bonded child labor is entrenched in certain cultures with long traditions of ethnic and religious discrimination. This heritage makes the eradication of bonded labor quite demanding. Bonded child labor is also extensive.

The Children's Rights Project claim that a high proportion of children working in India's hand-woven carpet industry are being held in some sort of bondage. But bonded child labor can be found in other countries besides India. Two agri-business firms, Nestlé USA and Cargill, were sued in 2020 by six individuals who claimed that they were trafficked into slavery as children. They allege that both companies knew that child slavery was a common practice on their Ivory Coast cocoa farms.[38]

Who is to blame for all of this oppressive child labor? The list of those at fault must begin with the parents who allow their children to work before they finish school. Employers who hire them, usually for very low wages, are also to blame. Also on this list are governments that refuse to protect their children. India's Child Labor Act of 1986, amended in 2016, prohibits employment of children (anyone below the age of fourteen) in any industry, including agriculture and domestic help. The law has not been well enforced, however, and so child labor remains widespread in that country. International corporations that source from these contractors using child labor cannot escape some accountability for the problem. Of course, the big culprit in child labor is poverty. Parents often send their children to work in "sweatshops" because they are destitute and need the income in order to survive.

The tacit assumption in the denunciation of children working long hours in sweatshops is that there are better opportunities for these children, such as attendance at school. In countries like Bangladesh, India, and Brazil, where child labor remains quite common, children are deprived of that essential opportunity. Most of the children work in agriculture or domestic service, but many also toil in sweatshops. And in these "sweatshop countries" a substantial proportion of children do not complete their primary education. But if children lose their jobs making sneakers or shirts, the alternative is not staying at home or going to school, but taking jobs in agriculture where there is lower pay and more injuries. Powell points out the paradox: "we do not help Third World Children by taking options away from them; we help them only when their options are expanded."[39] The exception, of course, is bonded labor, which severely harms children.

According to the ILO, child labor is not economically justified. Based on their careful estimates, it would cost about $760 billion over a twenty-year period to end child labor, but the benefits would be seven times as large. There would be significant gains in the quality and quantity of human capital, better health, and fewer lives lost due to lower accidents. Child labor prevents countries from investing in human capital, and this keeps many of their workers in low-level, unskilled jobs. Also, allowing child labor depresses wages for adults who have fewer options and lower pay. Thus, to some extent countries perpetuate poverty by tolerating child labor rather than trying to constrict it.[40]

But child labor will only decline when families in poor countries escape from poverty. Eliminating child labor in apparel and other industries and removing the "sweatshop" option for children may seem morally coherent, but it has unintended negative consequences, since it will force desperate children into worse alternatives. This reality greatly complicates the moral calculus. Arguably, conscientious multinationals should not necessarily terminate contracts with suppliers in countries like India and Pakistan where child labor may be present. One option is to work with suppliers to ensure that so long as there is no bonded labor, the children working in the factory work fewer hours so that they receive an education on site. IKEA, for example, formed a partnership with UNICEF to fund education for 24,000 children in India's "carpet belt" who were not in school. How far companies should go is a matter of debate, but the demanding issue of unintended consequences cannot be neglected.

Perhaps the best moral approach to all of these problems – safe working conditions, child labor, fair wages – is the simplest: the Golden Rule. This simple principle ensures that we look at moral dilemmas without partiality so we are more apt to choose the solution that promotes human well-being. Multinationals must not tolerate policies that unfairly remunerate workers, risk workers' health and safety, or unjustly exploit children. To judge what is unfair a corporation cannot just look at prevailing practices or local law. Rather, after considering the relevant facts and cultural issues, managers should apply the Golden Rule and imagine themselves or their families in the places of each of those affected by their choices. Even despite the grinding poverty and low living standards of Malaysia, would they consider it just to be paid a below-subsistence wage of $1 an hour?

Pegatron and Apple

Apple's troubled relationship with a key supplier in China illustrates many of the rights abuses presented in the last section. Unfortunately, Apple has been hesitant to rectify the situation despite its ample resources. For the last two decades, Apple has outsourced most of its production to a network of independent contractors, and one of its primary suppliers is the Taiwanese company Pegatron. Pegatron, founded in 2007, reported revenues of about $5 billion in 2020. Its products include desktop computers, smartphones, tablets, motherboards, and many other electronic components or devices.

Pegatron was chosen to produce the iPad mini along with several versions of its popular iPhone. But Pegatron has a history of inferior working conditions, especially in its Chinese factories. Severe abuses at several Pegatron facilities have been exposed by the NGO, China Labor Watch (CLW). In July 2013, CLW published a disturbing report called *Apple's Unkept Promises*. In that report it presented strong evidence that many Pegatron employees making iPhones and iPads were working excessive overtime. The report also highlighted low wages along with filthy, overcrowded dormitories.[41] An American reporter, who interviewed a number of Pegatron workers at the Shanghai factory, verified "a high-stress workplace marked by long hours and repetitive tasks, a factory where most hires last only about a year before quitting."[42]

Another CLW report issued in 2017 confirmed that conditions have not improved for Pegatron's workers. After reviewing a number of employee paystubs,

CLW concluded that over 60% of Pegatron employees producing Apple iPhones worked over 90 hours of overtime every month. Some worked as much as 109 hours in a given month. This amount of overtime is a violation of Apple's direct guidelines. Those guidelines prescribe that workers in Apple's supply chain should work no more than 60 hours per week with at least one day off. Monthly overtime should average no more than 80 hours. Pegatron has always insisted that overtime is "optional." But CLW investigators report that in peak production periods, requests to decline overtime work are routinely denied. The low base wages are also a perverse incentive for working many hours of overtime.[43]

These very low wages paid by Pegatron were also carefully studied by CLW. Pay-stubs revealed that most production line workers in Pegatron's Shanghai factory that produced Apple's iPhone 7 were being paid $304 per month. When the government raised the minimum wage to $330, Pegatron increased its monthly salary to $350. Pegatron employees who worked 80 hours of overtime a month earned $672, while those who worked 20 hours of overtime earned $407. These amounts include "compensation" and bonuses. In non-peak production periods there is a scarcity of overtime so most workers earn only $350 in a month. This below-subsistence wage is a formidable challenge for those living in the Shanghai area, where the average monthly salary is $895 per month. The average consumption expenditures of urban residents of Shanghai is about $464 per month. Thus, without excessive overtime, Pegatron workers making expensive Apple products would struggle to subsist in Shanghai on their low base salaries.[44] At the same time, Apple sells its iPhones at a premium price and generates huge profits. In 2017, the year of CLW's study, Apple, Inc. reported net profits of $47 billion.

In addition to inordinately low wages and excess overtime, a CLW investigator, who took a job at the Pegatron Shanghai factory, also uncovered sub-standard working conditions. Almost every production worker toiled for six days per week in 12-hour shifts. The overtime period ran from 5:30pm until 8:00pm, but workers were only paid for 10.5 hours because they were forced to attend unpaid meetings during the work day. After the long shift, workers were packed on to buses for a 30-minute ride back to their dormitories. Here fourteen people were crowded together in one small room where they all slept on soiled bunk beds. In these ill-kept dorms, "mold grows pervasively along the walls; bed bugs have spread throughout the dormitory, and many workers are covered in red bug bites."[45]

Finally, China Labor Watch and other NGOs have accused Pegatron of persistently mistreating its interns. Chinese vocational and technical schools require internships for students that can run from three months to a full year. Many of these eight million student workers find employment in coastal cities like Shenzen and Shanghai where the minimum wage is higher than in rural areas. Pegatron assigns these interns monotonous tasks such as wiping down screens or assembling products. According to Chinese law, interns are forbidden from working overtime. But some Pegatron interns worked more overtime than full-time employees. A Fair

Labor Association study confirmed that many of Pegatron's interns routinely worked an overtime shift. In addition, students are required to do work and perform tasks that are related to their studies. However, instead of providing relevant internships, Pegatron assigns its interns to routine work, usually on assembly lines making smart-phones or laptops.[46]

Despite the criticism of NGOs like China Labor Watch, abuses of factory workers have continued. In late 2020, Pegatron Kunshan announced a reduction of 10% of the promised bonuses for all dispatch workers who started producing iPhones at the factory in September. Thousands of temporary workers were recruited during the peak production season of Apple's new iPhones. These workers were promised that they would receive a bonus of more than 10,000 yuan after working for fifty-five work days. The bonus compensates for the low salaries paid to workers in Kushan. But at the end of the fifty-five-day period, the workers were told that they could not receive their promised bonuses in full. In a formal protest workers assembled and demanded justice: "We refuse to accept the 10% reduction, give back our wages," but to no avail. Withholding bonus wages to force people to work at factories where the regular wage is quite low is disputably a form of forced labor. The company is enticing people to work with a stipulated bonus and then reneges on its promise.[47]

Li Qiang, executive director of China Labor Watch, wrote to Apple CEO Tim Cook about this issue, but Apple replied that they had found no issues regarding the non-payment of wages. The frequent large-scale protests at Apple's supplier factories over unpaid wages in China strongly suggest the failure of Apple's audit system to uncover abuses that violate workers' rights.[48]

Despite this disappointing response, Apple has not neglected its supply chain problems. Cook and other executives have often reaffirmed the rights of those workers to a fair wage and decent working conditions. This rhetoric, however, has not led to decisive reforms. Apple has conducted 640 audits across its vast supply chain, but those audits suggested modest compliance with Apple's standards. For example, there was only a 66% compliance with Apple's standard of "excellence" for "wages, benefits, and contracts." There were similar compliance rates for occupational health and safety standards and for hazard prevention.[49]

In late 2020, Apple put Pegatron on probation for transgressions of labor rules for students working as interns in its factories. The students worked at night and worked overtime in violation of Apple's policies. They also continue to engage in work unrelated to their studies, and that practice is now forbidden by Apple's guidelines. To make matters worse, Pegatron falsified documents to cover up these labor rule violations. Apple has decided that Pegatron is not eligible to receive new contracts until it takes corrective measures. But the bigger question is whether a temporary suspension is adequate. Should an unscrupulous company like Pegatron continue as an Apple supplier, given its history of labor and environmental abuses over the years?[50]

Case study: Mattel's China conundrum

Mattel, Inc. founded in 1945 and headquartered in El Segundo California, designs, manufactures, and markets a broad variety of toy products. Its main rivals include LEGO and Hasbro. Rivalry is intense in an industry environment where low production costs are essential thanks to powerful distributors like Walmart and Amazon. The company's brands and products include Barbie fashion dolls and accessories, Angelina Ballerina, Barney, Disney Classics, Monster High, Hot Wheels, Matchbox, CARS, Toy Story, American Girl, and Max Steel. Mattel produces video games under its own brands and under a license agreement with Nintendo. Mattel boasts that its toy brands "have been inspiring generations of consumers and have deep emotional connections with a large fan base of children everywhere." The corporation also owns Fisher-Price Brands, which specializes in toys for small children. Global net sales for Mattel were $4.58 billion in 2020.[51]

Mattel operates through its North America and International divisions. It sells toys in the U.S. and Canada through the Mattel Girls & Boys Brands and Fisher-Price Brands categories. The International division includes the products marketed by the North America segment, although some are developed or adapted for particular international markets.

Some of Mattel's toys are made in its own factory in China. Mattel has also outsourced production of its toys to another factory, the Dongguan Dongyao Toy Co., which is located in Dongguan City in the province of Guandong. That factory employs 1,000 workers during peak periods and provides Mattel with its Fisher-Price product line along with other best-selling toys. The factory also makes Chicco baby products. Dongyao employs both short- and long-term workers. Long-term workers sign a contract that spells out work content, location, work hours, and compensation.

Conditions within both of these factories are quite inferior to their counterparts in the West. Despite some media attention and headlines highlighting how Chinese factories are making toys for privileged Western children under miserable conditions, there has been no ostensible improvement in those conditions. There are low wages, too much overtime, and dismal living conditions in worker dormitories. According to one labor activist, "We can't tolerate that children's dreams are based on workers' nightmares, and we must fight against the unfair oppression of workers who manufacture toys."[52]

China Labor Watch (CLW) has carefully documented the low wages and excessive overtime that have become commonplace at the Dongyao plant. Workers in most departments (such as coloring) begin work at 7:30am with a rest at 11:30am; they work from 1:00pm until 5:00pm, take another break, and then work overtime from 6:00pm until 8:00pm. During peak seasons, workers usually work 3–4 hours of overtime each weekday. They typically work overtime on Saturdays, usually 11–12 hours during peak periods. The company tries to limit overtime to 66 hours per month, but often most workers exceed this amount. Working as much as 110 overtime hours per month is quite common and even expected by managers. With this amount of overtime, workers could earn 6,000 RMB/month ($900). Labor contracts stipulate that employees can opt out of overtime, but if a worker makes such a request when the factory is busy, he or she is usually ignored. Also, workers and teams have production targets, but those who do not work overtime are recorded as having below average production levels.[53]

The company pays an hourly wage of $1.48; the regular overtime hourly wage is $2.22; and the weekend overtime wage is $2.97. Each position has different allowances and benefits. Workers frequently express discontent with the low wages and excess overtime, but feel they have little recourse and no other good options. CLW examined a number of paystubs to see what kind of monthly wages were being earned. For example, here is what a worker in the hand-sewing department earned during the month of July (2020): 184 regular hours at $1.48/hour; 69 regular overtime hours and 23 weekend overtime hours – for a total of $498 in monthly wages. He also received a $31 over-production award and had $3 deducted for dormitory fees for a net salary of $526.[54]

Workers tell CLW that they struggle to survive on these paltry wages, which are especially bad during off-peak times when overtime is scarce. The average monthly cost of living in the Guandong province is $1,433.[55] Some workers do odd jobs on weekends to earn extra income. Although Mattel has lost money in the competitive toy industry from 2017–2019, it reported $127 million in net profits in its 2020 fiscal year.[56]

Study question

1. What, if anything, should Mattel do about the low wages and extreme overtime at the Dongguan Dongyao factory?

Conclusions

The pace of offshoring and outsourcing has increased over the last several decades as companies zealously search for low-cost venues to produce their products. This process is driven to some extent by the rising power of discount retailers (like Walmart) and their relentless drive to cut costs in their supply chains. Virtually all segments of the apparel industry, including designer fashion houses, have been in the forefront of this trend. China, the world's largest clothing exporter, remains a popular location for companies looking for low wages, along with other emerging markets such as Bangladesh and Vietnam. But wages in China have been rising, and there are signs that China is losing its competitive edge as the ideal low-cost manufacturing location.

In the past, companies have tried to defuse criticism of sweatshop conditions at their suppliers' factories by contending that they are not morally liable for the labor abuses that occurred outside their own corporate boundaries. Our ethical analysis demonstrated the disingenuousness of such arguments. The brand owner–supplier relationship is not reducible to an arm's-length contract. Rather, this is a principal–agent relationship where the principal has vicarious liability for the actions of its agents who produce their clothing (or other goods). International companies also have leverage over these suppliers, and hence they have the capability to prescribe acceptable working conditions as a condition of future contracts. Moreover, with indifferent and dysfunctional governments usually involved, these multinationals often represent the only recourse for justice. These factors such as proximity and capability impose a clear duty to protect the rights of workers in their supply chain.

The scope of that obligation is open to some debate, however, since monitoring an entire intricate supply chain is expensive and exceedingly difficult. However, companies should be motivated by both economic and humanitarian reasons to purge those supply chains of abusive labor practices wherever this is feasible and morally reasonable.

International corporations, therefore, must help ensure adequate working conditions in the factories of their suppliers. Priority must be given to safety so that the workers' health and physical security is not subject to unreasonable risk. There must be decent working conditions with limits on hours worked, vacations with pay, and the right to form a union if the workers determine this is in their best interest. Every worker is entitled to just compensation that will provide enough money to support herself and her family with the basic necessities of life. Most of these moral demands entail rights that must be honored by contractors and protected by international corporations that source from those contractors. In addition, international enterprises cannot tolerate any type of bonded labor in their supply chains. Because of the unintended consequences, it may not be prudent to take away the "sweatshop" option for children of a certain age. But companies can at least ensure that those children are getting some education at their place of employment.

The Apple and Mattel cases indicate that there is much work to be done in improving the work environment of emerging economies. Shifting production to low-wage countries has improved the economic conditions of those countries, but it has also caused too many multinationals to lose their moral bearings. They become too focused on low cost and ignore the plight of workers who make their goods in these sweatshops. More attention must be paid to human rights and to securing justice for both direct and indirect employees.

Notes

1 Peter Goodman, Vivian Wang, and Elizabeth Paton, "Use of Cotton from Xinjiang Carries a Cost," *New York Times*, April 6, 2021, A1, A10.
2 Ibid.
3 Scumpeter, "Supply Chained and Bound," *Economist*, August 22, 2020, 56.
4 Mark Clifford, "Pain in Pusan," *Far Eastern Economic Review*, November 5, 1992, 59.
5 John Cushman, "Nike Pledges to End Child Labor and Apply U.S. Rules Abroad," *New York Times*, May 13, 1998, D1.
6 Kathy Chu, "Not Made in China," *Wall Street Journal*, May 1, 2013, B1–2. See also "Here, There, and Everywhere: Outsourcing and Offshoring," *Economist*, January 19, 2013, 3–5.
7 "Here, There, and Everywhere," 5.
8 Allen Myerson, "In Principle, a Case for More Sweatshops," *New York Times*, June 22, 1997, E5.
9 Larry Rohter, "To U.S. Critics, a Sweatshop: To Hondurans, a Better Life," *New York Times*, A1, A14.
10 Syed Zain Al-Mahmood, Kathy Chu, and Tripti Lahiri, "After Fire, Pressure on Bangladesh," *Wall Street Journal*, December 15, 2012, B1, B4.
11 Syed Zain Al-Mahmood, "Bangladesh Factory Toll Passes 800," *Wall Street Journal*, May 9, 2013, A10.
12 Benjamin Powell, *Out of Poverty* (New York: Cambridge University Press, 2014), 56–64.
13 Rubana Huq, "The Economics of a $6.75 Shirt," *Wall Street Journal*, May 12, 2013, A15.
14 Kathy Chu, "Tough Options for Apparel Retailers," *Wall Street Journal*, May 8, 2013, B1.
15 Quoted in Tim Larimer, "Sneaker Gulag: Are Asian Workers Really Exploited?" *Time International*, May 11, 1998, 30.
16 Quoted in Richard Spinello, "Human Rights and World Markets," *Boston Business Journal*, August 2, 1996, 17.
17 Timothy Perkins, et al., "Levi Strauss & Co. and China," in *Perspectives in Business Ethics*, 2nd ed., ed. Laura Hartman (New York: McGraw-Hill, 2002), 764–769.
18 Albino Barrera, *Market Complicity and Christian Ethics* (New York: Cambridge University Press, 2011), 128–133.
19 Ibid., 128–130.
20 Jeremy Bentham, *Introduction to the Principles of Morals and Legislation* (Oxford: Oxford University Press, 1907), 312. See also Keith Baier, *The Moral Point of View* (Ithaca, NY: Cornell University Press, 1958).
21 Eric D'Arcy, *Human Acts: An Essay in Their Moral Evaluation* (Oxford: Oxford University Press, 1963), 56–57. Also quite helpful is the discussion of these factors in John Simon, Charles Powers, and Jon Gunnemann, *The Ethical Investor* (New Haven, CT: Yale University Press, 1972), 22–26.
22 D'Arcy, *Human Acts*, 55.
23 Germain Grisez, *Living a Christian Life* (Quincy, IL: Franciscan Press, 1993), 532–533. See also John Finnis, *Natural Law and Natural Rights* (Oxford: Oxford University Press, 1980), 223–226.
24 Matt Moffett, "Underage Laborers Fill Mexican Factories, Stir U.S. Trade Debate," *Wall Street Journal*, April 8, 1991, A1.
25 Joseph Kahn, "China's Workers Risk Limbs in Export Drive," *New York Times*, April 7, 2003, A3.
26 Huq, "The Economics of a $6.75 Shirt."

27 Henry Shue, "Transnational Transgressions," in *Just Business: New Introductory Essays in Business Ethics* ed. Tom Regan (New York: Random House, 1984), 271–279.

28 Shue, "Transnational Transgressions," 278.

29 William Quigley, *Enduring Poverty as We Know It: Guaranteeing a Right to a Job at a Living Wage* (Philadelphia, PA: Temple University Press, 2003).

30 See Edwin Hartman, "Donaldson on Rights and Corporate Obligations," in *Business Ethics: The State of the Art* ed. R. Edward Freeman (Oxford: Oxford University Press, 1991), 163–172.

31 Pope John Paul II, *Laborem Exercens* (Boston, MA: Pauline Books and Media, 1981), §19.

32 Ibid.

33 John Rawls, *A Theory of Justice* (Cambridge, MA: Harvard University Press, 1971), 298.

34 Ibid., 303. According to Rawls, "The intuitive idea is that the social order is not to establish and secure the more attractive prospects of those better off unless doing so is to the advantage of those less fortunate," 75. Although Rawls did not have in mind a global social order, his ideas about justice still apply to issues like wages, especially when the economy is so globalized and national economies so closely interconnected.

35 International Labor Organization, "What is Child Labor." Available at ilo.org/ipec/facts/lang-en/index.htm.

36 "Sickness or Symptom," *Economist*, February 7, 2004, 73.

37 Megha Bahree, "Your Beautiful Indian Rug Was Probably Made by Child Labor," *Forbes*, February 2014, 31–33.

38 Adam Liptak, "Corporations Watch Case on Human Rights Suits," *New York Times*, December 2, 2020, A20.

39 Powell, *Out of Poverty*, 89. This discussion on child labor relies on the insights and data in a chapter of this book called "Save the Children," 83–96.

40 "Sickness or Symptom." See also International Labor Organization, "Investing in Every Child: An Economic Study of the Costs and Benefits of Eliminating Child Labor," Working Paper, December 2003.

41 China Labor Watch, *Apple's Unkept Promises: Investigation of Three Pegatron Group Factories Supplying Apple*, July 29, 2013. Available at www.chinalaborwatch.org/report/68.

42 Brian Merchant, *The One Device: The Secret History of the iPhone* (Boston, MA: Little Brown, 2017), 267.

43 China Labor Watch, "Apple Making Big Profits but Chinese Workers' Wage on the Slide," August 24, 2016. Available at www.chinalaborwatch.org/report/77. See also Nicki Lisa Cole, "iPhone or iExploit? Rampant Labor Violations in Apple's Supply Chain," *Truthout*, August 25, 2016. Available at www.truthout.org/news/item/37363.

44 Jack Schofield, "Pegatron is Exploiting Workers Making Apple iPhone in China," ZDNET.com, August 28, 2016. Available at www.zdnet.com/article/pegatron-is-exploiting-workers-making-apple-iphone. See also China Labor Watch, "Apple Making Big Profits," 10.

45 Asian Century Institute, "Working for Apple in China," July 10, 2016. Available at www.asiacenturyinstitute/development/1191-working-for-apple-in-china.

46 Eva Dou, "China Fills Tech Factories with Student Labor," *Wall Street Journal*, September 25, 2014, B1–2. See also Schofield, "Pegatron is Exploiting Workers Making Apple iPhone in China."

47 "Apple Supplier Pegatron: Workers in Kushan Stage Protest over Wages," China Labor Watch, December 31, 2020.

48 Ibid.
49 See Asian Century Institute, "Working for Apple in China."
50 Paul Mozur, "Apple Puts Contractor on Probation over Abuses," *New York Times*, November 10, 2020, B4.
51 See Mattel corporate web site, especially "Brand Portfolio." Available at corporate. mattel.com/en-us/brand_portfolio.
52 Gethin Chamberlain, "The Grim Truth of Chinese Factories Producing the West's Christmas Toys," *Guardian*, December 3, 2016, 1, 22.
53 "Workers in Misery: an Investigation into Two Toy Factories," China Labor Watch, December 3, 2020, 102–112.
54 Ibid.
55 "Cost of Living in Guandong China," China Admissions. Available at china-admissions.com/cost-of-living-in-guandong-china.
56 Tyler Clifford, "Strong Holiday Sales Give Mattel its 'Best Performance in Years,' CEO Says," CNBC.com, February 10, 2021.

Index